ALSO BY RICHARD HOWARD

Inner Voices: Selected Poems, 1963–2003

Talking Cures

Trappings

Like Most Revelations

No Traveller

Lining Up

Misgivings

Fellow Feelings

Two-Part Inventions

Findings

Untitled Subjects

*Alone with America: Essays on the Art of Poetry
in the United States Since 1950*

Damages

Quantities

PAPER TRAIL

PAPER TRAIL

SELECTED PROSE

1965–2003

RICHARD HOWARD

FARRAR, STRAUS AND GIROUX

NEW YORK

Farrar, Straus and Giroux
19 Union Square West, New York 10003

Library of Congress Cataloging-in-Publication Data
Howard, Richard, 1929–
    Paper trail : selected prose, 1965–2003 / Richard Howard.
        p.   cm.
    ISBN-13: 978-0-374-25885-6
    ISBN-10: 0-374-25885-6 (hc. : alk. paper)
        I. Title.

PS3558.O8826P37 2004

814'.54—dc22   2004047126

Designed by Jonathan D. Lippincott

www.fsgbooks.com

1   3   5   7   9   10   8   6   4   2

For
Anne Hollander, Susan Sontag, Rosalind Krauss
in admiration and emulation

Contents

ON POETRY

A Consideration of the Writings
of Emily Dickinson

[1973]

I

Until Thomas Johnson published his integral edition of her poems ("including variant readings" in 1955) and of her surviving letters (in 1958), Emily Dickinson had not readers but addicts, not critics but emendators; indeed since 1890, when Mrs. Todd and Colonel Higginson published the silently altered "First Series" of her poems (ignoring her prophecy that "it does not fit so well / when altered frequently"), Emily Dickinson's audience has proved as insatiable as it has been undiscerning—witness the subsequent sixty-year serial, precisely, of her publishing history, ever since Lavinia's discovery of the Locked Box (a little gothic novel in itself, the Other maiden sister who had lived under the same roof with the poet all her life, yet quite unsuspecting of the quantity or the quality of her enterprise, put to the cliff-hanging question: should she destroy the contents, just as she had been instructed to destroy Emily's papers?). We shall return to this dilemma, this differentiation between papers and poems in the leavings of an unpublished writer; but for now, by the diligence of Professor Johnson and his handwriting experts, as well as by the fortune of our own incomparable modernity, we have been released from the scandal of other people's good intentions—Lavinia's, Helen Hunt Jackson's, Colonel Higginson's and Mrs. Todd's, Mrs. Bianchi's and Mr. Hampson's. We confront, at last, the poet's own—Emily Dickinson's intentions, a much more troublesome affair.

For it must be confessed that as long as we could be merely scandalized, we were ensnared—indeed that is the initial sense of a scandal, a *skandalon*, a snare, reminding us that *scansion* too may be a stumbling block. Scandalized we have been, then, by the parcelling-out of the texts, by the editorial tampering responsible for so many mysterious breaches with success, so many apparent compromises with failure. Until Professor Johnson completed his vast undertaking in behalf of the graduate students of the world, one might say that Emily Dickinson's case was one of publish *and* perish. We have been further entrapped by our necessarily discrepant versions—considering our informants—of the poet herself: the pining recluse who wrote to Higginson, "Nothing has happened but loneliness, perhaps too daily to relate"; the breathless tomboy who once remarked to the same correspondent, "I sing, as the Boy does by the Burying Ground—because I am afraid"; the Juliet of Amherst (if not actually the Cleopatra) who gasped, "Had we less to say to those we love, perhaps we should say it oftener, but the attempt comes, then the inundation, then it is all over": the wayward bluestocking who could exult, "I am glad there are Books. They are better than Heaven for that is unavoidable while one may miss these"; the illiterate thrush who insisted that "Nature is a Haunted House—but Art—a House that tries to be haunted"; the vinegar-tongued spinster who declared, "It is essential to the sanity of mankind that each one should think the other crazy"; the metaphysical poet who, having read Vaughan, could yet write that "to have been immortal transcends to become so"; the symbolist poet who acknowledged that "the Ear is the last Face. We hear after we see"; the surrealist who called herself "the only Kangaroo among the Beauty"; the nun; the lesbian; the mystic of the *via negativa* who announced that "*no* is the wildest word we consign to Language"; the Puritan; the quietist who prayed, "We thank thee Father for these strange Minds, that enamor us against thee"; the atheist who wrote, "We cannot believe for each other. I suppose there are depths in every Consciousness, from which we cannot rescue ourselves—to which none can go with us"; the witch who knew that "nothing is so old as a dilapidated charm." Given all these impersonations, which by a few more extracts can be made to seem impostures, we should be thankful that Claude Lévi-Strauss has not yet fixed his attentions on this poet. Or perhaps not: a structuralist Dickinson (the one hinted at by her late confession that "orthography always baffled me, and to N's I had an especial aversion, as they always seemed unfinished M's") would further saturate the possibilities which have proved, or which in the nature of the case have insinuated themselves, to be nearly as attractive as the seductions of that other, that supreme, literary enigma whose name stands for so much and, biographically, so little. "Why is any other book but Shakespeare needed?" Dickinson asked—but of course she knew why: the one that was needed was the one she had to write, for did she not say, "My wars are laid away in Books— / I have one Battle more"? And it is only when we have amassed the same kind of speculative redundance about Dickinson which we have survived about Shakespeare that we have some chance of slipping out from under the net of partial identifications, of loosening the character-ological toils in which it has been so easy to imprison her and ourselves.

Easy, because we find what we intend to find in a writer. (And we blame what fails to correspond to our intentions—if it is our intention to find the poems of Mallarmé or Herrick, we censure a poet by allowing her to have written "perhaps a dozen perfect lyrics," though it is that poet herself who reminds us that "to multiply the Harbors does not reduce the Sea.") But if we have been facilitated in *our* intentions, hitherto, by the mere scandal of Emily Dickinson's poetry among us which so masked her own intentions, now we confront not the scandal but *the problem of Emily Dickinson*. The problem of her poetry, as it has been raised since the Johnson edition by her great critics and by her diligent ones, may be seen to menace every avenue of judgment, and most alleyways of enjoyment as well.

The fact that she never published her poems nor even, apparently, *wanted* to publish them—what she wanted to know, indeed what she inquired about in appropriate quarters, was whether they were "alive," whether they "breathed"; no more than that, barely protesting when such respiration was affected by an editor's tampering with her punctuation—the phenomenon of her forbidding privacy ("in all the circumference of Expression," she wrote at the end of her life, "these guileless words of Adam and Eve were never surpassed, *I was afraid and hid Myself*"), the care she took to keep herself to herself (explaining to Higginson, "I do not cross my Father's ground to any House or town," and indeed refusing to visit her father's grave until she herself was laid in the ground beside it)—is but the beginning of the problem of Emily Dickinson, but the beginning is perhaps a good place at which to start.

I mentioned just now that with the Johnson edition, at last, and for the first time, Dickinson's own intentions are before us. But was it her intention to be before us? Did she really write, as she is so often asserted to have written, her *letter to the world*? We must be wary about the "I" in her poems, the word which occurs there, the concordance tells us, 1,682 times, twice as often as any other word. Like all the Victorians—one thinks at once of Browning and Tennyson, particular victims of the identification of authorship with authenticity—Dickinson was troubled by the notion that her poems would be taken as confessional. She was so troubled that she took further trouble to be explicit about the matter, and wrote Higginson: "When I state myself, as the Representative of the Verse—it does not mean—me—but a supposed person." If then Dickinson wrote a letter to the world, she never mailed it; and in its present, final form, there is no finality to her work—there is only presence. By the time she was thirty and decided to take her writing seriously (seriously enough to keep it for herself, to lock it in a box), there is no point at which Dickinson's letters can be differentiated in consequence from her poems—the letters *become* poems before our eyes and ears, the prose talk becomes poetry torn up by the roots, as Colonel Higginson used to say, cartilaginous, bleeding even, tumescent with a freight which is undelivered.

In such a case, unique in the history of literature—for compared to this "solitary prowess / of a Silent Life," as she called it, Hopkins seems as eager for publicity as Norman Mailer, and Emily Brontë as comfortable in the limelight as Anne Sexton—in a circumstance where the poet could say:

> Though None be on our Side—
> Suffice Us—for a Crowd—
> Ourself—

what is the peculiar unity—amalgam, colloidal suspension, gist—which we call *the work of an author*? If Dickinson is, even, an author ("we must be careful what we say," she warned: "No bird resumes its egg"), is everything she wrote or said, everything she left behind in order to get on to everything else, to be regarded as part of "the works of Emily Dickinson"? "I am whom you infer," she would sign letters, permitting us the wildest liberties—and we have taken them. I shall take a number myself. For the six volumes of her poems and her letters stand on our shelves with the other great problematic works, unfinished, complete with Pascal's *Pensées* and with Nietzsche's *Will to Power*, a monumental indetermination, a reminder such as not even the pseudonymous masters Stendhal and Kierkegaard, nor even the orthonymous ones Rimbaud and Kafka (who published *and then* perished *in propria persona*), can afford to offer, in the nakedness of pure possibility—a reminder that the meaning of literary works is not the fixed meaning of their writing, but the undisclosed meaning of reading and of memory. The meaning of books lies before them and not behind: it is in us. A book is not a ready-made, terminal meaning, a revelation which we must undergo and assume; it is a reservoir of forms which receive their meaning; it is what Borges has called *the imminence of a revelation which does not occur*; it is an asymptote. Thus the work of an author is as problematic as his individuality, and in Dickinson's astonishing case, the poetry is as individual as its problematics.

Consider briefly, beyond the existence of the poems themselves, beyond the *existence* of Dickinson's work, that work's problems—how they press in upon us! There is the problem of titles, right at the top of the list: she did not use them, did not set off her poems *as* poems by this traditional literary device. Indeed she seems to reject anything so determinative as a label, the scab of experience, preferring, as she said, "no scar, / but internal difference, / where the Meanings, are—." Observing that "most of our Moments are Moments of Preface," she simply had no time for a title:

> Ended, ere it begun—
> The Title was scarcely told
> When the Preface perished from Consciousness
> The Story, unrevealed—

and in a variant of a poem sent to Mrs. Tuckerman in 1884—a variant
she kept for herself—she altered the final line, "The Mutineer / whose
title is 'the Soul,'" in a manner significant of her tastes in this matter: "the
Mutineer / discreetly called 'the Soul.'" Things—including such things
as poems—do not "have" titles, then; they are *discreetly called*, provi-
sionally, tentatively, asymptotically identified. The only title, as her most
famous use of the noun indicates, is the "Title divine" of wife, for which
there is no sign: as Blackmur says, Emily Dickinson married herself.

And hard upon the problem of titles comes the harder problem of
beginnings. She was forever starting up, beginning over, and always it
is the initiation which is her strength; she was not a new critic, and she
did not care, always or even often, to work out the implications of
those stunning first lines. After the example of Vaughan, she fastens
her poem to its first flash, and the rest of the poem may well . . . rest.
"The second half of joy," she said in one of her last poems, "is shorter
than the first"; and it is always the inauguration of her utterance that
energizes her, or at least that interests her. "The mind is such a new
place, last night feels obsolete," she wrote to Higginson, and it is that
new place she was forever looking for on the pillow, the breaking
open of the egg, the tmetic or splitting power of speech:

> I cling to nowhere till I fall—
> The crash of nothing yet of all
> How similar appears—

And as this last citation shows, if there was no time for a title, there
was little enough occasion for a period. "I would eat evanescence
slowly," she said, resisting anything like a full stop. Indeed the problem of Dickinson's punctuation is a mounting one (rather than constant, as in her rejection of titles), for she appears to have decided as
early as poem 7, written in 1858, upon an idiosyncratic though increasingly organized use of the dash, the comma, and of capital letters as
her preferred indications as to how her writings, prose and verse,
should be taken, should not be *mistaken*:

> My classics vail their faces—
> My faith that Dark adores—

And by the end of her flood period, in 1866, when she had written over a thousand of all her poems, it is astonishing how varied her use of the dash had grown—long, short, high, low, slanting up and down; the comma too becomes an elocutionary sign rather than a grammatical one, and the capital letter is as often withheld from the expected word as it is bestowed with subversive importance. There was no stopping her: punctuation was not a signal for pausing or pointing, but a means of extension; not a holding action but a creeping asymptote, the means of approach to an absolute. There was no point except to be at the hinge-point, where everything kept dying out to be reborn. "*It is finished* can never be said of us," she said, and if her dashes—her lunges at continuity—were various, what can then be said of her *variants*?

Here is one of the greatest Dickinson problems. An unpublished poet, she was under no necessity to prepare her work for the printer; indeed she was immensely *above* such a necessity of sacrificing the possibility which is not only "a fairer house than prose," as she called it, but than printed verse as well. "In adequate Music," she remarked, with characteristic insolence, "there is a Major and a Minor—should there not also be a Private?" Professor Johnson warns us that among her variants it is often impossible to determine Dickinson's own choice. He means she *would not choose*—"life is so rotatory," she said, "that the wilderness falls to each, sometime. It is safe to remember that"—and in his three-volume edition of her poems he prints them all, all her choices. Such profusion, in its very bewilderment, was her intention, I believe, though it is so very problematic that in his one-volume "reading" edition, Johnson, like the earlier editors, omits the suggested changes, the variants, the alternate possibilities as too much for us. They were barely enough for Dickinson, who makes a whole stanza out of them once, speaking of that central ecstasy which puts everything else beside the point:

> 'Tis this—invites—appalls—endows—
> Flits—glimmers—proves—dissolves—
> Returns—suggests—convicts—enchants—
> Then—flings in Paradise—

This kind of incremental pleonasm distresses us, for whom poetry is a *chastening* of the Word, not its superfetation; and a century of literary modernism brandishes its fiery sword at the gates of our thesaurus. Hopkins is the last great poet for whom language offered access to the polymorphous-perverse, and Hopkins is a Victorian poet. "Blessed are they that play, for theirs is the kingdom of heaven," Dickinson wrote on several occasions, and for her this refusal to settle for the singular sense, this failure to *determine*, is a kind of playing. Here a minute example must suffice to reveal how vast a field she could range by *leaving open* what, in the conventional practice of her art, is *invariably* a closed case.

Poem 1328, written about 1874, is an elegiac quatrain jotted down in pencil on the torn flap of an envelope:

> The vastest earthly Day
> Is shrunken small
> By one Defaulting Face
> Behind a Pall—

Artisanal variants are supplied for "shrunken" in the second line: first *shrivelled* and then *dwindled*; then the entire notion of agency in the second and third lines is rehandled in a variant which quite transforms the poem: "Is *chastened* small / By one *heroic* face"; lastly, the last line suffers a metamorphosis from which the tiny poem never recovers itself—the mortal face, first defaulting and then heroic, first dwindling and then chastening the earthly day, is twitched away from its fate and transfigured: one face, whether defaulting *or* heroic, is said to be the face "*That owned it all*—" rather than merely the face "Behind a Pall." We shall never know an ulterior version of this little verse ("True Poems flee," its author said), nor are we intended to: we have only the problem of its endless permutations, its trajectory from a mild piety of mourning to an heretical, a blasphemous solipsism. Or rather, from the attitude and aspect of the living to the enthralling viewpoint of the dead: Dickinson could never decide if the dead owned it all or if they were merely put away, appalled indeed. It is her great conflict, articulated here by the undetermined variants, between stasis and process, between sitting tight and letting go. The fascination with fixity involves, as Yvor Winters long ago observed about her, an element of horror, and the agony of moving is I think the impulse preferred, in-dicated, *dramatized* by her choice of not choosing.

As I have said, many of Dickinson's alterations and variants are merely artisanal, and afford us no more (though no less) than the op-portunity of spying on the maker at work, focusing intention, con-centrating effect, rehearsing surprise. But many more of these suggested changes are indeed extensions, blurrings, casting off the limitations of *le mot juste*: for Dickinson there was no justice, there was only mercy ("love, like literature," she said, "is its own 'exceeding great reward'"). Even when she copied out fair versions for her packets, the little booklets she sewed together for her own keeping, she could not or would not resist the further intimations of reality as they came to her from an already existing, already "finished" poem, "for reality itself is a dream with which no dreaming can compare," she said, "a dream from which but a portion of Mankind have yet waked, and part of us is a not familiar Peninsula."

So she left her poems undiscriminated, refused to give up alterna-tives, to forfeit the chance of coming closer to her method by merely editing. Her true Flaubert was Penelope, to invert a famous allusion, forever unravelling what she had figured on the loom the day before: "Night's capacity *varies*," she said, "but morning is inevitable." She was not finicky, I think, but instead obsessed with an infinity which had to be unfinished. As she said in 1880, when nearly all her work was done, "A spell cannot be tattered, and mended like a Coat." In such carmina-tion as hers, I am not certain if the spell can even bear to be woven at all: the loom is there, and the yarns, and a vast impatience with final-ity. "I had no monarch in my life," she condescended to explain to Higginson when he asked why she did not write more correctly, "and cannot rule myself, and when I try to organize—my little force explodes—and leaves me bare and charred." To enjoy the force (the *little* force, one gasps) yet to evade the explosion, the defoliation and the slag, she refused to prefer variants, to choose one in place of another. She wanted to be *in leaf*, to be one over the other, as leaves are, and she leaves us with the problem of her brief poems as epic palimpsests, overdetermined as dreams are, as all the motives of our deep psychic life are discovered to be ("In a life that stopped guessing," she wrote to her sister-in-law next door, "you and I should not feel at home"), never single or simple, for all their topiary deceptions on the page, but multiple, complicated, encircling, likely, dense.

"Low at my problem bending," she says, "another problem comes." It is true of her readers, too. No sooner are we perplexed, as we are very soon indeed, by the options with which she floods us, of-ten in the merest scrap of her work, than we must confess that the merest scrap is, even so, empowered to exploit, or at least to employ, the same conventions (and violations and variations) as the major screed. More than 1,700 poems written in the same Common Mea-sure, virtually all within the four margins of a page—to read Emily Dickinson through is to be pecked to death by Phoenixes! "The little sentences I began and never finished—the little wells I dug and never filled—," the everyday diminutiveness of this aporia is a problem for us, one more in the endless series. As Mark Van Doren's poem says of her, "the fine nerve, inquiring, did not stay for the long anthem." Never, I suppose, have so many readers so determined to confer upon their poet a majority status been so persistently confronted, flaunted, bullied with minority determinations in the poems. We thirst for greatness on our terms rather than on hers, and we exclaim in exas-peration: Why *would* she not hover over her cause a little longer, like her hummingbird, "a route of evanescence"? Why would she not *hold still* until we could tell where to take hold of her? And why, Bible-reader, Bardolater, fervent adept of George Eliot, why would she not let her lines *out*, why would she never write long or at least wide—there is not one iambic pentameter in her work, not one set of verses that assumes the page with that pre-emption of breadth *we* assume, or presume, to characterize a great poet—why would she, who by "eas-ing her famine / at her Lexicon," had won so astonishingly what she called "this consent of Language / this loved Philology," why would she write only short and teasingly deep, *flinging the problem back*, as she says in one of her first poems, *at you and I*?

How impatient we grow with the stubborn phenomenology of lit-tleness in the writing, the thematics of the bit-by-bit ("*Always* begins by degrees," she says, and in another place, "Even the Possible has its insoluble particle"—that is when she irritates us most, I think, when she is so complacent about not just the insolubility, but about the *particles*); how trying her fascination with the diminutive and the discardable, *the leavings*: even in describing herself to Higginson, Emily Dickinson says she is "small, like the Wren . . . and my eyes, like the Sherry in the Glass, that the Guest leaves." Her favorite quotation from *Antony and Cleopatra*, one of the few Shakespearean tags she does not distort for her own purposes—probably because this one serves her own purpose just as it stands—is a version of this problem of leavings; Antony says, as she reminds several of her correspondents, "take the hint / which my despair proclaims. Let that be left / which leaves itself." Dickinson took the hint, proclaiming a perpetual departure, forever leaving off, in order to get on: "Going is a drama / Staying cannot confer." Her poems, then, are to be little, and they are to be left—left behind, left over, left out, finally; elided from a life whose energy, as we shall see, is committed to getting rid of itself, to a reverence reserved for process—and for its neighborhood to presence—but never for persons merely, for personality, or for place. Indeed, place is nothing but what is left when presence is withdrawn or overcome, as at the end of her famous poem about the birds at dawn:

> And Place was where the Presence was
> Circumference between.

Flinging the problem back / at you and I! There, right there, is another problem involved with (and perhaps exposed by) her determined brevity of utterance, her dogged monotony of form: the problem of Dickinson's syntactical waywardness, her outright solecisms: *at you and I*! If she could not spell, she was a grammatical whizz bang, and there is something *to the life* about her lapses from acknowledged usage, even the acknowledged usage of the Connecticut Valley where she was so determined to "see New Englandly"; bad grammar, like bad spelling, *means something*, and we must not disregard the problem until we have given it a hard look. The tendency of her pronouns to lose the objective case is analogous to the tendency of her verbs to lose number, mood and tense, to become pure indication of process, no more than indicative verbality. Just as her pronouns tend toward the first person singular, so what at first seems to be her sub-junctive mood might better be called a continuing or universal present indicative, as Professor Johnson suggests. "I only said the Syntax— / and left the Verb and the pronoun out," Emily Dickinson reports of this procedure, and though it is not true that she omitted quite so much as that, it is true that she advanced, always, toward what the classical rhetoricians called an *oratio soluta*, wherein no element could stand for and by itself:

> Crumbling is not an instant's Act
> A fundamental pause—
> Delapidation's processes
> Are organized Decays.

And just as Roman Jakobson defines poetry as a kind of *organized violence* worked upon language, so Dickinson's "organized decays" serve to propose, at least, the problem of her rhymes, their insistent unpredictability and their slant or scant allusion to fulfillment. The de-spair of high-school English teachers, Dickinson's rhymes are a mask pointing to itself: they tell us something is wrong, something has al-tered or blurred from an identity which, by the pronounced lapse *from* it, is thereby asserted to exist. The problem of Dickinson's rhymes—if she was going to rhyme, why did she not do it more consistently? if she was not going to, why did she do it so much?—is suggested by an astonishing utterance from her flood period, in which the nature of her *poetry as a mistake* is dramatized: "Creation seemed a mighty Crack— / to make me visible—."

Moreover, I brushed right by, just now, the problem of her quota-tions, or of her misquotations. The New Testament she gets right, al-most always, but so fragmentary, so tesseral, are her citations from it that they do not refer, except for the Fundamentalist in us, beyond themselves. The Bible did not mean enough to her, did not press against her sense of life enough, for her to misquote it. Only when it offered an analogy to her doubts—and we must recall her celebrated equation at the end of her life, "Faith is *Doubt*," to measure her religion—was the Bible invoked: "When Jesus tells us about his Father, we distrust him," she writes. "When he shows us his Home, we turn away," she continues, to our astonishment, "but when he confides to us that he is 'acquainted with grief' we listen, for that also is an Acquaintance of our own." More interesting than her Biblical are her Shakespearean references. One is in fact more than interesting: it is the most revealing personal statement ever made about her. Three times, at different periods of her life, to different correspondents, she writes, "Do you remember what the Physician said to Macbeth? *That sort must heal itself.*" Clearly the passage was so significant to her that she juggled up her own shorthand version of it—for as with grammar and with rhyme, we bother to *get it wrong* only when the misdemeanor is significant for us; we have to change the truth a little in order to remember it, as Santayana says. Let me recall the original passage—it has more bearing on the problem of Emily Dickinson than all the biographical snooping we have been able to do, particularly because she herself calls it to our attention so emphatically. In the last act of the play, Macbeth inquires after his wife's health (and I need scarcely remind you of Lady Macbeth's interesting relation to *her* father as it is given in this play):

MACBETH: How does your patient, doctor?
DOCTOR: Not so sick, my lord
As she is troubled with thick-coming fancies
That keep her from her rest.
MACBETH: Cure her of that!
Can'st thou not minister to a mind diseased,
Pluck from the memory a rooted sorrow,
Raze out the written troubles of the brain,
And with some sweet oblivious antidote
Cleanse the stuffed bosom of that perilous stuff
Which weighs upon the heart?
DOCTOR: Therein the patient
Must minister to himself.

The prognosis is clear in Dickinson's persistent misquotation of the Doctor's helpless admission—"that sort must heal itself"—the prognosis is clear and it is negative, determined though she was not merely to minister to herself but to *heal* herself, to recover from the thick-coming fancies which harrowed her life—the life of a woman who at forty could say "to live is so startling, it leaves but little room for other occupations . . . There are many people in the world (you must have noticed them in the street). How do they live. How do they get strength to put on their clothes in the morning . . . I find ecstasy in living—the mere sense of living is joy enough . . . " If life itself was asymptotic to this joy, then self-healing was to have nothing to do with distinguished cures of the past.* Had not Emerson, the Emerson she read, formulated the principle "Imitation is suicide"? She was convinced of it, observing that she "never consciously touched a paint, mixed by another person," but as always, she carried the principle to her own extremity—if imitation was suicide, originality was murder. It meant destroying the texts, overcoming the Bible by assimilation, as Charles Anderson has said, in order to promulgate her own scriptures over and against those of her divine adversary; it meant falsifying the utterances even of Shakespeare so that she could afford her own. ("Remembrance," she once said, "is the great tempter.") For all the minor references to *Religio Medici* and to Ruskin, to Keats, to the Brontës' *poems* even, there is a characteristic sterility about Emily Dickinson's relation to literature: there is a clearing around her, bare ground in which nothing will grow near the one tree in the center, the poet who wrote she "only knew of Universe— / It had created Her," capitalizing "Her" of course. She knew she must heal herself—had she not written, "We must be less than Death, to be lessened by it—for nothing is irrevocable but ourselves"?—so she made her trauma into the treatment:

> A not admitting of the wound
> Until it grew so wide

---

*Vernon Newton reminds me that the original Shakespeare is itself a reflection of Scripture—Christ's quoting of the proverb, "Physician, heal thyself" in the synagogue at Nazareth (Luke 4:23). It is here, most assuredly, that Dickinson found the word "heal"—going back to the original which the Elizabethan varied for his own purpose, even to the point of switching the roles of the physician and patient.

That all my Life had entered it
And there were troughs beside.

I mentioned just now the way Emily Dickinson avoided calcination, avoided what she called explosion by refusing to "organize" her poems—to organize them, I mean, the way it was expected, in the middle of the nineteenth century, that poems should be organized. (The word is characteristically hers, not at all Colonel Higginson's: what *he* expected was decorum and regularity; cosmetics, not cosmos. When he advised Dickinson to drop rhymes altogether if she could not make them perfect, she thanked him for his "justice" but added, "I could not drop the Bells whose jingling cooled my Tramp.") "Life set me larger problems," she wrote in a central poem, and so she appears to have set larger ones for us. As I said, she wanted to be *in leaf*, even if she was the only tree standing—so much so that I am led by her own urgency to a final and representative problem, one which troubles me more than some of her other readers, for until lately it had seemed to me, like her preoccupation with the Interesting Deathbed, no more than a problem of her conventionality, of her submission to the Victorian identification of virginity with verdure, of maidens with lilies—in short, the problem of Emily Dickinson's relation to *flowers*. They were for her, in a different sense than for her contemporaries, a language, an intercession. Not only did she write about flowers; not only did she send her poems—*when* she sent them—to friends with flowers (after all, she also sent poems with gingerbread, with preserves, with a dead bee); she actually used flowers to speak *for* her, since after all they spoke so significantly *to* her. Recall the sole account of an outsider's encounter with Emily Dickinson:

A step like a pattering child's in entry and in glided a little plain woman with two smooth bands of reddish hair and a face with no good feature in a very plain and exquisitely clean white piqué. She came to me with two day lilies which she put in a sort of childlike way into my hand and said "These are my introduction" in a soft frightened breathless childlike voice—" and added under her breath "Forgive me if I am frightened; I never see strangers and hardly know what I say." But she talked soon and thenceforward continuously—and deferentially—sometimes stopping to ask me to talk instead of her—but readily recommencing.

The day lilies, then, were her introduction to Colonel Higginson; they spoke for and about her, precisely because they *were* the ecstasy which is there for a day and then is not there, a perfected moment which can be got rid of, which dies and blooms again, a recurring growth, like certain kinds of poems. The flower was the ecstatic embodiment of Eden—it was obligatory, of course, that her favorite Biblical quotation be Matthew, chapter 6, the "lilies of the field" passage celebrating "the grass which today is, and tomorrow is cast into the oven"—the realization of Being without reference to time. As she said, "There is no first, or last, in Forever—It is Centre, there, *all the time.*"

Like another American artist who about a century later as diligently burrowed into the spousal center of a rose, a morning glory, a lily until she had found the lineaments of mortality within the compass of her experience—like Georgia O'Keeffe, Dickinson was patient with flowers, for their evanescence fascinated her as much as their efflorescence, teaching, as she said, "How much can come / and much can go, / and yet abide the World!" Nor let us be misled by her inversion here, and her idiosyncratic verb form—she means, primarily, "and yet *the World does abide*"—she is celebrating process, the dying out and the reappearance of experience. "Bloom—is Result" she starts a poem in her great period of productivity; here is the whole poem:

> Bloom—is Result—to meet a Flower
> And casually glance
> Would cause one scarcely to suspect
> The minor Circumstance
>
> Assisting in the Bright Affair
> So intricately done
> Then offered as a Butterfly
> To the Meridian—

> To pack the Bud—oppose the Worm—
> Obtain its right of Dew—
> Adjust the Heat—elude the Wind—
> Escape the prowling Bee
>
> Great Nature not to disappoint
> Awaiting Her that Day—
> To be a Flower, is profound
> Responsibility—

Like her birds and bugs, these blossoms are a problem to us, for they put what she calls "the suggestion sinister / Things are not what they are."

If the day lilies are Emily Dickinson's introduction, if they *must be* her statement, then that statement in words, in her words, is that "forever is deciduous." Over and over, with these transient glories, comes the reminder: "Finer is a going / than a remaining face," or again: "To disappear enhances," and once more: " . . . going out of sight in itself has a peculiar charm. It is true that the unknown is the largest need of the intellect, though for it, no one thinks to thank God. . . ." Such eclipses, occultations, vanishings, *leavings* again, had something to do, in her mind, with the divinity of Earth, for she increasingly suspected that a proper study of evanescence would reveal

> The Fact that Earth is Heaven—
> Whether Heaven is Heaven or not.

The true eternity, indeed, would be a release from stasis, that "quartz contentment" which made her exclaim, "I don't like Paradise!" The true immortality would be a recognition and thence a recuperation of passage by certain rites—for that is what her poems are, of course, rites of passage, hinges whereby ecstasy might be accommodated, circumference engrossed, while

> . . . during its electric gale—
> The body is a soul—

as she said not long before her death. What mattered, what counted, what *amounted* to something was to proceed, to provide, in order for her poems to become process and provisional, improvisational even, so that, as she put it as early as 1860,

> Instead of getting to Heaven, at last—
> I'm going, all along.

II

Released by the Johnson edition from the scandal of Emily Dickinson's publication, we are impounded by the *problem* of Emily Dickinson's poetry; so many lions stand in our paths, as I have attempted to characterize them, that we are intimidated, not merely in reading but in understanding and enjoying her poems as she meant them to be understood and enjoyed, at least by herself. In fact, we conjecture that what loom as problems to us were also problems *to her*, that she was endeavoring to solve the same problems which we attribute to her work when we compare it with other poems, other poetry. Here we are mistaken, I believe, have been mistaken all along, but especially now, when we have before us just what it was she was doing. "We cannot assist another's Night," she said, but we *can* see that it *is* another's, without obscuring its stars and meteors by our own darkness. That is why I have called my paper a *consideration*, a word which first meant seeing the stars together as significant constellations, in relation to one another.

It was Freud who first taught us that a perversion is the *opposite* of a neurosis, that homosexuality, for instance, is not a problem but the *solution* to a problem. We have learned more—we have learned, quite as sensationally, that madness itself (what we call, nowadays, schizophrenia) is a *language*, is an attempt to communicate rather than a refusal to do so. We have begun to learn the language of the mad, to enter into a dialogue with them. Now writing is a social act, and it is, paradoxically, harder for us to acknowledge its idiosyncratic features, harder for us to escape the sense of menace and misgiving it affords us, when it exceeds the proprieties by which we recognize its functions, than it is to sustain relations with the socially banished psychotic. Dickinson was not mad, but her language must be entered with the recognition that it is *her* language—"the mind of the Heart must live," as she said—and we must take up a position within her utterance that will allow it such an autonomous life, recognizing too that she wrote her poems in a society in which, as Henry James remarked, introspection played almost the part of a social resource.

The one generalization I should care to hazard as to how we *should* respond to literature is that when we are troubled—bored, provoked, offended—by characteristic features of a writer's work, it is precisely those features which, if we yield to them, if we treat them as significance rather than as defect, will turn out to be that writer's *solution* to his own problems of composition and utterance. The problem of Dickinson's poetry *for us* is the solution to the problem of that poetry *for her*, as we shall see. By an agreeable coincidence, in the years Thomas Johnson was completing his edition of Dickinson's poems, I met Jean Cocteau, who gave me some advice: "*Ce que les autres vous reprochent, cultivez cela: c'est vous-même* (What other people reproach you for, cultivate: it is yourself)." As Emily Dickinson's contemporaries Lowell and Longfellow have so drastically demonstrated, there is only one thing worse than to be reproachable as a writer—it is to be irreproachable. In literature, if not in the salon, the posture Cocteau advocated is precisely the posture to which I aspire, for it suggest the means whereby all the lions which threaten our introgression into the work of Emily Dickinson, all the *problems* I have raised, or at least tilted upward, become rather guides and familiars in the enterprise, which is to see her poetry as it is; become answers, solutions, explanations of a poet who said, "My need—was all I had."

The poems were not written for publication; they were not subjected to that tidying reduction by which we acknowledge a literary profession; she made the poems to replace the habit of experience in the world—as Blackmur said, she made the poems of a withdrawal without a return. The phenomenology which governs her life as a poet is one of inundation. From the first, when she declared,

"My foot is on the Tide," to the last, when she said (and I think she was speaking of the fact that she no longer wrote more than perhaps a dozen poems a year, whereas once she had been obliged to write a poem a day—to keep afloat), "When Water ceases to rise—it has commenced falling. That is the law of Flood"; all her life long, she submitted to engulfment, she mastered it in her own terms, and when at last the deluge left her high and dry, she recorded that abandonment, too, in one of her greatest utterances: "The consciousness of subsiding power is too startling to be admitted by men—but best comprehended by the meadow over which the Flood has quivered, when the waters return to their kindred, and the tillage is left alone." The poems locked in the box Lavinia discovered after Emily Dickinson's death were the record of a struggle—"a Something overtakes the mind," she said, as if to account for her engagement, "we do not hear it coming"—a way of emptying the self, leaving off, cancelling out. "I sing to use the waiting," she said, and once she discovered her means, once she developed her method, she went on with it: "The appetite for silence," she wrote in the last year of her life, "is seldom an acquired taste."

Without what she called "the incident of Fame / or accident of Noise," she knew what she was doing, and what she was not doing. Her poems could not be longer than they were, they could not take another form than the one they had, for their length and their form were the way in which she could, by which she must, *pass them*. When she claimed that the predicament of mortality left us "as exempt from exultation as the Stones," she proceeded to get rid of the stones and on with the exultation. Her poems were calculated, for were they not calculuses, solid concretions formed in the body— especially, as the medical dictionaries tell us, in the organs which act as reservoirs?

When she sent her poems to friends, she sometimes stuck a title onto them—for herself, the poems in the packets are never titled; for herself, the poems are endless approximations, in part throwaways, in part provisional stays and props against ecstasy—what she called "an unfinished Pleasure." For her, each poem written was merely a way of proceeding to the next one, a release from bonds, a transition:

It is the Past's supreme italic
Makes this Present mean—

And in such a procession, titles were not only an irrelevant distraction but a betrayal, foreclosing what was to be perpetually dissolved, kept open. She finished a poem not *because* she had done with it ("Abyss has no Biographer," she asserted) but so that she could deal with the next one, would be ready to. A provisional process, her poetry was not to be stopped by mere attainment.

It was the starting that interested her; it was raising her voice, lifting the utterance. "Higher," she said, "is the doom of the High." Once she had initiated her poem, broken the eggshell, she was not commited to a program of elaboration; "To feed upon the Retrograde— / Enfeebles the Advance—" is a typical epigram of her productive years. The point was to advance, indeed to proceed, to get on with it, which of course meant getting off with it. Hence her dashes, her lurches into enjambment, her variants, her inclusive indicatives: there was no received standard version; experience was not to be assessed in terms of order and degree ("degreeless Noon" is one of her synonyms for the Earthly Paradise). Scripture was no help—"sustenance is of the spirit," she insisted, "the Gods but Dregs." What mattered was to expel what had accumulated and to make ready for what would:

The human heart is told
Of Nothing—
"Nothing" is the force
That renovates the World.

Her poems, then, are just that renovation, the negative force which made life itself accessible to her, day after day. They insist in their form upon that symmetry which is at one and the same time a principle of control and a power of vertigo. "Ruin is formal—Devil's work," remarked this *anima naturaliter negativa*: had her lines been *let out* long enough to slacken the tension, to withhold the formality, the poems would not function as she needed them to—would not ablate, not erase with the same unerring fascination, or rather with the fascination, precisely, of the errant. "Things so gay / pierce by the very Press / of imagery," she said, as veraciously of her poems as of the flowers which were to intercede for her:

> Bliss' early shape
> Deforming—Dwindling—Gulfing up
> Time's possibility.

These literally overwrought verses, palimpsests of a privacy committed to obliterating itself, vestiges merely of a presence so circumspect that we echo her terrible wonder: "To Whom the Mornings stand for Nights, / What must the Midnights—be!"—these poems are the cancelling forces which enable her life. "Softly my Future climbs the Stair," she noted, until there came an interval when it was no longer needful to write a poem every day, or every week, or every month. The life survived—

> Time does go on—
> I tell it gay to those who suffer now—
> They shall survive—

and the poems were put away, having served. The typical somatic gesture of each Emily Dickinson poem is in what William Carlos Williams calls her distaste for lingering: that twiddling of the thumb and fingers which seeks to remove something stuck to them. "Beauty is often timidity—perhaps, oftener, Pain," she wrote at the end of her days, having learned the rewards of such withdrawal. Her extensions had to be wily, secret, and so she offered variants for her experience, she refused to judge. "Good to know, and not tell," she exulted, "best to know and tell." She had solved her problem.

III

"It would be hard to name another poet in the history of the English language," Northrop Frye observes in a splendid essay on Dickinson, "with so little interest in social or political events." It is true: there was only one event, herself; the rest was what she called "the World that opens and shuts, like the Eye of the Wax Doll." For her, *to have lived is a Bliss so powerful*, as she wrote ten years before she died, *we must die— to adjust it*. However astonished to find herself singing her own "Song of Myself" off charnel steps, Dickinson produced, day by day, produced and then rid herself of—it was in fact a by-product, a sideline, an obliquity—the most relentless epic of identity in our literature; compared to her, Whitman is an epigrammatist. If you believe, as she did, in *the Nothing that renovates the World*, then an elusive form of communication is the only adequate one—a direct form is based upon the security of social continuity, while the elusiveness of existence— the astonishment, as Dickinson called it, that the Body contains the Spirit—isolates you wherever you apprehend it. If you are conscious of this and if you are content to be human, you will avoid a direct form. You become what Kierkegaard calls, in a passage which offers the best account I know of Dickinson's enterprise, if not of her achievement, *a genuine subjective existing thinker*. Having pointed out that Socrates, too, was a self-absorbed idler who concerned himself with neither world history nor astronomy, but solely with what it meant to be a human being, Kierkegaard goes on to describe such a thinker as

> always in the negative. He continues to be as negative as he is positive as long as he exists, not once and for all. His mode of communication is made to conform (lest through being too extraordinarily communicative he should succeed in transforming a learner's existence into something different from what a human existence in general has any right to be). He is conscious of the negativity of the infinite in existence, and he constantly keeps the wound of the negative open, which in the bodily realm is sometimes the condition for a cure. Others let the wound heal over and become positive; that is to say, they are deceived. In his form of communication, he expresses the same principle. He is therefore never a teacher but a learner; and since he is always just as negative as he is positive, he is always striving.

I hope you recognize in that description the poet who wrote once to the man to whom she always signed herself "your Scholar" this amazing sentence: "I found you were gone, by accident, as I find Systems are, or Seasons of the year, and obtain no cause—but suppose it a treason of Progress—that dissolves as it goes."

To Be, While Still Becoming: A Note on the Lyric Verse of Mark Van Doren

[1973]

In the second half of the twentieth century, we expect—and it is the first half which has whetted, which has exasperated our expectation—we expect, then, if we do not quite require, a lyric poem to have the dramatic impact upon us of suddenness, the convulsive energy of a pang, and we look in the poem's disposition as we listen to its discords for that excitement which lurks round the edges of things, trembling on the verge, thrilling at the margin. Modernism, as we have come to conceive it in the century of its life, is not opposed to lyric, but insists that the implicit qualities of such a poetry be made explicit, demands that the drama inhabiting the simplest utterance, the slightest acknowledgment of experience organized above "the tension of the lyre," dwell there in full view, outrageous, insistent, inescapable. Even at its most joyous, even when it *celebrates* loss and severance in an ecstasy, a transport, the modern lyric is committed to a *tragic role*, a role in which communication with the divine—and in Western culture such communication generally takes the disputed form of a protest, a conflict—is determinant. Love and death, then, in the modern American lyric are to be excruciating or they are, perhaps, not love and death at all. Only as it approaches the point of severance from experience is expression considered severe enough, extreme enough, to be authentic. This is our modernist heritage, the orthodoxy of a terrible faith in excluded middles; if there is heresy among us, it has not prevailed—or of course it would no longer be heresy then; heresies are doomed to minority status in poetry, the equivalent of persecution in religion.

But suppose we are confronted with a body, indeed with an anatomy of lyric verse which heretically rejects the tragic immediacy; which prefers to be interesting (the conscious) rather than to be excruciating (the unconscious); which prefers centers to edges, meetings to sunderings; which states—and statement will be a chief tenet of this heretical art:

> Freedom is the mean of those
> Extremes that fence all effort in;

which chooses—as Mark Van Doren says Shakespeare chose in *The Tempest*, that phantasmagoria of the temporal, as the very title indicates in its root—not so much to tell a story as to fix a vision. Suppose we are to read nearly fifty years' abundance—

> Leave them all there,
> Old lover. Live on

—of a man's lyric poems (and abundance appears to accompany statement as the idiosyncrasy of the heresy, its necessary condition) and find the drama, or the dramatic, at least, occluded, elided, no more than implicit in the old way. Why then, for us, such a man's poems would be as problematic as, say, Donne's songs and sonnets must have seemed to an admirer of Campion's, a "saying" indeed, when what was listened for was a song; whereas here the expectation is the bright incision that proceeds from the broken speech, the fragmented oracle, and what we are given is the integrity of the fabric, the one vision:

> To wish a word unsaid,
> To wish a deed undone—
> Be careful, for the whole
> World that was is one.

Calling a poetry problematic, whether Donne's or Van Doren's, is merely an acceptable, modernist way, of course, of calling it unfashionable. What is meant is that, insofar as we are "modernists," we are troubled by characteristic features of that poetry, in this case by its ease, profusion, recurrent pattern, confidence in the evidence:

> Eternity is now or not at all:
> Waited for, a wisp: remembered, shadows.
> Eternity is solid as the sun:
> As present; as familiar; as immense.

I have suggested that two of the characteristic features of this problematical poetry, this heretical lyricism, are the willingness to make statements and the necessity to be prolific; there are others, especially the commitment to that schedule of repetitions and returns we call, significantly, verse. In fact, there would seem to be a tradition or at least a convention for dealing with a world to which the poet refuses to grant our convulsive tragic lineaments, a convention of recurrence, of insistent pattern whereby the world is held in thrall to humble engagements, attentions that come back again, "submissive to each part / till it becomes the all," as Mark Van Doren says.

Now a heresy or a problematics which has its own convention is already a very special kind of heresy—it is more likely to be a discredited but not really lost religion, like matriarchy, which cannot quite be stamped out of our experience because it has somehow, at some level, enabled that experience in the first place, the first time, despite the orthodox practices which would rewrite history in terms of patrimonies, which would *invent* history to replace authentic experience. Enabling in its dealings with duration, its transactions with time (for Van Doren, explicitly, there is always another occasion, a chance to return to the form: "my mind," he exults, "will survive this song," ready and willing to find its further life in yet another song), the lyric poetry which is not singularizing or sundering in its effect, its effort, the "minor" utterance which is profuse and even didactically assertive in its animal integrations—such a poetry probably antedates, certainly underlies our modern orthodoxy of *terribilità* and its searing wisdom of confines, of transgressed limits, for it is the song of

> . . . the middle world
> That was made as if by children,
> Nor is changed with growing old.

We may trace the articulation of such a convention for dealing with the acknowledged bonds of life which the Romans called *pietas* and we call religion when we think of religion as a binding, a *ligament* uniting all experience, from its most exalted reaches to its meekest resignations—in our century we may honor this heresy in poems by Hardy, by Walter de la Mare, by Robert Graves, by Yeats before 1916, by Robinson and Frost in their lower registers, and by almost the entire lyric corpus of Mark Van Doren. The decorum of this kind of poetry admits of sharp observation but not much experiment or originality with the tools of that observation, either words or senses. The language of this poetry, a language invariably accessible to children and to enchantment—to spells and charms and invocations—is one already received by poets (all magic depends on repetition), not invented to satisfy new needs. Hence the many *poetical* words, the archaic turns, the inversions for the sake of a rhyme, the cunning topiary of the verses. "What was habit," as Mark Van Doren says in a poem from this convention of counting, "now is myth."

Indeed, in one of his very first collected poems, dating from 1924, appropriately in the form of directions or signals to a child, initiating the new being into that cycle of expectations which concerns, explicitly, the sense that experience is not single, drastic, separable, but rather recurrent, connective, predictable—experience is versification—in "To a Child with Eyes," Van Doren gives a determinative order for this kind of poetry:

> Run and see, and say how many.
> There are more if there is any.

Which will be true, and Van Doren true to it, for fifty years: the poet inventories the world ("omission is murder"), loyal to each perception, willing to loiter over each notation, each node on the humming wire which communicates the felt life, confident that all will come round again if only the immediate experience is cherished, embraced, *espoused*; no mere exercise in technical ingenuity, as Theodore Roethke marveled over a poem like "Private Worship," a single metaphor is carried without a break "through thirty lines to a true climax; the theme is not exhausted but enriched by the successful application of the single figure." "There are more" is the faithful corollary of a final prayer, that characteristic vocative of "Mark Van Doren, who grows daily older,"

> . . . O world
> Stay with me till I die.

Throughout is the trust in accompaniment, the fealty of body to earth, of flesh to spirit, of mind to matter ("my reason is mortality, and dim / senses"); the religion of this poetry is an entirely earthly *matter* ("this life of mine . . . lives only here, in this old / building," the poet says toward the end of his life, resolute to abide by the given, his faith in appearances never precluding his fondness for secrets: "Consult the shown, / Believe in the unshown"). Between that first assertion of plurality and the last plea for plenitude, there loom—surely the right word here, a constant weaving of the speech shuttle, as Sophocles calls it—more than six hundred pages of just that middle, that central life which is so ruthlessly excluded from the "modern" lyric, that connective tissue, cartilage, sticking plaster, call it, of a life which is indeed between—the one life to be found, as the title of Van Doren's median poem calls it, "Midland":

> Under the great cold lakes, under the midmost
> Parallel that Lisbon too lies under—
> Vesuvius and Corinth, Ararat,
> Peking and Chosen, yellow and blue seas
> Enormous, then the redwoods, then high Denver—
> Under the wet midnorth, under cool Canada,
> Swings my own West, directionless; the temperate,
> The tacit, the untold. There was I born,
> There fed upon the dish of dreaming land

That feeds upon itself, forever sunk
From the far rim, from crust and outer taste,
Forever lost and pleased, as circling currents
Swim to themselves, renumbering Sargasso
Centuries a wind brings round the world.
There am I still, if no thought can escape
To edges from that soft and moving center,
That home, that floating grave of what would fly
Yet did not, my own boyhood, meditating
Unto no end, eternal where I was.

If we are, in what Henry James once called our incomparable modernity, vexed by characteristic features of a writer's work, as I have begun to limn them here, for example, we have the comfort of knowing that it is precisely such features which, if we regard them as intention rather than insufficiency, will become that writer's *solution* to what we have called his problematics of composition. In the case of Mark Van Doren, our difficulties are, then, his ease, the imperturbable grace, the clarity and radiance of an undismembered self— rather of an ego that remembers, or as he calls it, "The Middle Creature":

> Man is the one most caught
> Between not knowing and knowing:
> Neither a beast today
> Nor archangel tomorrow.
>
> Man has most need of order
> Lest he be nothing now;
> So builds to the farthest future;
> Yet least is lord of the years . . .

Our problem, our vexation, in all the smoothness of this resigned *sagesse*, is our sense of the lack of tragic contention; our dilemma is, just so, the denial of extremity. The poetry of Mark Van Doren, so carefully administered by eye and ear and pulse, is not exciting

(it is not on the brink, imperiled, jeopardized by its proximity
to the void; in these poems, as lion and lamb in the Peaceable Kingdom,

> Experience lies down with doom,
> That sleeps again, as history uses);

it is merely—merely! the adverb stands for a world of historical reversals, fashions turned inside out—interesting. And as that word itself
tells us at its root, to be *interesting* means to be among and in the
midst of things, at the center, *mediate*. We are unaccustomed to the
enormous modesty of this position, a modesty which amounts to a repudiation; if one writes from the midst of life, then one must accept,
as in Scripture, that we are in death. How rare, then, Van Doren's reticence, and how apt:

> Time still is to be
> When I am not I.
> The speech death makes
> Is not special for me.

This is not a poetry of compromise—nothing is left out, the awful
is not omitted; what marks Van Doren's particular stance is that it is
not opposed:

> Compounded of all tones, including these
> Of stricken ground and hideous green seas,

this music, rather, accommodates the extremities of experience in order to get it all together, as we say now, and to keep it there. Integrity,
wholeness, that is never the tragic goal, the pitch of doom which is the
reward of struggle, of denial. "Fate," as Van Doren observes, "comes
double if we deny." Rather it is the slow guerdon of centrality—"half
between is holy ghost"—which this poet is out for, and into, as he
makes the odd invocation to the only divinity forever at his elbow, the
least glamorous in all the pantheon:

Monotony, be thou my god.
Humdrum, lie close and watch me well . . .
Bind me to what I most desire,
    No matter how I twist and frown.
    The smile you wear as I say this,
    Monotony, is all I wish.

The answer to such a petition is a peril for poetry—for modern po-etry, at least. For the poet who "would have each moment's name / be musical, and sound the same," there is the constant temptation of the lithic mode, that inhumanity of earth where a poet can sit

    . . . among the stones, himself a stone,
    Watching an empty heaven till his mind
    Passed out of him and poured the silence full.

Sometimes the requirements of the fully human—the demands of an emotionally saturated life—are arduous; sometimes the poet falters: "I think I'll sit / till the stones turn empty. / They don't mind." But to become no more than immortal is too easy, the trance which sustains the flesh beyond centuries omits too much for Van Doren, and his poetry murmurs and rustles on, *past* the stones, though it notes that "the spirit best remembers being mute"—passes on to the life which includes but does not oppose death:

    Death is our outline, and a stillness seals
    Even the living heart that loudest feels.
    I am in love with joy, but find it wrapped
    In a queer earth, at languages unapt;
    With shadows sprinkled over, and no mind
    To speak for them and prove they are designed.
    I sing of men and shadows, and the light
    That none the less shines under them by night.

As long ago as 1939, such couplets, their ease and sanity, made it clear that Van Doren was the appropriate heir of Dryden—a relationship to which I shall return; but what most caught the attention of Van Doren's (generally admiring) critics was his accommodation of extremes in the general tenor—one recalls Edmund Wilson and then John Peale Bishop, especially, who marveled at the poet's apparently out-of-the-way concern with such old-fashioned fidelities as family, region, and the enduring of mortality rather than the striving against it. Since the romantic movement, we have been so accustomed to the imagination as a borderer, dwelling in risk and self-loathing upon the contours and verges of experience, that the impulse toward centrality, toward integrity and accommodation rather than alienation and exclusion ("that's me in the middle," Van Doren exclaims, as anyone might on glimpsing himself in a group photograph, and again, apostrophizing the doleful Don and his lumpy Squire, "halfway between them, that will do"—though who else has the choice,

> Who else could be serene at truth's circumference
> When only the known center of it sings?),

the undertaking to unite seems to us an alien, an inadequate account of our situation, unpromising in drama when it is the dramatic conflict which promises to redeem. A life so firmly natural, so happily given over to the leagues and affections of family, of filiation and paternity, of marriage and companionship, of fraternity most of all, and so proudly committed to its own failing body as well—a life unalienated by the kind of demonic aspirations which have created an entire literature of fragmentation and partiality among us—is an exotic indeed, and what is more, a *mild* exotic, the hardest kind to entertain, to appease, to answer!

It will go easier for us if, as a prolegomenon to any future reading of Mark Van Doren, we trace even for a moment his profoundly acknowledged debt to the English tradition; almost alone among his contemporaries in this country, as John Peale Bishop pointed out, Van Doren shows no trace of French influence. T. S. Eliot commended Van Doren's 1920 study of Dryden (written, then, well before any of the poetry Van Doren included in his collected work), especially for il-

lustrating "the very wide range of Dryden's work," not just the satire
but the achievement in almost every department, every species of poetry. Dryden is not suggestive, Dryden is everywhere explicit; his verse
says what he means it to say ("poets are by too much force betray'd,"
as Dryden himself observed) and not more than that. Yet Eliot was
characteristically prophetic to admire Van Doren's breadth of response, for Dryden's is a range paralleled by Van Doren's own—in
fiction, in drama, in criticism, and in almost every department, every
species of poetry. The summer before he died, I asked Mark Van
Doren for a choice—to adorn an anthology I was compiling—of
a preferred poem of his own and of a poem from the past with
which his own might sustain interesting relations. With a certain
asperity, the poet, who had been my teacher and perhaps my only
teacher who thought it worth his while to show that he found fools
insufferable, chose Dryden's celebrated elegy on Oldham but refused
to specify in his own work beyond that preference of fifty years ago for
Dryden. In fact, he insisted that his former student select on his own,
out of what is not so much an embarrassment as an embodiment of
riches, the *Collected and New Poems 1924–1963*, these quiet yet queerly
fierce couplets which belong to the sustained middle register of Van
Doren's art:

> Envy the young who have no words at all,
> And the old, for they have had them. Now by wall
> In sunshine, or by candle at the dance,
> Or corner-warm, stillness is circumstance
> Conclusive: there they sit, and no one says
> They should be heedful of bright sentences.
> Their silence, innocent of insult, tries
> For how much truth? Who knows? It may be wise
> Or sleepy, may be amorous of death
> Or heavy with remembrance—the slow breath
> Of sluggards at the goal. Who blames them here
> For blinking? They are privileged to peer
> Past us, past Him, past anyone at all,
> And speak no word, those sitters by the wall.

On the face of it—the face of language heightened beyond mere speech ("if nothing were to be raised above that level," Dryden warns, "the foundation of poetry would be destroyed"), yet beneath any suspicion of mere spellbinding ("a man is not to be cheated into Passion," says Dryden again, "but reasoned into Truth")—on the face of it, this verse appears docile enough, even decorous in diction, a convention, as I have called it, for dealing with what a man means to say. It is a decorum, though, which admits of—which enforces—a terrible knowledge, rather a wisdom to be had only when language is "received," is handed down, and when a poet knows what is in his hands from another's. This kind of poetry, the poetry of a received idiom, is not, as I have said, a matter of experiment (which is merely experience) or even of originality (which is merely a reversion to origins), but of the chastened admission that his language is the poet's fate as well as his fortune, his doom and not merely his discretion. Hence envy of the young who have no words and of the old who have had them: the silence of the old in Van Doren's poem—like Dryden's farewell to a poet his junior by some twenty-two years—is a kind of valedictory to poetry itself, the acknowledgment that utterance is no more than a task, an obligation, that the uncheated passion is all in the silence. Dryden says somewhere, "To invent a probability and to make it wonderful is the most difficult undertaking in the art of Poetry." That is Mark Van Doren's invention in the poem I have quoted here, the invention in speech of the wonderful probability of silence.

I have not intended my appreciation of Mark Van Doren's lyric canon to serve, in particular, as an introduction to the last book of lyrics. In terms of circumstance, these final poems do represent a departure, for they represent The Departure; unlike the many, many other poems of his long life, the vivid, deciduous poems of *Good Morning* are not written in the midst of life, they are written from the acknowledged edge, they are poems everywhere resonant with the prescience and the presence of death. Yet the awareness of a threshold beside him, like Pascal's abyss, does not cause Mark Van Doren to recoil, to withdraw from life. Rather it is as if the very energies and impulses of his being—remembered, imagined, speculated upon, brooded over—were closer to language, to the one embrace he had always mastered, than ever before. There is no program to these moments of almost visionary awareness, these singular last devotions, save one: to come unpropped, undefended to the moment, to the encounter with life itself. That is why the poet can say:

> This is the first poem. There was none
> Before it. Do not misunderstand me. This
> Is the first poem ever.

Exactly: we shall not misunderstand if we realize that *only* when each poem is the first poem can there be a thousand poems. Otherwise, there is only one poem. It is precisely because he acknowledges the primacy of poems—other men's poems, his own poems—that Mark Van Doren can write each new, first one with "an odd secret excitement, a strange need / to be there with words when the heartbeat happened." He is the precious spokesman, mouthpiece and prolocutor of the single life at that moment when it knows itself to sum up the significance of what is more than single, the meaning of what is many.

Dreadful Alternatives:
A Note on Robert Penn Warren

[1975]

In all our societies, the hold the dead have over the living is the subject of literature; in the American South, or in the mind of that South, which made the discovery for America that when you live without the past you do not live in the present but in some imaginary (and unpromising) future—in the South, the hold the dead have over the living is the subjection of literature. Death is perceived, of course, as a standstill, life as a falling away from such perfection. The tension generated between that immobility and that erratic descent is the famous tension of poetry, its irony, even its disease: one tends to turn to stone, or to water. One petrifies, or one liquefies. Though he has his lithic moments, they occur early on in Robert Penn Warren's abundant oeuvre—back in the poems of "Kentucky Mountain Farm":

> Instruct the heart, lean men, of a rocky place
> That even the little flesh and fevered bone
> May keep the sweet sterility of stone.

And from almost as long a way back, the impulse is against the stone, and toward the water, against what stands and toward what runs. The poet is of course a novelist, a teller, and the poems which constitute such a continuing part of his production are just that: they continue, they persist against their own concretion, their own calculus. "This book is conceived as a single long poem composed of a number of shorter poems as sections or chapters," Warren carefully tells us at the beginning of *Or Else*, and the very alternative of such a title ominously suggests what bothers him into poetry: on the one hand, we exist only by getting on with it, only by continuity; yet on the other hand, "only in discontinuity do we know that we exist." And surely poetry is the knowledge of our existence! Yet just as surely poetry is more than death, more than discontinuity, more than one damned thing next to another: poetry is one damned thing *after* another, it is what happens next as well as what has happened once and for all. The tug of these polarities, the tactic of concessions now to this extremity, now to that one, are the matter of all Robert Penn Warren's various manners—are why he has so many. With *Promises* (1954–56) came a great renewal, and for the past twenty years the poems have been "brought in" in a steady stream, eagerly receiving signals from the deciduous world: the golden sycamore, the white dogwood, emblems of an acknowledged mortality, a complicity with death accepted by life, the narrated detail and the abstract knowledge made one.

The stream can be traced to its source fifty years back, when in 1924, Allen Tate wrote to Donald Davidson: "That boy's a wonder— has more sheer genius than any of us; watch him: his work from now on will have what none of us can achieve—power." Well of course "any of us" meant not only Davidson and Tate but John Crowe Ransom as well, and in such a case we are as reluctant as Warren would be to mea- sure out the "sheer genius." But if by "power" Tate intended that hon- orable skirmish between life and death, between the hold the dead have over the living and the hopes the living have over the (mere) dead, then he was prophetic and not only in the sense of seeing what was coming, but in the sense of saying what was there.

Robert Penn Warren has indeed the power to keep himself going, to write with an ease and outrage which cancels out rather than con- ceals the strictures which operate between poetry and prose (I mean that *verse* means very little to him now; what means very much is the movement of the voice as it glows over images, a prose voice most of the time, obstructed only at transcendent moments into the stoppages of significant line-breaks). It is a poetry, often, of statement below the tension of the lyre, though it acknowledges that tension as, indeed, above itself; toward the end of *Or Else* comes this statement: "This moment is non-sequential and absolute, and admits of no definition, for it subsumes all other, and sequential, moments, by which definition might be possible." Warren is talking about ecstatic recognition, which takes place out of time, against time, which takes the form of a kind of death ("this moment is . . . absolute"), and he cannot endure to versify such recognition, though the lines I have just quoted as prose here are set up on the page in a kind of fancy articulation which has nothing to do with that ceremony of recuperations we have agreed to call verse. He cannot bear, I think, to bring together the statement of death with the form of death (Tate's poems, Ransom's), for at such a confluence the flow will cease, he will stop writing poems, the ecstatic identification will choke him off. He says this very deliberately, very gently, at the end of one of the poems about his dead and their possession of him:

> All items above belong in the world
> In which all things are continuous,
> And are parts of the original dream which
> I am now trying to discover the logic of. This
> Is the process whereby the pain of the past in its pastness
> May be converted into the future tense
>
> Of Joy.

Such conversion is the effort and is the success, by and large (largeness is what most interests Warren now, his impatience with the finicky characterizes a man who knows his own mind, who knows what to expect of his own senses), of this newest installment of Warren's *poème-fleuve*, though installment is scarcely the word—let me say this new view from the next bend in the river, always the same water in which we can step any number of times: "he is telling himself his own old story."

The invoked masters for the present pursuit of joy are Dreiser and Flaubert. Dreiser because "his only gift to enact / all that his deepest self abhors"; and Flaubert because he offers "a solemn thanksgiving to

God for the fact he could perceive the worth of the world with such joy." Abhorrence *becomes* joy by the perception, the enactment, and of course by a kind of reverence in receiving what I have called the signals from mortal things: "Reality / is hard enough to come by, but even / in its absence we need not blaspheme / it." The two great realists, the Frenchman transfiguring even Egypt and syphilis ("Man lives by images. They lean at us from the world's wall . . . "), the American failing, and in his abasement coming to a kind of glory ("let us note how glory, like gasoline spilled / on the cement in a garage, may flare, of a sudden, up / in a blinding blaze, from the filth of the world's floor"), are superb emblems of invocation here, psycho-pomps, and the rest of the poem/poems hence fall or flow under the sign of the one redemption or the other loss. The paradox is that it is the redeemed experience, the transfigured image which literally stands for death, and that it is the lost experience, the abased and abhorred continuity which melts away into a life merely lived and thereby eluded. "Virtue is rewarded, that / is the nightmare," the book begins, and characteristically goes on: "and I must tell you . . . " Such telling, then, is the way out of the nightmare, the clue to the labyrinth:

> All day, I had wandered in the glittering metaphor
> For which I could find no referent.
> All night, that night, asleep, I would wander, lost in a dream . . .

whereas "the glittering metaphor" is no more than the scandalous image of death, the patience, the suffering, just so, of the ecstasy.

The drama of a life's work *resumes*, then, in both senses of that verb—continues and is summed up—in these new poems which are so much anti-verse because they seek to be universe, poems of autobiography and devotion, despairing illuminations of a man who turns from the rock, from the crystal, from the death, and at the end of the very poem addressed to John Crowe Ransom adjures himself and his old friend and all of us with that half-century of his "power":

> I advise you to detach your gaze from
> that fragment of rock. Not all witnesses

of the phenomenon survive unchanged
the moment when, at last, the object screams

in an ecstasy of

being.

So may the revelations of a man be cast, the energies of metonymy,
continuity, prose opposing the energies of metaphor, ecstasy, verse (or
at least separation), the water running out of the rock, the narrative es-
caping mere (mere!) being. *Survive unchanged*—who would want
to?—the terms are contradictions, survival requires just that change
which can withstand the scream of the object in its ecstasy. I said earlier that the impulse is against the stone and toward the water; it is reassuring to notice that at the front of his poem/poems Robert Penn
Warren has taken, from Psalm 78, this line as an epigraph: "He clave
the rocks in the wilderness, and gave them drink out of the great
depths." Not only reassuring to my assessed phenomenology of the
poet, but reassuring that there is more poetry to come.

The Resonance of Henry James
in American Poetry

[1988]

In 1895, before James had got round to his most emphatically Jamesian works, Oscar Wilde prophesied, with characteristically proleptic grace, the matter of the Jamesian manner. Why yes, says the heroine of *Lady Windermere's Fan* of the woman who turns out to be her mother, she is in Paris. She is an American, so she is in Paris. All good Americans go to Paris when they die. And where, asks the Wildean straight man, tortuous role—where do the bad Americans go? Oh, they go to America.

Think of the fate of Kate Croy, of Charlotte Stant, and think of the exchange in *The Portrait of a Lady* between Isabel Archer and Mme Merle. Isabel has just learned how deeply she has been deceived and manipulated by her vile husband and his former mistress, and she says to Serena Merle, "I believe I do not ever wish to see you again." And Mme Merle rejoins, pulling on her wonderful gloves, "I am leaving tomorrow—for America."

We are told so much of Isabel, whom we last see with diamonds in her hair, giving awful parties on Thursday evenings at the Palazzo Osmond, parties which exist to make people not invited to them uncomfortable. As always in James novels, the later life of the characters—the life they will lead outside the novel—is left suspended. No one dies, no one gets married; instead, like Strether, they go to America.

This was the clue which T. S. Eliot, who knew what being in America was like, collected from James's novels. Unviolated by any idea, he too was ravished by a situation, one which in *The Portrait of a Lady* he illustrated with unusual splendor. The speaker is, bluntly, Isabel Archer aged . . . well, my age. The novel was published in 1880, when James was the age of Dante's pilgrim, which would make Isabel, by 1910, in her mid-fifties. Ruined but irresistible, as we find her in Eliot's poem. One technical clincher, the "capricious monotone / that is at least one definite 'false note'"—those inverted commas refer to the moment in the novel when Isabel realizes that there is an intimacy between Osmond and Mme Merle (an intimacy expressed by the fact that Gilbert is sitting down while talking to the standing Mme Merle); Isabel doesn't know what is wrong, but she acknowledges one definite "false note." This is the tiny phrase Eliot puts in quotation marks, and it is enough for me, even though it is a false note registered by the young man struggling in the toils of the American spider who refers to her buried life and Paris in the spring and various other pathologies (life, what cauchemar!).

As Eliot recognized, Henry James was always a disaster for the novelists who succeeded him. We have some interesting testimony concerning the disaster from Cynthia Ozick. But as Eliot also, and more fruitfully, acknowledged, James was an inexhaustible quarry for the poets. Let me tip a few of the stones upward.

In 1944, the same year that Auden wrote a preface for the first reprint since 1907 of Henry James's *The American Scene*, he published *The Sea and the Mirror*, a commentary on *The Tempest* (also the one play by Shakespeare which Henry James himself commented upon). Here is my first picture then, from Auden. It is from the end of Caliban's speech to the audience:

Not that we have improved; everything, the massacres, the whippings, the lies, the twaddle, and all their carbon copies are still present, more obviously than ever; nothing has been reconstructed; our shame, our fear, our incorrigible staginess, all wish and no resolve, are still, and more intensely than ever, all we have: only now it is not in spite of them but with them that we are blessed by that Wholly Other Life from which we are separated by an essential emphatic gulf of which our contrived fissures mirror and proscenium arch—we understand them at last—are feebly figurative signs, so that all our meanings are reversed and it is precisely in its negative image of Judgment that we can positively envisage Mercy; it is just here, among the ruins and the bones, that we may rejoice in the perfected Work which is not ours. Its great coherences stand out through our secular blur in all their overwhelmingly righteous obligation; its voice speaks through our muffling banks of artificial flowers and unflinchingly delivers its authentic molar pardon; its spaces greet us with all their grand old prospect of wonder and width; the working charm is the full bloom of the unbothered state; the sounded note is the restored relation.

The discussion appears—through a welter of grammatical subversions, as down a corridor of dramatic diminutions—to concern life as it is transformed by art. That it should be Caliban who so addresses us, the audience, might surprise us at first, till we find that it is in James's essay that reference is made to "the ineffable delicacy, a delicacy positively at its highest in the conception and execution of Caliban." No, Auden, whose apostrophe to James as the "master of nuance and scruple," is not having his little joke, merely; he is expressing a loyalty. A loyalty to the extraordinary hypertrophy of myth and dialectic, as L. C. Knights once called the stratagem of James's late prose, revealed, or rather exhibited here in these two (parallel) sentences from James's own essay on *The Tempest*, written the same year as *The American Scene*:

It is for Shakespeare's power of constitutive speech quite as if he had swum into our ken with it from another planet, gathering it up there, in its wealth, as something antecedent to the occasion and the need, and if possible quite in excess of them; something that was to make of our poor world a great flat table for receiving the glitter and clink of outpoured treasure. The idea and the motive are more often than not so smothered in it that they scarce know themselves, and the resources of such a style, the provision of images, emblems, energies of every sort, laid up in advance affects us as the storehouse of a kind before a famine or a siege—which not only, by its scale, braves depletion or exhaustion, but bursts, through mere excess of quantity or presence, out of all doors and windows.

What Auden gets from James, and he gets it in his prose from James's prose, though he sets the stage for other poets to get it in their verse—for it is a thing to be had equally in prose or verse, as I hope to show—what Auden gets is the notion that language, poetic language, say, is what it does: that the saying of something can be enacted by its movement in the sentence, a great looping, spiralled boa draped upon the thorns of pronomination. What James says Shakespeare does *he* does in the action of his prose account, and what Auden's Caliban says that art does to life is indeed done to language by the sustained metaphors and the carefully subordinated members of the long and idiorhythmic sentence.

It is not always grammar, actually no more than a variant of glamour, that the American poet found he could take, or take back, from James. At the start of the century, it was a theme, the encounter of innocence with experience which was the renewal of Oedipus's triumph over the sphinx:

> And the great domed head, *con gli occhi onesti e tardi*,
> Moves before me, phantom with weighted motion,
> *Grave incessu*, drinking the tone of things,
> And the old voice lifts itself
>   weaving an endless sentence.
> We also made ghostly visits, and the stair
> That knew us, found us again on the turn of it,
> Knocking at empty rooms, seeking for buried beauty.

The seventh canto, down to its tags of Italian and Latin, is of course an account of Pound's own visit to James, and occurs in my series of portraits not as a parallel vision, but an instance of special pleading, one worth hearing specifically for the theme announced, the matter rehearsed.

I want to skip past it and back to my chronology: back to the late 1950s, in fact, and to a poet from a grudging northern urbanity confronted with the overwhelming ease of meridional life. Here is Elizabeth Bishop in 1956, in *Ouro Preto*:

> . . . Women in red dresses
>
> and plastic sandals, carrying their almost
> invisible babies—muffled to the eyes
> in all the heat—unwrap them, lower them,
>
> and give them drinks of water lovingly
> from dirty hands, here where there used to be
> a fountain, here where all the world still stops.
>
> The water used to run out of the mouths
> of three green soapstone faces. (One face laughed
> and one face cried, the middle one just looked.
>
> Patched up with plaster, they're in the museum.)
> It runs now from a single iron pipe,
> a strong and ropy stream . . .

A kind of enchanted wringing of the hands might be the tone, one very clearly sounded in 1909 by Henry James in Capri. Listen for the resonance of helpless seduction in the awfulness of it all:

> The saint comes out at last, borne aloft in long procession and under a high canopy; a rejoicing, staring, smiling saint, openly delighted with the one happy hour in the year on which he may take his own walk. Frocked and tonsured, but not at all macerated, he holds in his hand a small wax puppet of an infant Jesus and shows him to all their friends, to whom he nods and bows: to whom, in the dazzle of the sun he literally seems to grin and

wink, while his litter sways and his banners flap and everyone gaily greets him.

It is not disgust, it is not even distaste, but in all of Bishop's Brazilian intimeries there will be that resonance, the immitigably alien, "separate" septentrional consciousness just a little shocked, just a little thrilled by the promiscuous availability of it all, registered in a prose accurate to the last degree, and a verse made even more so by the telling enjambments and the barest kind of iambic pentameter among the easy observations ("It runs now from a single iron pipe"). Auden used to wonder what Henry would have said, faced with the spectacle of a drum majorette . . . One suspects he would have been equal to it, and that equality is measured, is registered, in the capacity of the fussy grammar, the implacable advance of the huge periods, the overwhelming alliterative barrage, the annihilating adverbial postponement to be found, to be heard in Bishop's exactitudes.

I can make my point best, I think, by erasing the lines. Here is Bishop on Brazil, set up in prose:

> Januaries, Nature greets our eyes exactly as she must have greeted theirs: every square inch filling in with foliage—big leaves, little leaves, and giant leaves, blue, blue-green, and olive, with occasional lighter veins and edges, or a satin underleaf turned over; monster ferns in silver-grey relief, and flowers, too, like giant water lilies up in the air—up, rather, in the leaves—purple, yellow, two yellows, pink, rust red and greenish white; solid but airy; fresh as if just finished and taken off the frame.

And here is James's adieu, or a little of his adieu, to Florida:

> . . . The whole impression, for simply sitting there in the softest lap the whole South had to offer, seemed to me to dispense with any aid but that of its absolute felicity. It was, for the late return at least, the return in the divine dusk, with the flushed West at one's right, a concert of but two or three

notes—the alignment, against the golden sky, of the individual black palms, a frieze of chiselled ebony, and the texture,
for faintly-brushed cheek and brow, of an air of such silki-
ness of velvet, the very throne-robe of the star-crowned night,
as one can scarce commemorate but in the language of the
loom.

It will be the language of the loom, or the embroidery-frame, which
brings us up short. Bishop follows James in her resolute capacity to
hold the experience within a governing metaphor, a "fix" of relations
within which the view can be tweaked and poked at, quite relentlessly,
until it becomes a vision.

I hear the tonalities, and the strategies, of Henry James in the poetry
of my own generation. Let me elicit examples, with their opposite
numbers, or routines, in Henry James, from four of them: Anthony
Hecht, James Merrill, Howard Moss, and John Hollander, withholding my own practice only as too much of a damned good thing. Here,
for starters, is a smidgin of James in Venice, on the Grand Canal,
in 1890:

> ... These things at present are almost equally touching in
> their good faith; they have each in their degree so effectually
> parted with their pride. They have lived on as they could and
> lasted as they might, and we hold them to no account of
> their infirmities, for even those of them whose blank eyes to-
> day meet criticism with most submission are far less vulgar than
> the uses we have mainly managed to put them to. We have
> botched them and patched them and covered them with sor-
> did signs; we have restored and improved them with a merci-
> less taste, and the best of them we have made over to the
> pedlars.

Against which, or out of which, to use the veterinary phrase, how easy
it is to hear Hecht writing at just the same age, of the Serenissima:

                    Meanwhile,
Space must be made for all ephemera,
Our cast-offs, foulings, whatever has gone soft
With age, or age has hardened to a stone,
Our city sweepings. Venice has no curbs
At which to curb a dog, so underfoot
The ochre pastes and puddings of dogshit
Keep us earthbound in half a dozen ways,
Curbing the spirit's tendency to pride.
The palaces decay. Venice is rich
Chiefly in the deposits of her dogs.
A wealth swept up and gathered with its makers.

Except for "dogshit," which I don't think James would use, though surely those ochre pastes and puddings are within his reach, and his rights, there is a kind of travel account, a discourse of pilgrimage which James instituted for us—past Hawthorne, past Ruskin, past Pater— there is no nineteenth-century writer in prose who so figures the individual words in their run upon the mind ("we have botched them and patched them and covered them with sordid signs") that can be of such service to the describing poet. Now of course that very category is not altogether, in my generation, a frequent one. *The describing poet* is the poet who has truck, or some vehicle or other, with the past, with the permanent, even when it is a permanence jeopardized. For the American poet since 1950, any descriptive account of *anything* will be Jamesian, insofar as the Jamesian tone, the muster of language under the ravaging wing of memory and credence, will afford an access to the physical world which prosody has funked. I am saying that only a certain kind of prose can be employed, in its careful tortuosity, to accomplish what was once the very genre of the lyric necessity in its aspect of memorial associations. Hence, with all its guarded qualifiers, Howard Moss's "Buried City"—of which here is but one of twenty-three stanzas:

    Slowly this buried city came to light
    Up from its ruins, all its riddles blank

(Its verses, too), with no one to look out
While all of us looked in. We were the mere
Observers, really, not the partisans
Of life. At the exit, sign the pledge
Forbidding you to say that we exist at all.

Moss's very good verses must still observe the decorums of very
good prose as well, the particular, even finicky prose which
James has turned into *the* American idiom for the past, its theory and practice, as here in evoking Pompeii, circa 1908:

. . . Even Pompeii, in fine, haunt of *all* the cockneys of creation,
burned itself, in the warm still eventide, as clear as glass, or as
the glow of a pale topaz, and the particular cockney who
roamed without a plan and at his ease, but with his feet on Roman slabs, his hands on Roman stones, his eyes on the Roman
void, his consciousness really at last of some good to him,
could open himself as never before to the fond luxurious fallacy
of a close communion, a direct revelation.

The paradox of the reversal I am celebrating here, the attribution
of memorial intensities to prose and of spontaneous discoveries to
verse, may be an accident in the history of our poetry, but it has ne-
cessitated recourse to the American expatriate novelist in more than
one kind of work. The note of satire, even of outright comedy and certainly of character, is one that resorts most readily to the Jamesian
prosateur for outrage, for insight:

Mr. Cashmore, who would have been very red-headed if he had
not been very bald, showed a single eyeglass and a long upper
lip; he was large and jaunty, with little petulant movements and
intense ejaculations that were not in the line of his type.

That is a character making his entrance in *The Awkward Age*, much to
William Glass's delight in his destructive variations on "The Concept
of Character in Fiction"; it is not precisely the same theory of not so

much what is given but what is left out that makes not only the Jamesian character but James Merrill's as well:

> Lodeizen, Hans, 1925–50,
> Dutch poet. Author of *Het immerlijk*
> *Behang*, Etc. Studies in America.
> Clever, goodnatured, solitary, blond,
> All to a disquieting degree.
> Plays a recording of the "Spring" Sonata
> One May night when JM has a fever;
> Unspoken things divide them from then on.
> Dies of leukemia in Switzerland,
> The country of a thousand years of peace.

One more set of pictures, then, one more exhibition not of "influences," God forbid, but of strategies shared, learned, adopted, effected! My last showing then takes us to the Jersey shore, revisited by James, remembered by John Hollander, both with that embracing intensity we now call Proustian, but only because we have not first or far more recently read *The American Scene*:

> These influences then were present, as a source of glamour, at every turn of our drive, and especially present, I imagined, during that longest perspective when the road took no turn, but showed us, with a large, calm consistency, the straight blue band of summer sea, between the sandy shore and the reclaimed margin of which the chain of big villas was stretched tight, or at least kept straight, almost as for the close stringing of more or less monstrous pearls. The association of the monstrous thrusts itself somehow into my retrospect, for all the decent humility of the low, quiet coast, where the shadows of the waning afternoon could lengthen at their will and the chariots of Israel, on the wide and admirable road, could advance, in the glittering eye of each array of extraordinary exposed windows, as though an harmonious golden haze.

It is from within such structures, in Deal, New Jersey, during a summer at the shore, on the ninth of July specifically, that Hollander has his epiphany, afforded him as to all our poets, by the sentencing of Henry James:

> This is the time most real: for unreeling time there are no
> Moments, there are no points, but only the lines of memory
> Streaking across the black film of the mind's night.
> But here in the darkness between two great explosions of light,
> Midway between the fourth of July and the fourteenth,
> Suspended somewhere in summer between the ceremonies
> remembered from childhood and the historical conflagrations
> imagined in sad, learned youth—somewhere there always hangs
> The American moment.
>   Burning, restless, between the deed
> And the dream is the life remembered . . . On the ninth of July
> I have been most alive: world and I, in making each other
> As always, make fewer mistakes . . .

And Hollander gives me, at the end of this magnificent passage from his most neglected book, *Visions from the Ramble*, which like James's own books will kick off its tombstone one day—Hollander gives me my farewell to these pairings in tribute with his great judgment of the Master, or should I say *from* the Master, which accounts for why James is so present, so presiding a force in the work of some of our finest and most forceful poets:

> To imagine a language means to imagine a form of life.

Marianne Moore and
the Monkey Business of Modernism

[1990]

T here is only one figure, a single poet (and of course a single woman) in the entire cavalcade of the American literary vanguard who from the first—and in some instances, from well before the first—was acknowledged, was prized, was in fact and in fancy *adored* by a plurality of eminences in that critical and poetical company, on both sides of the Atlantic, which we now, with some readiness, some show of conviction, call Modernism. By its exemplars she was greeted and ingratiatingly seized upon as one of their own: by Ezra Pound, who dubbed her—invoking a specifically Modernist desideratum—"a protagonist for the rights of vitrification and petrifaxis" (for had she not admitted: "my writing is a collection of flies in amber"?); by T. S. Eliot, who said she was "too good to be appreciated anywhere" (and had she not remarked on her utter isolation: "the cure for loneliness is solitude"?); by Wallace Stevens, who called her "not only a complete disintegrator, but an equally complete reintegrator" (and had she not observed: "the objective is architecture, not demolition"?); by William Carlos Williams, who called her poetry "a multiplication of impulses, distressingly broken up, which by their several flights, crossing at eccentric angles, might enlighten" (and had she not admitted that "to doubt is merely a part of liking and of feeling"?); by Kenneth Burke, who delightedly recorded how she, "by the gentle mastery of her ways of writing, had terrified me over and over again" (and did she not confess that "willingness to baffle the crass

reader sometimes baffles the right one"?); and by R. P. Blackmur, who
defined hers as "a sensibility which constitutes the perfection of standing aside" (for had she not all apodictically announced that "those
who have the power to renounce life are those who have it"?). Even
Gertrude Stein, as we discover with some surprise in her correspondence with Carl Van Vechten, was eager to have her admiring respects
wafted to the author of, at the time, a single book of fifty-three poems
published in 1924, the poet then being thirty-seven years old.

I have woven a tendentious chaplet from the unweeded garden of
accolades which sprouted around Marianne Moore at the very inception of her poetic career and which has tended to hypertrophy and
overgrow the embowered personage it was intended to honor and
embellish; let me lead you up that garden path only a moment longer,
and perhaps out of the precincts of encomium—always a little stifling,
a little blinding—by noting that there is, simply, no comparable instance of such unanimity of favor among our canonical Modernists
and their substantiating critics (as the mere mention of Gertrude Stein
may remind us: just consider the bouquet of hostilities these same
gentlemen, as well as the rest of the reading world, presented to Miss
Stein, whose monolithic insistence that you were with her and for her,
or else out of the running altogether, made her so much less likely to
be honored as a literary master, or even as a literary mascot, than the
decorous Miss Moore. Indeed, I believe we are entitled to some small
wonder that the subject of our musings—for all her propriety, her
gentility—was not *subjected*, just so, to a share in the mass of obloquy
and derision visited upon her three notable contemporaries—Gertrude
Stein, Eleanor Roosevelt, and Martha Graham—so monumentally
mocked in their prime for all the eventual homage accorded them
in their superannuation). There is no analogous instance of such general recognition, reverence, and *commitment* as that showered upon
Marianne Moore by those masters whom my high-school English
teacher, Miss Gail Wickwire, used to call, in fear and trembling, "the
Moderns."

They appeared, those Moderns, at about the same time in the
spring term as short sleeves, and to us they seemed, at Shaker Heights
High School, to bulk or to bulge large chiefly by their differences and

disparities, their mutual repulsions, and even more by their differences from everything which had preceded them. Thus, it was all the more astonishing to encounter—by the time I made it to Columbia University in Miss Moore's own New York, where in another borough the poet was a frequently visible specimen in the literary zoo, and even in the zoo itself—such a concord of approval and even veneration as was evidently hers. Not that we understood, precisely, what she was being praised for. It was hard to know what to make of Mr. Blackmur's entrancement with her method, what he called "her system of counting which stands for more than it shows, and shows, when you are on to it, more than it can possibly stand for." We could see that she was concerned with an attention to detail, to observable experience which seemed, often, pathological. Her strategies were so evasive, so deliberately oblique, for all the immediacy of her concern with the animal kingdom. Her splendor, as Geoffrey Hartmann was to point out years later, was menagerie. She had discovered in the world of creatures a vocabulary, a nomenclature of analogies, for herself. The trouble was that her poems were not really about animals— they were about the poet and about themselves, of course. She used this extraordinary manner of apparently exact description to render, in what we might call a zoophrasty or a zoophrasis, a world of suffused statement about herself. It was the most personal poetry ever written, yet it had become so by a refusal to be autobiographical. There was always a double resistance—on the one hand, to what she called "this disease, myself" and, on the other, to external menace. The animal poems, which Miss Wickwire was so eager to call to our attention and which the Moderns had so praised, were the confessions and acknowledgments of a compromised and vulnerable self. They were not a bestiary at all, or not like any other bestiary we could read. As for these praise-givers, our Miss Wickwire had known, of course, who they were, the concurring Moderns. She had recognized them—as she recognized the subject of their concurrence and the object of their delectation, Miss Marianne Moore herself—just because they were so different, altogether dissimilar, and even discrepant from the Elizabethans and the Augustans and the Romantics and the Victorians she had been "doing" with us every day, all year long. The Moderns, it was true, may not have appeared quite so different from the Metaphysicals or from the Mad Poets at the end of the eighteenth century, but neither madness nor metaphysics, I should tell you, buttered much hay with Miss Wickwire, who had us and the warm weather to contend with, and the syllabus to get through, *including the Moderns*, by June 10, 1947. . . .

For Miss Wickwire, by and large, any poet was modern—and consequently was modern for us, looming up on the other side of the Great Divide of literature as she professed it: disaffected, alien, dumb—if he (and even if *she*, a relatively singular instance) sustained or suffered an apparent scission from the poetry of the past; and all the more modern if he (and she) insisted upon the appearance and the publicizing of that scission. Such insistances upon a discontinuity with past masters, an excision from the acknowledged fabric, struck Miss Wickwire—and struck us—as particularly ominous in matters of form, for matters of form were so much more than merely that: were in poetry (and were we not reading poems, even if they were modern poems?) and in our transactions with poetry so very distinctive. Matters of form, after all, were how we managed to know it was poetry, and we clung to those formal recognitions with the desperation of the shipwrecked, discovering our vessel coming apart at the joints and the seams, just when we had learned—however sketchily, however academically—its anatomy, its framing. So that even though I believe Miss Wickwire enjoyed being able to dissert, as she had disserted earlier in the year upon the recognizable achievements of Christina Rossetti or of Emily Dickinson—for after all, she was Miss Wickwire, as they were Miss Rossetti and Miss Dickinson, with a certain emphasis: she was Miss Gail Wickwire, part of that American Maiden Tradition to which, from Louisa Alcott to Amy Clampitt, we entrust the instruction of our young people and the ecstatic impulse of our lyric selves—there was, nonetheless, in the encounter with the poetry of the Moderns, and chiefly in the collision with the poetry of Miss Moore, an interval of panic obstruction, for unlike the poetry of any earlier Miss, this poetry was unlike ANY POETRY WHATEVER! How, Miss Wickwire asked, flinging out her short-sleeved arms in a pretty gesture of despair—how were we to know that it was poetry at all?

Even if a certain assurance of harmlessness (much to be desired, in dealing with the responses of midwestern high-school seniors) was apparently vouchsafed by Mr. Blackmur's assertion that "there is no sex anywhere in her poetry, no poet has been so chaste; but it is not the chastity that rises from an awareness—healthy or morbid—of the flesh, it is a special chastity aside from the flesh, a purity by birth and from the void"—was this much help to Miss Wickwire, when it was her task to persuade us—even to bully herself into acknowledging— that these verbal objects Miss Moore had produced with such apparent detachment were or must be poems, even as Shakespeare's sonnets and Shelley's "Ode to the West Wind" and Swinburne's "Hymn to Proserpine" were recognizably and identifiably and *even in their titles* poems? Nor was it much more help when Miss Moore herself, from whom help should certainly be forthcoming, told us (or told someone; everything gets repeated: the walls have ears): "it never occurred to me that anyone might think I imagined myself a poet; if what I write is called poetry it is because there is no other category in which to put it." Really no help at all! This was, lamentably enough, poetry by default, and it cut a preposterous swath, a pitiful figure indeed, in the world of bards and laureates. . . .

Yet there it was: Marianne Moore's poems were precisely the ones which elicited, it appeared, among the very figures we so mistrusted and so misconstrued, among the mysterious Moderns, a perfect anthem of approbation and advocacy, a paean which was to echo down through the generations of American poetry, with confirming *fioriture* appended by Auden and Lowell, by Jarrell and Merrill and Ashbery, by Kenner and Davenport. . . . And what was unanimity among such disparate, even such discordant voices if not—as Miss Moore herself had said in another connection—a good sign if not always a good thing!

Miss Wickwire has gone to join Miss Moore among those gracious, life-enhancing presences who enable us, if we listen to their voices, to fend for ourselves in their absence. No longer am I faced, as I was at Shaker High, with four or five anthology favorites (if that is the word, given our mystification, our muddle when confronted with "No Swan So Fine" or "An Octopus"), but with the crisp Penguin that purports, in a plausible mendacity of 247 pages, to be *The Complete Poems of Marianne Moore*. This is a scandal, comparable to the seizure of revisionary zeal which appears to have overcome John Crowe Ransom, too, in his eighties; perhaps old writers cannot let their early poems alone because they cannot endure the revelations they believe they have permitted. In Miss Moore's case, the choppings and changings are disastrous, and I must urge any reader not to believe the old poet against her younger, wiser self. She warns us, the old poet, taking a whole page for the ominous four-word message, that "omissions are not accidents," a notification that has all the demure severity of a message from Hamlet's father's ghost: we are to put up with excisions, with renamings, with revisions out of all recognition—in short, with losses that no poet's achievement should be compelled to sustain. Let me remind you—and Miss Moore's editors and publishers, if ever my voice could reach so far—that what we need is not this absurd (though self-inflicted) travesty of the poet's accomplishment, nor even its superior predecessor of 1951, the so-called *Collected Poems*, which includes none of her mascot poems that so disfigure the later book, poems written, or assembled, when she had become resigned to the absurd charm of her appearance among us—her costume, her correspondence with the Ford Motor Company about the naming of the damn Edsel, her fanaticism about baseball, her general adorableness. For she had become a kind of Mary Poppins in our literary life, brutally irrelevant; and even someone who admired and understood her truly subversive and wrenchingly emotional qualities, someone like Elizabeth Bishop, did the remaining work great harm with her "invitation to please come flying," that invocation to a kind of benevolent witch, Glinda the Good, who might visit Manhattan and fix everything up with her "glittering collection of morals." No, what we need is a textual reprint of the 1924 *Observations* and of each subsequent book *as it first appeared*, without the deleterious cutting and fussing which the misguided and somewhat craven poet perpetrated upon her true genius.

There are, as it happens, three phases in the natural history of a poet: the phase of the constitution of the poetic canon; then the phase (occasionally elided) of the prose canon; and finally the phase of the poet's letters, sometimes not quite prose or poetry, but poetry torn up by the roots, as in the case of Emily Dickinson. Those of us who have developed an appetite for Marianne Moore's major work have learned to assemble the poems of the first phase for ourselves, without the help of their author or of The Viking Press; and in her centennial year, by a happy labor, Patricia Willis assembled the complete prose of the second phase, which must make a great difference, a great accrual, in our estimation of the poet. Not in our reading of the poetry, of course, but in our appraisal of the mind and heart, and indeed the body, which created it. From my own experience, I should suppose that the third phase will be quite as vital, quite as rewarding as the second. Back in 1947, not long after I had slid from Miss Wickwire's hands, the editors of *Columbia Review* invited Marianne Moore to judge their annual Boar's Head Poetry Contest. This was the year, I believe, when Miss Moore's mother, with whom she had lived her whole life (the poet was then sixty years old), was in failing health. Miss Moore wrote us (I was one of the editors) a note explaining in some detail why she could not take part in our revels—a postcard it was, inspissated with capitals and distributed with astonishing axiological intention over its entire surface: the mysterious thing was an unmistakable message from the poet. For like Henry James, Miss Moore was always entirely present, entirely herself, whether she were meeting a friend (or a dog) in the street, or writing a note of social obligation, or a poem, or a review. She never put "something of herself" into what she wrote—she put it all. I deduce from the note refusing our invitation—a note I stole from the archives of the *Columbia Review*, for I coveted the resemblance of contours to the late poems of Stéphane Mallarmé—that the letters of Marianne Moore will amount to an overpowering affair, an enlargement of this deceptively modest figure who insisted that "she would rather be told too little than too much," for whom "the power of implication" (to which I shall return, for it is a key to her mystery, that implicative power) "was insured by compactness," and who readily acknowledged: "writing is difficult—at least it is for me." In other words, the woman who said she would like to have invented the zipper.

But until the texts of phase three are collected (from private hands, from restricted library collections, and from the Rosenbach Foundation holdings of Moore papers in Philadelphia), we cannot altogether speak of Marianne Moore the poet in the way in which we speak of Yeats, or Stevens, or Hart Crane. It appears that a poet's letters constitute a crucial dimension of the poet—Pope thought so to the point of editing and rewriting and publishing his own—one we cannot well do without, though we are perhaps compelled to do so, or to make believe we do so, for a very long time. Since we have also had to make do with a pernicious selection of the poems, how consoling (her word, one she uses almost as often as *elate*, as *rapt*) that we have, this year, so full and fulfilling an edition of Marianne Moore's prose. Here I have fed, and found the kind of pasturage which the poet's own debilitations of her poems have so frequently denied me. That is, "superlatives and certainties so sanguine as somehow to seem like uncertainties," as well as "a naturalness so studied as to annihilate itself," and the claim that "we must have the courage of our peculiarities" simultaneous with the insistence that "we must be as clear as our natural reticence allows us to be."

What is it we can learn about Moore and modernity (so nearly synonymous, as I intend further to assert) in these hundreds of pieces, often confronting for the first time new works by Yeats, by Pound, by Stevens, by Eliot, by Williams, by Stein? Marianne Moore did not have a great mind, but she aspired to have a whole one, and a whole mind is rarer still, and more important than mere greatness. It is this wholeness of mind, this integrity of Being, which enabled her to say, with such exemplary fierceness: "the thing is to see the vision and not deny it; to care and admit that we do." Everyone knows, by now, those great ethical crystallizations which occur like geodes in her poems, culminating in the volume—and the poem—*What Are Years* (1941). They have become a significant part of the poetic morality of our time. Here are the ones that come to me, merely by murmuring her eminent name and letting the fine words float to the surface:

hope not being hope / until all ground for hope has / vanished

the project / of wings uniting levity with strength

The chasm-side is / dead. / Repeated / evidence has proved that it can live / on what can not revive / its youth. The sea grows old in it.

the haggish, uncompanionable drawl / of certitude

his byplay was more terrible in its effectiveness / that the fiercest frontal attack

as if a death mask ever could replace / life's faulty excellence!

complexity is not a crime, but carry / it to the point of murkiness, and nothing is plain.

the dismal / fallacy that insistence / is the measure of achievement and that all truth must be dark

when one is frank, one's very presence is a compliment

one detects creative power by its capacity to conquer one's detachment

The passion for setting people right is in itself an afflictive disease. Distaste which takes no credit to itself is best.

Ecstasy affords / the occasion and expediency determines the form.

He sees deep and is glad, who / accedes to mortality / and in his imprisonment rises / upon himself as the sea in a chasm, struggling to be / free and unable to be, in its surrendering / finds its continuing.

The power of the visible is the invisible

To explain grace requires / a curious hand

Victory won't come / to me unless I go / to it

The weak overcomes its / menace, the strong overcomes itself

As if, as if, it is all ifs

When what we hoped for came to nothing, we revived.

memory's ear / that can hear without / having to hear

There never was a war that was not inward

A formula safer than an armorer's: the power of relinquishing / what one would keep; that is freedom.

But in *The Complete Prose of Marianne Moore*, we are discovering how such wisdom was come by. Classical in its emphasis—as when she says, "in any matter pertaining to writing we should remember that major value outweighs minor defects"—it is also stoical in its submission to humility and concentration and steadfastness—as when she says, "if one cannot strike when the iron is hot, one can strike *till* the iron is hot." There is, further, in this prose, the spirit that, as Wallace Stevens described it, wears the poem's guise at last. It is, though without the stiffening of doctrine, a spirit profoundly Christian, for it is the spirit which invokes the strength "to surmount defeat by submitting to defeat"; and again, it is the spirit which acknowledges that "to be hindered is to succeed." At its greatest reach, it is the spirit (and I note that Helen Vendler has already seized upon this passage as rising to the passion of religious oratory while keeping its distance from the conventionality of predictable religious utterance) which says: "We need not be told that life is never going to be free from trouble and that there are no substitutes for the dead; but it is a fact as well as a mystery that weakness is power, that handicap is proficiency, that the scar is a credential, that indignation is no adversary for gratitude, or heroism for joy. There are medicines." No religion in history has enabled such *sagesse* except Christianity, though this is a strain of

Christian sentiment not to be found over Dante's gate, nor over Saint Peter's portal. It is quietism, and it is a sentiment which has enormous aesthetic—or poetical—consequences, for it makes Miss Moore say that "no work of art is old which was ever new, as no one is dead who was ever alive."

Here, I think, is manifest the consciousness which makes Marianne Moore speak so frequently, and so zealously, as if she had failed; as if for all the admiration and honor of her fellow Moderns, she were not with the elect; "I seem to myself an interested hack," she once said, "rather than an author." She abided by such humility because she believed authorship had to do with continuity, had to do with perpetuation and with union. In this she was with Miss Wickwire. "Insofar as a thing is really a work of art," Miss Moore believed, "it confirms other works of art." So here was the issue. It was the issue Miss Wickwire and her class of seniors at Shaker Heights High School perceived in their confusion. Indeed, it is the issue which even Robert Lowell perceived, quite as confused, when he referred to her "terrible and private and strangely revolutionary poetry." For whatever Modernism may be, we know this much about it, that its modes and mechanisms are those of fragmentation, dissociation, erasure, and opposition. In a word, of collage, an abrupt dispersal without modulation, without continuity, functioning not by transformation but by . . . transgression, very likely. The mosaic of citations and shifting focuses which constituted Marianne Moore's poems from the first was, of course, a device of what might be called primitive Modernism, immediately recognized by more sophisticated—less isolated—practitioners. What they recognized was the inmost struggle to reassemble a whole, to reconstitute ecstasy, to regain, by a project of faceting and assemblage, that rapt elation which Yeats inveterately called unity of being. Characteristically, Miss Moore quotes another author when she wants most succinctly to identify her own enterprise: "One cannot too much encourage artists," she cites Christian Zervos as saying, "who strive to bring back unity, who perceive new sources of ecstasy, who all their lives love something not to be found in this world."

I believe this invoked (and unattainable) unity is the cause, or at least the source, of Marianne Moore's immitigable self-distrust, her conviction that "everything added is something taken away" (one of her rare iambic pentameters). How reticent, how wary she was about the originality so often, and so rightly, attributed to her by her peers! She did not want to be original; she wanted to be whole. As she said, "originality is not a thing sealed and incapable of enlargement, but that an author may write newly while continuing the decorums and abilities of the past." And again, with searching self-knowledge: "we cannot ever be wholly original." One understands that this is said with relief, not with regret. Placing together two things perceived as unrelated but capable of creating a third, indissociable thing—this is the characteristic Moore operation, an enterprise of salvage, a venture toward that integrity she so much adored. Indeed, the invention of the zipper.

"The emended theme compels development," she said, and not till we have a proper edition of all her poems shall we comprehend the extent of her emendation. When I say she was a primitive Modernist, I use the adjective in the sense used when we speak of primitive Christianity; nothing unconsidered or crude is meant. Miss Moore was always eager to seek out the consolations of an order, a discipline, a restraint, and though she loved spontaneity and cherished impulse, she mistrusted the tendencies of pleasure ("satisfaction is a lowly / thing, how pure a thing is joy"). They tended to get out of hand—tendencies indeed. We all remember the famous dismissal: "nor can we dignify confusion by calling it baroque," though I suspect that is just what we can do, and in her case as in others, what some of us, as classifying readers, have done.

This matter of the senses, and ultimately of sexuality, is one which recurs in any consideration of this poet. "Some are not interested in sex pathology," she writes with characteristic impersonality, though we know who is meant, do we not? She even extends the figure of a disease I have already quoted in her terrible condemnation, "innate sensuality is a mildew." By 1928, four years after *Observations* was published, and during the five years as editor of the *Dial* when she wrote no poetry, she mustered her editorial "we" to decisive effect: "We confess to admiring instinctiveness, concentration, and tentativeness; to favoring opulence in asceticism." *Opulence in asceticism*—it is a memorable phrase, and to its memory must be added that stoic corollary: "We fail in some degree, and know that we do, if we are competent; but can prevail." The point was not pleasure, or even gratification. The point was joy. Indeed, I believe the only sexually revealing (or betraying) locution Marianne Moore makes in the seven hundred pages of her prose—the only Freudian slip, if you like—is in this discrimination. "Pleasure," she asserts, "is not joy, it is a strangling horror—the serpent that thrusts forward rigid—and does not know it ever was anything else." What a reproof to the phallic consciousness! No wonder she observed—speaking of versification, or course—"the interiorized climax usually pleases me better than the insisted-on climax." It was joy, it was unity, it was wholeness which was the issue, the ecstatic outcome, the event, and she discerned that she could not reach it by what she once called "the courage of too much nudity on the part of waitresses conveying champagne to clothed patrons."

There is a sense in which the history of Modernism is precisely the history of those figures whom we initially read as if they had no erotic charge—like Henry James, like Virginia Woolf, like Santayana—and whom we ultimately, learning to read better, come to find suffused with erotic life. After all, the use of language itself is a manifestation, an expression of eros. And Marianne Moore is not only no exception to this law (as Mr. Blackmur had supposed); she is a thrilling *example* of a writer charged with erotic energy, sometimes with specifically sexual energy. As I perceive it, her sexuality is expressed in terms of the observed pulsion and response of tissues within the self rather than in terms of the exchange of epidermal sensations between two selves; but such writing is nonetheless as erotic, or as eroticized, as any I know, and has a kind of sensuous enchantment or gusto, to use a word she lingered over. I am uneasy, of course, in discussing the eroticism or the lack of it in Marianne Moore. I think we all are. As with Dickinson or O'Keeffe, I feel that in talking about women artists—or in talking about men such as Henry James or George Santayana—we have not yet devised or developed a vocabulary in which we can readily express or understand the erotics of withdrawal or recessiveness or obliquity, or the refusal of explicit sexual gesture. And consequently, I don't believe any of us can easily say: this is, or this is not, a fulfilled and rewarding sexual life. Nor is it correct for us to deny such a possibility to a life we ourselves perceive as unpromising.

Yet I have my mite to add to the confusion, for I would make an observation or two about Marianne Moore's life with her mother. Like that other primitive Modernist, like Constantine Cavafy, Moore lived until she was sixty with her mother. Yet in a sense she was the converse of the great Alexandrian poet, for it was the entire drama of Cavafy's apparently placid life that, although he shared his social and domestic existence with Fat One, as he called his extraordinary mother Harikleia, he never once revealed to her that he wrote poems. He never showed her his work, whereas Moore never wrote a word, or at least never wrote a poem, which did not pass—in every sense—her mother's austere scrutiny. This is what she meant by *implicative*, I believe. And when she said, "the iron hand of unconvention can be heavier than the iron hand of convention," I suspect she was speaking, in her characteristically oblique way, of the rewarding sense of Mary Warner Moore's approval. According to commonly acknowledged schemes of development, the mother is seen as powerful, and her power is seen as one that must be overcome, outgrown, escaped. Whether nurturing or smothering, the mother's power is perceived as a threat to autonomy. And, of course, autonomy has come to stand as the very structure of maturity. Any theory of identity which sees maturity as the achievement of separation is bound to regard the mother's power as inferior to—and as less desirable than—the father's power, which stands for distance and the world, whereas the mother's power stands for closeness and the home. According to this popular hierarchy of development, a woman who lives with her mother all her life would by definition never achieve full maturity. But perhaps such development to maturity is being measured here by the standard of only one gender. Perhaps we should reconceive the notion of maturity to include more of the spectrum of relationships than an idealized—and largely male-oriented—version of autonomy. A tolerance for incomplete separation (to put it negatively) could be perceived as differently mature from an insistence on total independence, on separation.

I invoke these clinical reflections because it seems to me that the one real blunder Marianne Moore ever made in her literary life was related to—was occasioned by—the death of her mother. For it was in her grief, casting about for some sort of prop or stay in the period of mourning, that she hit upon La Fontaine. Her decision, her determination to translate the *Fables*, and her commitment to doing so, "rendering" every last one, produced one of the most dispiriting failures in the history of verse translation. Howard Nemerov put it correctly, over thirty years ago: as poems to be read in English, Moore's *Fables* are "irritatingly awkward, elliptical, complicated and very jittery as to the meter"; as renderings of the French, they "vacillate between pedantic strictness and strange liberty." We know the labor must have been long and hard, and indeed it was required to be so, for these translations were not of La Fontaine at all, but of grief. They are the labor of mourning, and implicate the poet's needs, not her narrative intentions or nonchalant originals. "The mind resists a language it is not used to," Miss Moore wrote in another connection, and added what is the best judgment I know on this task we do not call Herculean only because Hercules could not have done it: "The conflict between the tendency to aesthetic anarchy and the necessity for self-imposed discipline must take care of itself." It has taken care of itself, and finally it released Marianne Moore for the last decades of her life's career in literature. Work done during this period is not equal to the style or standard of the remarkable poems created before her mother's death. The way of writing has become something of a tic, the product of *books and verisimilitude*, as she liked to say. But she did not project as valuable— this is what she once remarked of Pavlova, and it goes for herself twice over—the personality from which she could not escape. There was something more that she wanted, something further that she was trying for. "Nothing so eludes portraiture as ecstasy," she once observed, and that is her great truth. It was her felicity and her flaw—it was her fate—to create a poetry of Modernism which was the fruit of ardor, of diligence, and of refusing to be false. Yet all the while her impulse was toward ecstatic wholeness, unity of being, and what she called "the vision." Her struggle was a great one, and it is responsible for the supple tension, the resilience of her finest poems, which "move themselves with spotlight swiftness / into the crevices— / in and out, illuminating." The conflict, the opposition between what I have called the monkey business of Modernism—its dissociations, fragmentations, abrupt juxtapositions, and entangling oppositions—and the mind enamored of wholeness is Marianne Moore's immense arena, the proving-ground which she filled with grand work, ineluctably unlike anything ever written before or since. It is her doom to have cultivated an imaginary garden, in which she has become, for our literary histories, a misapprehended shibboleth. The garden happily remains—an imaginary garden with a real token in it.

Sharing Secrets

[1992]

The young woman at Bard College told me, "I don't like your poems." I was hanging around, or in there, as we say, after a reading of those poems, waiting to give a talk—like this one—about modern American poetry, or about the modernity of American poetry, which would be anything but a defense *pro domo*— but how should she have known that? Well, she would have known had she stayed to hear my talk. The best I could manage, the retort positive, as it were, was, "I don't either, a lot of the time," but that was insufficient. "I don't like your poems," she returned to the charge with an insistence not so much surprising as disagreeable. "I don't like them because there's too much history in them." "*Too much* history?"

My astonishment was not altogether an affectation—though I do not wish to appear to put affectation down—rather it was a kind of stupor, in part the consequence of a certain amount of expert grilling over the years as to my inaccuracies: Mrs. Cameron had died twenty years before I made her take Lord Tennyson's portrait; Ravel was in Madagascar when Strauss conducted Salomé in Paris, not in the next box, etc. etc. Why, when a professor of English came up to me with triumph gleaming in his eyes to say, "I'm the Victorian chair," a locution peculiar to our profession, I knew what was coming. It came: "I used to be so moved by your Ruskin poem, and then I happened to be reading some Ruskin letters and I realized how much Ruskin you appropriated for your poem, and (let's give credit where credit is rated low) I was even more moved by your poem in a different way." So the Victorian chair and I have one little secret which we share already. But whether mistakes or plagiarism, such waverings with regard to ascertainable fact are invariable liabilities discerned in my work by those who regard such work as anything more than the slavish tracings of Clio's hemline; hence my astonishment with the Bard contingent.

"*Too much* history?" "Yes," she said, "too much. I don't like history. History is oppressive to women. There never was a woman who wasn't oppressed by history." "Never? Not even Queen Elizabeth?" "Which Queen Elizabeth?"—this she put narrowly, as if I were trying to sneak through some casuistical loophole. "Oh, you know," I weaseled out of it, "Queen Elizabeth the First, of England . . . in the Renaissance?" "When was the Renaissance?"

I quote this little colloquy to its appalling end to take the burden off my poems, of course—the sublimity of such ignorance, like Heidegger's rationalism, cannot be sufficiently praised *or* blamed. But I also think—now, after a certain amount of scar tissue has formed— that my interlocutress had something. Something more, I mean, than a vast doubt about the location of the Renaissance. She felt, if I may give her the benefit of my suspicions, of my susceptibilities, that there was, in the poetry I so much enjoyed writing, stealing, reading, *performing*, too much hardware, the excessive realia of lives which inevitably reminded her of just those household bonds which, like so many women, she had determined to cast off. My critic was, if I may say so, kicking against the pricks. For surely my poetry as she heard it was all clanking and clattering, scratchy and thorny with the intimation, the positive insistence, of facts, features, names of occasions and even—history indeed!—with *dates*, the very data of circumstance.

And was such a thing, ontologically ripped from the gossip column, the chronicle, the matrix of our records of each other which the French so wisely call *commèrage*—was such a thing poetry? Wasn't poetry, rather, an immediacy unencumbered, unconditioned by the circumstantial? Wasn't lyric poetry, precisely, the eternal Now, or even the immediate Then . . . but experienced without—literally— impedimenta, without the mere baggage of our lives?

I speak of course of American poetry, and the mere mention of baggage affords me the occasion for a little excursus—the constatation of a geography: American poetry is no better than it has ever been, for there is no improvement, no progress in what must be no more (if no less) than itself, immitigably on its own terms, those terms being what it is; the end of utterance as a term is an end, as well as the utterance itself. No, American poetry is no better than it was with Emerson or Dickinson or Melville or Whitman, but it is discrepant, there is a difference. One remarks that it comes to us, now, from every point on the continent, from every condition of social life, from every source of regional speech—and *that* is at least a departure from the classical locality of articulation in these states, as the four names I have just mentioned indicate. That our poets should now be inspissated in every county (almost, one has to say, in every university) of these fifty states is no argument for their being less alone—less without baggage—with America than before; rather it is an evidence of why they must be the more so, the more isolated within their so unconnected elsewheres. For the poetry of America begins only in the face of the unnameable, it begins with the giving of names to what has not been named, as Gertrude Stein once said, and such an assignment commences only upon the perception of an *elsewhere* alien to the very language which seeks it out. One welcomes the diversity, the difference, the discrepancy as I have called it, not because it will unite us but because it will refresh the terms of our division, our selfhood, our reality.

And here I should like to hover, to loiter a little over my declared perception of a generalized impulse in all this poetry of ours—all except mine, I mean; mine and perhaps the poetry of half a dozen contemporaries—Mr. Hecht, Mr. Hollander, and Mr. Merrill among them, fortunately. Let me say, then, that I want to brood upon the nature of something in the work of poets in the United States who are *under fifty*, thus exposing myself and Mr. Hollander and Mr. Hecht and Mr. Merrill completely. Something in the burden, to use an old word for subject or content when it takes a special form, the burden, then, of most of our American poets as I see them. And I see them as an editor of poetry magazines for the last twelve years, receiving about a thousand poems a month; as a teacher; and as a publisher of a series of poetry books I choose from all the clamorous manuscripts (they even come from agents!) that fill the publisher's mail room, poets who hang or fall or even lie together in their mistrust, their questioning, indeed their indictment of all the overt ceremonies which constitute—which always have constituted—the means of poetry. A burden indeed, when each poet must be his or her own devil's advocate, or rather must advocate within his or her own expression precisely the opposition to everything in that expression which constitutes its continuity as itself. The burden of our poets—and it is, I once said, speaking of one of the most touching figures among them, the first time in the history of poetry that human beings have been concerned and even compelled to write a *poetry of forgetting*—is to rise against the form in which they are writing; their burden is their longing to lose the gifts of order, recovery, convergence upon an end so that all might begin again; their burden is their aspiration to gainsay, to despoil the self of all that had been, merely, propriety.

No recurrence, no reversion, no verse—not the turn but the errant line. When the mind is thus released from its old subservience to repetition, when no experience is reverted to, recuperated, then we get a poetry of revelation without memory, a poetry of centripetal illumination, a poetry without any of the axiological signs and spells which served, once, to hold it in the mind—and which implied there was a mind to hold it; a poetry whose imagery, hugged close to the self, is often in that repository pulverized beyond the recognition of shared contours; a poetry without rhyme, but rather with a sonority parodied beyond belief into instances of mockery and Hellenism, a music jeering at conventional accords; a poetry without constants in rhythmical behavior, but a kind of insistent unpredictability which affords the singled-out self its final locus, an ultimate accommodation of what Shelley said was "conscious, separable, one."

Such a poetry—and my description of it here is only a provisional and polemical cast of the net, deliberately harsh to exceptions and resemblances, to hopes—has jettisoned *verse*, that angelic ceremonial of beginnings and endings which make up the entire justice of prosody. It bears instead the weight of a fallen angel, a Luciferian responsibility to cancel out itself (and its information); to use itself up even as it speaks, the way prose does; to write itself in water or even in rivers of fire, anyway in some inconstant element which will not allow us ever to step into it more than once. Conventions, even such conventions of memory as dates, are . . . conveniences, and without them, without baggage, the poet, alone with America, as I have described him or her, must draw upon the automatism of exclusion—the poet's exclusion, the poetry's exclusion, it is the same—as if on a bonus talent unimaginable in "normal social life." The poet must fall back on his un-propped nature, on the terms, merely—merely! yet how much they determine!—of a temperament, of an identity.

If I am at all correct in my characterization of American poetry, then I am correct in confirming that young woman at Bard in her scorn of history in my work—history as a kind of hardware, then, what might be said to be a trope for all those disciplines (from Lévy-Bruhl to Lévi-Strauss) which characterize our century—psychoanaly-sis, anthropology, comparative religion, criticism itself as practiced, as perfected by Northrop Frye, say. That such things once turned up *inside* certain poems is a specific consequence of modernism, or perhaps—since this is how we now consider modernism, is it not?—as a specific consequence of the high romantic tradition which leads to modernism. But in the American poetry of my juniors, in the post-modernist poetry I am called upon to examine with such exemplary thoroughness, I perceive a new courage. No longer the courage to live on everything (which requires a tradition or at least a convention, and a memory), but the courage to live on nothing. Nothing but our bodies and the weather—that is the courage of American poetry in our moment. We Americans have, and have had, a certain asceticism which renounces the past, renounces whatever is too much with us—even when it is the Word which is too much with us: our poetry renounces the Word as well. Forgetting—the blank of not knowing, of dismem-bering rather than remembering—is precisely the ground of our wis-dom, what Geoffrey Hartman would call an apotropaic relation to language, whereby we invite or inveigle into speech itself the energies of unmaking, of forgetting, or negation, that negation which Hegel said was our task, for with it, when the plenitude of Being fails, when the Void becomes a power in itself, Man is most fully himself. Forget-ting, for us, is the condition of all creative thought. In all "advanced" art of our moment, we are to forget before we confront the new work, which, as in the initiation ceremonies of the Orphic adepts, not only requires us not to know anything in advance—for the first time in three thousand years, art proceeds without habits of shared recognition, without the (often obligatory) negotiation of common awareness—but also requires us to forget anything we might happen to know. Perhaps that is our lyric poetry, the burden of the present of which I spoke: the responsibility of forgetting.

Consider the two poems I bring before you. One is by precisely that laureate of enormous repudiations and dispossessions whom I mentioned, or did not mention but alluded to just now: W. S. Merwin. In the blankly named "The Approaches" is a world of which we are, by living in it, dispossessed. That is Merwin's world, "made up of less and less," as he says, unless we can bring ourselves to forget. For in this world, it is insofar as we remember things that we are conscious of their passing from us; if we forget them, we have them forever—no strain, no sweat, as we so insufferably say these days, no problem. But there is a discipline, a constant calisthenics of oblivion here, a workout and an erasure extending from mere numbers, counting, as he says in a late poem,

> going on to the alphabet
> until everything is continuous again
> go on to forgetting elements
> starting with water
> proceeding to earth
> rising in fire
> forget fire

a characteristic process in this poetry of deprivals and effacements. Indeed it is all process: without punctuation, without predictable prosody, which is to say without prosody, without companions, "speaking another language / as the earth does," he pursues his asymptotic phenomenology of thresholds and doors and passages, "the gates about to close / that never do."

It is a man's relation to the transcendent, unknowable mode of existence which Merwin apostrophizes in his trance-poem: a mode of existence hinted at by the startling and violating occurrence of the word *Canaan* (the Promised Land), though for Merwin that is where the fighting is: there is a sacramental violence, then, in this eruption of precisely the hardware I am claiming Merwin generally chooses to elide, to elude. (For him, history exists only when the story it has to tell comes to its end, and he is left with his body and the poems of our climate.) A sacramental violence as well as an initiatory peace about the enterprise, and a terrible void. For there are no persons here, nor even personifications. There are presences, and they support processes which afford the speaking voice—not disembodied, but disenfranchised, always—an access to prophecy, as prophetics are without honor; an access to the capacity to release the present. It is the coercion of this poem and of all Merwin's later work to resist hopes and assurance ("trying to remember what the present / can bless with," as he says). The exultation must be *now*, it must not depend on what we have had, it must not count on what we may have. . . . And NOW, as we all know, is *never*, untenable, untenantable. The exultation, therefore, will be an ecstasy of loss, the sense so different from the Proustian memory and its losses, of what Wordsworth called fallings from us, vanishings, yet experienced as a revelation of the self, a birth. There is no story here, no history, or if there is it requires us to revise our old sense of Story, of History, which in all Western culture has meant a lie: *ce sont des histoires*, the French say of such fabrications, legends, fables, fictions, a history of departed things, a story was once what was told by a man or woman who knew what he or she was telling to an audience who knew what they were being told. It had become, by the eighteenth century (say, after the fourteen centuries between the Confessions of Augustine to the Confessions of Rousseau), what was told by a man or woman who knew what he or she was telling to an audience who did *not* know what they were being told. A story is now what is being told by a man or woman who does not know what he or she is telling to an audience who does not know what they are being told; nor does the man or woman telling what he or she does not know, know even if he or she *has* an audience who does not know what he or she is telling.

The real focus of "The Approaches," what the poem is approaching, is a quality of life which used to be called visionary and which Merwin would call, I think, provisional—hence its virtually derisive utilization of the historical category, the capitalized noun with its Biblical association. He addresses a life which must be characterized by negatives, by what it is not; for what it is cannot be remembered or known or communicated to others. A phenomenology of cold and darkness there, of loss, absence, and removal which governs this imagery, even governs the tone, for a prosody of pauses, halts and silences—if, as I say, this is a prosody at all—will let the language thicken to unaccustomed suspensions, enjambments which reveal, chiefly, weight to the ear, hasty for conclusions:

> I may never
> get there but should get
> closer and hear the sound

as they show disparity (on the page) to the eye, seeking recurrence:

> they make off
> birds
> no one to guide me
> afraid
> to the warm ruins
> Canaan
> where the fighting is

The use of single words to form a line here is a use which goes against the sanctioned practice of poetry as we have understood it for three millennia. It is a counter-mnemonic device.

What Merwin gives us is an irreversible course toward an undivided, unqualified life, a life unmediated by any expectation but that of obliteration; erasure and an awareness that whatever is said of such a life, is not *that life*. Whence a saving tension in the poem, the tension of saying "no, not that," as we feel a tension in Chekhov's play when Nina says, "I'm a seagull—no, that's not it," and we wait for a refining elucidation: if she's not a seagull, what is she? We might call this cate-

gory the symbolics of inadequate postulation, and I believe this negative poetics forms a powerful dimension of our post-modernity. The
tension in Merwin is that of a continuing struggle between the cry and
the crater, between the hymn and the silence. The source of Merwin's
singing is the deciduous life, but its seal is elsewhere, its justification is
a forbidden or unjustifiable Canaan of which the poet with characteristic asymptotic despair says: "I may never / get there but should get /
closer and hear the sound."

And now, as Hamlet says, "Look here upon this picture and on
this—can you on this fair mountain leave to feed, and batten on this
moor?" Our second poet does not determine—even from their loss—
but rather derives his terms as given. In my poem "Fra Angelico's *Last
Judgment*," a painting is postulated—a "Last Judgment," to be seen in
the world, in Florence, which is the world for its painter. This world.
And the poet, compelled by something outside himself into acknowledgment, seeks to make terms with the painting. He begins in front of
the painting; he writes his poem from the already created picture. The
phenomenon—*ekphrasis*, an old convention of which such poets as
Hecht and Hollander and Van Duyn provide us sublime examples—
suggests a passivity, an assumption that the known, the remembered,
the revisited—as Henry James would say, the *visitable past*, as it stands
now in the picture, pledged to be *there*—will disclose its significance.

This passivity might elsewhere and otherwise be called trust, a confidence in what Yeats names a natural momentum in the syntax, a cu-
mulus he said enabled a poem to carry "any amount of elaborate
English." And elaborate the English is, faceted with turns and returns
("Hell, which I leave / in its own right, where it will be left"), with an
alliteration struggling to become the master-principle of the meter
("Now / we go, we are leaving this garden / of colors and gowns . . .
we walk into that / gold success"), and a playful consciousness (am I
being self-indulgent in calling it playful? At least I insist that it *is* a consciousness) of the diversions to be made available in the difference between the language written and the language spoken ("How to behold
what cannot be held? / Make believe you hold it"). The confidence
shared, the saving grace, if that is what it is, is all in the capacity of language itself—compulsively qualified, idiosyncratic in address, entirely
given over to conventions and observed usages and allusive reliances—

to carry the impulse, the effort of the poem (the received memory, the *history* of Western consciousness, not to put too fine a point on it) by the *energeia* which words hold within themselves, by the dynamics they generate "among one another" line by line rather than one at a time—by a secret plot.

It is this plot, this conspiracy, the notion that there *is* a story, which our friend from Bard—and I am making her into a symbolic public now—finds so objectionable, whereupon I must adore the fact that her college's name is BARD. It is by no means my secret alone, but it is, as I practice and concoct it, sufficiently out of the way to produce a specific response. When that response is not outright, Bardic hostility, indeed when that response is in fact favor, it tends to go something like this: "I like your poems, but why don't you—since you write so many poems about the Victorians, or about pictures, or about what is *already there*—why don't you write a poem about Thomas Hardy after the death of his first wife? Or about Lewis Carroll taking photographs of those naked little girls in the studio? Why don't you write about what I've always wanted to read about?" Now, can you imagine anyone ever suggesting a "subject" to W. S. Merwin? Or to Mark Strand? Or to John Ashbery? to name but three of our post-modernist practitioners of the art of forgetting. No—it is only to the remembering writer, to the poet tainted by history, that the occasionally entertained public will tender such an offer—an offer which so often, when tendered to me, seems like an offer of the last straw. For oddly enough, the dramatic monologue, the apostrophe, the poem of helpless trust in remembering what is there, the poem of "derived terms," the poem of the "placed persona" appears to be the most suggestible of poems, though in actuality it is always a mystery.

Such poems have appeared in the history of literature as a genre coeval with the poet's need for secrecy. (Hence Tennyson, who knew he had secrets; hence Browning, who appears not to have known but who probably knew—I refer you to Henry James's story "The Private Life," which takes up the matter with contemporary relevance.) The poem of historical memory and of the placed person always concerns the poet's need for secrecy.

In France, great examples frame the last period in which a placed persona in verse (and even in a prose avatar like *In Search of Lost Time*, the longest dramatic monologue in literature) could be exploited without a maker incurring an excessive risk of giving "himself" away. This safety period, 1873–1917, is bracketed by two huge verse monologues, Mallarmé's "Afternoon of a Faun" and Valéry's "Young Fate." Both these great poems are monologic utterances of figures without a past, without an acknowledgment of history other than that of their own flesh, figures who must consequently question the reliability of memory, of "real life" as it is filtered by consciousness, the Faun interrogating the self as to what "actually" happened ("did I love a dream?") in at least a recognizable landscape (Sicily) with the identifiable apparatus of classical mythology (faun, nymphs, volcano, grove, swamp), all of which, by the second poem, thirty-five years later, dissolves into a "no one" (what else is a Fate, even a young one?) who doesn't know where she is (is that the wind, is this a beach, is it dawn?), only that she has a body and that there is weather.

This dissolution leads poetry—emphatically our modern American poetry—toward the obsolescence of the hardware, as I like to call it, though perhaps software is the likelier term, of historical memory, and concomitantly of our ability and our need to dream forward, to hope, which makes us unique among living forms on the planet.

So that when the resentful young woman at Bard asked me, in what I took for good faith, "When was the Renaissance?" I began, in the manner of one who spends a good deal of his life moving from one classroom into another—I began to tell her about the revival of learning, the rediscovery of the old world and the discovery of the new, the invention of perspective and the concomitant inference that the world was round, thereby closing God out of the picture, and so on. Well, I did go on, as I do, and my interlocturess—you remember, she had approached *me* with the intelligence that she did not like my poems—in a gesture of fatigue and boredom and disgust, said (I think she felt I was patronizing her by answering her question), "Oh, fuck off." Hold that expression in your minds a moment, we shall revert to it. I have spoken of the prevailing mode of poetry in our time as a poetry of forgetting, as a poetry which posits forgetting, as in the Merwin poem, as *the* condition of all making.

As this little story reminds us, there is a terrible dialectic between memory and forgetting, and the entire victory of hardware would be just as disastrous as the triumph now celebrated by our contemporary Song of Myself, that generalized American epic of forgetting. Yet there is the impossibility, for us, of total forgetting as well; that is the dilemma of having a body. For the body exists according to a structure of recurrences: the body is verse. And if our poetry is nowadays largely written out of a horror of repetition, there is on the other hand the horror of a world without recurrence. Wallace Stevens once said it is the greatest poverty not to live in the physical world. But there is a greater poverty yet: to live in a world where everything happens only once. The body teaches—our breathing, our heartbeat, our periods teach us—recurrence, and the making of the circle. Joy, as Nietzsche remarked, joy has the ring's will in it, but how does this ringmaking occur? It occurs by the word, by the life of the text, by the energy of grammar. In the beginning, we are told, was the word. We are given no assurance as to the end, but I believe we see it all around us. Certainly I heard it there at Bard, the living end, an art without memory, an expression without linguistic culture, a paroxysm without grammar: *Fuck off.*

After all, it is the temporal structure of language which makes us insist there is a past, that is separate from the present and from what we call the future. Our capacity to articulate a future tense—in itself a metaphysical and logical scandal, as Nabokov reflects in *Ada*—our ability and our need to dream forward, to hope, makes us unique among living forms on the planet. Such capacity is inseparable from grammar, from the conventional power of language to exist in advance of what it designates. Analogously, our sense of the past, the past as a shaped selection of remembrance, is radically linguistic. History is language cast backward. No animal remembers. Its temporality is the eternal present tense of the speechless.

The cult of immediacy—represented and empowered by our magnificent poetry of forgetting, by the demand that each of us do his thing with complete vehemence of personal being—is actually a reverse elitism. For the very derivative nature of what we condemn as "classical culture" used to mean an equal measure of participation in apprehensions decidedly greater than those which most of us can discover for ourselves. The demand, for example, that every erotic experience be "orgasmic" and "creative" is precisely a parallel piece of blackmail against our common resources.

We are beginning—the linguists and psycholinguists tell us—to understand that certain patterns of affectlessness, of antisocial and anarchic conduct, are related to verbal inadequacy, to the inability of the grammatically underprivileged to plug into a society whose codes of communication and idiom of values are too sophisticated.

Most advanced forms of art today—aleatory, improvisational, artifacts made only to be destroyed or abandoned or forgotten—are all strategic denials of the future tense, even as the derision of precedent, the unsaying of history, and a contemptuous indifference toward it are refusals of the past. Hatred of the past. In the grammar of the freakout, it is always now. So my Bardic Hostess rightly showed her insight when she abrogated all discussion by saying, "Fuck off."

She no longer shares the language of those she regards as her enemies. She wants nothing to do with it. She would break free from language as from her own shadow. She must stop her ears to all the ceremonious ironic voices from the past which are in books—books that will outlive if not outlast her, books that speak of death.

Yet an art without death, which is art without memory, is either autistic or else it is megaphonic. Either it is implosive, like Gertrude Stein and John Cage, or it is stadium kabbalism, like the poems of Ginsberg and Yevtushenko.

But here I hear my own voice getting shrill in the aspirations of my philippic. Let me conclude with other overtones, accents of alterity. Here are three quotations, which by collage make my point. First, from Goethe:

> Who cannot give himself an accounting
> for the past three thousand years
> remains in darkness, without experience
> living from day to day.

From Nabokov: "To be means to know one has been."

And from Northrop Frye:

The culture of the past is not only the memory of mankind but our own buried life, and study of it leads to a recognition scene, a discovery in which we see not our past lives, but the total cultural form of our present life.

The matter here, the point to take, the line to follow is not one of being on the side of memory and death and the past, or on the side of the moment and forgetting and of life, but one of recognizing and identifying the dialectic between them. That is what constitutes the tension, the irony and the interest of an authentic art, now or ever. What we want is the recognition of both energies, constituted by our assent to them. How I should like to give you an example from my own work, but I cannot, for with the exception of one poem, my work fails to give Forgetting its due, as my friend from Bard pointed out. I am too much in the pay of the past. But I can read you a poem which suggests supremely the ideal interpenetration of forgetting and remembering I am trying to locate. It is—and here I shall leave you— Elizabeth Bishop's "In the Waiting Room."

Things Forgot:
The Education of the Poet

[1996]

We must be taught as if you taught us not,
And things unknown proposed as things forgot.
—Alexander Pope

Seventy-five years ago, Edmund Wilson wrote an essay which asked a rhetorical question—as we have come to call questions which assume their own answers—with a flourish we recognize in comparable interrogations, for instance, as to the use and abuse of family values so vehemently put by Senator Jesse Helms. Wilson's question was: Is Verse a Dying Technique?

To which, at the end of the twentieth century in these United States, the short answer is that Verse lives, flourishes even, because it is no longer a technique. (The extended answer is this essay.) What is known as verse is a propitiatory gesture made nowadays in obeisance—sometimes deferential, sometimes scornful—to practices once understood as an artistic engagement but presently regarded as insignificant, nugatory, oppressive, trifling, dumb. By students of poetry, those with some intention of becoming poets, verse is ignored—by which I mean that they are ignorant of it. In the practice of new poets, verse is no longer perceived as what the word itself means, a ceremony of recapitulation, recurrence and return, a periodic rhythm, but as a purely allusive performance; and what it alludes to is the assumption that the text thus handled, or fingered, or in fact nailed, is not prose, and therefore not to be subjected to the same expectations or demands which we impose, still, on what Dryden called "The Other Harmony." If there is time, I shall insert a coda on our modernist approbation of prose, an art form which since Flaubert we have learned to esteem as, indeed, a technique, not merely a referential vestige.

Of course this verse of "ours"—and by the plural possessive I refer to the almost universal phenomenon among practicing (if imperfect) poets of what is called "free verse," that crowning enterprise which at the end of the nineteenth century followed upon free trade and free love, and which has overtaken the field—indeed, which *is* the field, so far as the poetry sent to our literary magazines with the intention of seeing print is concerned: this verse of "ours" is not all there is. No technique is ever entirely unemployed, entirely without honor in the modern eclecticon: somewhere in the darkness, there is a woman who has recovered the secret of stained glass and is clandestinely re-creating the glory of Chartres in disconcerting contemporary terms. Analogously there are some twenty-five verse-writers in this country who continue, even since the deaths of James Merrill and Howard Moss, to further the mystery and the mastery of verse, exemplars of prosody by whom the secrets of Milton and Dryden will be preserved. Names upon request.

But having thus deplored the situation of verse, its practical desuetude and its academic relegation, before I light into what my title announces as my subject, I had better provide something like a context in which my remarks will take their place with a certain seemliness, or at least a certain perspective. Allow me to shake the froth out of the bottle. I am not merely a poet, though I am that, and I am not merely a critic of poetry, though I am that; I am not merely an anthologist of poetry, though I have been that, and I am not merely a publisher of poetry, though I am that, and I am not merely a teacher of poetry, though I shall continue to be that. I am—and what I am entitles or condemns me to everything that follows—an editor of poetry for two literary magazines, having been an editor of poetry for three other such magazines over the two decades before this one, so that I address you now as a man who has scrutinized the current product (product!— I use the word with a certain compliant twinge) *in extenso* for thirty dutifully attentive years.

I bring you, then, a report from those fields—playing fields, killing fields, the risk of your choice is mine—with the same despairing assiduity that Mallarmé brought to that Oxford audience of his when he announced that he had epochal news to communicate. *On a touché au vers!* Mallarmé exclaimed: "They have tampered with verse!" Of course Mallarmé believed, good Platonist that he was, that each time the modes of music alter, the walls of the City tremble, and he felt that the introduction of *vers libre* into the traditional armory of French prosody, he himself being one of the introducers, one of the offenders, was an alarming event. But in my corrupt and cynical way, I am something of a Platonist too, and I believe, at least, that the poetry we have is the poetry we deserve, the poetry we literally bargained for: the shelves of the Library of Congress will not buckle under the weight of our heterodox practice, but they will block out the light.

And in such darkness, what is to be done? Out of the thousands of poems, or texts bearing the aspect of poems, at least along the justified left-hand margin, offered in such incredible volume to any and every organ of publication, how—by what impossible filter, what empirical or abstract grid pressed upon the helpless, aspiring words—are the sixteen (or even the sixty) poems to be selected, which will appear as superior achievements in each number of our little magazines, those periodicals of which Gertrude Stein once remarked, so cogently, that they repeatedly died to make verse free? How, in the absence of proper verse—verse of an estimable propriety and its concomitant registration of competence—are these mountains of submitted free verses to be discriminated? By—precisely—submission: by an editorial yielding to the invoked impulse itself as it appears, written (or so often, merely typed up, blocked out in every sense) on the page. By having patience with the poem! *Patience, hard thing*, Hopkins calls it, for patience, even literary patience is, quite exemplarily, suffering; and the poem—each poem—is to be suffered in all its eccentric lineation for the sake of that moment when it will, or when it may, speak.

Indeed that is how the winnowing is done, the *triage* made; that is the education of the poetry editor. A moment comes in the course of reading a submitted poem (and of course there must be enough of a poem *there* to permit such a moment to come: reading five hundred haiku is to be nibbled to death by guppies) when the language of the poem ceases to be language of the poem's author, when indeed the language of the poem becomes only—only!—its own, an autonomous voice heard in the passion, or in the refusal of passion, which its energies inaugurate and sustain. Most likely, these days, they will not be the energies of regular verse.

Let me move further along in this attempt to describe what it is the poetry editor has to be doing these unversed days (I am convinced it will lead us more securely, less abruptly, to the matter of the poet's education). If not actually upbraided in the matter of what so many of the besieging new poets like to call *experimental form*, the poetry editor (of, say, a gilt-edged, *bon bourgeois*, blue-chip magazine like *The Paris Review*) is pretty often laced into—I have seen it said, in a distinctly antibourgeois periodical, in *Fuck You, A Magazine of the Arts*, in fact, that only iambic pentameter was acceptable to the editor of *The Paris Review*—so that it is with regard to a stance, or at least a leaning, toward the experimental that I would extend my foregoing "submissive" gloss on that dialogue between two interlocutors who never speak, their *pre-text* being, quite literally, on the one hand the poems submitted in all their thousands, and their *text*—their post-text, really—being the poems eventually printed on the other. Well, so one hand does wash the other, then; and it is just the quality—soapy? oleaginous? abrasive?—of such laundering that I want to examine in public.

Is there such a thing, as so many of our new poets insist there is—or perhaps not so much a thing as, like electricity, a way things behave—as *experimental form* in poetry? And if there should be, if it were to turn up or to bed down among all this "new writing," which to these old ears seems merely an echo (the resonance, momentarily sustained, of the "old modernism"), how might the poetry editor set about recognizing it? Is he gingerly, or just rueful? Or are there no fresh spices in order here at all, if there is no constituted order to sweeten or to sharpen, but merely—O merely!—to seek? For I am convinced (revealing myself completely) that it is *because* poetry operates by means of conventions, is governed by techniques (the very ones whose life expectancy Wilson has questioned), that it can become the instrument not only of *instant expression* but of enduring significance. Where *anything* and indeed *everything* is possible and nothing is unexpected (even if such expectation is only to be flouted), significance falters and fades, and any continuing communication must diminish . . . if it does not collapse.

What then might experimental poetry be; what is an experimental form? In the earliest sense this naughty word has in our language, the sense it has carried since 1570 (when Ascham's *Scholemaster* was published) as "based on or derived from experience, founded on experience only," *experimental poetry* is either a tautology or a teratism, either a necessity or nonsense. For of course poetry is based on or derived from experience; but it is just insofar as poetry escapes from its derivation, its basis, that it becomes poetry and not merely a tryst, a joust, a grope, a broken engagement, or a *mésalliance*. For it is just to the degree that poetry is confided to language, to culture, that it escapes from nature and becomes, instead of something tentative and approximate, a tryst, a joust, a grope, a *mésalliance*, something we recognize, something we can identify and acknowledge as part of the order of our experience, even if it is the order of our experience of chaos. A poem is a victory *over* experience arrived at (and often fled from) by transforming it, and the terms of that victory and that transformation are the terms, these days, for our new poets, of experimental form.

Thus the poetry editor might endeavor to recognize (such recognition having the same look of *Realpolitik* about it as the "recognition" of Serbia by the United Nations) authentically experimental forms among the welter and dither of prefabrication on hand. Let me exemplify one such inflection of achieved resource as sighted from this vantage point (duck-blind or conning-tower, it all depends); one experimental form I can recognize—and have pretty widely published— is the poem which is *an answer*, echo or after-image, in terms of some extra-poetical, certainly extra-literary convention, some way of *getting across* from the private life to the public image by means, for once, of the media, the very forms which so promiscuously surround when they do not smother us. Poems are now, and will be, submitted, and published, which do not in fact *look* like "poems," the verse so free, indeed, that it can barely be identified, poems which are no longer what John Hollander likes to call (and I wish you could see his face when he does call them: they seldom dare to come) "poem-shaped objects," but they do have a shape, a form, a response to what is not themselves: sometimes as a slide-show, sometimes as the response to a questionnaire, as a television schedule, as a multiple-choice exam, as a market-research spread, as an obituary, you name it . . . For that is the purpose, not merely the occasion: the poet names it (Gertrude Stein liked to say that poetry is naming—prose just relating), and by thus naming the poet constitutes the cherished identity of experience and experiment which is (under the sign of danger, the etymological aegis of *peril*) an identity indeed—the calling into being, not into doubt, of the made thing (the *poem*, the *fiction*: these two words have a like meaning) which is the true vocation, the mouth and the myth of the poet.

Of course it is the endemic and tyrannical prevalence of free verse which has obligated the extreme discovery, the desperate invention, the sensational contrivance of these experimental forms: our new poets are driven to experiment by their urgent need for precisely that periodic ceremony which verse (unliberated verse, bound and thereby determined) forces upon mere expression in order to arrive at memorable speech (by memorable speech I mean something like the grin of the Cheshire cat, "which remained," Lewis Carroll remarks, "some time after the rest of it had gone"). Poets, rare birds, are searching for the cages which are the only sites in which they can sing. For art, as Gide once said, is born of constraint and dies of liberty. If we have fled or are determined to flout the acknowledged, the conventional, the traditional versions of such constraint—that is, if we have so enthusiastically done away with verse—then our poets will be obliged to invent new ways of encaging their utterance, new artifices, new contraptions. Their experiments are sometimes noble, inspired even, and some will endure, though they present one great difficulty. They are *inimitable*. Each experiment is the unique and dangerous *trouvaille* of each new poet, his alone, hers alone. Jorie Graham and John Ashbery, to instance two fashionable names, are without lineage, and in the nature of the case they cannot become founders; they are what a friend of my mother's, examining the (to her) baffling art of Agnes Martin, called "singularly unique." Examining the exhibition of what for all the world seemed no more than giant sheets of graph-paper, my mother asked indignantly, "Who Authorized These?" Such poets—and are there *other* such poets?—cannot be classic because they cannot form a "class." Such a reading of classicism would constitute the ultimate defense of verse, of course, that periodic rhythm of recurrences which I am here to propose—surely you have seen this coming, a tiny bright vehicle making its way toward you through my umbrageous sentences—as the Education of the Poet. The Education of the Poet is Verse, a discipline, an order, a contraption which has been, by and large, jettisoned by our Writing Programs, those academies of freedom functioning across our country at a Stakhanovite level, if level is the word I want.

Of course we have made the ritual genuflections. Every Creative Writing Program has its version of a "Forms" course, in which what John Hollander (again!—it is no accident that this poet, this scholar, this literary avatar of a Scud Missile, appears so cooperatively in what I like to flatter myself is my argument) calls "Rhyme's Reason" is dissected and exhibited, principally as the work of the Great Dead, the villanelles and sestinas of all that poetry which has been got behind us, like Satan. It is my impression that our new poets, free versifiers all, are good-naturedly willing to inspect the nostalgias, to explore the monuments. (It affords them, if they are to be known as poets, a certain *cachet* that indeed poets *used to be known* for making such things, for exhibiting such preposterous virtuosity, if not such potent virtues as the heroic couplet, anapestic trimeter, and the variable caesura.) But see how these same new poets have neatly confounded their instructors by licking the sugar off the pills: they have acknowledged that verse is what poets *used to write*. But almost no one who writes today with any serious intention of being or becoming a poet will write with any investment in verse, that lapsed and depressed enterprise. Or will write anything but free verse, which as I have been saying, is the great escape, the ultimate alibi of our modernity.

For poetry is already a problematic if not a despised art in modern times. Despised because popular. More people are writing what they believe to be poetry, what is even called poetry by their readers, their publishers, their detractors, than ever before in our history—many more are writing poetry than are reading poetry, as you have so often heard. This situation is not a paradox, it is a necessary consequence of our cultural structure. Our academies offer their M.F.A.'s in unprecedented numbers, for we write, these days, not what we want to keep but what we wish to dispose of. We read only what we value and enjoy. So abject, and so absurd, has the situation of poetry-writing become in our polity—unread though occasionally exhibited, despised

though invariably ritualized, as at certain inaugurations—that not
only are we determined to put the poor thing out of its misery, but we
have made it a patriotic duty to do so, declaring A National Poetry
Month, for example, to signalize the end of the affair.

We have not yet gone all the way; and though grave, the situation
has not yet passed beyond the possibilities of a sort of recovery. I am
here not only in my costume of Cassandra, or of Jeremiah, but with
my prophetic robes of dawn about me too. You can discern them if
you attend: I am here to offer, while there is still time enough and
world, a modest proposal which may yet restore that art which was
once the glory and the consolation of humanity to something like its
ulterior status. My proposal is simply this: to make poetry, once again,
an order of returns, a relation to that ceremony of recurrence we have
always called, with a certain discipline, a certain strictness, VERSE.

Of course part of that relation to verse will be, now, a study of the
escapes from it. All our incomparable modernity has been achieved by
those struggling to release themselves from precisely the order of reversion, so that they might gain access to the order of advance. It is
their struggles which constitute modern poetry, and I advocate its
frequentation, not its abandonment.

Indeed, as all our best critics of poetry tell us in the brilliant and
exasperated terms to which Mrs. Vendler and Mr. Bloom have been
reduced (or enlarged?) by our determined mugwumpery, the frequentation of the poets of the past is remarkable for the unity of its
demonstration. There has never been a poet, a strong poet, who has
not been observed to have studied all the other strong poets—neither
Walt Whitman, nor Emily Dickinson, nor Arthur Rimbaud are exceptions to this program of concern: all the greatest rebels and secession-
ists and singletons have been imminent participants in the one
pedagogic enterprise. The education of the poet has been poetry, and
it is my notion, my observation indeed that it is not just—just!—
poetry, but that once nearly-universal propulsive mechanism of poetry
we call verse which is the poet's proper study, and which is the entire
justice of any poetic study.

Ours is a generation of poets which knows not the Law, and
though the results of such ignorance are often brilliant, and certainly
worth our often delighted attention, they are desperate measures,

dreadful freedoms which only the strongest and most resolute talents can endure. Of course that is what such a culture as ours may require— only the strongest and most resolute talents. Yet what a wasteful method of discovering, of obtaining them! It is my purpose here to propound another dispensation, a different mode. The study of, the submission to, the mastery of verse, that form of poetry in which a periodic rhythm is paramount, is the education of the poet, and almost the entire poetry of education as well.

And what of the study of prose? Certainly with the loss of verse as a constant order of experience, it is admissible, it is evident that our prose has become—consider the enterprise of Mr. Gass, of Mr. Pynchon, of Mr. Alexander Theroux, of Mr. Guy Davenport—our prose has become a New Order, has taken up the slack, has eliminated the slack, and become what our poetry might have been.

This has always been imminent—a promise if not a threat, and we might bestow a brief retrospect upon the matter. The term *prose* first appeared in English in about 1330, but was not actually opposed to *poetry* until 1561. It was thus used by Milton, who describes himself "sitting here below in the cool element of prose." And even then, relating that when in his youth he set himself a task in composition "whether prosing or versing," he makes no sharp distinction between them. And so intense has the pressure been, among the artists of prose from Flaubert and Henry James to Ford Madox Ford and Conrad, to discern and even to exemplify a poetics of prose, that we are not surprised, in the excruciation of high modernity, to find Ezra Pound insisting *that poetry should be at least as well written as prose.* Clearly the shoe is on the other foot, and any sequent metrical syllabic groups—of iambs, trochees, dactyls, and so forth—more closely resemble, henceforth, shoes than feet! It will take a good deal of what I have called frequentation to recall the energies of expression to a versified poetry after a hundred years of prose mastery, of prose discipline. Let me leave you with two passages by the same writer, and with a question of how we might construct, or reconstruct a bridge as our President says which leads from the one achievement to the other. Here is the prose:

"The scene darkens and the fires of the bivouacs shine up ruddily, those of the French near at hand, those of the Russians in a long line across the mid-distance, and throwing a flapping glare into the heavens. As the night grows stiller the ballad-singing and laughter from the French mixes with a slow singing of psalms from their adversaries. The two multitudes lie down to sleep, and all is quiet but for the sputtering of the green wood fires, which, now that the human tongues are still, seem to hold a conversation of their own."

And here is the verse:

SNOW IN THE SUBURBS

Every branch big with it
Bent every twig with it;
Every fork like a white web-foot
Every street and pavement mute:
Some flakes have lost their way, and grope back upward, when
Meeting those meandering down they turn and descend again.
The palings are glued together like a wall,
And there is no waft of wind with the fleecy fall.

A sparrow enters the tree
Whereon immediately
A snow-lump thrice his own slight size
Descends on him and showers his head and eyes,
And overturns him
And near inurns him
And lights on a nether twig, when its brush
Starts off a volley of other lodging lumps with a rush.

The steps are a blanched slope,
Up which, with feeble hope,
A black cat comes, wide-eyed and thin;
And we take him in.

To write, as Thomas Hardy has written, early in this century, this prose and this verse is the manifestation of genius, but it is also the possibility of talent; as an example, it remains the responsibility of the education of the poet.

ON FRENCH LITERATURE

Childhood Amnesia

[1969]

for Laurent de Brunhoff

The French do not have children. Or childhood. What they have, as all of us know who have accepted Baudelaire's invitation, is infants. And infancy. Not childsplay—*enfantillage*. The French have sons and daughters, the schools are full of boys and girls, but there are no *children*. In other words, in *one* other word, the French have what their language has foisted upon them, for every culture has the vocabulary it reserves: they have *relations*.

ENFANT. From the Latin *infans*; from *in* (not) and *fari* (to speak): the one who does not speak.
FABLE. From the Latin *fabula* (narrative, story), from *fari* (to speak).

Put them together and it spells . . . silence. Secrecy—perhaps the only secret ever kept in France. The Gentlemen's Agreement, the *tacit* complicity of the French concerning childhood is as absolute and reliable as the understanding of two of Sade's characters concerning the use of the garrotte or the presence of the mother. As in most Mediterranean cultures, there is no French word for *child*, no word for the human young taken, or given, not as a relation, not as an element in a structure, but as a reality, a self, a center, a surd.

It is noticeable that writers who concern themselves with explaining the characteristics and reactions of the adult have devoted much more attention to the primeval period comprised in the life of the individual's ancestors—have, that is, ascribed much more influence to heredity—than to the other primeval period which falls within the lifetime of the individual him-self—that is, to childhood. —Freud (1905)

Of course there are evasions, disclaimers, disguises, colloquial prox-ies. The French employ—invent, invoke, indulge—their celebrated *argot* (a "secret jargon," as of thieves; the word's origin is unknown) whenever they seek to conceal, to distract attention from, what they are doing. That is why they have the richest slang in the world.

Yet it is only an expedient, their argot, a cover-up: it must be rein-vented every generation or so, for it sinks into the sand of experience and is lost, like the origin of the word *argot* itself. *Gosse* is a stopgap, a makeshift, a *circumlocution* which is a way of talking around . . . a se-cret. What matters is what is done with the language in its central range, not around the edges—what matters is not Francis Carco but Jean Genet:

> My first impulse was to point out to him that it was ridiculous to put words and phrases between quotation marks, for that prevents them from entering the language. When I received his letters, his quotation marks made me shudder—a shudder of shame. Those quotation marks were the flaw . . . whereby my friend showed that he was himself, and that he was wounded.
> —*Miracle of the Rose* (1951)

And in the central range of the French language, there is no word for *child*; no childishness in that closed circuit, that strict discourse which is the entire justice of French Literature. A literature of rela-tions, in which all are *members*, marvellously combined, subordinated, distributed: a continuum.

It was Gide, with his splendidly personal sense of Vicissitude, of di-verging, opposing, and ultimately complementary . . . ultimates ("*les extrêmes me touchent*"), who perfectly characterized French Literature (which he could not escape any better than could Genet or Sade, the world's freest minds in the world's most imprisoned bodies) as one immense and endless conversation. And if to eavesdroppers like ourselves it sounds more like an argument than a *causerie*, that is merely because we have not been listening long enough. For the dialogue continues, the unappeasable do-it-yourself dialectic proceeds, asking questions not to be answered for five hundred years, answering others the season before they are asked—a system of provocation and response without a temporal variable:

> Hydre absolue, ivre de ta chair bleue,
> Qui te remords l'étincelante queue
> Dans un tumulte au silence pareil.

At any given point of entry, the reader of this Literature has the encircling, often constricting awareness—has the *conviction*—that he is inside a completed structure, as the foreign visitor to Paris frequently has the suspicion, crossing even the broadest steppes the city affords—the Place de la Concorde under a stormy sky, the Jardin du Luxembourg on a sunny afternoon—that all of Paris is really *inside*, somehow preposterously enclosed and housed in one enormous chamber, and a *salon* at that!

The pride of it all, and the horror, is that it keeps going on, apparently able to assimilate whatever is proposed, even whatever is opposed (as Gide opposed to it the Bible, Shakespeare, Dostoievsky, even Dashiell Hammett), a myth of our human happening. Endless this sense of stylization; the only unpunished French vice and certainly the only unpublicized one, such accommodation may operate either upward or downward, as F. W. Dupee once pointed out—we may get something like *Steinbeck-ou-les-nobles-sauvages*, or we may get *Hamlet-ou-le-distrait*. And if the great solitaries of modern British and American literature are still unknown in France, it is because the French have not yet found the right stylistic frame for Hardy and Yeats, for Stevens and Frost. *Ça viendra*.

French Literature, like Sainte-Beuve, is "inclined to accumulate incompatibles"—whereat they are found to lie down together, like Villon and Genet, like Bossuet and Péguy, who harmonize with each

other more closely than with analogous figures outside the fold. Recuperative, burrowing, exorbitantly metropolitan, in this voice is the
resonance of an entire human survival, the interminable, unnameable
gossip in which Mr. Beckett, of course, has the last word—last, because it is also the first:

> I'll go on, you must say words, as long as there are any, until
> they find me, until they say me, strange pain, strange sin, you
> must go on, perhaps it is done already, perhaps they have said
> me already, perhaps they have carried me to the threshold of my
> story, before the door that opens on my story, that would sur-
> prise me, if it opens, it will be I, it will be the silence, where I
> am, I don't know, I'll never know, in the silence you don't
> know, you must go on, I can't go on. —*The Unnameable* (1949)

A literature of childhood? The words have not found it, no word
has uttered it. Not yet. For the child—momentarily: how long is
childhood?—is not a member, is not accommodated, is not an infant,
an *enfant*. The child *has* his word to say, has to say *his* word, a word
that carries him to the threshold of his story, before the door that
opens on his story, and it will be a word unknown—for how long?—
to French Literature. Precisely: as Mr. Beckett is at such pains to reveal, speech begins only in the face of the unnameable, upon the
perception of an *elsewhere* alien to the very language which seeks it out.
It is this creative doubt of the child, this fecund aporia of his language
which French Literature, until very recently, has condemned to silence
in its "central range" and exorcized around the edges.

If there had been children in French Literature, they are there as
mere instances of acculturation; as victims (Hugo, Renard), as cult
objects (Hugo again, Gide); either assimilated by Society as infants
(speechless) or transformed into members (remembered) or extruded
as freaks (Minou Drouet). Until yesterday, the child as an acceptable (utterable) metaphor of human life had no place, no word, in
France.

When we think of what Shakespeare and Goethe, Blake and Dostoievsky invented—remembering that to invent is to find, *invenire* to

come upon—we may be startled that *l'Opoponax* is the first book—
however trivial, however complacent—of its kind in French, the first
to acknowledge *another language*.

But we will understand why there has been no children's literature
in France.

A Note on Roland Barthes's *S/Z*

[1974]

British reviewer of the French text of *S/Z* writes, "It will afford profit and pleasure to that numerous class of persons
who have no instinctive enjoyment of literature." *Instinctive
enjoyment of literature!* Surely all of Roland Barthes's ten books exist
to unmask such an expression, to expose such a myth. It is precisely
our "instinctive enjoyment" which is acculturated, determined, in
bondage. Only when we know—and it is a knowledge gained by taking pains, by renouncing what Freud calls instinctual gratification—
what we are doing when we read, are we free to enjoy what we read.
As long as our enjoyment is—or is said to be—instinctive it is not enjoyment, it is terrorism. For literature is like love in La Rochefoucauld: no one would ever have experienced it if he had not first read
about it in books. We require an education in literature as in the sen-
timents in order to discover that what we assumed—with the complicity of our teachers—was nature is in fact culture, that what was
given is no more than a way of taking. And we must learn, when we
take, the cost of our participation, or else we shall pay much more.
We shall pay our capacity to read at all.

Barthes calls his study an essay, and in it a consideration of more
than just the tale by Balzac is desirable if we hope to discern what it
is that is being *tried* here. For the work on the text by Balzac, the
dissection—into 561 numbered fragments, or lexias, varying in length
from one word to several lines—of *Sarrasine*, is not performed for the

sake of identifying the five notorious codes (hermeneutic, semantic, proairetic, cultural, and symbolic), or even for the sake of discriminating the classical text (with its *parsimonious* plurality of interpretation and its closure of significance) from the modern text which has no such restrictions, no such closure (for the final closure of the modern text is *suspension*). Rather, the work so joyously performed here is undertaken for the sake of the 93 divagations (I use Mallarmé's term advisedly, for it is with Mallarmé, Barthes has said, that our "modernity" begins) identified by Roman numerals and printed in large type, amounting in each case to a page or two. These divagations, taken together, as they interrupt and are generated by the lexias of the analyzed text, constitute the most sustained yet pulverized meditation on *reading* I know in all of Western critical literature. They afford—though Barthes can afford *them* only because of the scrupulous density of his attention, his presence of mind where one is used to little more than pasturage—a convinced, euphoric, even a militant critique of what it is we do when we read. For reading is still the principal thing we do by ourselves in culture, and it has too long been granted—as when Valery Larbaud calls it the one unpunished vice—the amnesty of our society. We have "forgiven" masturbation in our erotic jurisdiction, but have we even learned to "indict" reading?

"What do you read now?" the hungry interviewer asked the famous writer, a woman of commercial success in the theater whose autobiography has defined a character of considerable literary sophistication. And the famous writer answered: "I don't read novels any more, I'm sorry to say. A writer should read novels. When I do, I go back to the ones I've read before. Dickens. Balzac . . . I find now when I go to get a book off the shelf, I pick something I've read before, as if I didn't dare try anything new."

Aside from the underlining fact that it is a writer speaking, this is a familiar experience, this preference for what Barthes calls the *readerly* over what he calls the *writerly* (I believe Richard Miller has been both plausible and adroit in his translation of *lisible* and *scriptible*; the dilemma is characteristic of the problem any translator of Barthes confronts, and the solution is characteristic of Mr. Miller, properly concerned with his reader's comprehension, not his comfort). It is a familiar experience because only what is authentically writerly can *become* readerly. If we were to set out to write a readerly text, we should be no more than hacks in bad faith; yet, as readers, how hard it is to face the open text, the plurality of signification, the suspension of meaning. It explains that hesitation at the bookshelf, the hand falling on the Balzac story, the known quantity. Known . . . How often we need to be assured of what we know in the old ways of knowing—how seldom we can afford to venture beyond the pale into that chromatic fantasy where, as Rilke said (in 1908!), "begins the revision of categories, where something past comes again, as though out of the future; something formerly accomplished as something to be completed." (A perfect description, by the way, of *S/Z*.) *Why* we read in this repressed and repressive way; what it is, in the very nature of reading, which fences us in, which closes us off, it is Barthes's genius to explore, not merely to deplore. His researches into the structure of narrative have granted him a conviction (or a reprieve), a conviction that all telling modifies what is being told, so that what the linguists call the message is a parameter of its performance. Indeed, his conviction of reading is that what is told is always the telling. And this he does not arraign, he celebrates.

So exact are Barthes's divagations, so exacting are their discoveries about the nature of reading, that we may now and again be dismayed—if we are in the main readers of the *readerly*—by the terms he has come to (he usually assumes Greek has a word for it) in which they must be rendered. For Barthes's text is *writerly*—at least his divagations are. This criticism is literature. It makes upon us strenuous demands, exactions. And because of them, precisely, we too are released, reprieved; we are free to read both the readerly (and can we ever again read Balzac *in all innocence*? can we ever want to?) and the writerly, *en connaissance de cause*, knowing the reason why. Essentially an erotic meditation, then, because it concerns what is inexpressible (which is the essence of eros), Barthes's essay is the most useful, the most intimate, and the most suggestive book I have ever read about why I have ever read a book. It is, by the way, useful, intimate, and suggestive about Balzac's tale *Sarrasine*, which the reader of the readerly finds reassembled at the end of this writerly book, *en appendice*, as the French say.

A Note on Renaud Camus's *Tricks*

[1981]

Over twenty years ago, I wrote: "It is more difficult to translate French texts dealing with pornographic subjects and low life than anything else. The French have developed a middle language somewhere between the smell of the sewer and the smell of the lamp, which in English is mostly unavailable. We have either the coarse or the very clinical, and I do not see how we can produce an English version of a masterpiece like *Histoire d'O* until we work up a language as pure and precise—though as suggestive and colorful—as that of Pauline Réage, whose French, for all the scabrous horror of her subject, is among the finest of the century." Only a very young or a very naive young man could have supposed it was possible so rapidly to "work up a language"—as if a language were no more than an emotion or an erection—and indeed the subsequent translation of *Story of O* rather proved his point *a contrario*: direct dealings with high pornography tend—I am referring to *linguistic* transactions—to lower the tone, to reduce the patina, to falsify the tempo.

Why should this be so? Perhaps the American version of *Tricks* (so-called in the original—the French do not have it all their own way) will suggest an answer. Not that I want to apologize for my text, which must stand on its own merits and fall on its defects, nor do I wish to intervene between the reader and Renaud Camus, who sounds, I am certain, a sufficiently idiosyncratic note to obviate any explanatory hocus-pocus on the part of his hard-driven translator. But these twenty-five *relations* do give us an indication of the problems all good writing about sex must contend with, in translation. The French words for sexual parts—and this is what I think I was trying to say, back in the censorable 1950s—are not metaphorical, or at least they are *immediate metaphors*: to call the penis a *verge* (rod, staff, as in our word *verger*, who carries the rod or wand of office) is still within easy reach of the most modest associative capacity. But to call it a *cock* is to invoke an entire range of imagery outside the immediate concern (unless we are talking about chickens). Almost every English word at the colloquial level for the sexual parts, male and female, is thus extravagantly metaphorical, even—am I stretching it?—poetic. I believe that our Anglo-American uneasiness, in the upper-middle class, about the words for sexual parts, and even for the unexposed corners of the body likely to become the focus or the fetish of sexual attention, is entirely characteristic of a certain social problematic. Perhaps the jitters are always responsible for metaphorical treatment; perhaps we always use *other words* when we are afraid. This differentiates us from French literary culture, which has here—and indeed traditionally so—the advantage. "They order these things better in France," Sterne claimed, and is this not how they ordered them? Called a spade a spade, and a penis a penis, when we who use English are "happy to say," like Cecily in Wilde's play, "that we have never seen a spade: it is obvious that our social spheres have been widely different."

And there are minor difficulties (though it is always minor points which constitute the major claims of writing to be literature). English has not separate names for the hair growing on the head and the hair growing elsewhere on the body. Of course we supply the lack by adjectives, but the simplicity of that *poil / cheveu* opposition escapes us. To conceal such discrepancies is any translator's business, and I am not offering excuses, I think, when I note that writing about sex explores the genius of a language in its most intimate recesses, its most subtle emergencies. All that is not mere sociology, all that is not mere exploitive eroticism, is what tends to fall between the medical and the foul-mouthed. And surely it is not just wringing one's hands in public (though considering what is done these days in public . . .) to point out that we have not, in English, even a simple verb for "getting an erection" unless we resort, again, to metaphorical equivalents of dubious charm.

No matter: the translation attempts to offer a clear view into Renaud Camus's drastic world, and though I no longer believe we can work our way up to the proper expression straightaway, perhaps this book affords one more occasion to make the effort, to round the corner, to fill the gap—if you see what I mean.

A Note on *Les Fleurs du Mal*

[1982]

Here is one more translation of Baudelaire's poetry. If the reader is tempted to smile, I can avow I smile as well (and if to sigh, even so . . .); it is for such a reader I would express here the principles to which that smile appeals.

It is a translation of the whole of *Les Fleurs du Mal* with twenty additional poems not included in either edition published in the poet's lifetime. It is a translation of one poet by one poet, with constant reference to the Concordance, by which the Frenchman's lexical practices may be acknowledged if not recovered. Thus to proceed with a *corpus* engages the translator in a different attitude—compels a different enterprise—from a rendering of individual poems chosen out of that corpus. The emphasis here is not on the varnish to which a single poem is susceptible, but on the hope of articulating a sustained structure among all the poems. Like *Leaves of Grass*, *Les Fleurs du Mal* is a recognizable (if variable) entity, proposed by the poet as a cumulative whole. Some of the methods by which the poet arrives at such a unity, such a unison at least, are not within my reach. The reader will notice that for the most part I have not sought to make the verses rhyme (whereas Baudelaire *always* rhymes when he writes in verse). Yet I have schemed, conscious as I am of the obloquy James Agate once cast upon a translator of *Cyrano*: "He refuses to rhyme and takes refuge in blank verse, like a tight-rope walker whose wire is stretched along the floor." My scheming has sought other means of getting the wire into the air; I have employed all the artifices in my power to make up for, even to suggest, the consentaneous regularities that the persistent use of rhyme affords. Here was an occasion, it seemed to me, when the sacrifice of a minor stratagem to a major one was in order—eschewing "terminal consonance" for the sake of cumulative effects, that "secret architecture" Baudelaire so prided himself upon. Even in the slenderest lyrics, when a rhyming music appears to be the justification for everything—or at least for anything—I have investigated other tactics for keeping the poem suspended: for it has been my study to acknowledge, first of all, a thematics that overshadows and underlies the melos.

His attention to thematics, however compensated for, however blandished, implies the translator's trust in the accessibility of what the poetry is "about"—call it the *mythology* of poetry. And surely the mythology of Baudelaire, like the mythology of Whitman, is as powerful as that of any poetry to be found within the modernity that these two helpless masters have—from our perspective—founded. The adjective formed from his name joins that extreme company—Platonic, Byronic, Rabelaisian, Freudian—of words that suggest a world without our having had to read the writers who have bestowed such qualifiers upon us. To be "Baudelairean" in the fashion of Arthur Symons, a fashion of sensational Satanism, is of course not the same thing as to be "Baudelairean" in that of Robert Lowell, a fashion of convulsive and confessional energy; implied mythologies rather than mere melodies are at variance. But it is in any case the translator's responsibility, and his doom, to engender a notion—the better for being the more conscious—of what the implications might be, though he himself cannot say what they are. Translating the work entire has suggested to me that there are so many more notes to be struck, or at least to be sounded, than my predecessors had intimated. Indeed the *intimate* was the first note which was new to me: a certain *private register*, which Gide compares to Chopin's and which I have tried for in especial.

Throughout, certainly, the undertaking has constrained me to an acknowledgment of the splendor and misery of cities, of bodies, an assent to the vast background of negativity against which finally rises the success of *Les Fleurs du Mal*. If I could not always love my originals, I have endeavored to serve them by an attempt to leave them alone, to get out of their way rather than to domesticate them. Baudelaire's poetry concerns us much more, and much more valuably, by its strangeness than by its familiarity: its authentic relation to us is its remoteness. Wanting to keep Baudelaire, I wanted to keep him at a certain distance.

The *Pléiade* edition of Baudelaire, established and annotated by Yves-Gérard Le Dantec, has been my source. I have attempted to dispense with notes, trusting to the understanding of the translation rather than to its overbearing gloss; in a great poet as in a great nation, to borrow Keats's phrase, "the work of an individual is of so little importance; his pleadings and excuses are so uninteresting; his 'way of life' such a nothing: that a preface seems a sort of impertinent bow to Strangers . . ." Thus chastened, or charged with the sublimity of his office, the translator eagerly makes way for his poet, proud and humble in the necessary dosages.

A Note on *Past Tense:*
The Cocteau Diaries, Volume One

[1987]

In this first of several volumes of late journals, covering the years 1951–52, we enter with Cocteau upon the last decade of his life. Nor will it come as a surprise, to those of us who have followed him (at a distance) through the most metamorphic career in Western culture since Merlin, yet the most single-minded poetic vocation since Orpheus, that Cocteau here repeats himself—indeed cannibalizes himself. The last two volumes of prose, half journal and half essay, excellent in their Montaigne-like sagacity, draw upon the life registered in these journals, the complex and harried existence of a man who could *stage* anything.

Perhaps it is of some use, certainly it is of great pride, to his translator that 1953 was the year I myself met Jean Cocteau. It must have been during one of the very few days the poet allowed himself in Paris, and I recall my pilgrimage as an effort to resolve, by application to a master, the conflict between concentration and dispersion. At the end of what I might call in the full sense of the word *audience*, I remember how the poet gave me some advice which it turns out he gave to a great many others as well—perhaps because it was such good counsel in his own case. Dryly, wryly, as he spread his famous hands between us, Cocteau said: "What other people reproach you for, cultivate: it is yourself." I see now that there was an answer—or at least, a response—in the impatient poet's words, and I have translated his journals in order to keep faith with his . . . faith, the faith of a poet in his unpersuadable calling.

The specific merit of these journals is, of course, the *energy* of the life displayed, excruciated, fallen upon the thorns of its own creative impulse. Beyond the discontents of the sixty-year-old *grande vedette*, beyond the ill-tempered sniping at Gide, at Proust, even at Genet, there is a fundamental action in these journals which makes them Exhibit A in the alphabet of our exemplary dedications: *poein*, "to make." Indeed, in accounting for the works which constitute no more than episodes of his career, Cocteau assigns to them a series of variations on the notion of *poetry*: *poésie de roman, poésie critique, poésie de théâtre, poésie graphique, poésie cinématographique*, etc. We are to understand that once a Cocteau produces novels, criticism, plays, drawings, films, they cease being these things and become part of *poetry*, which, like electricity, is not so much a thing as the way things behave once they are made by a human being. (Of course, this is not the same as saying that they become merely Jean Cocteau, though that is always—dangerously—the next step.) The splendor of this distracted existence is the generosity of an inveterately creative impulse. On almost every page Cocteau responds to his own necessities (". . . finished the new poem . . .") and to the demands of others (". . . sent off the introduction to Apollinaire . . ."). Drawings, films, poems (and the management of their appearance in the world), an endless stream of objects and texts, of *works and plays* are secreted by the poet as the cocoon within which he will stave off death (even if at times it is no more than silence that he defeats). The charm and the *lesson* of this journal are there, in the dedication to work, even in these late years, the work of recuperating his own past. . . .

In this particular volume Cocteau undertakes a new *mise-en-scène* for the opera-oratorio *Oedipus Rex*, upon which Stravinsky invited Cocteau to collaborate back in 1925 (". . . because I greatly admired his *Antigone*. . . . Cocteau's stagecraft is excellent. He has a sense of values and an eye and feeling for detail which always become of primary importance with him. This applies alike to the movements of the actors, the setting, the costumes, and indeed all the accessories . . ."). In a sense, this final staging is the completion of a cycle which had made many demands: in 1928 Cocteau published his French text for the opera-oratorio (originally performed in Latin) and six years later came to terms with the myth of Oedipus, or rather the cycle of myths that extends, as Cocteau himself points out, from the hero's "Siegfried-like youth, consumed with curiosity and ambition . . . to the transfiguration of this playing-card king," who triumphs over his conflict by submitting to it, who emerges from his tragedy by sinking *through* it, who passes from "the livid, mythical light of quicksilver" out into sunlight—blind, ignorant, and guided by his daughter, Antigone, who speaks with the voice of his mother and wife, Jocasta. The terms Cocteau came to are generally regarded as his finest work for the stage, a masterpiece of the modern theater, *The Infernal Machine*, a crowning expression of that truly Parisian gift for an encompassing style in which all of Cocteau's long career flourished (floundered?) at times so flagrantly as to seem—who has not resisted *all* those seductions, but who has not yielded to *some* of them?—frivolous, but always with the true *lacrimae rerum* note. Appropriate, then, that in these late journals Cocteau should return to *Oedipus*, to himself. For it is not only an exploitation of his *patrimony* that Cocteau stages anew for his old master and friend, a symbolic murder of his father (as classical literature is received and devoured as the ancestor of French literature), but the other great inheritance, the other great theme of descent that he *realizes* here: the theme of the Possession of the Mothers. All of modern French literature is under this sign, of course; that is why so many of the greatest works of the twentieth century are by homosexuals: Gide, Proust, Cocteau, Jouhandeau, Genet. Deposing Daddy, marrying Mommy: that is the great occidental undertaking, and in Cocteau's Oedipus cycle, from *Antigone* to the final *tableaux* for Stravinsky's great music, all the instruments concur, all the influences converge to create beyond the incest taboo as beyond the stigma of sexual heterodoxy, a dazzling emblem of parricide and piety as we have traditionally known it in our cultures. Now that Jocasta is internalized into no more than a voice, speaking only when her daughter and granddaughter, Antigone, speaks, now that Oedipus is mutilated, the marital conflict is at an end, and the pair are simply—simply!—mother and son, or father and daughter, again. Purified, they pass, with Antigone, into what Cocteau's voice (he narrated the work with Stravinsky conducting, in Paris and in Germany, in the course of these journals) properly calls *gloire classique*.

The reader will be interested to find Cocteau projecting these roles onto the odd family he has reconstituted for himself: his adopted (younger than himself) mother, Francine Weisweiller; his adopted son, Édouard Dermit. There is an extraordinary psychodrama taking place in the course of these often vexed, vehement, vociferous pages, a reworking of the Sophoclean recognition scene at Colonus (Santo Sospir—Paris was his Athens), a domestication of the sublime—an inclusion within the household bonds of life of precisely what had loomed as inaccessible, ecstatic, aloof. In this volume we find Cocteau accommodating his life to myth with all the insolent familiarity of a rightful heir. *Spectateurs, vous allez entendre.* . . .

A Note on Julien Gracq's
Balcony in the Forest
[1987]

N either document nor testimony (Gracq's own experiences in World War II were on an entirely different front, and in altogether other circumstances), *Balcony in the Forest*, Gracq's fourth novel, and actually the *precipitate* of the encounter between a certain historical situation, one that was very unstable and indeed fugitive, and the inclination of the author's fantasy, is the only one of this author's fictions—among so many legends, romances, *gestes*—which can be presumed to be realistic.

In the little forest outpost at the beginning of World War II, Lieutenant Grange has a passionate yet detached affair, during the fall and winter months, with Mona, a lovely child-widow whom he encounters in the forest much the way Golaud encounters Mélisande. Then spring comes, and with it the murderous reality of the German avalanche. History, for an interval, becomes a kind of pure awaiting, in which Gracq is enabled to feel, for the first time, what he calls "imaginative communication with reality." All his other novels—*The Castle of Argol* (1938), *A Dark Stranger* (1945), and *The Opposing Shore* (1951, translated in 1986)—are so many myths of abeyance and interregnum in which the characters, or rather the *figures* (as we might say of any human silhouettes moving in darkness against a sanguinary light, within a singular silence) expunge each other's energies during a period of suspense, of transgressive daring, until the Unspeakable Event engulfs them in a longed-for yet deferred catastrophe. For this novelist has what might be called a Parsifal Complex (indeed, *Balcony in the Forest* opens with the adjuration by which Gurnemantz begins that music-drama: "Forest Guardians, guardians of sleep as well—waken at least with the dawn!"), an imagination so structured that any action is merely the delusive interlude, the masque of misapprehension, before a ravaging revelation. For Gracq, of course, the Grail is indeed revealed as a cup of trembling, a ruinous chalice—but perhaps we never did put much credence in Wagner's stagey salvation. Hadn't Nietzsche warned us that with Amfortas, with Kundry, with Parsifal himself, we were only two steps away from the hospital? The astonishing thing about Gracq's novel, the last full-length fiction he was to write (in 1958, some eighteen years after the occurrences it is concerned to adumbrate), is that it has been able to transcribe in terms of contemporary life, of contemporary death, precisely those images and incidents which in all of Gracq's other works are assigned the distancing labels "gothic" or "surreal" or certainly "magical." Such a transformation has come about not because Gracq has changed—for he has not: no novelist ever remained so true to his esoteric inspirations as Monsieur Poirier, a geography professor who chooses to create his poems, his play, his essays, and his fictions, even his translation of Kleist's *Penthisilea* and his study of André Breton, under that mysterious, Breton-sounding pseudonym *Gracq*. But because reality changed.

In English we called it the "phony war." In France it was called, with varying degrees of validity, the *drôle de guerre*. For nine months after the declaration of war between Germany and the Allies, hostilities were suspended, were not engaged. And in that gestation, there was a great silence, a terrible holding of a continent's breath until the blow fell in the easy June 1940, and France fell with it, as if there were no such fierce thing as combat—only surrender, only collapse, only defeat. But in the bated September 1939 there was no knowing, no telling; the mobilized troops were sent to the various frontiers—those famous and "impregnable" lines that were to be so readily erased—where they waited in a demoralizing silence for month after month. This is the interval Gracq chose; it took him nearly two decades to write his way into it, to let reality speak in the terms of his somber enchantment. As he says: "Things were suspended, but there was no clearing, no perspective. It was not impossible (or so people thought) that things might end without hostilities. There might, then, be a 'white' peace. And there were also all kinds of catastrophic possibilities, including the one that came to pass. We found ourselves, truly, on the brink of a sort of mist-filled chasm, out of which it was very difficult to see what would emerge. It is, I think, quite an *original* situation, that of a declared war that does not get itself fought, that cannot begin."

Hence it is this novel of the phony war, of the inauthentic peace and the inactual hostilities, which is the least oneiric of Gracq's works. It is the least oneiric *book* because the period it treats was itself a kind of waking dream. The France of 1939–40 was living as if there had been no military necessity. "There was," Gracq observed in 1971, "the sentiment of a void, the sense of an enormous blank. Nothing occurred: there was an utterly somnambulistic aspect to everything. For everything continued as if nothing had happened. There was a paralysis, a putting-in-parenthesis, a prelude—to what? No one knew. It was *pure anticipation.*" The story of Lieutenant Grange (*lieu-tenant*, place-saving: even his rank is a kind of mystery, a holding action), assigned to command the isolated French blockhouse at Hautes Falizes, in the middle of the forest—the Forest of Arden!—and, closer still, the Ardennes of the last Great War, near the Belgian border and the Meuse river. The story of Lieutenant Grange is nothing but the story of Any-man in a vacant moment whereof the true occurrences are the vast metamorphoses of nature (the turn of the seasons, the sullen erosion of rock to sand, the woodland murmurs of sprouting and decay), and the minuscule transformations within a single body (". . . when he put his weight on his heel, a sharp spear of pain leaped up to his hips; against the harsh cloth that bound his skin, he felt the faint velvety shudder of fever, still almost voluptuous.").

It is of interest to note that this is Gracq's one novel to have been "made into" a movie, whereas *The Opposing Shore*, for example, has been produced as an opera: opera is of course the apposite "realization" for Gracq's work. Yet in the film of *Balcony in the Forest*, the author was amused to discover that the soldiers, the *other soldiers*, have much more continuous presence than in his book itself, though that presence has no effect on the process of the narrative. "Simply," as Gracq is pleased to say, "because in a scene in a novel, a character about whom the author has ceased to speak immediately becomes an *absent presence*, while in the film such a character remains caught in the camera field—he is still *there*." Gracq was astonished to find *the others* dragged into the visual field, for in his text, his imaginative substance, there are never others unless they are *named*, unless they are audible as language. However capital the images, however striking the visions, Gracq is the purest of novelists, and there is a sense in which he cannot be reduced, transferred, or even translated into other versions, other forms of art.

He can, of course, be translated, in the absolute sense; the coincidence of Gracq's privileged fantasmatics with an actual historical sequence affords his (third) translator a particular opportunity, one of which Gracq himself appears to be quite conscious, as in this passage where Lieutenant Grange studies a pamphlet describing the German offensive weapons:

> The ponderous gray silhouettes . . . seemed curiously exotic—another world—with their simultaneously baroque, theatrical and sinister quality of German war machines which, despite all the requirements of technology, still managed to remind him of Fafnir. "*Unheimlich*," he thought: there was no French word; he studied them with a mixture of repugnance and fascination. Outside, the heavy rain of the Ardennes was beginning to fall with the darkness, its drumming muffled by the snow. Unconsciously, he strained to hear the occasional noises from the crew room, afraid of being surprised, as if he were poring over obscene photographs.

Grange, then, is a kind of Amfortas, a Fisher King (the title of Gracq's play of 1948), wishing for, yet reading against, the arrival of the Germans. As Kundry says: *I await the conqueror*. "Never before," muses Grange as he wonders over the war's suspension, "never before had France pulled the sheet over her head with this feverish hand, this taste of nausea in her mouth." And what a boon to the translator of 1958, then, in what became the novel's final sentence, suggesting the kind of overdetermined, lyric necessity of this musical, mysterious text: "He lay for a moment more with his eyes wide open in the darkness . . . then he pulled the blanket up over his head and went to sleep."

From Exoticism to Homosexuality

[1989]

Written over a seven-year period (1896–1903), the four little texts that constitute *Amyntas* (1904) range from an initial Loti-like incantation to the disenchanted scrutiny we recognize today in the "travel writing" of a Graham Greene or a V. S. Naipaul. The little book, largely overlooked in the canon, is a sort of hinge in André Gide's career, for it marks—under a name borrowed from Theocritus and later assigned by Virgil to a shepherd of enterprising but melancholy eros—an articulation of consciousness: far from being a merely decorative opuscule whose rhapsodies have hitherto evaded translation and even commentary because of their apparent submersion in local and exotic color, *Amyntas* accounts for how the author of *Les nourritures terrestres* (1897; *The Fruits of the Earth*), that Nietzschean apostrophe to hedonist liberation, became the author of *Corydon* (1911), those insistently subversive dialogues on the nature of human sexuality and on the place of the homosexual in society. Gide began writing *Corydon* as soon as *Amyntas* was published, and hoped for a preface to this "second shepherd's play" from Freud himself.

Amyntas, then, is a work of disintoxication, in which Gide attempts to separate himself—ruefully, gingerly—from the North African prospects and panoramas that had hitherto formed his entire erotic spectrum. Of course he was working in a great French convention—Flaubert and Eugène Fromentin, Eugène Delacroix and Pierre Loti had shown him the way; yet only Gide achieved the right tonality of eros in his ecstatic dedication to certain landscapes, certain desolations of weather and light. Perhaps Gide's commitment, his ardor, was so tenacious precisely because the desert is the one place where a man's thirst cannot be quenched.

Years later, when considering the possibility of a reprint with illustrations, Gide was to murmur reproaches in his *Journal* (to others? to himself?) about the reception of *Amyntas*: "Few realize I have never written anything more perfect than *Amyntas*. People look for descriptions, for the picturesque, for information about the country and its customs. Yet there is virtually nothing in the book I could not just as well have written elsewhere—in France, anywhere. To whom could the secret value of the book speak? Only to the select few. Others were disappointed" (December 1910).

In *Amyntas* the stupefying rhetoric of exoticism collapses; the identification with a certain "primitive" languor falters. The book is the secret narrative of one more impoverishment, a destitution that will lead the author to his authentic riches, his characteristic fictions: *Les caves du Vatican* (1914; *Lafcadio's Adventures*), *Les faux-monnayeurs* (1925; *The Counterfeiters*). Exorcism is perhaps the one constant in Gide's metamorphic career, an anthology of returns—from symbolism, from exoticism, from homosexuality, from communism. And of course, in order to return, one must make a departure. From his very first work, *Les cahiers d'André Walter* (1891; *The Notebooks of André Walter*), published before he was twenty, Gide was concerned with wrenching himself from his comforts, chronicling his consequent lacerations, and accepting no easy solace. André Walter, like Rainer Maria Rilke's Malte Laurids Brigge (fragments of whose diaries Gide was to translate in 1911), would commit suicide; Gide, like Rilke, would survive into a new realism, a new reality. By tracing the decline of the substitutive persona, Gide managed to save himself, to become, as he put it early on, the most irreplaceable of beings.

It was not easy. The disappointments of the insistently returning lover—the connoisseur of landscape, of *Stimmung*—are bitter, sometimes comical in the chronicling. But these are undergone in *Amyntas* for the sake of grander claims, intimations—to be made clear in *L'im-*

moraliste (1902; *The Immoralist*)—of a more active eros: adulthood! Indeed, the value of *Les nourritures terrestres* is only in the subsequent transcending of its message. The modest *Amyntas* is an enactment of just such manumission; it ends in the Normandy autumn, Gide's persona racked by his longing for that discarded polymorphous perversity he had once discovered for himself in "De Biskra à Touggourt" ("From Biskra to Touggourt," the first piece in *Amyntas*). The opposite of a neurosis, Freud was to say, is a perversion. So Gide was to discover, and *Amyntas* represents the lyrical working out of that maturation which I should call *barbarism and its discontents* if I had not already called it *Gide's Way*.

L'immoraliste was finished in 1901, a year after Freud's *The Interpretation of Dreams*, and published—"so far behind me," Gide wrote in his *Journal*, "that I cannot bear to correct the proofs" (2 March 1902)—in an edition of three hundred copies in 1902, a year before Nietzsche's posthumous *The Will to Power*. Whereas *Amyntas* is dedicated to Gide's wife, *L'immoraliste* is dedicated to destroying her. Freud and Nietzsche are the landmarks by which to locate this narrative, this voice raised almost to the tension of the lyre as it fills the night on the terrace of Sidi b. M. If there is anything immoral about Michel it is his style—languorous, sometimes complacent, yet with all the terrible energy of a man who has made it his duty to be happy. In it we recognize Gide's very charged sense that only excess may be recompensed, that only *too much* thirst is to be slaked. This recital might as well be called "Civilization and Its Discontents" as "Toward a Genealogy of Morals."

Certainly skepticism is what resonates at the end of the trajectory beginning with *Les nourritures terrestres* and ending with *Corydon*. Who was this last, so hemmed and hawed over? Certainly he was a shepherd in Virgil's second Eclogue, in the first line of which we learn that he burned for fair Alexis (another shepherd). To the classically educated Frenchman, the name alone would be, even now, an indication of sexual status, although in the Anglo-Saxon pastoral tradition—in Spenser, for example—Corydon is merely a shepherd and quite as susceptible of being matched with a shepherdess.

Gide was fond of the names that strew the Theocritean canon. One of the most important is that of Ménalque (Menalchas), who first appears in 1895 in a prose fragment of that name, later incorporated into *Les nourritures terrestres*. Apparently *L'immoraliste* was to have been a life of Ménalque before it became Michel's interior drama; the rather "nineties" tempter and catalyst, evidently drawn from Gide's entranced observations of Oscar Wilde, is yet endowed with a resonance we recognize in another connection:

> Lately an absurd, a shameful lawsuit with scandalous repercussions had given the newspapers a convenient occasion to besmirch his name; those whom his scorn and superiority offended seized this opportunity for their revenge; and what irritated them most was that he seemed quite unaffected. "You have to let other people be right," was his answer to their insults. "It consoles them for not being anything else." But Society was outraged, and those who, as the saying goes, "respect themselves" felt obliged to cut him, thereby requiting his contempt. (*L'immoraliste*, p. 425)

Obviously this is the same man who, "I had been told, made no objection to certain unnatural tendencies attributed to him" (*Corydon*, p. 3). Gide has managed to accommodate much of what remains outside his fictions in the figure of Ménalque, and not only the "I" of *Corydon*—a frequently boorish, utterly un-Gidean bigot—but also Corydon himself are the book's real success (as we so often feel that Plato's real success is the figure of Socrates and the décor of the polis, the attribution to philosophy of a site and a voice). Some of the best comic touches occur at the very beginning of Gide's little subversion, already adumbrated so subtly in *Corydon* (p. 4):

> On entering his apartment, I admit I received none of the unfortunate impressions I had feared. Nor did Corydon afford any such impression by the way he dressed, which was quite conventional, even a touch austere perhaps. I glanced around the room in vain for signs of that effeminacy which experts manage to discover in everything connected with inverts and by which they claim they are never deceived. However I did

notice, over his mahogany desk, a huge photographic reproduction of Michelangelo's *Creation of Man*, showing Adam
naked on the primeval slime, reaching up to the divine Hand
and turning toward God a dazzled look of gratitude. Corydon's
vaunted love of art would have accounted for any surprise I
might have shown at the choice of this particular subject. On
the desk, the portrait of an old man with a long white beard
whom I immediately recognized as the American poet Walt
Whitman.

In *Lolita* (1955) Vladimir Nabokov provides a parody of this scene.
Humbert Humbert is delighted to discover some comfort in the analogous sufferer and pederast Gaston Godin, who "always wore black,
even his tie was black; he seldom bathed . . . Upstairs, he had a
studio—he painted a little, the old fraud. He had decorated its sloping
wall with large photographs of pensive André Gide, Tchaikovsky,
Norman Douglas, two other well-known English writers, Nijinsky
(all thighs and fig leaves) and Marcel Proust. All these poor people
seemed about to fall on you from their inclined plane" (p. 166).

By the time Gide had reached *Corydon*, the century had turned and
the pervert's lair was no longer represented as the incense-blued den of
decadence. Corydon's asceticisms are just as clear props and signs.
Only the narrator is taken in.

To be taken in—to be deceived, especially self-deceived—was for
Gide an abomination. It was what he knew to be wrong with his culture (even with symbolism, which he declared to Valéry left too much
out). And this was the realm of lies and fraudulence, which alone
could rouse Gide from his own lair by any number of youthful solicitations. As the years have gone by, his steadfast refusal to lie has
glowed steadily like a declarative beacon played on a much-vexed
darkness. The pursuit of truth and its essential Gidean corollary, the
refusal to lie, make *Corydon* worth reading. For despite his painstaking
recourse to an appallingly rigged and anthropomorphized zoology,
despite his other recourse—the two are always found together in the
period's apologies for the homosexual in society—to the literary and
historical vestiges of Greek culture, Gide was on to something; in-

deed, the very indecisiveness of his vocabulary affords a clue that his translators have often chosen to overlook. Precisely when we are discovering that there is no such massive and unitary object of discourse (or experience) as homosexuality, Gide's fluctuations in nomenclature must be rendered as an index of a mind reluctant to dignify confusion by calling it uniformity. The terms he uses in *Corydon* may seem to us merely quaint—*uranism, pederasty, inversion, degeneracy*, not to mention *urnings* and *the third sex*—but at least they question, they even jeopardize, conventions of classification that impose a false unity of conceptualization. Like the Freud he had not read and the D. H. Lawrence who never read him, Gide suggests, in the very variety (instability) of his nomenclature as well as in his liberalizing proposals to a relentlessly repressive and therefore libertine society, that the language of desire is not "about" a continuous unitary sexual experience. Rather, as we learn from *Amyntas*, that language produces and constitutes such experience. What we say structures "instinct" and generates the scripts in which experience and sensation, in themselves, are registered and understood. Or at least received.

Begun in 1907, *Corydon* gestated for thirteen years. It was first published in 1911 in an unsigned private edition of twelve copies with the title *C.R.D.N.* and consisted of only the first two dialogues and a bit of the third; in 1920 another unsigned private edition of twenty-one copies contained all four dialogues and a preface; finally, in 1925, it was published, titled *Corydon*, in a signed, commercial edition, much reprinted subsequently. In 1921, determined upon its general publication (partly as a result of the wrenching alienation from his wife, who had burned all his letters to her upon realizing that Gide had accompanied young Marc Allégret to England), Gide made a great discovery. He began to read Freud, the Freud who seemed to echo his own thoughts when he had written: "Psychoanalysis resists entirely the attempt to regard homosexuals as a specially formed group and to separate them from other men . . . It finds that all men are capable of a homosexual object choice and that they have in fact performed it unconsciously . . . The exclusive sexual interest of a man for a woman is equally in need of explanation and cannot be taken for granted as an underlying chemical attraction." So delighted was Gide to learn that

Freud regarded a man who experienced *no* homosexual desires rather than one who did as the oddity, that he asked his translator, Dorothy Bussy, to consider whether her brother, James Strachey, Freud's English translator, might not intercede for him: would not Freud be the ideal authority to supply a preface to *Corydon*, thereby sheltering it from many of the misconceptions and antagonisms it was bound to provoke? Apparently communication broke down somewhere between Bussy, Strachey, and Vienna, but it is noteworthy that Gide began psychoanalysis (five sessions) at about this time, and that he went so far as to speculate: "Perhaps I might present *Corydon* as 'translated from the German' . . . a preface by Freud might emphasize the book's usefulness and timeliness" (*Journal*, April 1921). The perceived congruity of purpose between Freud and Gide echoes a larger historical structure: the apprehension of unity within apparently opposed or agonistic energies, whether sexual or psychic. *Corydon* remains one of the books crucial to an understanding of the development of the Western mind in the first quarter of the twentieth century.

Corydon participates in the intuition of ecstatic wholeness that appears to be the ruling metaphysical pathos of its period. From *L'immoraliste* and *Les nourritures terrestres* to *Si le grain ne meurt* (1921; *If It Die*), Gide's first autobiography, Gide's apprehension of discursively determined rhapsodic experience remains unequaled in French literature for the scope and frankness of its scrutiny. Gide's secret, as Camus once remarked, is that he never lost, among all his doubts, the pride of being human. His is not a great mind, wrote E. M. Forster in 1951, in his obituary of Gide, but a free one—"and free minds are as rare as great, and even more valuable at the present moment."

Like other works of the period, *Corydon* explores not the nature of human sexuality but the history of its repression; it peers, sometimes gracefully, sometimes grotesquely, beneath what Gide called the veil of lies, convention, and hypocrisy that still stifles an important and not contemptible part of humanity.

The same year that Hitler published *Mein Kampf*, Gide published *Si le grain ne meurt*, the program of another battle, another subversion. Indeed, the strategy had been laid four years before, when Gide first spoke of these memoirs to Marcel Proust: "Spent an hour of

yesterday evening with Proust . . . I take him *Corydon* of which he
promises not to speak to anyone; and when I say a word or two about
my memoirs: 'You can tell everything' he exclaims, 'but on condition
you never say: *I.*' Which does not suit me" (*Journal*, May 1921). During the years in which Gide enabled the discussion of homosexuality
with *Amyntas*, *Les nourritures terrestres*, *L'immoraliste*, *Corydon*, and *Si le
grain ne meurt*, Jean Cocteau, Marcel Jouhandeau, and Jean Genet devised and perfected their own idiolects of heterodoxy. The argument
implied by Proust's comment to Gide has in fact little significance in
comparison to the enormous freedom that the Marcel of *A la recherche*
acknowledges and enjoys in speaking of sexual subjects. Thenceforth
the dialogue among Gide, Proust, and these writers was just that, a
dialogue, in contrast to the previous series of sensational (and sometimes preposterous) soliloquies. Frequently the tone was snappish:
Gide portrayed Cocteau in *Les faux-monnayeurs* as Count Robert de
Passavant; Genet dismissed Gide with "I do not like judges who bend
amorously over their victims"; Jouhandeau bandwagoned, "How
amused I was, reading *Les faux-monnayeurs*, to see that we have dealt
with the same scene, you know, the 'child suicide,' and perhaps at the
same moment. It is an episode in my tale that Kahnweiler is to publish
next autumn, and which has as its epigraph: Everyone wakes with a
minor preoccupation: that of murdering God." But these were intra-
mural sports. Much later, as a result of their struggles, the subject
of homosexuality acquired the status of legitimate literature.

In the last twenty-five years, largely as a result of Gide's work, there
has been a change in both the status and the language of the homosexual writer in France. The homosexual writer in France today is
born simultaneously with his text: or rather, his text brings him into
being. He does not exist as a glorious or scandalous progenitor; he is
not supplied with a being that precedes or transcends his writing. If
there is a certain invisibility about him, it is because he no longer
needs to present himself as a *monstre sacré*. When the homosexual is no
longer the subject of which his book is the predicate, then he eludes
the scandal and parade of *before* and *after*: there is the time of writing,
which is also the time of our reading, and the problem (is this not
what Gide was trying to tell us?) becomes the solution. Of course so-

lutions raise other problems, but that is no more than the dialectics of life itself; in our oedipal tradition of parricide and piety, as Cocteau has shown, one stages a symbolic murder of one's father (as classical literature is received and devoured as the ancestor of French literature), but the other great inheritance, the other great theme of descent, is then realized: the theme of the Possession of the Mothers.

Invitation to the Voyages
of Xavier de Maistre

[1994]

In 1790 Count Xavier de Maistre, a twenty-seven-year-old Savoyard officer stationed in Turin, fought a duel with a Piedmontese officer and was put under house arrest for forty-two days, an interval during which he wrote a text to beguile the languors of his solitude—having hitherto shown no trace of a literary vocation—and in 1794 he left the manuscript of *Voyage autour de ma chambre* in Lausanne with his older brother Joseph, who published it there the following year without the author's knowledge. Two centuries later we are astonished by the many anomalies which these circumstances present to current notions of authorship, of intellectuality, and of what we might call the military necessity. Our amazement at the oddities of the young count's career will be enhanced by our discovery that he was an early enthusiast of the brothers Montgolfier, that he flew in a hot-air balloon at the age of twenty-one, and that he described the ascent in a "Letter Containing an Account of the Aerostatic Experiment of Chambéry" (1784).

In 1798 Count Xavier, delighted by his unsuspected status as a *littérateur*, began writing a sequel, *Expédition nocturne autour de ma chambre*, which his brother advised against publishing—"according to the Spanish proverb, Part II is always bad"—and which remained in manuscript until 1825, four years after Joseph's death, when the (inaccurately titled) *Oeuvres complètes de Xavier de Maistre* appeared in Paris with considerable success. Subsequently these brief texts have been accorded a certain classical, or academic, success; they are *récits*, a genre which has long been appreciated in France (from Constant to Camus, with brilliant illustrations by Gide and Blanchot) and exemplified as well in Russia (*Notes from Underground*, for example), in Italy, and of course in England, where the personal essay invariably threatens to spill over into this protean form. A *récit* is a sort of dramatic monologue in prose concerned with the problematics of narrative, questioning the nature of such pronouns as "I," "he," and "you," and given, as Northrop Frye has determined, to notions of literature as process rather than as product. De Maistre's versions are among the liveliest and the most lenient in the repertoire.

In 1810 Count Xavier—whose brother, now plenipotentiary envoy of the Kingdom of Sardinia to St. Petersburg, has arranged for him to be appointed director of the Admiralty Museum while serving as a colonel in the tsar's army—attends a gathering where, during a discussion of leprosy in Scripture, someone asserts that the disease no longer exists; Xavier excitedly describes a leper he had known in Aosta. Joseph encourages him to write the account, which is published the following year as *Le Lépreux de la Cité d'Aoste*, along with *Voyage autor de ma chambre*, in St. Petersburg.

It is necessary to recall the qualities of this overwhelming older brother, whose genius for provocation was matched only by the eloquence of his umbrage and the dogmatic vehemence of his contempt. Embodying Catholic reaction against the doctrines of the *philosophes*, Joseph de Maistre, in a series of scathing works beginning with *Considérations sur la France* (1796) and culminating in *Du Pape* (1819) and *Les Soirées de Saint-Pétersbourg* (1820), brandished anathemas with enthusiastic cruelty, and raised his repudiations of science, of progress, of democracy, and of tolerance to the dignity of scandal. It is to him that the roots of French fascism descend, and it is no surprise to find this apologist for capital punishment praised by Baudelaire, who once said that "de Maistre and Edgar Poe taught me to reason." Nothing of his aggressive, indeed his insolent lucidity is shared by the younger brother, but the charm and amenity of Xavier's texts provide a kind of responsive alternative to the arrogance of Joseph's prejudices.

In 1838 Count Xavier—having served with distinction in the Russian armies against Napoleon ("the man from Hell"), whose retreat in 1812 his letters eloquently describe; having married a Russian woman in 1813 and had a son in 1817; having given up his military career in 1816 and having lived a tranquil family life in St. Petersburg for ten years; having returned to Italy in 1826, after his brother's death in 1821, leading in his beloved Turin the life of an important man of the world—visits Paris for the first time (and meets Sainte-Beuve, who consecrates his literary success by an essay in 1839).

Savoy, Sardinia, Switzerland, Italy, Russia: in pre-Bonaparte Europe it is possible to express (and to feel) allegiances to all these protonational entities and still be (or become) a French writer, readily acknowledged, even proclaimed, as Xavier de Maistre has been, a characteristic practitioner of a certain engaging resonance, informal and even capricious, yet immitigably a part of the realm of "polite letters."

Virtually unknown to English-speaking readers today (though there have been earlier translations), *Voyage autour de ma chambre* flaunts its filiations (as in Chapter XIX, Chapter XXVIII) with the powerful model of deviation and even of subversion established by Sterne, a resonance that would be echoed throughout Europe and even in Latin America (from Goncharov to Machado de Assis); Sainte-Beuve detected even more of the *grace souriante et sensible* of Charles Lamb in these whimsical chapters, and managed, as well, to find in de Maistre's incidental verses something of the *lucky* innocence of La Fontaine, as in these first lines of his *épitaphe*:

> Under this gray stone, Xavier lies
> To whom everything was a surprise:

> Where did the wind come from, he wondered,
> And why was it that Jupiter thundered?

How flabbergasting is it that the young count should also have been a passionate admirer of Ossian!

Certainly the point of Xavier's *voyages* is not to keep us wondering what will happen next, but what the author will think of next: this is a literature of the irregular and unpredictable, tending to brief or even fragmentary utterance. The qualities of consciousness are recessive, and operate in flashes, in explosions of insight which are not likely to sustain any sort of continuous development.

But such explosions are often of an astonishing brilliance in themselves, unlikely to quit the memory, and they foreshadow, so to speak, much that has been more laboriously and systematically discovered by our ulterior science, our psychology of the unconscious. I refer, for example, to what in Chapter VI de Maistre calls his "system of *the soul and the beast*." Here he accounts, in the blithest fashion, for that entire Faustian division of the self which was to become one of the great tragic themes in Western culture:

> I have conducted I know not how many experiments on the union of these two heterogeneous creatures. For example, I have clearly determined that the soul can command obedience from the beast, and that, by an unfortunate reciprocity, the latter can very often compel the soul to act against her will. . . . When you are reading a book, Monsieur, and a thought more agreeable than the rest suddenly enters your mind, your soul clings to it at once and forgets the book. As your eyes mechanically follow the words and lines, you reach the end of the page without understanding or remembering what you have just read; and this is because your soul, having ordered her companion to do the reading in her place, did not inform him that she was about to absent herself briefly, and thus the *other* continued reading while your soul no longer listened.

With what imperturbable amenity de Maistre plays on this theme, that we are not always ourselves! How wickedly he articulates some of the consequences of such dichotomy, such role-playing:

> Gentlemen: Never forget that on the day of a ball, your mistress is no longer yours.
> The moment the dressing begins, the lover becomes nothing more than a husband: the ball alone is the lover. . . . have no illusions: if she shows great delight in seeing you at the ball, it is not as a lover that you give such pleasure, for you are a husband: it is because you are part of the ball, and because you are, therefore, a fraction of her new conquest, a *decimal* of a lover . . .

But the perceptions are never permitted to extend themselves into anything so formal as a method, a system. Even the direst insights are playfully made, glancing, hit or miss. And the game of intimate relations—identity's Marivaudage—is played to the bittersweet end, relentless, heartbreaking. It is an extraordinary moment of equilibrium, somewhere between the Misanthrope and Manfred, that Xavier de Maistre occupies, a moment which merits our modern perscrutation.

Having returned to Russia in 1839, two years after the much-lamented death of his twenty-year-old son, Count Xavier established a salon which became the meeting-place of French society in the capital, until his wife died in 1851, leaving him despondent. In 1852 Xavier de Maistre died in St. Petersburg at the age of eighty-nine, having survived his entire family, his century, and in some sense himself.

Yourcenar Composed

[1994]

In 1909 the possibility of electing a woman to membership in the Academie Française was for the first time discussed in serious, in plausible terms. Of course the notion of such an exploit had frequently occurred, in the crypto-feminism of the *belle époque*, to many men and to many women as well, but serious discussion could supervene only when adversaries and partisans could acknowledge an inevitable choice. If the police rubric was *cherchez la femme*, the literary motto was *choisessez-la*!

And in the first decade of the new century, such a choice appeared inevitable. If the Forty were ever to open their exalted ranks to a member of the sex, the poet Anna de Noailles (by no means forgotten in France today, where she figures prominently in the Proust Follies, but by no means a consensually admired *writer*) was surely the designated candidate: for the first third of this century it appeared beyond dispute that her poems of an *innumerable heart*, her diffusely sensuous novels, her memorial reflections on an aristocratic and solitary adolescence (by birth a princess, by marriage a countess, by inclination a conversational imperialist), her essays in tribute to distinguished contemporaries with whom, as in the case of Maurice Barrèz, she had been notoriously intimate—all these productions seemed not only to warrant but to require elevation to what would be a no more than acknowledged Immortality. Discussion of the issue was indeed serious, yet the election did not occur, and as the years passed and the suffrage passed her by, the nature of the Countess's achievement appeared increasingly nugatory—the productions were found to be no more than effusions—the Countess breathed, she talked, she wrote: it was all quite natural. She was not so much an authority as that unwarrantable entity, a mere if memorable . . . authoress.

During the next seven decades, parallel or analogous qualifications were adduced to support the candidacy of Colette (who like Mme de Noailles and, in 1970 like Yourcenar herself, had already been inducted into the more gynophiliac Belgian Academy), of Simone de Beauvoir, of Nathalie Sarraute, even of Louise de Vilmorin; but it was Marguerite Yourcenar (born de Crayencour, a distinguished family name of northern France, which the young writer transformed into the curious anagram so characteristic of her self-invention in every department) who turned out to be the first woman inducted, in 1981, into this holiest and hoariest bastion of French literary and intellectual eminence, regarded for three hundred years as the ultimate redoubt of masculine privilege, though she was shortly and shadowily followed there by the classical scholar Jacqueline de Romilly. No women have subsequently been elected to membership.

Like that of the Countess de Noailles, Marguerite Yourcenar's standing is not uncontested. She is, indeed, one of those French writers whose authentic distinction is frequently indiscernible to anglophone readers dependent upon translation for a fair representation of literary authority. And here is one of the indications of our modernity, and the difference it makes in our apprehension; for whereas Goethe had famously—and to us, almost incredibly—declared to Eckermann that the crucial virtues and values of any writer are inveterately apparent in translation, it is Robert Frost who gains *our* credence by quite as famously remarking that the poetry is just what is lost in translation. Since I myself have translated into English Yourcenar's first volume of discursive prose, I am evidently in no position to decide the issue either way, but I should like to loiter over the *invidium* of this author's remarkable case—over, that is, the reluctance of many American readers to acknowledge her *grandeur* (or perhaps it is just *grandeur* and only *grandeur* they *will* acknowledge, the kind of ceremonial distinction that got the lady into the Academy in the first place).

Perhaps some analysis of our frequently noted recalcitrance with regard to Yourcenar will convince us of more than merely her own virtues or visitations—perhaps by some consideration of this kind of problematic fame (even more problematic than the erstwhile celebrity of Mme de Noailles, whose fall from a widely acknowledged salon vogue was no more than a matter, like that of Edmond Rostand, of a waning period manner) I can identify the difficulty some of us have with a writer so evidently comfortable with being *official*; perhaps by breathing on it a little I can clear the lens through which we regard (or are prevented from regarding) literary stature beyond provincial applications of celebrity and neglect, of sanction and subversion.

Well then; now that the froth is out of the bottle . . . In this country Yourcenar's most widely praised, indeed most nearly popular achievement is a sort of historical novel, *Memoirs of Hadrian* (1951), purporting to be that emperor's recollections bequeathed as a sort of experiential enchiridion to the nephew who was to become Marcus Aurelius; learned and lapidary though it is, this text is often compared— in merit as in accessibility—to the explicitly "entertaining" *Claudius* books by Robert Graves and to Thornton Wilder's *Ides of March*, though as a marker of popularity it might be noted that two of Yourcenar's many other fictions, one antecedent, one subsequent to *Hadrian's Memoirs*, have been made into interesting films, always a register of a writer's vitality in our era. Yet even *Hadrian's Memoirs*, a quasi best-seller translated into twenty-five languages and, more significantly, still in print in most of them over forty years later, has its detractors, who in this instance as in so many other productions of her *oeuvre*, find the classicizing prose ponderous, the historicizing psychology portentous, and the homosexual preoccupations pestilential.

They are wrong, I believe, but it is certainly evident that the virtues of Yourcenar's finest books (there are many virtues and many books— novels, tales, poems, essays, plays, translations, autobiographies) have been realized, so to speak, not by plethoric talent and overwhelming appeal, but by pervasive and strenuous effort, by a sometimes rebarbative concentration of will, an application perceived to operate against the very grain of a demanding, even a distressing temperament. Yourcenar is a writer who has composed her career as carefully as any of the works

which constitute it; she has revised, rejected, and revived various com-
ponents of the *oeuvre* until they have established, to her by no means
concealed satisfaction, an harmonious image of impulses which were
once entertained on entirely different, and latterly despised, premises.

We tend to call such writers "conflicted," and it is they who constitute the subjects of engrossing biographies, even when their careers
are apparently serene in terms of incident, for there is a constant agon
in the life as in the work, an evidenced struggle to emerge from mere
authorship into some kind of apprehended peace, an Olympian perspective granted by the structure of the collected works, an ultimate
poetry, so to speak, of reappraisal. There is not a moment of humor in
the trajectory formed by such insistent reassessment, and no more
than a modicum of grace, but there is passion, and wisdom, and,
against all odds, truth to the demands of art.

In the interests of a different truth, a truth to the demands of life,
Yourcenar's biographers and critics have often been obliged to contra-
dict, even to upbraid their subject; they have found it necessary to remark such chinks in the ostentatiously donned intellectual armor as
her youthful efforts at versification, so reminiscent of George Eliot's
clumsy poems (though Yourcenar's later translations of classical and
demotic Greek and of American poetry and African-American spiritu-
als into French verse and French prose are another thing: hers was the
gift to learn from her mistakes, or rather from her *maladresse*), or to
deprecate her improbable musicianship in those insipid essays on
Mozart or on Beethoven which resemble nothing so much as the
mundanities of Mme Verdurin—or of Mme de Noailles; these are the
readily remarked liabilities of a writer determined to present herself as
totally equipped to contend with—indeed to overcome—all the challenges of culture. Moreover, in the seven years since Yourcenar's
death, we have been made aware of the damages done to her own
character and to the confidence of her intimates, the blows dealt out,
round an embattled figure, by a felt need to present herself not sym-
pathetically but heroically (as in the case of Katherine Anne Porter,
whose biographers have similarly revelled in their discovery of like discrepancies between the velvet glove and the iron fist)—the need, in
short, to produce an image of triumphant prowess.

I once had in my hands a copy of Miss Porter's collected stories which belonged to her friend Donald Windham. In the blank spaces between the end of one story and the beginning of the next, as a kind of exultant gloss, Katherine Anne Porter had written brief accounts not of the anecdotal genesis of her fictions, but of how long it took to create, say, *Noon Wine* or *Pale Horse, Pale Rider*. "I wrote *Flowering Judas* early one morning in 1937"—that kind of thing. If we were to believe her (and of course we are not), none of the famous tales was the work of more than a few hours. In Yourcenar we discover a similar, or perhaps a converse impulse, for the desire to heroize the *made thing*— the fiction, the poem, both words mean the same—applies not, as in the American author's case, to a virtually clandestine instancing of the claims of spontaneity, of creative immediacy, but rather to a mythology of will, arduous, extended, and not inscribed somewhere in the margins but printed on the back of every copy, an indication that what had been published initially was merely a trial run, a rescindable enterprise, not to be regarded as part of the final design, the ultimate structure.

Indeed when I first began reading Yourcenar in 1953, I was struck by the fact that most of the works she had written before 1940 were no longer in print and apparently not to be reprinted *as such*, for even if they were not being rewritten, reconceived, ultimately replaced, the important thing for this author's readers to know was that certain works had once existed, though they were no longer to be laid hold of. For instance her first fiction *Alexis*, published in 1929 when she was twenty-six, was not reprinted in what Yourcenar would regard as its final form for thirty-five years. It was merely indicated, on all her subsequent books, as *épuisé*. The little novel affords proof of remarkable talents which required this kind of ripening into significance through a shadowy life of repudiation, a patient career in correctability. "The Treatise of Futile Combat," as it is subtitled in the French edition, concerns a young man's attempt to achieve self-awareness, and thereby self-acceptance, and thereby self-fulfillment. His discovery of sexual tastes which Alexis, an impoverished central European of noble stock, regards as unacceptably fixed on "beauty," decisively thwarts this nineteenth-century life, in which marriage and paternity fail to mend matters, and

only art—musical composition, as it somewhat vaguely turns out—
succeeds in releasing Alexis from his bad faith. The work assumes the
form of a confession, a long letter to the wife he is "abandoning," and
it concludes on a devastated note of triumph: "With the utmost humility I ask you now to forgive me, not for leaving you, but for having stayed so long."

Choosing for what she calls her "portrait of a voice" the tonality of
the classical French moralists, the young author secured for herself, as
ventriloquist, the possibility of a unity of tone exceptional in a beginner, and also the possibility of an aphoristic glamour which might
compensate for a certain meagerness of incident. Not even *The Princess
of Cleves* or *Adolphe* strews each page, each paragraph, with so many
lustrous nuggets, so many neat lucidities. In the "definitive" preface of
1965 (which rather condescendingly dilutes what she had written for
the second French edition of 1952, so that "for readers who may have
forgotten Virgil" becomes "for those who may have forgotten the
Latin of their schooldays") Yourcenar denies the influence of Gide's
"great books" but acknowledges certain filiations with the author of
Corydon and indeed devises formal parallels with the speaker of *The
Immoralist*, whose confession antedates that of Alexis by some quarter
of a century. Like Gide's Michel as he wrenches himself away from his
wife Marceline in that celebrated breviary of estrangement (similarly
unknown in its first edition to the public at large, but later to become
a sort of classic), Alexis prompts his reader, even prompts his creator,
to wonder about his wife Monique's possible response to such defec-
tion. "But for now," Yourcenar reports in her preface, "I have abandoned that project. Nothing is more secret than a woman's existence."

Uninterrupted, then, by any conflicting utterance—precisely in
the manner of all those early Gidean "treatises"—Alexis tells his own
story with the mild fluency of the eighteenth-century *maximistes*.
Thereby he cuts down the blood supply to the brain and instead max-
imizes, in another sense, a more general application of this cautionary
tale. Given the stipulations of her chosen vocabulary and of the period
taste to which she was admittedly appealing, Yourcenar could not use
the word *homosexual*, or any of the rest of that technical vocabulary for
"aberrations of the senses," as she observes they were called at the
time: invert, pederast, pervert, uranist. Hence there is, for the reader,

a certain mystification in all this "futile combat," without any very vivid apprehension of what it is that Alexis eventually surrenders to. Dostoievsky would not so leave us, as the French say, on our hunger.

Yet even granting a specifically *pallid* tonality, much transformed in later recitals into Hadrian's austere vivacity and the abrupt lyric cries of *Fires*, I should claim for this first tale in Yourcenar's canon a certain precision and an authentic power in her hero's admissions which derive from just the degree of ironic detachment so handsomely administered. In her preface she cites, helpfully and not a little vaingloriously, the influence of Rilke's *Notebooks of Malte Laurids Brigge* (1910), and indeed the recurrence of devices normally considered "poetic" is a pervasive character of this and of all Yourcenar's subsequent fictions. The alternation of narrative and aphorism is a much-honored procedure throughout, and if we recall that *aphorism* is etymologically a "wisdom broken," and that narrative is the healing impulse of language to put things together, we may observe how nicely this first brief recital fulfills the requirements of Yourcenar's ulterior imaginative genius, critical and lyric in close array.

Quite as instructive, in this kind of creative reorganization, is the fate of what Yourcenar calls one of her "forgotten texts," her first extended essay, the study of Pindar written in 1927, published in 1931 and withheld from subsequent readers until its posthumous appearance sixty years later in the Pléiade edition of her essays and memoirs. During the 1950s and '60s, Yourcenar had prepared—first for her own pleasure, then for publication, a series of translations of the Greek poets, from Homer to the Mimes of Herondas and beyond, to the lyrics of Byzantium, each selection provided with a brief but trenchant commentary, in her liveliest manner; these prose glosses, like the notes for *Hadrian*, are among her most striking works, and indeed she once suggested that these few pages on Pindar were a suitable substitute for that now unavailable early book. Here is a fragment of that later Pindar scholia, which gives some notion how inclusive as well as how incisive her criticism can be:

Happy to the end, the poet is said to have died in his eighties on the steps of the theater at Argos, during a performance, his head resting on the shoulder of his young friend Theoxenos, for whom he had just composed an admirable erotic *Eulogium*. Granting the changes with regard to sentiment and propriety in the course of the centuries, this Theoxenos of Tenedos was for the old Pindar the equivalent of Ulrika von Levetzow for the old Goethe, and the poem for Theoxenos his *Marienbad Elegy* . . . The learned men of the Renaissance exulted in this brilliant and difficult *oeuvre*, which corresponded to their thirst for sublimity, and represented a sort of challenge to their erudition. Among the poets, Ronsard imitated him, but on a smaller scale and by quite external means; subsequent "Pindaric" odes, for all their obligatory "splendid disorder" escaped, in France, neither platitude nor absurdity. Seventeenth-century England was more fortunate, thanks to the Milton of *Lycidas* and the *Ode on the Morning of Christ's Nativity*, with their breadth of diction and their rhythmic virtuosity, the rare and somehow abrupt inclusion of a cogitation or of a personal emotion, at least in the former poem, and their religious fervor, at once magnificent and grave. Later, Dryden's *Ode to Saint Cecilia* was to imitate, somewhat academically perhaps, the form of the Pindaric ode and its rich deployment of sacred legends. With romanticism, a frequently mandatory admiration for "the great Ancients" occasionally gave way, with regard to Pindar, to a deeper understanding. In German-speaking lands, the young Goethe of *Prometheus*, of *Ganymede*, of *The Wanderer*, Hölderlin, and latterly Spitteler, splendidly attest to his more or less internalized influence. Hugo, with his startling critical flair, has defined the Theban poet in a single verse: ". . . serene Pindar filled with epic echoes," more aptly than any number of commentators, the five words summing up Pindar's two main aspects, majestic tranquillity and the perpetual murmur of epic transpiring through lyric song.

But before Yourcenar published her homage to a millennium of Greek poetry, including the seven or eight pages on Pindar, in 1970, she was still concerned about what she regarded as that unsatisfactory early essay: "I am currently working on revising, or rather rewriting," she re-

ports to an archeologist friend, "a work I had the naiveté and audacity
to undertake in my early twenties on Pindar's poetry, which both my
French and my foreign publisher want to reissue. Since I clearly cannot let it be published as it stands, which is to say full of gaps only too
obvious to me now, I am deeply involved in an enormous reconstruction job." Yet out of weariness or perhaps clearheadedness, that particular "reconstruction" never saw the light of day.

Despite Yourcenar's continuous disavowals of the little book, there
are many clues in it to what would be her universe, her thought, even
her style, as when she speaks—remember, Yourcenar is twenty-two
when she is writing—of Pindar as "reaching the age where egoism is as
much a virtue as a necessity" or again "every life contains a failure, and
glory, in coming, only serves to call more attention to it." Finally, in
evoking Pindar's old age and his amorous passions late in life, the young
woman Yourcenar was when she wrote this book made some astonishingly premonitory remarks. Through Pindar, she sketched something of
a self-portrait of the old woman she would become. "At all stages of his
life, one could glimpse a lively sensuality in Pindar. This is a positive
quality . . . That simple sensuality disciplined itself in art . . . With age,
as always, his rather haughty reserve diminished: a weakening will could
no longer hold instinct in check. It is toward the end, in the formless
writing on the final pages, that intimate tastes and torments are revealed. Regret, that remembrance of desire . . . Let the reader not consider himself obliged to exhibit at this inappropriate juncture what few
remaining principles he has. This taste for young beauty is a frequent
one in those who are getting on in years." She who had her Alexis say,
"As a child, I yearned for glory"—and who would admit much later on
to having spoken of herself in this way—ends her first essay on Pindar
with this sentence: "The only lesson we can learn from this life, so dis-
tant from our own, is that glory after all is nothing more than a temporary concession." Notice, though, how she revises away from the
too-revealing confessional mode and in that later introduction to her
translation of Pindaric fragments fastens her painful analysis of desire
and regret to the old Goethe and the *Marienbad Elegy*.

Comparable revisions occur in the biography, of course. I have
noted how several of Yourcenar's friends, lovers, and allies in the great

campaign of cultural supremacy fell victim to the determined scission this author created in her life, much abetted by the drastic necessities of World War II: how the free-ranging, autonomous pre-1940 Marguerite seems an altogether different woman, and an altogether different writer, from the remote and hypochondriacal consort of Grace Frick, for the next forty years her translator, her domestic mainstay, and her unacknowledged lover. But perhaps, less sensationally, I can indicate the kind of transformation Yourcenar is always attempting—so that it becomes permissible, say, to print (and posthumously, at that) that early Pindar essay only when the later and shapelier and more stringent text is in place at the end of her career—by a more literary example which I believe has evaded Yourcenar's biographers.

On Tuesday, February 23, 1937, Virginia Woolf laments a lost opportunity to write in her journal, thus: "This extraordinary scribble means, I suppose, the translator coming. Mme or Mlle Youniac (?) Not her name." And then, after a page or so about what couldn't be written while indeed she was actually writing it, Woolf returns to the charge: "So I've no time or room to describe the translator, save that she wore some nice gold leaves on her black dress; is a woman I suppose with a past; amorous; intellectual; lives half the year in Athens; is in with Edmond Jaloux &c, red-lipped, strenuous; a working Frenchwoman; matter of fact; intellectual; we went through *The Waves*. What does 'See here he comes?' mean & so on." And then on the next day, writing to the composer Ethel Smyth (a difficult friend, whom Woolf was probably eager to put off at anyone else's expense), she concludes the dossier thus: "Yes, Ethel dear, I'd like to see you, but what's the use of seeing you against some intolerable necessary bore—this refers to a French translator who's wasted one of my rare solitary evenings." So much for the encounter, at least on Woolf's side, between these two women who were to become, each in her national fashion, Major Writers, insofar as majority status is conferred by academic consensus, critical esteem, and a continuous readership.

On Yourcenar's side, something more significant than a missed opportunity, an accidental oversight, is registered, indeed is enacted. For the encounter with Woolf and its treatment in Yourcenar's texts represents in little the characteristic procedure of this writer, its finesse and its excess, which I regard as the central symbolic effort of her life's work, and even of her life: the will to compose a figure of Olympian equilibrium which, as Dr. Johnson said of Milton, would be "great by design."

In the essay which served as a preface to *Les Vagues*, first published as an article in *Les Nouvelles Litteraires* in 1937, Yourcenar sketches a portrait quite as telling as Woolf's informal one, though evidently given a high gloss for her French readers whom she assumes to be unfamiliar with the achievements of Leslie Stephen's daughter: "Only a few days ago, in the sitting-room dimly lit by firelight where Mrs Woolf had been so kind as to welcome me, I watched in the half-light as the profile of that young Fate's face emerged, hardly aged [Woolf was fifty-five, Yourcenar thirty-four] but delicately etched with signs of thought and lassitude, and I reminded myself that the reproach of intellectualism is often directed at the most sensitive natures, those most ardently alive, those obliged by their frailty or their excess of strength constantly to resort to the arduous disciplines of the mind."

Thirty-five years later, the high gloss has become something of a mirror in which Yourcenar (already incipiently identifying with Woolf's "sensitive nature," her "frailty or excess of strength," and most significantly with her "obligation to resort to the arduous disciplines of the mind"—though it is doubtful that Woolf would have characterized her own creative impulses in this highfalutin fashion) manages to articulate eternal contours for herself: "I translated *The Waves* into French, Virginia Woolf's next-to-last novel, and I am not sorry to have done so, since my recompense for ten months of work was a visit to Blooms-bury, and two short hours spent beside a woman at once sparkling and timid, who greeted me in a room taken over by twilight. We are always wrong about the writers of our time: either we overrate them or we run them down. I do not believe I am committing an error, however, when I put Virginia Woolf among the four or five great virtuosos of the English language and among the rare contemporary novelists whose work stands some chance of lasting more than ten years. And I even hope, despite so many signs to the contrary, that there will be a few minds aware enough in around the year 2500 to savor the subtleties of her art." Being overrated or run down—this was, as Yourcenar's latest biographer observes, a premonitory diagnosis: between the fetishists of her own productions, ever ready to launch into easy raptures, and those who regard her as in the worst sense an academic, even a *pompier* writer, Yourcenar has not yet been afforded a determinate status, nor do we possess, for all her rank as an "immortal," a satisfactory clue to how her work will be regarded "in the year 2500."

As for those subtleties of Woolf's art, Yourcenar seems to have been remarkably off-hand about them. In a letter written some forty years after her translation was published she comments: "I don't think the translation of *Les Vagues* caused me any particular problems, it was merely a question of letting oneself drift along with the current, not always too clearly aware of where that current was taking one; but Virginia Woolf herself seems to have desired that impression of vagueness (no play on words intended). In an attempt to be a conscientious translator, I went to see her at the time, to ask her certain questions about how she would prefer that I translate certain sentences containing allusions to themes or images from English poetry: literally, or by trying to achieve the same effects with similar themes familiar to French readers. But this problem was quite alien to her, as were problems of translation in general."

There is a discrepancy here, between Woolf's response to the encounter, which is described, however hastily, as a rather elementary process of textual scrutiny ("What does 'See, here he comes' mean, & so on"), and Yourcenar's lofty and perhaps after-the-fact discussion of French equivalents to "themes or images from English poetry." It is hard to believe that Mrs Woolf would be so obtuse about questions of equivalence in the translated language, if they had been presented to her. (As early as 1923, she writes in her journal: "I wonder if this next lap of my fiction will be influenced by Proust? I think his French language, tradition, &c, prevents that, yet his command of every resource is so extravagant that one can hardly fail to profit, & must not flinch, through cowardice.")

Yourcenar, however, was anything but a "conscientious translator," though she was frequently an inspired one, as we know from the testimony of her friend Constantin Dimaras, with whom, a year before her encounter with Woolf, she had collaborated on a translation of

Cavafy's poems, a task perhaps facilitated by the fact that she did not know modern Greek, though as Dimaras tells us, "Marguerite was solely concerned with what she thought sounded good in French . . . I would give her word-for-word translations and she would 'arrange' things." In the case of her version of *What Maisie Knew*, completed in 1939 though not published in France until 1947, it may be of some interest to confront the texts, however briefly.

Here is James in 1897, on page 3 of the novel, suspended over Maisie's parents' divorce: "It was a society in which for the most part people were occupied only with chatter, but the disunited couple had at last grounds for expecting a time of high activity. They girded their loins, they felt as if the quarrel had only begun. They felt indeed more married than ever, inasmuch as what marriage had mainly suggested to them was the unbroken opportunity to quarrel."

And here is Yourcenar's version: "Dans ce monde là, les gens étaient presque uniquement occupés de commérages, mais ce couple désuni avait au moins devant lui de sérieuses occupations. Ils se ceignirent les reins, avec le sentiment que la lutte ne faisait que commencer. En vérité, ils se sentaient plus mariés que jamais, d'autant plus que le mariage n'avait jamais signifié pour eux qu'une perpétuelle occasion de disputes." The one slip in that first sentence, where "at last" is translated as "at least," is plausibly compensated for by the nice play on *occupied* which substitutes "sérieuses occupations" for "a time of high activity," nattily playing the phrase off "uniquement occupés" and giving a bit more point to a passage which in English seems to chew more than is bitten off.

More conclusive, though, than any inspection of Yourcenar's verbal surfaces is her continued interest—we are now in 1965, twenty-six years after the translation of *Maisie*—in James's thematics, the inveterate presentation of a child, especially of a girl, in a corrupt world of unloving adults. There are no children in Yourcenar's fictions, and all the more reason, then, to consider her own circumstances as a virtually motherless only daughter educated by her father in the manner of Montaigne and of Gargantua, of Mme de Sévigné and of Émile, when she discusses, with characteristic high-handedness, the procedures of Henry James: "[*The Turn of the Screw*] struck me yet again as a masterpiece and interests me all the more because, having translated *What Maisie Knew* into French quite some time ago, it prompted me to reflect on that other tale of childhood voyeurism, in which this time it is not with specters but with adults who are very much alive that the little girl forges strange bonds of complicitous knowledge. *The Turn of the Screw* goes much further than this nonetheless extraordinary novel because it is not, this time, only the problem of childhood innocence and perversity that preoccupies James, but that of our dealings with evil. James goes beyond the psychological, at once consciously and unconsciously, to enter into the theological and metaphysical as well as the occult. How right . . . to eliminate disdainfully Edmund Wilson's hypothesis reducing everything to hysterical fantasies on the part of the governess. A fine example of the flat and rudimentary aspect that spiritual problems take on in the minds of certain of our contemporaries. In reality [*sic*], sexual obsession fills *The Turn of the Screw* by virtue of the very fact that it is in the form of contacts with fornicators that James (typically a man of the nineteenth century) treats this problem of connivance with evil, and the first chapter, so offhandedly worldly, strikes me as proving *a contrario* that he knew how dangerous from all points of view was the terrain upon which he was advancing." It is hard to keep from feeling that Yourcenar's scornful dismissal of Wilson and of an emphatically psychoanalytical reading of James's tale is defensive, and that her own excitement about these texts is fueled by other concerns than "the problem of connivance with evil." Yet there is a certain grandeur, perverse perhaps but undeniable, in her approach to James—one consonant with her own metaphysical and religious traffic in *The Abyss*, which is both the *Salammbo* and the *Sentimental Education* of her career, accounting thereby for the curious dryness of this willed descent into chaos.

To return briefly to the matter of translation as an evidence of self-invention. My own dealings with Yourcenar, when I had occasion to translate her splendid volume of essays *The Dark Brain of Piranesi*, made me realize how troublesome, indeed how manipulative, as we have learned to say, such intercourse with a great writer can be. Yet it was evident throughout that all "our" efforts were to be in the service of the art, of a high and unyielding standard which would determine not only the nature of an author's prose but of her presence, as it were, in the English speaking world.

It is clear to me now that such demands were made continuously by Yourcenar, to the very end of a very long life, to good purpose: I believe that at least three of her novels (*Coup de Grâce, Memoirs of Hadrian,* and *The Abyss* (for all its *acedie*), three volumes of her essays, the lyric prose of *Fires,* the French translations of Cavafy and of Greek poetry with its glosses, and the volume of *Oriental Tales,* are as likely to abide as any literature produced in the last fifty years. Moreover the arrangement, the design of these works and of all the lesser others which sustain them are as much the product of the maker's imaginative energy as the writing itself, though I also believe the author's determination to achieve the impregnable status of a monument will strike most of us as anything but sympathetic. With the help of her biographers, we may conjugate (surely the right word here) the largely concealed intimate drama of Yourcenar's life with the intensely intellectual drama of her literary progress, discerning how the nature of this astonishingly isolated woman—isolated by family circumstance, by sexual preference, and by actual exile from the comforting occasions of ordinary success—generated her writing and how such writing created her name, her body, and her life. I believe such an enterprise is worth our attention and our esteem.

Implicit in our modern cultural mythology is the assumption that the author is at the disposal of her works, servant of her inspiration, *umile ancella,* as Adrienne Lecouvreur puts it in the opera, of some external power, not hers at all. Like Nabokov, like Thomas Mann, Yourcenar opposes these assumptions; she has chosen, at the cost of how many grandiose inspirations of youth, of how many thwarted plans of maturity, of how many eloquent deliriums of her old age, to do nothing which is not a disposition of a conscious creative will. The two Pléiade volumes of Marguerite Yourcenar's works, the fictions and the essays, is a monument as purposefully determined as the Hanging Gardens of Babylon, laid out by Semiramis. Nowadays we are not so beguiled by monuments as we were once taught to be; they remain, nonetheless, among the wonders of the world.

Divination by Ashes:
An Introduction to Claude Simon

[1995]

When he was awarded the Nobel Prize for Literature in 1985, Claude Simon was seventy-two years old and the author of fourteen extended prose texts which he, or his publishers, or his critics, or perhaps his readers, chose to call novels; a fifteenth, *The Acacia*, which the author regards as a sort of consummation of the last eleven, was published in 1989. These works constitute the bulk and body of his production, though there are by now a considerable number of interviews and essays concerned with artists (Rodin, Poussin, Novelli), with photographs, with writing—which shine like erratic stars among an identifiable constellation of "advanced" fictions that for fifty years has not wavered in its expansion: the legible sky of Claude Simon, where we can easily pick out the Horseman, the Whore, the Bride, the Saint, the Fool, the Cyclops, Mother Earth, and Father Time.

Yet inclusive and far-reaching as it is, this career of five decades did not begin with writing. "I tried painting, and failed, I tried revolution, and failed. Only then did I try literature," Simon has observed with characteristic ruefulness, his resonance ever that of the dutiful artisan doing his best but aware that better still remains to be accomplished.

Parenthetically, some of his graphic work is to be found in the French editions of his writings, though after studying painting with André Lhote in the late 1930s, Simon had abandoned any ambitions to be an artist; he continues making collages, drawings, and photographs; as late as 1970 a line drawing appeared as the frontispiece for *Orion aveugle*, and in 1988 another served as the cover for the autobiographical *Album d'un amateur*, a collection of his photographs with commentaries. Simon's exhaustive utilization in his work of the plastic arts (solicited, anatomized, apostrophized), and even of their mechanical reproduction (postcards, museum prints, postage stamps), is probably a consequence of his failed career as a painter—one more aporetic adaptation of a forlorn hope. There is no other novelist of the century, not even Proust, who has made so much of works of art, imaginary and real, name-dropped and deconstructed. Claude Simon has drawn on the work of man's hand from the crudest graffito to the Parthenon frieze, from anonymous newspaper photographs to the decorative rococo emblems of a cigar box, all "rendered" in that discontinuous magma which history—individual, national, human—has come to figure.

As for his "revolutionary" impulses, Simon's sympathy with the unprogrammatic Left (if the oxymoron may pass) continued to find expression—though one quite different from occasional gunrunning for the Republican cause in the Spanish Civil War—when in 1960 he signed the "Declaration of the 121," an intellectuals' manifesto declaring the right of insubordination in Algeria.

And if Simon's literary life began later in his biography than is usual in the career of someone we have come to regard as a "born writer," like Yeats, say, or Gide (Simon's first novel was not published until he was thirty-two), his writings were not acknowledged by the author himself as authentically his own—the books *he* wanted to write—until much later still. It was first necessary, or inescapable, that he produce three long, rather conventional novels—unreprinted, untranslated, unheeded one might say, though a couple of dogged French critics have violated Simon's (admittedly mild) repudiations and gone so far as to find in *Le Tricheur* of 1945 (actually written in 1941, the same year as Camus's *L'Étranger*)—in *Gulliver* of 1952, and in *Le Sacre du printemps* of 1954, the seeds as well as the husks of all ulterior productions of this "new novelist."

Since Simon himself wishes us to consider his writing as beginning with *The Wind* of 1957 (when the author was forty-four), I shall not loiter over these three precocious works and the similarly disclaimed, more or less autobiographical text of 1947 called *La Corde raide* (*The Tightrope*), except to note the allusive resonance of such titles as "Gulliver" and "Rite of Spring," which foreshadow the extremely literary references to be found in all of Simon's subsequent works—epigraphs from Descartes, from Pasternak, and from T. S. Eliot, titles from Virgil and from Roman history, evident manipulations of Conrad, Orwell, and Dostoievsky ("*The Wind* is simply a remake of *The Idiot*," Simon once told an interviewer)—all of which serve to remind us that this insistently unbookish and even anti-intellectual writer is a passionate reader and a tireless *bricoleur* of those shards and shreds of the world's literature and art which constitute the substance and notabilia of that vast, much-canceled palimpsest, the *libretto* of the Claude Simon opera.

If, like Graham Greene, Claude Simon forswore his early novels, he has persisted in what we might call his artisanal intertextuality, so it would not be far-fetched to observe that though all his works since *The Wind* "verge on the autobiographical" (as he has acknowledged), what takes them to the verge is their participation in an epic literary project, "irreducible," he claims, "to any realistic schema" yet clearly part of a shared rhetorical project—shared and acknowledged as shared with Joyce, with Proust, with Faulkner, with all writers who attempt by language, specifically by prose, to represent, indeed to create, the human experience of time and mortality, and in narratives of war, imprisonment, and disease to achieve a consciousness of the body's tragedy, the spirit's ecstasy, the meaningless splendor of the physical world.*

I want to emphasize the phrase "human experience in prose" be-

---

*"Compared to the simplest object (a leaf, a shell, a feather) or the most banal human action (a walk, a conversation overheard in a café), what we customarily call, in art or literature, 'the marvellous' has always seemed to me to be laborious and childishly deficient. Far from fading with age, this grateful wonder I feel before things and life grows ever greater. I noticed this same phenomenon when I was in prison or seriously ill: it seems that everything limiting our freedom sharpens our faculties for apprehending the world as a result. The smallest detail stands out. . . . Peeling an apple for dessert distresses me now (the chef-d'oeuvre I am about to destroy!), and I spend a long time turning it and contemplating it regretfully before I can bring myself to pick up my knife." —Claude Simon, from an interview, 1977.

cause of a mounting uneasiness we feel, I believe, about designating as
novels such works as these increasingly discontinuous, lyrical, nondis-
crete texts by Claude Simon, though that is the label most persistently
employed (even by the Nobel committee) to identify their genre.
There have been any number of fictions since, say, *Wuthering Heights*,
Moby-Dick, and *Salammbo*, which we are evidently more comfortable
calling "dramatic poems," "mythological frescoes," "historical palimpsests," or "archetypal collages" rather than novels—and indeed I believe Simon shares with any number of authors, from Laurence Sterne
to Samuel Beckett, a conception of his work that ultimately discards
most of the meanings ordinarily accorded to the novel except for the
etymological one: something new! Perhaps, indeed, that is why Simon has ultimately conformed to the commercial usage, espousing as
he does Harold Rosenberg's dictum that the only valid tradition in art
is the Tradition of the New. Certainly Simon has not been content
with forays into the other genres—the play "*La Séparation*," which in
1963 he based on *The Grass*, though it was produced with the veteran
trouper Françoise Rosay in the cast, was not successful enough to inspire Simon to write for the stage again; and the film scenario he
based on *The Palace* remains unexploited (more significant to the author, perhaps, as his sixth recycling of Barcelona during the Spanish
Civil War than as a venture into a new medium).

My notion may be illustrated with a certain vividness by this
episode: a writer friend of mine was invited, in the service of an irreproachable cause, to one of those benefit dinner parties where each literary lion is seated at a table of plausible benefactors. "And what do
you write?" asked my friend's decidedly unliterary neighbor. "I write . . .
novels," replied Francine Prose (I betray her identity for the splendor
of her cognomen). "Oh, novels," came the rejoinder: "fiction or non-
fiction?"

There is a real clinch of truth within such preposterous uncertainty,
and if I am to characterize the writings of Claude Simon with any veracity of identification, I believe it is critically principled of me to suggest that he does not actually write novels (the way Mauriac or Martin
du Gard wrote novels, to name a couple of previous French Nobel
laureates); he writes, as we immediately realize when we read any-

where in the last dozen works (and part of the quality of the achievement is that we *can* read anywhere, rather than being constrained to proceed from beginning to end in pliably linear fashion)—he writes *a voice*, an utterance that rises from (and perhaps justifies) the debacle which is our consciousness of our history, our contention with our bodies, and our mistrust of the mind, the body's old enemy and friend.

Simon himself had an impulse to seek elsewhere for a more exegetic characterization of his enterprise, we may note, in presenting the first work he regarded as worthy to constitute the cornerstone of his own *oeuvre*: in 1957 he subtitled *The Wind* (in letters as large as the title) not "a novel" but a "Tentative Reconstruction of a Baroque Altarpiece"—a genre classification that puts us on much firmer ground, I believe, in enabling us to recognize the nature of Simon's subsequent volumes, though such a problematic identification with the lineaments of art history was not of much comfort to booksellers. Decades have passed, and *The Wind*, with perhaps more justification than is attributable to its successors, is now declared, on its cover, to be "a novel." (If I were to make a personal choice, I should call the genre of Simon's *oeuvre a tephromancy*, i.e., a divination by ashes.) Of the ensuing volumes, half a dozen are associated with a single ruined, aristocratic family in southwest France, intricate in its ramifications, polychronous in its allegiances, so that the by now considerable accumulation of Simon criticism has agreed to call these books "the de Reixach cycle." (Notoriously, it was that "realist" novelist Balzac, in one of his more visionary moments, who first came up with the notion that characters, families, buildings, institutions could spill over from book to book in the effort to account for human experience, implying a kind of reality beyond the postulation of mere works, a reality to be located rather in the entire fresco of language itself—what Merleau-Ponty calls *la prose du monde*, committed to just such Balzacian accountings.)

From the second of the de Reixach chronicles, written in 1958, I want to offer a characteristic swatch, a brief sounding of prose, before I attempt to explain—or at least to explore—why it functions the way, or the ways, it does, and to confront it with a comparable swatch written some thirty years later. Here is page 118 of *The Grass*, concerned with the account book of Marie de Reixach:

... Repairs for the clock in the salon 21 Fr. the pages, the columns of figures and descriptions extending, rising, accumulating in a kind of patient tomb constructed stone by stone, as if some legal arrangements, some meddlesome and interfering administration only allowed our exhausted bones to lie down at last in order to return to the original dust after having erected this kind of fabulous mausoleum consisting of time heaped upon a few ashes: ashes, nothingness, and on top, a pinnacle of vacancy in or upon which the ghosts of actions performed appear with a grim insignificance, made concrete not by those ambitious inscriptions written on tombstones but by the absurd symbols of money, in a debased coinage which conferred upon the old account books, as upon the actions of Balzac's heroes, that sort of fallacious, laughable, and tiny unreality at the heart of which generals, bankers, countesses, and prostitutes seem to struggle and scratch each other's eyes out for the sake of a handful of pennies rattling in a street-arab's pocket.

It is generally acknowledged that when adjectives appear so luxuriantly in a piece of language, we are being confronted with the sign of that which is without language. Hypertrophy of the adjective is the symptom which betrays a nostalgia for that reality which precedes all language, for the otherness of language, the intransmissible image—the message remaining "on the tip of the tongue." This is the eloquence which declares itself inarticulate, and it is the most evident, indeed the most frequent characteristic of the writing of Claude Simon. The Greeks had a word for it: *aporia*, the acknowledgment of failure even in the effort to succeed. In modernity, aporia is more than a figure of speech, it is a mode of discourse, a version of energy. In Simon's prose, as just demonstrated in this work of his early success, the process is one of erasure, of the elimination of expression *by* expression (in the manner, as Simon would say, of a Giacometti drawing which deletes its lines by their very excess, so that the image is somehow canceled by the very means intended to call it into being). It is one of the two modernist techniques of which Simon makes pervasive use, the other being collage, increasingly manifest in the later works. By collage I mean the unmodulated, direct confrontation of already existing entities, usually drawn *as is* from the "real world" and, as Lévi-Strauss has said of *bricolage*, used as members of discourse instead of more intimately invented elements.

In Simon's later works the aporia of erasure is overwhelmed by those energies of collage or palimpsest which insist that it is among the *already made* (in the fashion of true *bricolage*) where the effort of expression is to be exerted. Let me confront that shard from *The Grass* with this culmination from *The Acacia* of 1989, in which the character who has assumed the physiognomy of the author finally (it is the last page) faces the task of creating all the books he will have written in the decades since that first baroque altarpiece:

> At a bookseller's he bought the fifteen or twenty volumes of the *Comédie Humaine* bound in reddish-brown morocco, which he read patiently, without pleasure, one after the other, not skipping one, listening to the wind noisily rubbing against the roof, banging a shutter somewhere. Except for a few relatives, he knew only an old painter in town, a perpetual drunkard who endlessly repeated the same flowering peach trees and in whose house he met a few people stranded there like himself. Gradually he began to change. He began reading the newspapers again, looking at the maps they printed, the names of the cities, coasts, or deserts where battles were still being fought. One night he sat down at his desk in front of a sheet of blank paper. It was spring now. The bedroom window was open on the warm night. One of the branches of the big acacia growing in the garden almost touched the wall of the house, and he could see the closest fronds lit by his lamp, their leaves like feathers faintly palpitating against the darkness, the oval leaflets tinged a raw green by the electric light and occasionally stirring like *aigrettes*, as though suddenly animated with a movement of their own, as if the whole tree were waking, shaking itself, freeing itself, after which everything subsided and they became motionless again.

Here, as I say, the endlessly self-correcting adjectives are allowed a certain *standing*, rather than rushing to replace one another—the film, so to speak, has become a photograph—largely because of the weight and power of the collage elements, the register of cultural artifacts: a set of Balzac (so deliberately dismissed!), a drunken artist obsessed with peach trees, newspapers with their maps and names ("of cities, coasts, or deserts where battles were still being fought"), and finally the acacia itself: ultimate emblem of the process to which the writer is indentured.

Though I cannot imagine (nor is it suitable to do so) how *The Acacia*, avowedly a summative work, can be succeeded (and transcended) by further novels or even novelties, it is perhaps prudent to end with a reminder that Simon's is an oeuvre which stubbornly rejects closure. I have remarked how the Character—what the French call the Personage—in Simon's latest novel has become the Narrator who, if I am correct in assuming that this is Simon's last novel as well, has become the Author. But my own conclusion is best arrived at by evoking the infinitely suspended ending of all Simonian fiction: there is no resolution, no final solution, there is only, and always, that pedal point, *sostenuto*, which momentarily freezes the narrative flux—a final vision of a figure on a bench, a last raindrop, a row of shoeshine boys in Barcelona, or an increasingly motionless branch of acacia. . . . Each new work finds its support and sustenance in the preceding ones. It refers to them explicitly, from one chapter, from one novel, from one period to the next: that branch of the acacia tree, at the end of its eponymous text just quoted, rejoins the same branch and renews the story of *History* from twenty years earlier. With minuscule and yet crucial variants, Simon sends us from one avatar to the next of the same *subject*: that horseman who tirelessly traverses his whole oeuvre, thwarting, *abolishing* the very notion of a beginning, of an ending. There is only the utterance, what Ezra Pound called the "voice raised, weaving an endless sentence," endlessly erasing itself and trying again.

A Note on *The Charterhouse of Parma*

[1999]

Englishspeaking readers invariably characterize Stendhal's works, and especially *The Charterhouse of Parma*, by the words *gusto, brio, élan, verve, panache*. These are, of course, all foreign terms, never translated, though so necessary that they have been readily naturalized. It will be the translator's aim, indeed the translator's responsibility, so to characterize any future translation of Stendhal, who wrote his last completed novel in fifty-two days, a miracle of gusto, brio, élan, verve, panache.

Like miracles generally, the novel is mysterious, beginning with its title: the Carthusian Monastery of Parma, the Charterhouse, appears only on the last page of the book, three paragraphs from the end. To this sequestration Fabrizio del Dongo retires, lives there a year, dies there (he is twenty-seven years old—the age of the oldest French generals in Napoleon's army entering Milan in Chapter One). Stendhal had initially wanted to call his novel *The Black Charterhouse*, a clue: in the prison from which Fabrizio so spectacularly escapes, there is indeed a *black chapel*. Fabrizio's *nine months' imprisonment* in the Farnese Tower—more than one critic has observed—is analogous to the Carthusian monks' discipline in their monastery: by this means he is reborn, he achieves freedom, happiness, and love.

Throughout the novel, incidents and details recur, repeat themselves, recall some earlier instance. Certain verbal echoes may keep the reader conscious of the pattern: Fabrizio's first imprisonment and his night with the jailer's wife will "become" Fabrizio in the Farnese Tower, loving Clélia; the del Dongo castle at Grianta towering above Lake Como "becomes" the Citadel of Parma; the astronomy lessons on the platform of one of the castle's gothic towers "become" Abbé Blanès's observatory on top of the town bell tower, then the platform of the citadel on which the Farnese Tower is erected. Towers, platforms, windows; height, imprisonment, flight; divination, hiding, visions: these images and themes weave the novel together. The same words are used in widely separated situations: the translator must make sure they recur in his version. . . .

Nothing fixed. "The man," Nietzsche said, "was a human question-mark." And he suggested the tone, the reason for it and the consequence of it: "Objection, evasion, joyous distrust, and love of irony are signs of health; everything absolute belongs to pathology."

Consider Gina's two husbands: Count Pietranera, who prefers living in poverty to political compromise, and Count Mosca, for whom politics is a game and any conviction a liability. All political life is marked by incoherence. As Professor Talbot puts it, conservatives become liberals when out of power, and liberals become conservatives when in power.

Consider, again, Fabrizio's roles; in the first third of the novel he claims to be a barometer merchant, a captain of the Fourth Regiment of hussars, a young bourgeois in love with that captain's wife, Teulier, Boulot, Cavi, Ascanio Pietranera, and an unnamed peasant. Further, he will assume a disguise to visit Marietta's apartment, will use Giletti's name and passport to go through customs, assume another disguise as a rich country bourgeois; then claim to be Ludovic's brother, then Joseph Bossi, a theology student. With Fausta, he passes himself off as the valet of an English lord; in the duel with Count M——he calls himself Bombace. And under all this, his conviction that he is a del Dongo. Nor is he even that—he is the son of a French lieutenant named Robert billeted in the del Dongo palace in Milan during the French occupation; therefore Gina is not his aunt, though on one occasion early in the novel she passes Fabrizio off as her *son!* . . . Evading the love of a woman he believes to be his aunt, Fabrizio ends in a prison originally built to house a crown prince guilty of incest.

Nothing fixed: Fabrizio is not a soldier, though he may have fought at Waterloo; not for a moment do we believe he is a cleric, though he is made archbishop of Parma; he is pure becoming, and the language he uses must show him to us in that form, that formlessness. . . .

Translate this book to exorcise the fetishism of the Work conceived as an hermetic object, finished, absolute . . . (Beyle, the anti-Flaubert). Nothing in this novel, "complete" though it may be, is quite closed over itself, autonomous in its genesis, and its signification. Hence Balzac's suggestion to erase Parma altogether and call the book something like "Adventures of a typical Italian youth. . . ." Remember that the novel opens as the story of the Duchess Sanseverina. And ends with the "throttled" disappearance (Beyle's phrase, in protest against the publisher's insistence that the book fit in two volumes) of everyone but Mosca, "immensely rich." Such vacillation is never satisfied. More than *Vanity Fair*, this is a Novel Without a Hero, without a Heroine, a novel without . . .

Realism, but no reality. The first text by him I ever translated, for Ben Sonnenberg's *Grand Street*, was that extraordinary list of twenty-three articles headed *Les Privilèges*. That ought to have done it: God would exist and Beyle would believe in Him if he never had to suffer a serious illness, only three days' indisposition a year. . . . If his penis would be allowed to grow erect at will, be two inches longer, and give him pleasure twice a week . . . If he could change into any animal he chose . . . If he would no longer be plagued by fleas, mosquitoes, and mice . . . etc., etc.

Then I translated one of the dozens of unfinished books "by" one of dozens of pseudonyms (as many as Kierkegaard, as many as Pessoa!), texts abandoned after no more than a torso had been molded, the armature of inspiration forsworn once the rapture waned (*The Pink and the Green*).

The invitation in both these texts, preposterous and unfinished alike, to enter (and for the translator, it is virtually a welcome) into the banausics of the affair . . . A kind of painful tension under the disguise of the driest, or the wettest, style. What Valéry calls the restlessness of a superior mind; in any case an ineloquent one. You could "place" Stendhal by saying he is utterly alien to eloquence (Hugo, who had no use for him, said he lacked "style"; Stendhal delighted in the compliment, as in this scribbled note: "A young woman murdered right next to me—she is lying in the middle of the street and beside her head a puddle of blood about a foot across. This is what M. Victor Hugo calls being bathed in one's own blood"). An author who must be continually *reread*, for he never repeats, and as Alain observes, never *develops*.

It's not style he lacks, but rhythm: Stendhal never sweeps you away—he doesn't want to sweep you away: that would be against his principles. He engages your complicity, and for that you must be all attention. Follow him down the page, in the sentence, across the synapses of the amazing clauses, and the sense, the wit, the *literature* occurs in the gaps between the statements, very abruptly juxtaposed:

> A man of parts, he had formerly shown courage in battle; now he was inveterately in a state of alarm, suspecting he lacked that presence of mind commonly deemed necessary to the role of ambassador—M. de Talleyrand has spoilt the profession—and imagining he might give evidence of wit by talking incessantly.

Grasshopper prose, and there is no pleasure to be taken in it if it is not attended to by *presence of mind*. As the reference to Talleyrand suggests, we are being taken into the author's confidence, entrusted with the supposition of intellect—what other author flatters us to this degree?

A translator observes that the scansion of the Stendhal phrase is almost always dependent on that tendency of the French language to accent its abstract nouns on the final syllable: *la logique, le bonheur, l'esprit* (the Beylist trinity). This gives a certain determination to the run of the words, a certain *frappe*, as if the words were minted by a very sure mind. In a language so disposed, may the translator find means to afford evidences of an analogous *mentality*, a power which separates, which suspends, which excludes.

Reading aloud the chapters of *The Chartreuse* to Ben Sonnenberg as I translated them, week by week (fifty-two days to write, twenty-eight weeks to translate), I reveled with him in Beyle's strange elevation of bastardy, the rejection of the Father, the return, with Italy always, to the Mothers. Silly often, goofy even, but always *on*. Adored by Proust, envied by Gide ("He is the cuttlebone on which I sharpen my beak—what I envy in him is that he doesn't have to put on his track shoes before he starts running"), Stendhal withstands translation yet again, a stage in his continued life.

A Welcome Return: On Gide's *Journals*

[2000]

> In no way superficial, a great Frenchman nonetheless always preserves his surface, a natural envelope which surrounds his depths.
> —Nietzsche, *The Dawn*

It is a great assuagement—indeed, for a whole new generation of readers, it will prove a great resource—to have all of Gide's journals in print once again, for they constitute the cartilaginous tissue that secures and sustains the otherwise discrepant and (particularly for Americans who must rely on the vagaries of translation) diffuse oeuvre of the most enantiotropic writer of Western culture. André Gide was a creature of conflicts, reversals, contradictions, and antitheses so marked that without the "natural envelope" of the *Journals*, we run the risk of missing, in the flagrant multiformity of his production, those inveterately sounded notes that constitute, as Auden once observed, *the restored relation*.

The journal was the first form of writing to occur to him. From his own intermittent but inexhaustible text, which began with a single entry for the year 1889 when he was twenty, to *Les cahiers d'André Walter*, published anonymously in 1891, when he was twenty-two, to *Strait Is the Gate*, a 1909 *récit* concluded by the Alissa's lyric diary (later set to music as a solo cantata by Darius Milhaud), the *La symphonie pastorale* (1919), another *récit* entirely narrated in the pastor's two diaries, all the way to *Ainsi soit-il*, a dateless deathbed meditation published posthumously in 1951, André Gide continually experimented with the genre. He kept a journal of his progress—and his setbacks—in writing his only novel (a large portion of which consists of the journal of a novelist writing a novel to be called *The Counterfeiters*) and eventually published this journal as a sort of appendix to the (real?) *Counterfeiters* (1926); he kept a journal of his travels in the Congo to study—and to criticize severely—French colonization in Africa; and he even aspired to keep a journal of his translation of *Hamlet*. Indeed, any enterprise Gide could conceive of as constituting an independent effort, a moral and aesthetic project, he subjected to the record (and the erosion) of his progress in consciousness, thereby articulating the first of many besetting contradictions, for it is the nature of a journal to be successive, and Gide was the most simultaneous of beings in modern literature. After the first twenty years of journal keeping, he was painfully conscious of the dilemma: "It is hard for [my critics] to admit that these books cohabited, still cohabit, in my mind. They follow each other only on paper and through the great impossibility of letting them be written together. Whatever the book I am writing, I never give myself to it utterly, and the subject that claims me most insistently immediately afterward, develops meanwhile at the other extremity of me" (*Journals*, 1909). Not only is all of Gide somehow present in any one work, but all of Gide is present in that initial diary kept by that suicidal, alter ego André Walter, and futhermore André Walter is still present in Gide in 1947. That is why I doubt his journal has much interest if reading Gide's work has not awakened some initial curiosity as to the man who kept it.

Certainly Gide's journal is the one work that affords the mucilage or masking tape to hold the diverging works together, affording us this man's central determination to see himself as being forever dual "and therefore not to be confined within any one thing." It is by means of the *Journals* that we can accompany Gide, or at least pursue him, through that remarkable pattern of "returns" that characterize his labyrinthine life and can be identified by his remarkably conflictory works: the return from puritanism (*Fruits of the Earth* [1897] and *The Pastoral Symphony* [1919]), from marriage (*The Immoralist* [1902] and *The School for Wives* [1929]), and from narcissism (*Les cahiers d'André Walter* [1891] and *Le retour de l'efant prodigue* [1907]); the return from Symbolism (*Le voyage d'Urien* [1893] and *Paludes* [1896]) and from Christianity (*Strait Is the Gate* [1909] and *Numquid et tu . . . ?* [1926]); from absurdist comedy (*Prometheus Ill-bound* [1899] and *Lafacadio's Adventures* [1914]) and from the "grand machines" of classicism (*Philoc-*

tetes [1899], *Oedipus* [1931], and *Theseus* [1946]); from exotic dramatic gestures (*Saül* [1895] and *King Candaules* [1901]) and from drama itself (stage versions of Kafka's *Trial* and of his own *Lafcadio*); from literary responsibility (founding and directing the *Nouvelle revue française* [1908]) and from homosexuality as well as from "family values" (*Corydon* [1924] and fathering a daughter); from the critique of capitalism (*Travels in the Congo* [1927–28]) and of communism (*Return from the U.S.S.R.* [1936]); and from controversiality, or at least from controversy (translations of Shakespeare, Whitman, Conrad, Blake, Goethe, Pushkin, and Tagore). Even Gide's sole novel, *The Counterfeiters*, might well be counted a return from Dostoievski, whose cult Gide had so eagerly furthered in lectures and articles in 1923.

I would emphasize by the word *return* that Gide does not *retreat from* passions and positions espoused, however experimentally, in the fluctuations of a notoriously self-conscious life and literary career; rather he *returns to* a core of ironic fervors (it is not irrelevant to invoke a Nietzschean intensity here) that afford him the possibility, ever and again, of escape from ideology, from fanaticism, from whatever Gide perceives as falsehood and fixity. The unremitting journal inveterately serves as an argumentative, sometimes lyrical, and often drastic corrective to any residual—and fallacious—commitment.

Along the way, almost as an incident in the journal enterprise, occurs Gide's life—"life too," as Alan Sheridan, Gide's latest and best biographer, reminds us, "has its autonomy: it does not require justification by works." Here the journal, with what can only be qualified as a thick-skinned intimacy (by 1916 Gide knew that every word he wrote in the journal would eventually and often immediately be published; a set of "pages de Journal" often jump-started *La nouvelle revue française* between the wars), articulates the life's notorious intimacies and alienations (Valéry, Claudel); hopeless forbearance and happy infatuation (Madeleine Gide, Marc Allégret); the exemplary instances of conscience and corruption (ascendancy of Mallarmé and of Oscar Wilde); the collaborative amities and collegial betrayals (Martin du Gard, Cocteau); the excursions into a permissive exoticism (*Amyntas* [1906]) and the withdrawals to an equally permissive family seat in Normandy (*Souvenirs de la Cour d'Assises* [1912]); and year by year, month by month, the inveterate vacillation—the constant autocritique, really—between modish classicism and modernist contraption, the reading lists and grammatical disputes, the education not only carried out but also ceremonially paraded in public.

An inveterate lineament of Gide's insisted-upon "life in the present," we have discovered since his death in 1951, was the letters. To the solicitations of the world's friendship and the world's hostility, Gide *corresponded*. In a hastier age, one wonders how he managed it. Between his works and his journal, between a simmering professional life in Paris and a lacerating private one in Cuverville, between his elaborately staged travels and a vast program of reading and rereading fanatically pursued over seven decades and faithfully glossed in the *Journals*, how did he ever find or make time for thousands and thousands of letters, letters written and, perhaps just as besetting, letters *read and answered*—over thirty complete correspondences published so far, some in two volumes, constituting another range altogether, often a corrective one, of the biographical dimension that so many of us had assumed was to be simply—simply!—accounted for in the *Journals*, 1889–1949. To think that these diaries are only a partial reticulation of the social and literary and political web in which this inky spider loomed over some sixty years of his generation!

Besides the correspondence, there is another body of writing that has released Gide's journal to be read not as a source, a disclosure, but as a work of concentrated and harmonious—no, *harmonized*—experience. This is *someone else*'s journal, *Les cahiers de la petite dame* (the "little lady" being Maria van Rysselberghe, intrepid widow of a Belgian painter, whose daughter, Élisabeth, was to become the mother of Gide's only child, Catherine), four volumes covering the period from 1918 to Gide's death in 1951. *Covering* is the apposite word, for the incessant, accurate, and mercilessly affectionate reportage by this clear-eyed friend, amassed without the knowledge of her unwitting "subject" and published only after his death, has probably done more to eclipse and to disenchant Gide's demonic self-image than all the attacks from Rome and Moscow or all the horrified attentions of an offended literary orthodoxy; henceforth no biographer can resist these quotidian intimate revelations, but no heroic figure—especially the figure of an author committed to the unique presentation of an authentic, a "sincere" self—can withstand them. And of course such testimony from the rim discloses the *Journals'* core workings to be faulty—not precisely fraudulent, but not precise either: fallacious, if we are reading for the facts, ma'am. This will come as a veritable liberation to new readers of Gide's *Journals*, now to be attended as a truly Goethean muster of "poetry and truth," as opposed to scandal and parade. For the first time, we may come unburdened to the intersection at which Gide has remained, the most important and populous carrefour, where the two greatest roads of the Western world cross—the Greek and the Christian; here is the total situation Gide preferred, enclosed by nothing and protected by nothing, subject to every attack, accessible to every affection. To survive, to perdure in so perilous a situation—it is only "natural" that the very word *experience* should have the notion of *peril* at its root—required a certain hardness, out of which masterpieces are made.

"It is from the point of view of art that it is most fitting to judge what I write—a point of view the critic never, or almost never, takes. . . . It is, moreover, the only point of view that does not exclude any of the others" (*Journals*, 1918). Gide's works are the depths to which Nietzsche refers in the epigraph I have given to these remarks, depths surrounded by the "natural envelope" of his journal, which as Roland Barthes pointed out long ago, we must not suppose is in opposition to the work and not itself a work of art. The journal is not an explanatory, an external writing; it is not a chronicle like Saint-Simon's history but the masterpiece of a mind and body not free yet seeking to be free by means of those passionate inquiries, arguments, and contradictions that make him, rather, another Montaigne. Let us put an equal accent on both nouns to obtain his true portrait: Gide, or Civilization and its Discontents.

The Cruel Guest:
Alphonse Daudet's *In the Land of Pain*

[2003]

The "language requirement" in American high schools has always been something of a curricular curiosity, and the aboli-
tion nowadays of the hopeful competence it once proposed
is but another sign of the withering away of the State . . . of Literary
Studies. Even so, up until the end of World War II (*now when*, my
graduate students ask, *would that have been?*), the text inveterately proposed on which to teethe for linguistic mastery, if the "required language" happened to be French, was Alphonse Daudet's *Lettres de mon
Moulin*. Even in France these good-natured vignettes were a perennial
lycée favorite, the author having evinced an exemplary perfection in the
vexed matter of *sequence of tenses*, henceforth something of a Daudet
specialty. (After 1945, the already much-diminished French requirement probably shifted to Camus's *L'Étranger*; at present I cannot even
conceive of a plausible choice—perhaps Monique Wittig's *L'Opoponax*, a novel in the voice and vocabulary of a five-year-old girl.)

Daudet's letters from his windmill, a set of colorful family snap-
shots, were written just before the Franco-Prussian War (don't ask)
and, like their coeval *Silas Marner*, were deemed suitable for American
adolescents—no sex, no sordor, just vivaciously recounted peasant ca-
pers in closely observed though, as Zola pointed out, scandalously idealized Provençal landscapes (Daudet's realist phase would come later).

This folkish note, farcically sustained in the manner of Dickens,
was sounded again in *Tartarin de Tarascon*, in a sequel *Tartarin sur les*

Alpes, and even in a "further adventures," of Tartarin, *Port Tarascon,* eventually translated—for the money, he claimed—by Henry James, who had first met Daudet in the 1870s: "Yes, I have seen Daudet several times. He is a little fellow (very little) with a refined and picturesque head, of a Jewish type." Regardless of type, the acquaintance was pursued (how his elder son Léon, a founder of the Action Française, would have writhed at the racial slur), and James was to become something of a family friend (though he never like Léon), entertaining the Daudets in London when the "great little novelist," as James had called him in the *Atlantic Monthly,* let him glimpse the *inédit* annotations on the progress of his disease. (Mme Daudet herself was not to know it was tertiary syphilis that was killing her husband, though one wonders what she suspected on the many occasions she gave him the assuaging morphine injections which enabled Daudet to produce these disjunct texts, which were published in France only in 1931.) In 1889, when Daudet was forty-nine and had eight more years of torment to endure, Henry James reported to William on "Daudet's own queer, deplorable condition which he intensely converts into *art,* success, copy, etc.—taking professional notes about his constant suffering (terrible in degree) which is to make a book called *La Douleur,* the most detailed and pessimistic notation of pain *qui fût jamais.*"

But I am losing my sequence of tenses. The initial successes of what James called Daudet's "high-colored little Provençal *faconde*—like the waving of some spotted bright handkerchief," along with the coquettishly autobiographical tale *Le petit chose* (the *David Copperfield* of France), must have worked some slick magic on what are always known as young people of all ages, and in all languages, for I inherited from my grandfather Isaac (no reader of French) the *Works of Alphonse Daudet,* twenty turquoise shagreen tomes, supplemented by six identically bound memorial volumes by the author's brother, by his wife, and by his two sons (two volumes each). Evidently my grandfather, who also possessed a refined and picturesque head, of a Jewish type, was a bookish gent who liked to move among fine bindings.

If the renown of Alphonse Daudet had trickled down or bubbled up in Cleveland Heights to this extent—namely a turquoise shagreen shelf about half as long as the crimson morocco set of *Masterpieces of*

George Sand, there must have been something doing which no longer does. Who has read a book by Alphonse Daudet?

Well, I have. Indeed I have read most of them (in French, I admit, not in the awful English of my grandfather's splendid set in which James's translation did not figure and which I sold as soon as I came into that part of my inheritance), and I must approach the plausibly dismissive overtone of my question with some finesse, for my preening answer should afford reasons, or at least inducements, to read not only *In the Land of Pain* (which is not "a book by Alphonse Daudet" at all and does not of course appear in that turquoise set so handsomely supplemented by the rest of the great little novelist's family) but other, ulterior works by Daudet. After you, Alphonse.

The prodigy of Provence had arrived in Paris brimming with journalistic schemes and boulevard plays (which came to much the same thing); of the plays only *L'Arlésienne*—based on material from those windmill letters—survives (because of Bizet's incidental music), though many of Daudet's nine subsequent novels which had left Provence so far behind were dramatized, or better say "staged," in the flashy manner of the period. The journalism (fugitive and acidulous) and the first of the Paris novels, *Froment jeune et Risler aîné*, gained Daudet membership in that ardent group of "realists" who met regularly to talk about literature: Flaubert, Turgenev, Edmond de Goncourt, and Zola, and from that association his fate was determined, if "sealed" were not the better term.

For as Henry James was to say in a moment of exasperation with "realism" as it was so insistently rehearsed at the Magny dinners, "ignorance of everything but his little professional Paris horizon kept Daudet from the greater imagination, the imagination of the moralist." James is generous even here, however, adding that "Daudet was really more personal, more individual and more inimitable than anyone. None of the various descendants of Balzac who were to find in any degree the fortune that, under Balzac's great impulse, they often went so far to seek, has even perhaps equally arrived at that special success which consists in having drawn from one's talent, from one's whole organization and every attendant circumstance, every drop one was capable of giving." And he holds up for special admiration—this was how I came upon and immediately resolved to translate it: wait and see!—the singular "comic novel with a fine tragic movement" *Kings in Exile* (1879), in which several dispossessed monarchs take up their residence in the French capital—some waiting and plotting for a restoration and chafing under their disgrace, others indifferent, resigned, relieved, eager to console themselves with the pleasures of Paris. And I should even exceed James's "warm immortality of condonation" by recommending one further, very late novel before coming down to *La Doulu*; this is *The Immortal* (1888), Daudet's "Académie-Française" novel, harsh, bitter, and pervasively grim, without a single character whose virtues are admirable or who could represent simple decency or even command the reader's pity. The book, really a pamphlet-fiction summing up the complaints of three generations of novelists (Balzac to Goncourt) disdained by the Notables of Letters, was upon publication saluted as a deliciously wicked scandal-sheet which provided the season's favorite salon sport: attaching the presumed real names to its fictional characters. But *L'Immortel* transcends such entertainments, for its nugatory plot turns on the antithesis between a prototypical academician and an authentic artist; if there is a lot of Mary McCarthy in it, there is even more of Dostoievsky, and the three great chapters—the fifth, which describes the gala dinner of an Academy salon, the eighth, recounting the funeral of the Academy's Perpetual Secretary, and the last, articulating the suicide of the eponymous "hero" (the ironic send-up of the book's title)—articulate uniquely, among all Daudet's fictions, what it means to call the characters *possessed*.

In his efficient introduction to *La Doulu*, which he borrows a phrase from the book to call *In the Land of Pain*, Julian Barnes, its translator, remarks on certain disparities in these notes which Daudet began to take in the last ten years of his life, when the syphilis which he had contracted at seventeen, soon after his arrival in Paris, and which had gone into remission for so long, resurfaced in its tertiary (and mortal) form: "The manuscript is currently untraceable, having apparently been dispersed after Lucien Daudet's death in 1946. The text was certainly edited before first publication [in French]; how much was cut or rearranged is impossible to guess." To his literary friends, and even to his literary sons (though not to his literary wife, though everyone in the family, even Mme Daudet's father, was called upon to administer the frequent doses of morphine and chloral that enabled Alphonse to write, if not to walk), Daudet often spoke of accumulating these materials for an eventual book, perhaps even a novel. As my earlier quotation reveals, even Henry James, whom we might think of as averse to or at least remote from such intimacies, was invited to inspect the agonizing fragments and was aware of Daudet's heroic sacrifice to literary consciousness; in fact James regarded what he saw of *La Doulu* as part of the Flaubertian pathology of turning *everything* into art, at all costs.

Julian Barnes points out that the fifty-some pages of clear-headed, often comical notes that here distill a decade of acute suffering (Daudet apparently stopped recording what was happening to him about three years before he died; which interval, like that in Baudelaire's life and in Maupassant's, belongs to the inconceivable martyrology of syphilis, entirely off the literary record) are chiefly remarkable for their rare capacity, exactly suited to their fragmentary form, *to set down what life—life!—feels like*; in other words, to write pain.

Curiously, the agonized and agonizing record, chopped and checked as we have it, suggests the best novel Daudet never wrote, though he alluded to such a project not only to Henry James but to Parisian literary journalists not long before his death: a post-modern novel in which the conflict is reduced, as in those late Beckett texts and plays "for nothing," to the arena of the confiscated self, the valor of clenched teeth: "suffering is nothing," as he once murmured, "it's all a matter of preventing those you love from suffering." For the transcribing sufferer, pain is always new, fresh, inventive, *creative*; while for those around him—not cool-handed attendants protected by professional indifference but the very family the man's entire *oeuvre* was committed to cherishing—his unspecified illness is merely repetitive, banal, boring, *sterile*.

In his businesslike way (after all, the editor and translator of even this posthumous work is but one more professional), Julian Barnes adumbrates this ultimate project, but he is too dismissive of the kind of writer Daudet is nowadays perceived to be—"hard-working, popular, whose fame and relevance are largely used up in his own lifetime"—to attribute more than a skillful transcription of pain, terror, and even despair to the "vendor of happiness," as Daudet liked to call himself at the end. Of course I am grateful to Mr. Barnes for his crisp translation—"the first ever," the jacket exclaims—of this unsuspected text of Daudet's, but I find his account of its author, knowing and adept as it is, to be ultimately inadequate and certainly uncharitable (e.g., "the twenty-volume collected edition . . . seemed to have said [more than] it all"). I believe (revealing myself completely) that "the fame and relevance" of *any writer*—even one as clever and seasoned as the author of *Flaubert's Parrot*, even Flaubert, God help us—will always be "largely used up" unless readers attend to his works with some exploratory sense that the past is not inferior to the present just because we are alive and the past is dead; unless we grant the unexamined books of a bygone author what Blake called the equivalent of prayer—the charity of unmixed attention.

This was to be my little peroration, what the French would call a *prière pour le bon usage d'Alphonse Daudet*, but then I made a last-minute visit to my university's library (having sold my own library inheritance, as I admitted earlier, for a pot of message) in order to ascertain which chapters of *The Immortal* were the good ones, or at least the best bad ones, to recommend to readers innocent of Daudet's production. You see, I was feeling rather huffy about Mr. Barnes's clever identification of *In the Land of Pain* as an item of (acceptable) modernist textuality over Daudet's old-fashioned production of yarns (so much voice-writing, as it were). Then conceive my amazement when, mooning along the still-unravished shelves of Daudet *père et fils* (*et frère et femme*) in French and in English, I discovered—it turns out that my discovery may be repeated in all the major libraries of New York City: hardly a maverick *trouvaille*—a little gold-backed volume called *Suffering 1887–1895* by Alphonse Daudet, published by the Yale University Press in 1934—three years after the French edition—translated by one Milton Garver "at the request of Madame Alphonse Daudet who is still living in the same apartment where she spent many happy years with her illustrious husband." This first translation of the work is a little less brusque, a little more smoothed out than Barnes's very contemporary-sounding version. There are places where Garver does seem more concerned to make Daudet's meaning clear:

> *Garver*: Let us try and make the doctor beloved instead of as-
> signing him the role of a brutal and hard butcher.
> *Barnes*: Let's make people love the doctor, rather than play the
> tough and brutal butcher.

But certainly the Barnes version is sharper throughout and more spontaneous (Garver: "the mind becomes accustomed to this sinister state." Barnes: "the mind adjusts to this appalling condition.") Mr. Garver follows his translation by some pages of bibliographic detail regarding Daudet's plans for publication of the (possibly more extensive) text, of which he prints the same torso that appears in Mr. Barnes's version. He also includes a handsome though ravaged-looking photograph of Daudet and what he calls "the beautiful article of Marcel Proust, published in *La Presse*, August 11, 1897." Proust's article (one of several he devoted to Daudet, though he wrote even more rapturously of Lucien, the younger son) is a four-page meditation on the great man's countenance, "this work of art which is M. Daudet," and it is followed by a fifteen-page "appreciation of Alphonse Daudet by André Ebner, the last secretary of the author." Barnes cites Ebner several times but I did not realize that he was the amanuensis-*en-titre*, having inherited the position from his own father, who served as Daudet's secretary for fifteen years after the Franco-Prussian War. André Ebner appropriately concludes his 1930 tribute (Daudet had been dead for thirty-three years) and the entire little volume of the first translation of *La Doulu*, thus:

> I seem to see his delicate pale face with half-closed eyes, oppo-
> site me at the table, during those joyful hours when I wrote at
> his dictation, and when in moments of discouragement I try to
> draw up a balance of the happy moments of my life, I put in the
> first rank that of having known Alphonse Daudet and of having
> received the noble lesson of his life as an example. And at once
> my complainings cease.

I am not concerned to slap any wrists by pointing out the existence of the Yale edition of *La Doulu* (though it is naughty of Knopf to claim a "first-ever" translation which has actually been preceded by a handsome and valuable English edition—from a university press, no less!— of the same work some seventy-nine years ago). Mr. Barnes has afforded us a literary gem, and I am happy to recommend to readers of our incomparable modernity the efforts of everyone concerned with presenting, and presenting once again, this beautiful, agonized and agonizing little book. Especially the efforts of Alphonse Daudet.

An Introduction to *In Search of Lost Time*

[2003]

In old days books were written by men of letters and read by the public. Nowadays books are written by the public and read by nobody.
— Oscar Wilde

D ear Proust, I'd like you to meet your new readers. Most of
them have heard about you for some time (there have been
at least four films made of *In Search of Lost Time*; there has
even been a film about you, and your housekeeper, and your asthma,
and your cork-lined room—a film of course about the inaccessible last
years of your life), and certainly they have had many opportunities to
get acquainted with your great work—everyone has been told it is
great—but for one reason or another they haven't done so.

Why not? you'd like to know. Well, to begin with, your reputation
as a difficult author is widespread, and many readers are daunted. For
instance, you're said to have written the longest sentence in the history
of literature; there's even a parlor game that challenges people—bright
people!—to diagram it. And of course the *Search* itself is one of the
longest novels in modern literature—long and intricate and allusive;
why, there are even some critics (you know how we're all intimidated
by critics) who say it isn't a novel at all.

What do they say it is? Oh, a cultural cosmogony, a Menippean
satire, and most overwhelming of all, a sort of evangel. For you offer
us the postulation that we can, in the shadow, or rather the radiance,
of your own enchiridion, *go and do likewise*. Each reader, instructed
and inspired by your own salvationist exercises, has a capacity to redeem his own past, to regain the time. I myself have . . . or have
had . . . two friends, Jean Stafford and Roland Barthes, they're both

dead now, who felt your book was more like a gospel than a novel. Jean used to say she had to start your book over every five years because each time she read you she had already become a different person. And Roland, near the end of his own life in 1978, wrote that he

> like Proust ill, threatened by death (or believing himself so) came back to the phrase of Saint John which Proust quotes in *Contre Sainte-Beuve*: "Work, while you still have the light. . . ." Does this mean that I am going to write a novel? How should I know? I don't know if it will be possible still to call a "novel" the work which I desire to write and which I expect to break with the nature of my previous writings. It is important for me to act *as if* I were to write this utopian novel, to put myself in the position of the subject who *makes* something, and no longer of the subject who speaks *about* something.

It is more than incidental interest, with regard to the *Search* as this sort of gospel and prototype, that Roland Barthes found himself qualified to make certain reservations, certain *criticisms*, which do not alter his soterial purpose. He readily acknowledged that he preferred certain parts of the *Search* to others, but that each time he read the book again, the parts he then preferred were different ones, and that was why Proust was a great writer.

But the real trouble new readers have with your book is reading it for the first time. And most of that trouble, frankly, is the length—what you call *longueurs*. Now, if you get to know each other a little, there are ways of solving this problem. For instance, one could moderate the "academic" insistence that a reading of Proust has to be conducted straight through, from beginning to end, no dipping here and there, no looking ahead, or back. . . . There's no need to stipulate such draconian conditions for achieving some sort of intimacy with you. That's why I'm so eager to introduce you to your new readers. But for now, let me say that in introducing *them* to *you*, I want you to understand that there might be some problems—what appear to be contemporary problems.

Such as? Well, American readers are likely to be in a hurry—*they haven't time*, they often say. It's an expression you might appreciate. And you'll have to admit you're a very deliberate writer. You need to be patient with your American readers—actually, I think you are: you've already devised a technique for patience, at least for their patience. I've noticed that often on any one page or in any one passage—somewhere between a chant and a chapter—you manage to cast your spell, to sound your note, *to tell your truth*, for goodness sake! so that readers don't have to read all the way to the end of the whole book to get what Proust is about.

You've seen to it that the message is sent on every page. Readers can read, and stop, and then, another time, resume. There are other books like that; we call them "wisdom literature," and their matter is casually crystallized quite as often as it is likely to be exhaustively secreted. Of course I think there's a real advantage in building up sufficient momentum to read straight through from "For a long time I would go to bed early . . ." to (six volumes on) ". . . between which so many days have come to range themselves—in Time." But say you had provided (or permitted) a way of reading your book which took our new readers' impatience into consideration, which summed up *as they went along*—even that kind of epitomizing might well strike your new readers as a sort of jungle, a sort of maze—you remember all those comparisons critics have made of the *Search* to a Gothic cathedral, or a Wagner opera, or even a flying carpet. You're not generally considered pithy.

Yet all through the tangled volumes of your work, you do crystallize the world into aphorisms and epigrams—I think you're as succinct as any of those classic French moralists politely murmuring somewhere behind you. Why sometimes you're faster than La Rochefoucauld himself (as when you say, "It's from adolescents who last long enough that life makes its old men"). If I could admonish your new readers to watch out for those "moments of speed," as it were, among the prolonged dimensions and the plethoric details, I think they would find the going a lot easier than they'd expected.

But all I want to do, for now, is to make sure that in meeting your new readers you know what to expect of them, what you have to come to terms with—as I hope to tell them what to expect of you and what they have to come to terms with when they start reading the *Search*.

Oh, there *is* one more thing you ought to be aware of if you're going to confront these new readers of yours with a modicum of good will. Even though you managed to include, with a really Tolstoyan appetite, such "modern" manifestations as the Great War, and airplanes, and telephones (wonderful what you did with *them*), for new American readers in the twenty-first century, the time you keep referring to as lost—in French *lost* means "wasted" as well—is over and done with, of no account. And a search for the past, even one recent enough to include automobiles and airplanes, is an unlikely, even an unlikeable enterprise. You see, we have a kind of allergy to the past; it's our national disease, and the very assurance with which you insist that the past is *within the present* is likely to seem quite repellent, even offensive, to these new readers. I know you intend to be gentle with them—your ferocity is elsewhere—but I feel I must warn you about the reception you're likely to meet when you release one of your zingers on the subject. I think it will take the American readers of the twenty-first century a long frequentation of themselves as well as of you to believe it when you say:

> It's no use trying to evoke our past, all the efforts of our intelligence are futile. The past lies hidden beyond the mind's realm and reach, in some material object (in the sensation that material object gives us). And it depends entirely on chance whether or not we encounter that object before we die.

Finally, what your new readers will want to know is Who's saying such a thing? Who tells it like it is? Who is the *discoursing person*? And these questions bring me to the other part of my project: introducing your new readers to you, Proust.

You'll notice, dear new readers, that I haven't said, "introducing . . . *Marcel Proust* . . . ," for I don't believe that (biographical) person speaks in the *Search* at all. You'll find that the discoursing person who is in fact the Narrator of the *Search* is hardly ever named, and if indeed he seems to be called Marcel once or twice, it's extremely difficult to assign him the attributes of autobiography; he is *the self who writes*, and his relations with the self who votes and pays rent and has bad (or good) sex are uncertain and in some sense *displaced*. Proust himself has explained this neatly when he insists that Sainte-Beuve, for example, "fails to realize that a book is the product of a different 'self' from the one we manifest in our habits, in society, in our vices." In other words, it is futile to wonder if the Narrator of the *Search* is the Marcel Proust so many people remembered knowing after the book was published, and even before; the Narrator is simply *another* Proust, one quite frequently unrecognized by the author (in fact Marcel Proust *couldn't* recognize the Narrator, since this other Proust is created by *what is written*, not by the author's intention to write . . .).

For the Proust I want to introduce is a new, an odd, a *modern* kind of Narrator (I'll try to explain what I mean by modern in a little while), for if he does really narrate (rather than philosophize or write what are now called "personal essays"), the narrative he writes will not apprehend a life perceived in a linear course of time, from year to year until the moments he decides to write "the story" down.

What is narrated is not the Narrator's life, but his *desire to write*. Time thwarts this desire, tends it toward a conventional chronology (which must be continually subverted, for what is merely successive is surely lost: only the circle can be *retrouvé*, a word that means not only regained but rediscovered, recognized, repossessed) — and how many challenges, discouragements, and rivalries must be endured before *the desire to write* achieves an ultimate triumph (this is the best reason to read straight through to the end of *Le Temps retrouvé*, where the Narrator arrives at the Guermantes's party and discovers what it is that he has to write (time regained) and thereby realizes, indeed reassures himself, that he will be able to write, though as we all like to discover when we close the last volume, it is already written.

So the reader learns that what the *Search* contains is indeed the Narrator's life, but a life displaced, as I said. We've read a symbolic biography, or as one of Marcel Proust's early biographers (by now there have been so many) calls it, "a symbolic story of Proust's life." In one of his prophetic letters Keats wrote: "A man's life of any worth is a continual Allegory," and Keats seemed quite certain, actually quite sanguine, about the legibility of the allegory—it was plain and pleasing to such a poet. But Proust's favorite poet, Charles Baudelaire, had

been more doubtful, more pessimistic, in fact more *tragic* about reading the sense of the allegory out of the given life-experience:

> . . . as if in a shroud,
> my heart lay buried in this allegory:

> On Aphrodite's island all I found
> was a token gallows where my image hung . . .
> Love give me strength and courage to behold
> my body and my heart without disgust!

Of course Proust had the courage to behold anything in his or anyone
else's body and its behaviors, but he was not so sure about what
strength would be given him, or what strength remained of what had
been given, and indeed in terms of his health it was a narrow squeak:
Proust's textual revisions recovered in the last twenty-five years have
shown us how much was left to do, how much could not quite be
done.

There is a whole other poetic drama (*maker's* drama) in the recently published notebooks, the variant readings, the canceled (but
plausible) versions: Marcel Proust's wavering agon about where to
place this humiliation, that death, the other sudden revelation (for instance the discovery that the two "ways" are the same). Indeed whole
sections were wrested from what in linear terms would be their "right
place" in order to serve the design, to fulfill the allegory; and Proust
scholarship for the next twenty-five years will be instructing our inner
graduate student as to what some of the decisions (and the indeci-
sions) had been and what they became, more or less, finally. Certainly
the requirements—the logic—of the allegory allowed, actually *compelled*, Proust to erase the differences, the contradictions between the
novel and the discourse (as Descartes would have it), the treatise (as
Spinoza), the essay (as Montaigne). . . .

This recognition brings us to the figure of Proust as a modern
writer, which any introduction to the twentieth century's greatest novelist must engage. *Must*, because Proust was twenty-nine when he entered that century in which he lived only twenty-two years; indeed he

was thirty-five and had already written several unsuccessful versions of the *Search* before 1907. (Tolstoy was thirty when he completed *his* great autobiographical allegory *Childhood, Boyhood, and Youth* and began his career as a novelist.) We call Tolstoy the great(est?) novelist of the nineteenth century, though he lived a decade into the twentieth, and though the "essays" that finish off *War and Peace* (written the year Proust was born) seem obstructively "modern" on our first reading of that novel. Still, we do not regard Tolstoy as a "modern" novelist.

Yet Proust, who is as insistent about the "realism" of the world of the *Search* as anything in *Anna Karenina*, as inclusive about its "naturalism" as everything in *The Death of Ivan Ilyich*, is inveterately coupled or tripled—by Nabokov, for example—with Joyce and Biely and Kafka as indefectibly modern. I believe this is precisely because of the nature of that Narrator and his strangely absent presence, if I may put it that way. Proust's every gigantic effort is to subtract his "empty" Narrator's discovery (and possession) of time regained from what Gaston Bachelard calls the "false permanence" of biography. That is what pushes this enormous novel over the edge (the edge of encyclopedic allusion, of social chronicle, of literary emulation, of symbolist dithering, and of speculations concerning love, art, death, and time) into that enormous structure (abyss?) of repudiations which *is* our modernity.

This matter of locating Proust in such modernity is the most vexed question with which you must contend. For Proust is a writer between two centuries, between two aesthetic postulations (the "realism" of Balzac, Flaubert, Goncourt, etc., and the "symbolism" of Baudelaire, Huysmans, Mallarmé, etc., or, as Antoine Compagnon, the best critic of Proust-between-centuries, puts it, between etymology and allegory. Proust can be perceived as epitomizing the past achievements, but he can also be characterized as inaugurating new ones. His suspension between the fictional obligations of nineteenth-century masterpieces and those of twentieth-century "experiments" makes it difficult for his new readers to be comfortably aware of what he is doing; he seems on the one hand to be violating the laws (or at least the conventions) of an achieved program, and on the other hand to be regressing from explorations and discoveries into the tried-and-true (or at least the old reliable) methods of a familiar agenda.

I believe my introducing you to each other will be more convincing if I offer this notion of repudiations, of negativities, as the essential modernism of this great writer, for in the making of his gospel-novel, his fiction-as-evangel, Proust rejects, one after the other, precisely those realms of experience that have heretofore always constituted the claims of human success: the triumphs of worldliness, of friendship, and of love (all of which Proust declares to be failures, in fact disasters). It is only art, or rather the mediations to be found in art, that Proust urges as the means of regaining time, of recovering what is otherwise and always *lost*.

That is why he elevates to a special eminence in the *Search* four characters—Elstir, Vinteuil, Bergotte, and Berma: painter, composer, writer, and actress—artists whose creations point the way to redemption for the empty fifth character, the Narrator, who in several thousand pages reveals so few hints about his physical appearance that it is impossible to imagine what sort of man he is. He is frail and suffers from asthma and insomnia, we know that much, but all his other energies and perceptions are directed, under the pressure of the most exhaustive observation, to the acknowledgment that the human enterprise—in society, in friendship, and in love—is a failure, the source of exhaustion, ruin, and despair.

The other thirty-five? forty? fifty? characters who accompany us through the *Search* like so many grand and grotesque catastrophes— even Charlus, even the Duchess of Guermantes, even the Narrator's grandmother whose name we never learn—are relegated to tragedy or to farce with the same dismissive gesture by which Wotan repudiates Hunding in *Die Walküre* after he has killed Siegmund: with a wave of his hand, the god casts out the mortal who has served his pathetic turn: *Geh'! Geh'!*

Only the artist, or rather only what the artist creates, is triumphant, is exemplary, is enduring, is *successful*. And only such makings can persuade the Narrator to undertake one of his own, a persuasion in which—for three thousand pages or so—we must collude. His language (Proust's language, of course) surrounds us, penetrates us, so that these makings are not only the Narrator's redemptive moments but our own.

It is my fervent hope that by introducing, with some charity, you new readers to Proust, and by introducing, with an equivalent charity, Proust to his new readers, the parties may proceed some way together. To the emblematic fulfillment of this hope I am somewhat encouraged by the new street signs of Paris boulevards, which, as if they sought to celebrate the Proustian *sagesse* that asserts "we are like giants plunged in time," flash a message picked out in little red lights (for danger? for delectation?) to those seeking safe passage to the median strip between opposing directions of traffic, a haven that must be attained before reaching the seemingly inaccessible other side: *traversez en deux temps*, the red lights direct us, *cross over time and time again*.

ON THE
VISUAL ARTS

People Figures

[1970]

The diminutive is the last refuge of greatness.
—Bachelard

For the last three years at Christmas-time though without any dogmatic reference to the Holiday Season, as we have been conditioned to call the end of the year, New York's Museum of Contemporary Crafts has put on exhibitions of a specific diversional character that will be evident if I merely list the previous labels: "Amusements Is," "Puppets," and—almost notoriously—"The Art of the Baker: Cookies and Bread." This year, the Convention on Fifty-third Street is extended by a large show entitled "People Figures," a selection of doll forms (affording more or less complete representation of the human body) from contemporary art, religious figuration, and folk traditions.

The diversity of the sources is important. In fact, Thomas Kyle, the Museum's assistant director who has assembled this exhibition, is concerned to further his institution's impulse—if it is not an explicit policy—to dissolve the boundaries we conveniently but constrictingly raise between craft and art, between toy and idol, between cult and culture. There are, as all these Yuletide shows have dramatized, what we might call *interferences*, objects, places, and moments at which our categories collapse, and we must suddenly see the world the world in a new perspective, or without any perspective at all, as a child sees it. The works in this show, on loan from museums, private collections, galleries, and the artists themselves, provoke precisely such quandaries of genre: where does the doll leave off and the sculpture begin? Where does the plaything take over from the fetish? At what point does the individual maker assume responsibility for the folk pattern?

I have no solutions, of course—I am merely delighted the problem can be posed so effectively by the show itself. Surely the entire effort of contemporary art might be defined as Christian: "except ye become as little children, ye shall not enter the kingdom of heaven." With the significant heresy that we have discovered the vision of little children to accommodate "perversity" more readily than any other. Hence the terrifying, in fact the diabolical, nature of most of these "people fig-ures." Seeing the works—heterogeneous images, as Dr. Johnson said of metaphysical poetry, yoked by violence together, nature and art ransacked for illustrations—prompts me to reflections on my own re-sponses which varied, of course, with the items displayed from hilar-ity to horror, sometimes instancing both at once, hovering most of the time, though, in the range of wonder. We marvel, only partly in retro-spect, at these people-figures: they are ourselves, and arouse memo-ries of all the things we wish to do with ourselves.

Which is the point about children, of course. The doll transcends the idol because our transactions with it proceed in *both* directions. We can worship our doll, sacrifice to it, but we can wreak upon it, as well, all the expressive havoc that we feel toward ourselves and fear to inflict at such close quarters. Most of us, I think, can remember what it was to have had a doll *too long*. Bald, filthy, one-armed, often eyeless and speckled with nameless maculations, our beloved toy *had* to be taken to bed with us precisely because it was in such condition—it had truly become *ours*, the repository of our daydreams and the confidant of our terrors. Not every manufactured doll "takes" with a child, of course, but one of the evidences of this show, on the part of those ex-children who have created such dolls as are here, is that people-figures become works of art precisely at the moment they leave off being "suitable playthings for the young"—become art precisely when they stop being the manufactured dolls we buy and turn instead into what children have made of them. That messy poppet we refused to surren-der is just where Irena Martens, for example, begins her work—what was once regarded as the death of the doll (time to buy a new doll) is now seen to be its beginning. As soon as it can accommodate evil (time, change, others) the toy becomes art.

As for the votive aspect of these figures, one might say that the idol begins where the notion of reciprocity peters out. When a doll no longer has a countenance which corresponds to the facts of our suffering life, it becomes a ritual object, exempt from private experience, a matter for public worship. It is through facial expression, Sir Kenneth Clark has said, that every intimacy begins. That is why even the most "profane" items in this show—Clayton Bailey's latex images of Hell's Angels, grotesque leather-jacketed motorcyclists, larger-than-life-sized hoodlums—participate in the sacred: their faces are exempt from private experience and particularly from private pain: large or small, they transcend our intimacies, our exchanges (as we say that two people "exchange a glance"), and merely bestow upon us their grimaces. We have nothing to give them.

The folk pieces in the show remind us, as popular expression invariably does, that it is possible to *process* many—and many of the best—experiences of life according to a received idea, relying upon something *already* understood. Like the figure we call an idol, the folk images function only in one direction, but it is in the opposite direction: we must give them everything, for they can be said to afford no expression. They invite us to inhabit them, to inspire them with whatever meanings we have at hand. *They* do not have a meaning, except what we can put into them. That is why folk art is always cheerful, even when it consists of skeletons.

There are hundreds and hundreds of people-figures in this show, and if it is easy enough to decide whether they are toys, folk objects, or ritual instruments, it is hard to relate the emphasized aspect, finally, to one's own notions of what is art. Tell me what you think is "art," and I will tell you who you are, the saying might run today. We are learning more and more to use our eyes and our hands, less and less our minds and our memories in making such a decision. For the question of art can only be answered—in our culture, at least; and only a culture like ours could permit this show in the first place: half the things here would be burned by the exhibitors of the other half in any ethnic acceptation except that of our eclectic West—by each person who visits the "People Figures" show, for *him or herself.*

There is no answer any more, only the question; or rather, there are only *answers.* That is our weakness, and also our strength.

Fragments of a "Rodin"

[1974]

for Emma Joseph, who provided

In March 1970 an act of violence and vandalism was committed in Cleveland, Ohio, its victim a cast of Rodin's statue known as *The Thinker*: dynamite had been wedged between the grasping bronze toes, and sometime after midnight the figure was blown off its pedestal, the lower portion suffering considerable damage. Though put back in place, the statue itself has not been restored, and it looks—legs torn open, buttocks fused, the wonderful patina even more spectacular where the metal is gashed and split, a slender steel palisade boxing in the unbalanced torso—it looks like a "modern" statement now, something closer to a Reg Butler hominoid impaled on its thorns or a realization in the seething bronze of one of Francis Bacon's horrors, neatly jailed, keeping or kept at its distance, than to the celebrated figure created in 1879 and crouching, as we all know, before so many museums, colleges, and courthouses across the country.

Growing up in Cleveland, I had seen this particular *Thinker* at work in front of our art museum—had seen it every week, sometimes every day, and inside the museum I had seen other statues I was told Rodin had made, particularly a pair of creamy marble clumps, *The Kiss* and *The Hand of God* (modelled, Miss McFeelsy said, after the sculptor's own hand!)—which appeared very different indeed, lapped so smooth the light found nowhere to go but inward, from the rugosities of the image we visiting schoolchildren entitled, with an allegorical impulse quite as merciless as the Master's, *The Toilet*. And when I read in the papers, even in *The New York Times*, about the explosion of this childhood icon (by now I had seen its consessioner before Philosophy Hall at Columbia University, and I had visited the Rodin Museum in Philadelphia and even the Musée Rodin in Paris), I realized as surely as if I had heard the nymphs crying "the great god Pan is dead" when Christ was born, that an era was over, that a hinge had folded, and that life, as Rilke said apropos of another broken statue, must be changed.

Why, I wondered, had "they," nameless and faceless agents of Darkness, done the deed at all? No slogans scrawled on the pedestal indicated the provenance of such destruction, yet the mischief was too intricate to be no more than some Midwest version of an *acte gratuit*— it lacked the adorable spontaneity of the Absurd. At first I inclined to believe *The Thinker* had been blasted because it was *thinking*. This was 1970, after all, and anti-intellectualism is scarcely a minor tributary to the stream of American life. But there was a ruinous paradox in my reasoning—indeed had I not already noticed that the somewhat squashed effigy had a new pertinence, a deeper significance? The wound merely enhanced the wonder of thinking. The only way to overcome a thought is by . . . another thought. And the only victory over *The Thinker* would be, say, disposable earthworks or primary sculpture, some emblem of unthought—not the vandalization of a received emblem of thought.

Then, recalling that the figure had been enthroned, originally, above the lintel of *The Gates of Hell* and that Rodin intended it to be called *The Poet*, for it was to represent Dante conceiving the tormented universe of forms which writhed beneath him, I presumed that the same negating hostility to association, to history and to the very presentiment of the past had functioned here as had dictated the cancellation of the program-cover of the Republican Presidential Convention in 1956, when Rodin's *Three Shades*—chosen by a committee to illustrate Peace, Progress, and Prosperity—were discovered to be the guardians who point down into the same swirling inferno over which *The Thinker* so creatively broods. Yet most people have no notion that Rodin's most popular work is not seen by them as he intended it to be seen—as part of an encyclopedic, and unfinished, apocalypse; any more than they realize that Rodin never touched a chisel, never "carved" all those caramelized creations that came out of his *atelier* from the hands of Italian artisans busily producing sentimental marble facsimiles of what the master's hands had modelled in clay, plaster, and wax.

No, *The Thinker* had not been blown up because it was thinking, or because it was thinking about Hell or history, or because it would be fun to blow it up; *The Thinker*, I was obliged to conclude, had been blown up because it was a special kind of art, because it was by Rodin. What, then, had that come to mean—"by Rodin"?

The answer might lie in a name-dropping still-life with a title lifted from Kipling, who certainly belongs in the picture: *A sonata is only a sonata, but a cigar is a good smoke.* Under a framed lithograph of Brahms playing the piano and puffing on a cheroot—a Brahms bearded like Whitman, like Ibsen, like God, and like Rodin himself (whose hand, I knew, already partook of divinity)—there was a shelf of books in our house, and the biggest book, with the same luxuriant margins, the same gravure illustrations shielded by a wisp of tissue-paper, the same *propos* of the Master gathered as in a chalice of reverent inquirendo by Paul Gsell, was to be found in the houses of all my parents' friends, if not under Brahms then on top of the piano, among the folds of an art-scarf which might have been snatched from Isadora's chubby shoulders. This was the book republished now by Horizon Press, and on its spine were but two words, though they appeared in very large letters: ART, and beneath that, a trifle larger, RODIN.

For my family and their friends, for an aspiring middle-class America in the first four decades, say, of this century, the assumption was not that Rodin made art, but that Art was what Rodin made (as Poetry, for the preceding generation, had been what Tennyson wrote). Objects which came, or were said to come, from Rodin's hands were art because they were made by an artist (*cherchez l'homme* is the motto of the middle class), and they were great because they were made by a Great Artist—not because of their intrinsic qualities, formal properties, but because of a justifying aura of comment supplied by the Master. That is how the middle class has always recognized art: by the directives of the artist and his ape the critic. Only an aristocracy, of course, can afford to respond to such objects *unmediated*; even triumphant, the bourgeoisie never asks "is that what I like?" but only, anxiously, "what is it supposed to mean?" Rodin, among others, told us, and we believed, we recognized. This book is one of the places and ways in which he told us. But to determine an analogous recognition in the history of sculpture, to affix a *cachet* with the same complacent unanimity, we should have to look back as far as Canova, perhaps as far as Bernini—and that far back, no such recognition could be made by the middle classes, which were merely rising; by the time I was poring over ART by RODIN—or was it RODIN by ART?—they had risen.

Other books, as I mentioned, shared with Rodin that shelf which showed forth, until it showed up, the last word in middle-class taste, and though it appears to be period taste now (which means taste, period), who can afford to condescend to such choices when we consider our own last words? There were the works of Maeterlinck and Rostand and d'Annunzio and Anatole France (a long red row, the latter, from which I would learn, as again from Schnitzler, that *libertine* is a diminutive of liberty); there were the scores, on the piano, of Puccini and Massenet (the "Meditation" from *Thaïs* was played at my mother's wedding!); and there were certain numinous figures, living persons whose appearances and performances (often, as in the case of the Divine Sarah, identical) had to be granted the same inviolable veneration with which certain books were to be read: Nijinsky, Caruso, Duse . . . Certainly, after the Great War there was a Great Snobbery about the other side of the Atlantic, a great craving for spoils. But more than any other creative figure—even more than Richard Strauss (music, after all, even music orchestrated by Strauss, could not be *owned* in the way marble and bronze and mere clay could be owned, as chthonic trophies)—Rodin satisfied that craving, fulfilled the needs of the class and circumstance in which I grew up—the class defined, abruptly, by the circumstance of having "been"—by which was meant having been to Europe. A class which is, today, a has-been, for it has been had—by its own possessions, despoiled by its own spoils, among which few were so proudly carted home as the statues of Auguste Rodin.

There were, of course, several Rodins. There was the Rodin who did—if indeed he did them—marble busts of Mrs. Potter Palmer and her friends for colossal sums; there was the Rodin who scandalized the townspeople of Calais by insisting that civic virtue and patriotic sacrifice were not always noble and exalted, that heroism is a form of solitude—a suffering form; there was the Rodin who questioned the very pride of the body he glorified, who in *The Old Courtesan* articulated with unendurable persistence the miscarriage of life, the futility of effort, the impotence of the mind, the weakness of the flesh; and there was the Rodin who, taking a big mouthful of water and spitting it onto the clay to keep it constantly pliable, did not always aim well and soaked George Bernard Shaw:

> At the end of the first fifteen minutes, he produced by the action of his thumb a bust so living that I would have taken it away with me to relieve the sculptor of any further work. . . . But this phase vanished; within a month my bust passed successively, under my eyes, through all the stages of art's evolution. The careful reproduction of my features in their exact dimensions of life . . . went back mysteriously to the cradle of Christian art, and at this moment I had the desire to say again, stop and give me that. It is truly a Byzantine masterpiece. Then, little by little it seemed that Bernini intermingled with the work. Then, to my great horror, the bust softened in order to become a commendable eighteenth-century *morceau*, elegant enough to make one believe that Houdon had retouched a head by Canova. . . . Once again, a century rolled by in a single night, and the bust became a bust by Rodin and it was the living reproduction of the head that reposes on my shoulders. It was a process that seemed to belong to the study of an embryologist and not to an artist.

With characteristic acuity Shaw hits on what appealed to Rodin's public—not only to his patrons who wanted to be flattered, consoled, immortalized, but to a vast audience which knew what art ought to be, though it may not have known what it liked: art was science ("the study of an embryologist"), not the genesis of a vision, not revelation but realism, but the reproduction of what we see with our own eyes. By this dispensation, art need not—always—reassure, but it must tell the truth, and that was what Rodin the evolutionary biologist claimed to do: "I am not a dreamer," he said, "but a scientist . . . There is no need to create. Genius comes only to those who know how to use their eyes and their intelligence."

This, even more than the indulger of duchesses, was the Rodin that was detonated on the steps of the Cleveland Museum of Art—the mediator of an eternal human nature (that pretext of capitalism), the mouthpiece of the bourgeois aesthetic which makes art an art of detail. Based on a quantitative representation of the universe, this aesthetic demands that the truth of any whole be no more than the sum of the individual truths which constitute it—as Rodin used to say that a statue was the sum of all its profiles. In consequence, an emphatic significance is attributed to the greatest possible quantity of details, and the mimetic surface thus produced is one of literally sensational intensity. As Albert Elsen, Rodin's most scholarly critic, puts it:

> within an area confined to a few inches on the sculpture, each fingertip will encounter surface inflections of a different character; feeling one's own arm, one gains the impression that the surfaces conceived by Rodin are more richly complex.

It is an art which refuses to transform the world (choosing, as Elsen shrewdly suggests, to *enrich* it, to capitalize on our losses), which urges instead its obsessive record; indeed, an art which offers its hypertrophied mimetic surface not merely as an enrichment but as an homeopathy: to inoculate us with a contingent ill in order to forestall an essential one. This is what Roland Barthes calls the Essentialist Operation: to insinuate within an Order the complacent spectacle of its servitudes as a paradoxical but peremptory means of glorifying that Order. *The Age of Bronze, Eternal Spring, The Cathedral*—our middle-class *frisson* upon finding these "noble" titles affixed to works of a convulsive naturalism fades into acceptance, an acceptance of their ulterior and not their inherent function. To label *Dawn* (or *France* or even *Byzantine Princess*—it comes down, or climbs up, to the same) the semitransparent wax mask of Camille Claudel, the poet's sister and the sculptor's mistress, may rid us of a prejudice about the individual human countenance, but it is a prejudice which cost us dear, too dear, which cost us too many scruples, too many rebellions, and too many solitudes. To call an image of human flesh *The Thinker* is an allegorical holding-action, an alibi which manifests initially the tyranny and the injustice of that flesh, the torments it endures, the reproaches it incurs, only to rescue it at the last moment, *despite* or rather *with* the heavy fatality of its complaints, by calling it so. *Saving the appearances* by sovereign appellation, that is the Rodin who buttered up Puvis de Chavannes and his wan aristocratic allegories, that is the artist, and that the art, which passed—with its audience—from universal acclaim, from smug persuasion, in a flash of gunpowder. For it is written: I will show you fear in a handful of dust.

In the Print Room of the British Museum, if you have managed to murmur the proper words in the proper quarters, an attendant will set on the table before you any number of green buckram boxes, each large enough to contain an overcoat. Inside them, however, are not overcoats but the majority of the watercolors of Joseph Mallord William Turner, mounted though unframed, many with Ruskin's characteristic annotations ("nonsense picture") on the reverse—thousands and thousands of works, constituting one of the greatest achievements in art, though only a few of these pictures have been reproduced and a few more exhibited.

Here or in another such room, a deplorable scene occurred soon after the painter's death, at the age of seventy-six, in 1851—a scene which nothing but the profusion and perfection of what is in these boxes can keep us from mourning as more than an incidental loss: according to W. M. Rossetti, Ruskin (who was not yet thirty-five at the time) found among these works several indecent drawings "which from the nature of their subjects it seemed undesirable to preserve," and burned them "on the authority of the Trustees" of the National Gallery. Rossetti had been helping Ruskin to sort the Turner bequest, and neither he, Ruskin, nor the Trustees were swayed by the fact that Turner evidently considered the sketches *desirable to preserve.* Nevertheless, we find in these green boxes many rapid drawings and watercolors, executed after the artist's fiftieth year, of naked lovers copulating, of naked girls embracing. According to Turner's biographer, the genitals in many sketches are plainly shown, even enlarged. These erotic works illustrated what Turner himself, in a verse written much earlier, called "the critical moment no maid can withstand / when a bird in the bush is worth two in the hand." Apparently there were many more of these caprices than the ones which survived the Rosetti/Ruskin sifting, but as in the case of the great mass of the Turner watercolors, they were not executed for sale or for exhibition—they were executed for the artist's sole delectation. Turner was the first major artist to show this division between a public and a private art—between the astonishments of Varnishing Day and the unvarnished truth of the studio.

In the archives of the Musée Rodin, there are about seven thousand drawings and water-colors by the Master; no one may see them, for as anyone who knows who has attempted to undertake research in that country, France is a bureaucracy tempered by spitefulness, and though the canonical fifty years since Rodin's death have passed, the work has not been made accessible to students. About two hundred drawings and water-colors are exhibited in the museum, and there are perhaps as many in other collections. Nothing, apparently, had been destroyed, but we are in something of the same case as with Turner: the world lies all before us, where to choose?

Like most of Turner's water-colors, like all of his later ones, Rodin's were painted for himself; they are a private art. So often accused of melodrama, of oratory, of sensationalism, both men, we must remember, created an entire *oeuvre* apart in which nothing happens but in which nothing is kept from happening—the art of the late Turner, of the late Rodin (who first permitted a large group of his wash-drawing to be exhibited in 1907, when he was sixty-seven), is the greatest example with which I am familiar in the history of art of an art without history, an articulation of a life that can be lived without repression, without sublimation, in eternal delight, in endless play, in the undifferentiated beatitude of bodies and earth and water and light whose realm is eternity, not history. The eroticism, even, of Rodin's and of Turner's pictures has nothing to do with the drama of sex—it is the ecstatics of a condition, not of an action, and when we label it polymorphous-perverse we mean merely that it is playful, exuberant, gay.

In considering the pleasant symmetries of the two artists: that each

of them ended and began a century of taste; that each of them lived
over three-quarters of a century without ever marrying, though entertaining intractable relations with an "unsuitable" woman; that each of
them conducted two opposing careers, the first charged with virtuoso
scandal—it was Hazlitt who as early as 1814 saw "a waste of morbid
strength, visionary absurdities, affectation and refinement run mad"
in Turner, and an organizer of the American National Sculpture Society (in 1925!) who saw in Rodin "a moral sot" and in his *Walking Man*
"proof of the working of a mind tainted with sadism"—and the second entirely an interior rapture, no longer the assertion of selfhood
but rather the collection of an identity (motionless or moving, rapt or
reft, suggestive or stark) from the very lineaments of what is *other*: this
private creation of Turner and Rodin is the highest expression Western art can show of an identification with what is not the self but seen,
the making of an inwardness from what is outside—as I have said, an
ecstatics of art . . . In considering then the remarkable analogies between Rodin and Turner, let us not forget that to each genius was attached a young and voluble literary man whose attentions were not so
welcome to the artist as they are to us: Ruskin who by his late twenties was determined to dedicate his fortune and vocabularly (both
enormous) to the exposition of his "earthly master"; Rilke who at the
same age served as Rodin's secretary, and though ignominiously dismissed managed to patch up the misunderstanding by patience, admiration, servility even—and of course by one of the most beautiful
essays in the entire range of art criticism, which Rodin may never have
read. One sentence from each writer must suffice to manifest the degree of suffusion, the deep dye these passionate young men had taken:

> Rodin and Rodin only would follow and render that mystery
> of decided line, that distinct, sharp, visible but unintelligible
> and inextricable richness, which, examined part by part, is to
> the eye nothing but confusion and defeat, which, taken as a
> whole, is all unity, symmetry and truth.

> Turner was a worker whose only desire was to penetrate with
> all his forces into the humble and difficult significance of his

means; therein lay a certain renunciation of Life, but in just this renunciation lay his triumph, for Life entered into his work: his art was not built upon a great idea but upon a craft, in which the fundamental element was the surface, was what is seen.

Ah no, I have the names reversed: the first sentence is by Ruskin, the second by Rilke. There is always a confusion, is there not, when literary men meddle with art?

Between the "wrong" Rodin mutilated on the steps of the Cleveland Museum and the undivulged Rodin I have suggested as an antidote, between the emblem of an abject ideology and the ecstatics of a released identity, it is good—it is corrective—to stand a moment before the masterpiece of Rodin's sculpture and the supreme sculptural expression of the nineteenth century, *The Gates of Hell*, begun in 1880, left unfinished (in plaster) and cast only a decade after his death. The first cast is in Philadelphia, the second in Paris, both gifts of the same American millionaire who created the Rodin Museum in the former city and who restored Rodin's villa outside the latter, housing hundreds of original plaster studies and drawings which had been inadequately protected—a gesture never acknowledged by the French authorities. Looking at the spectacular patina of the bronze, the terrific shadows which are Dantesque indeed, one is easily distracted from the Master's intention:

> My sole idea is simply one of *color* and *effect* . . . I have revived the means employed by Renaissance artists, for example, this mélange of figures, some in low relief, others in the round, in order to obtain those beautiful blond shadows which produce all the softness . . .

Rodin had hoped to make the individual figures in wax, attaching them to the plaster frame, which would have created even subtler "blond shadows," but the technique was impracticable, and year after year the portal remained in his studio, endlessly altered, figures added, removed, shifting in scale and inclusiveness, the only fixed point being the tombs near the base of the doors, which were the last major additions before Rodin's death. Almost all the images we associate most readily—and not always with relish—with the sculptor are here, frequently in a context which challenges the connotations they have come to have for us: *The Thinker, Adam, Eve, The Prodigal Son, Crouching Woman, The Three Shades, The Old Courtesan, The Kiss, Fugit Amor, Ugolino* . . . In particular Man as *The Thinker* replaces Christ in the judgment seat, and in general chaos and flux supplant the hierarchies of doctrine. For Rodin himself, the work was as private as the swiftest of his drawings, the most summary of his clay sketches, and its inflection— though I have called it ecstatic, though I am certain it is exalted and even exultant—is catastrophic. Michelangelo called Ghiberti's doors *The Gates of Paradise*, and surely Rodin accepted the challenge in calling his own *The Gates of Hell*. They are the consummate expression of that encyclopedic impulse of the nineteenth century, that effort to gain access to prophecy by means of process, which we link to Courbet's *Atelier*, for example, and to the *Comédie Humaine* of Balzac—Balzac, of whom Rodin gives us the most *unwavering*, the most Promethean image—for their subject is not so much a version of Dante as an inversion: *La Tragédie Humaine*.

Corrective, then, to pre-empt this apocalyptic and yet intimate Rodin—apocalyptic in the sense that he creates a world of total metaphor, in which everything is potentially identical with everything else, as though it were all inside a single infinite and eternal body. The last great artist for whom art, nature, and religion are identical, Rodin was faithful to what Pater calls the culture, the administration of the visible world, and he merited Revelation, which might solace his heart in the inevitable fading of that. His delights, as it says in Scripture, were with the sons of men, and in *The Gates of Hell* we read their fortune; it is ours.

Eleven Caprices on
the Work of Michel Delacroix

[1990]

L*a Ville Lumière*—as these images yet again rehearse the old sweet songs, the old sharp sayings—had better first be engaged as *la ville nuage*. Let it be clear as day, the degree to which we do combat with clouds, for only then does the fabled city show its light against an outer darkness withstood. What the painter suavely determines is that shadows rise (it is *light* that falls), and so pressed are we for space (as if it were time!) that only upward can we seek those moments of release from our intersections and divisions—from ourselves.

For the landscapes of Paris, the urban tableaux, are to be read upside down: the city grows from its sky, that one sure thing, the great containing vessel. These paintings by Michel Delacroix confirm what I have always divined, often with delight, though sometimes in dread: that incessantly in this city, with its legislated proportions of house against house, roof upon roof, chimney echoing chimney, we are *indoors* (a word which does not exist in French), we are held within some vast but relentlessly enclosing chamber (what Barthes calls a *camera lucida*): and even on the city's broadest steppes—the Champ de Mars on a stormy day, the Place des Nations under July's Reign of Terror, the Seine itself as it takes an easy curve round the Jardin des Plantes—all Paris is at home, *chez elle*. And that is why M. Delacroix never (or hardly ever) sees the city's mass and movement from a room, out a window—his views of Paris are always exteriors because the city itself is an interior, and it would be a pleonasm to inspect it twice over from inside.

This particular Paris of M. Delacroix's is, of course, as unreal as Baudelaire's—

> Swarming city—city gorged with dreams,
> Where ghosts by day accost the passer-by

—for the haunted painter is as much a prisoner of his euphoric imagination as the haunted poet of his dystopic one; he knows the city he was born in not as it looks now, but as he has learned its aspects from his parents, from *their* memories and legends. Only a man born post-Proust, so to speak, could so vigilantly, so diligently pursue the lost paradise, the transformed city (Baudelaire again: "no human heart / changes half so fast as a city's face"). Therefore carts and carriages, therefore horses and dogs but no Citroën, and in that encompassing sky no Concorde, but a balloon, the world's most passive transport, the true *flâneur* (how appropriate that a Frenchman, Motgolfier, devised this lighter-than-air conveyance, and a German, Count Zeppelin, cancelled it out with his doomed will-to-power).

Yet for all the cobbled and shuttered anachronisms of the Paris of Michel Delacroix (b. 1933!), some corner of his imaginary city will always be correct if we have looked even once at the pervasive city's history with our own memories—some colonized fragment of that comprehensive sky is up-to-date, is exact, for the painter can only realize (make real), as the poet says, his desire:

> None of the famous landscapes that we saw
> Equalled the mysterious allure
> Of those that Chance arranges in the clouds.

SPORTS AND PROCESSIONS

Here is a festive city where no one seeks to get there merely, but *to make a spectacle* of the way—and of oneself into the bargain! Where competition is fierce, but only on the polo grounds, and where, on the diligently cobbled streets, there are no parked cars! Where a wedding, a circus, and a marching-band are reciprocal models of the splendors of filing past, the theater of being there!

An Englishman's home is his castle, we are told, and a Frenchman's street-life, as M. Delacroix delights in displaying, is his happiest home. Impossible to determine whether the springtime regatta is the focus of all those watching eyes along the boardwalk, or whether the eagerly manned boats are a grandstand for strolling couples and admiring belles, the much-embellished bystanding personnel. Even the lady on the margin of the links is on show, *en boutique*, and certainly (as the enlargement gratifyingly reveals) the parading elephant *et fils* are as conscious of our attentive presence as any of us—in the doorway of the dyeing establishment ("mourning in 24 hours") or on the skimpiest cafe terrace—may be riveted upon them. As any Parisian will tell you, we are certainly as remarkable to an elephant as an elephant, right here in the Rue Beaubour, may be to us!

Sitting outside, or standing in a favorable spot from which to watch, is probably the greatest (though unacknowledged) national sport: not staring but looking, or rather *onlooking* for life in public is what the French have called since the Middle Ages a *jeu*, not so much a game as a *game played*, a performance. Indeed, the principal pastime of M. Delacroix's Paris is the very first thing I discovered for myself a generation ago (after all, I had been raised in the Midwest and taught *not to stare*): when you sit on a cafe terrace, the street is your stage, but when you take to the street—cycling, walking, on horseback, even riding in the still-harmless, rather diffident automobiles—then the bysitters are *your* innocent performers. It is all urban theater, an articulation of the civic *gestus*. Even the dogs inspect our doings with the interest we accord menagerie: how entertaining the creatures are, human and otherwise! How delightful that the street brings them past us as they proceed round the fountain, under the trees and banners toward that tremendous focus, that triumphant span—

> For all experience is an arch wherethro'
> Gleams that untravell'd world, whose margin fades
> For ever and for ever when I move . . .

And how fortunate that our cobbled capital is so devised as to lead up to (and away from) such ordering cynosures! For in Michel Delacroix's Paris, the loftiest patriot is the liveliest citizen.

PORTRAITS

A Frenchman, or that anthological specimen of France a Parisian, may be identified by the consciousness of others, defined by an existence against the offing—it may be disregard or heed, favor or contempt—of a social configuration. He is a part not of all that he has met, like Ulysses, but of all who have met him, like Narcissus: *I am I* (and Gertrude Stein might well have been speaking of the painter's subjects) *because my little dog knows me.*

No one in these tableaux exists in isolation, for that is the *purpose* of the capital city—to construe a surround, to persuade a neighborhood into being, however alienated one may feel within it, however determined (like the painter's *clochard* in the Rue Degas, like his laundress crossing the Place des Vosges on a misty, smoky morning) to leave *all that* behind. No matter how sequestered, no matter how apparently extrinsic to the business of community you may believe yourself to be, there will always be a dog, *someone's* dog, to inspect your qualifications for separation and belonging (and then to look up at the painter, at the viewer, at *us*, who constitute a figment of this relentless society); there will always be a family watching from a doorway as the wild man departs, or a woman shovelling snow who notices the soldier returning to his barracks, the "audience" at an upper window for the pedlar so attentively beheld by the ubiquitous terrier . . . One of the painter's ingenuities of presentation, in this respect, is his reminder of *what has been here*: the vestige, the omnipresent scrap of poster on old walls, the graffito of commerce, and of course the intrusive *script*, persistence of human speech in its urgent manifestations throughout the city. However silent we may be (or wish to be) in our meditations, our eremitic project, we are surrounded by the record of discourse and the reminder of function: the pharmacy, the wine-shop, the dentist, the barber, the cabinet-maker (*ébéniste*), and the midwife all have their calligraphic claims to advance (and the torn and tacky residue of their signs have their claims to *withdraw*). It is as if our buildings themselves, and the scurf of our momentary occupancy of them, have assured the responsibility of our solitude, inflecting it to a recognized propriety, paralleling its singularity and thereby erasing it (as in the case of the lost lady on the near side of a foggy millpond, solaced by the reflected fieldstone manse behind her—who could *remain* lost in the vicinity of such residential composure?). The merest act of individual prowess, say the placing of a ladder against a wall in order for the boy in *velours* knickers and white stockings to scamper up and garner for himself a few of the neighbor's apples, must bring us into juxtaposition with the city's cries and whispers, as evident in the faded script of the baker's *enseigne*, replaced by the blood-red chirography of the horse-butcher, as in the almost audible proclamation of the glazier, so dear to Cocteau and Satie, with his poetical panes upon his back . . . You will notice that even when there is no writing on the wall, our *immeubles* (as the French call any multiple dwelling, suggesting its *immovability*) and even our most wretched hovel invariably inscribe upon the tender sky their text of breath-smoke: someone is there, and a person may be *portrayed* because the city keeps watch, keeps house, keeps faith.

BOATS

Woe unto the City whose name is not writ in water—so might the Psalmist have written, had he been urbanistically inclined. For not only is the waterway generally the source of the city, its historical justification, but the very script of its "message," whether utilized for transport, for recreation, or reflection: moving water is the emblem of life itself, and stands for what never stands still. It is our consolation, and our only hope against the stones.

Except, it seems, for Houston and Madrid (both cities created by fiat), all the great interior centers are riparian, and though their waterways may have ceased to defend and enrich them, the cities never lose their reliance on the *circulatory* analogies which even the grimiest canal affords. In Paris, the moderate Seine appears to offer the most docile functions, easy occasions for our commitment (hauling, fishing, even residence) and for our escape (locks, bridges, embankments), so easy that we tend to forget how often the river has forgotten itself, or perhaps remembered itself: and made terrible depredations on bankside life. Michel Delacroix has remembered almost every usage, even lifesaving and laundry. Though his parapet observations are leisurely and well-spaced, they are intricate and varied: the string of sulfur-barges cuts off the *bateau-mouche* at the point of the Ile Saint-Louis, in what is perhaps the grandest prospect the painter has taken (usually he settles for man's-eye views, with no more vantage than the city's apertures allow). It all makes a fine contrast to the intimate transverse by the rowboat from the Académie-Française to the fine pair of black cart-horses being held by the eight-year-old daughter while her father shovels sand into the two-wheeled cart, the scene framed by an oblivious fisherman—his dog is not oblivious, of course—and the bargeman's wife hanging out her seven shirts. In the very disparity of archaic water-craft, the painter reminds us, in the preponderance of work over pleasure, that until very lately the Seine was a toiling river. And even those of us who populate its banks offer every indication of our tasks (including the tasks of pleasure): item, the great bins of books and prints we must pore through, whether we are housemaids, a scarlet-epauletted officer, or a scholarly curé; item, the baby who must be promenaded; item, the gutter which much be cleared of the last linden-leaves; item, the ball which has just bounced across the cobblestones, ominously close to the great red cart filled with the evening papers—Jean-Pierre will run out and rescue his ball while Aunt Hortense and his little sister Marie watch in some alarm; Jean-Pierre wears a sailor-suit, and knows the names of all the tugboats on this stretch of the river. The dalmatian belonging to the newspaper-cart is quite accustomed to such dramas, and like the white *caniche* on the opposite bank, he knows this is a world where nothing can be lost or left behind. All has been brought to the surface of that other river, our life, which pursues its rippling course beneath those great iron rings set in the stone walls. To them we moor our boats and barges, but there is no mooring our experience, no tethering the seasons and ages which M. Delacroix has

so precisely selected and observed. That life runs on, as smooth and
luminous as the Seine between its careful quays, and who would ever
suspect its capacities to teem, to flood, to drown!

STREETS AND SQUARES

Even if, to a divine intelligence, everything in human life is of equal interest, to the utterly human painter our lives must discover and present some point of interest, some focus which rearranges whatever is
around it to afford a provisional signification: there, *right there!* before
it all escapes into incessance, is the hub which grants scale and scheme
to what is otherwise mere hubbub.

It must be eight o'clock, for the sky is not yet accustomed to cobalt,
and against it the smoke from thirteen chimneys on this early summer
evening (the trees still permit the lighted windows behind them to
show through: it must be May) bears off the traces of other lives elsewhere. But here, but now, something is notable enough to attract
three automobiles (one is a taxicab) as well as every variety of carriage,
and a flower-vendor, even a *gendarme* to direct the unusual affluence
of personnel: why yes, a closer look reveals it is the old Opéra-Comique
(torn down in the 1950s), and soon there will be a performance of
Mozart's *Così Fan Tutte*. No wonder there is so much light, so much
excitement, so much concentration of interest. What better than a *theater*, M. Delacroix reminds us, to beguile our attention from all the
tasks and trifles which so constantly solicit it, to gather us in and, once
gathered, to set about the nightly task of revelation!

It is one of the momentary features of city life, this discontinuance
of the usual scattering of our concerns, even if it is only to make us
aware of a couple of street-musicians on a smoky afternoon, serenad-
ing an audience of three, no, four—there is a critical dog—and any
number of enigmatic windows, behind which may be any number of
generous listeners. Momentary but momentous enough to constitute
a point of convergence for M. Delacroix, who must always have his
cynosure, his center, his *punctum*, even though the huge factory chimneys back there carry off their ignominious exhaust into the pinkening

oblivious west. Perhaps the best balance between an ongoing Everywhere and a fixed Here-and-Now—even better than the theater, than
street performances, though it is a street performance of a sort—is the
neighborhood market, the quotidian stalls and barrows (bright
awnings, even brighter heaps of tomatoes, lemons, aubergines!). In
this, Delacroix has a subject to his hand, for though the city extends
up and away, though the market itself is so disparate as to have no central issue, there are incidents which insist that we take heed, that our
awareness be enlarged. For all the discrepancies of the Paris streets,
and though the Église de Saint-Paul towers in the middle distance, we
cannot miss the Maison Blum (*Fondée en 1861*) with its Star of David
and its Hebrew characters to assure us of the kosher (*cacher*) quality of
its products, and next door the synagogue—look, there is the rabbi in
his prayer-shawl on the doorstep, and the bookish boys on their way
to *shul* . . . It is a world within a world, the Jewish street which for this
instant has seized our notice. But we have only to turn the corner and
we are back in the immense generality of things, all specifics blurred in
the chaos of another morning. As Baudelaire saw, with harsher though
no cleverer eyes than M. Delacroix:

> Shivering dawn in a wisp of pink and green
> Totters slowly across the empty Seine,
> And dingy Paris—old drudge rubbing her eyes—
> Picks up her tools to begin another day.

MOODS

The pressure of events, what the French call *la force des choses*, can be so
peremptory in city life that our moods come upon us not as a thief in
the night, a gradual guest by day, but with a kind of compulsive bus-
tle, as if by sorcery we were thrust into another state of soul. Everything reaches a halt, for a moment consciousness wavers and the
dream preponderates—a tyranny of light and shadow: the moods of
Paris, so sudden as to be almost a vertical phenomenon.

It is this vehement torpor that M. Delacroix has understood so
solicitously, perhaps because a painting—any representation of the

seized moment, life's process transacted—is already a sort of violence done to flux, an assault upon the tide. Capital instances are the three versions of a man overcome by his mood, suddenly the victim of *elsewhere*, entranced: 1) On the corner of the Rue Cézanne stands a sweeper, his broom held in both hands as if it were a votive candle, heedless of the cafe owner and her daughter ogling him from the doorway, of the granddaughter and her equally oblivious spaniel on the sidewalk—for out of the white sky, up from the pink pavements has appeared—to his eyes alone—that unappeasable visitant he now entertains, blind to the tasks of Paris, deaf to reason's appeal. 2) Is it the same man at the corner of the Rue Monet (these allusions are surely intended, by a painter named Delacroix! to remind us that his art is a succession of national magics), who leans on his snow-shovel in front of a rusty gate, his red kerchief the only sign of the life he must dig out once the fit has passed? Behind him extends the frozen butte of Montmartre, its gray houses icebergs this winter afternoon, seven-eighths submerged in the brief glory of a gold sky reflected in golden snow. Perhaps the hound running ahead of its mistress will knock the shovel from his hands, rousing the fellow from his mood . . . 3) This is the most tyrannical version, the least warranted: a man stands under a bare tree in some sort of open field, evidently in the outskirts of the city (the difficulty about liberation, Gide once said, is to get past the suburbs!). It is dawn, there is no more reason he should be here than that he should not: the stars have not faded yet, the busy chimneys tell how cold it must be, and there is no accounting for the facts: a man stands under a tree in a field—could that be a golf-club in his hands?—and he spares not one glance for the dubious houses behind him, reddening just now in the rising light. He is a captive of his mood.

Not always are a mood's represented victims the objects of M. Delacroix's attention, the subjects of his work. Here a coral moon (clearly diseased, the man in that unsteady orb) which has just floated free of the chimneys, saluted by the slanting scarves of smoke (there must be a west wind tonight), has made the viewer its only human votary, though the viewer must not forget the one face at a black window, the two radiant geraniums which have withstood the first frost. Ensorcelled all, quite as much as the densely populated square in front of the Saint-Michel fountain at five to eight on a summer evening (the clock leaves us in no doubt): for this one moment, everything is caught up in a twilight iridescence, everything contributes, everything belongs. It is the moment Baudelaire calls *harmonie du soir*, and the thirty-nine persons thus enclosed by the crepuscular trance, along with a horse, a poodle, two griffins, and five statues of indeterminate sex, will not stand for such scheming another moment—look hard, look fast, the sky will darken, the light will thicken, and the mood must be exorcized; only now is every cobblestone liable to glisten, every window to glow. *C'est l'heure exquise.*

MONUMENTS

It is an irony Clovis might have savored: the structure emblematic of Paris the world over is but the latest of her monuments (unless you count Pei's pyramid in the Louvre court—denounced as bitterly as Eiffel's tower ever was). That a city so marked by her venerable past should be signified by a commemoration of the future affords a clue to the paradoxical modernity of Paris, her dogmatic eagerness to be completed by the new, the next brilliant victory.

But in M. Delacroix's paintings, such triumphs are infallibly moderated by the resonance of habituation. The crepuscular Vendôme Column, the great Cathedral (mysteriously deprived of the Seine along its south side—as if the painter wanted to wrap Notre-Dame in lodgings *all round*, to naturalize the sacred edifice altogether), the Arc du Carrousel, and the Académie-Française are landmarks by which we live, and from them the city identifies its actions, distributes its movements. Everything is tempered by a film of frequentation, so that even the Eiffel Tower mounts not only out of the blue but into it as well, and adds a softened azure to the darkening vault: we are conscious of it from the most secular surround (no grand avenue leading up to it), rather as though we were merely going about our business (pharmacy, cafe, bakery, piano lessons) under its benign supercession. No one looks at it, indeed most of the public looks distinctly away. Come to think of it, there are no tourists in M. Delacroix's portraits of places, everyone *lives* there, and our interests are *vested*. How often these

views remind us—cropped as cunningly as any of Piranesi's metropolitan caprices—that the space around a monument, a determinative
building like the Académie as it faces across the Pont des Arts, is a kind
of countryside, a piece of pastoral reference: Paris, on this showing, is
an overcrowded solitude!

It was Dumas's Lady of the Camellias who first referred to the city
as a *populous desert*, a phrase Verdi was careful to retain in his opera of
modern Paris, and the pleasures of that half-world to which such ladies
resorted are given their monumental salutation of M. Delacroix's de-
piction of the Moulin Rouge, the Eiffel Tower's coeval and (inflected
by our recollections of Lautrec) feminine counterpart. It is an autumn
evening, there are still a few russet leaves on the sycamores, but
through them we can readily see the ebullient gas-globes of the Bal du
Moulin Rouge, crowded of course, though the crowd appears to be
coming out, seeking pleasure as much in the leaving of it as by the entering in; and how decorous, if not innocent, this handsome throng
appears, as one gentleman escorts his ladylike conquest into a waiting
taxi, *blinds down* . . . Most of the departing merrymakers are content
to hail the attendant carriages, or to tip the Zouave (sword and
horsetail-helmet indicating the sort of more-than-ornamental Zouave
he must be) to do so, and one or two couples are so impatient that
they utilize a decently obscure doorway for the first intimacies. The last
ones are still far in the future, the night is young, and the dance continues. Why, next door at that more sedate establishment the Brasserie
Graff, there is no hint of impropriety, or even of festivity: simply a
matter of serious drinking, a solid *choucroute garnie*, and an Alsatian
inflection of our Montmartre nocturne. Around the edges, domestic-
ity asserts its claims (laundry at the window four floors up, and a couple taking the air on their attic balcony—who could sleep with all that
racket, what Mistinguett would call *les flons-flons du bal*!) . . . And in
the foreground there is even a family doing the town in a cabriolet
(perhaps they are tourists, after all, venturing into the precincts of
pleasure just for the *frisson* of naughty vibrations), a strawberry-
woman endeavoring to convince a dubious housewife that her fruit is
fresh, and a fox-terrier riveted by the headlights of a speeding Delage
coupé. *On s'amuse, hein?* Monumentally wicked.

IN THE SNOW

In Paris, snow is not so much a substance as a process: it serves as a sort of developing fluid—reports the structures of our roofs, articulates the mass of our buildings, dramatizes the spaces where we may proceed and those where we may not. Generally transitory, a phenomenon of hours, Parisian snow hasn't time to muffle, to disguise the city as something else (the typical New York consequence of a blizzard—a transformation that can last weeks). *Time's whiter series* italicizes Paris a while, then the plain text shows through again, quite soon.

In a city of frequent Impasses, those alleys and courtyards where traffic drops dead, the meager snow makes more of a showing than on the Grand Boulevards (a recent feature of Paris, after all: M. Delacroix's city is post Haussmann, but tends to shy away from circulatory feats); the third act of *La Bohème* is the paradigm, the world over, of all such snow-scenes, even on the grandest scale, as in this painter's vast gray panorama (from what coign of vantage—can it be the Tour Saint-Jacques?) of the city coped in white, from Notre-Dame to Saint-Sulpice, and far in the rear a ghostly transparent Sacré-Coeur, linked by a thousand nameless edifices, each momentarily glorified with a silver sequestration. Only in the impasse does snow collect sufficiently to be shoveled away, or to be . . . snowballed by the children. Here Mimi can wait, coughing in the wilderness of her jealous passion, for her oblivious Rodolphe; here all the characters of Murger's sketches, like those of Du Maurier, stand out more vividly against the telling powder: how the colors glow! the red scarves and epaulettes, the sudden gold of lamps at the windows, and that curious mauve which appears on certain shutters, certain cafe corners, certain very worn overcoats. The merest wisp of cheer is heightened by such scenes, though the painter has provided one mournful view with no such note, no relief in sight—and *then*, of course, the snow in the city is a different affair, a discovery of all that is drear and daunted. There is not one lamp at the windows, the clock in the impasse says ten after six, and except for the man pushing a barrow across the white space (it is not open, it is *empty*), Paris is uninhabited (oh yes, one face at a fourth-floor window, momentarily captured by the patient flakes, but the rest is silence, dilapidation, mystery). It is the very definition of melancholy not to know whether this scene is ten after six in the morning or ten after six in the evening. Such are the despondencies of winter.

But on most occasions, M. Delacroix is eager to endow his signs of life with good cheer. Foremost among such views, of course, is the giant *arbre de Noël*, monumentally glistening in an odd little square somewhere north of the Tour Saint-Jacques (every Gothic crocket picked out with snow, the tower becomes an illustration of the style). The horses that brought the huge tree here are about to take away the wagon in which it must have rested as in a palanquin; there are little trees we can buy at the near corner, and there is no wind at all—every sleeve of smoke rises untroubled and vertical into the rosy sunset. The children have never seen a tree so tall—the four horses must have hauled it a long way, perhaps from the Forest of Compiègne, and certainly it is a message of metamorphosis since the days when Villon wrote about *Noël, morte saison*. Of course he never had such things as streetlamps, huge cast-iron guardians of all that is brave and bright. We shall stay out in the snow as long as the light lasts, the lovely apricot twilight over which (or under) falls the clarifying snow, disclosing for a while that radiant topography of our lives. It is the silence out of which every sound is heard more clearly, and the albescence which produces every chromatic fantasy: snow = revelation.

CLOSE-UPS

Where the city ends—a very different site from where it begins, for the city's inception is at its center, *downtown* always comes first—the tempo of life retards, and the artist necessarily dilates upon a more isolated subject. Around the edges of metropolitan life, vestiges of another rhythm can be felt, even if they make few *inroads* upon the humiliated suburbs. This *other metabolism*, neither pastoral nor oppidan, is what makes Delacroix's "close-ups" so touching. If something has slowed down, something else has not yet sprung up: images of a truce.

Easiest to convoke such meanings when the time of day is analogically transitional, when the light takes leave of our senses almost reluctantly, but parts company nonetheless. The street-lamps are on, yet their consolations have not yet begun except for the most local effect, a luminous puddle at the base of the black cast-iron shafts. The sky is still flushed, cerise to amethyst, behind the leafless plane-tree clogged with still-green mistletoe, and at such moments—understood so well by Magritte, too, as *surreal*, though for Delacroix they are merely *stopped*, the images of stanched life—the young man in black and his white poodle seem not merely to face us but to *confront* us with those questions about existence—the road turns around the salmon-colored house ever so symbolically—which we must answer hesitantly at twilight. It seems the challenge of Being itself, spied on by the shadowy mother in the doorway: do we make for the City, where great things have been done and may yet be done, or do we stay here, on this gentle, fuliginous corner, where nothing happens but time, and life passes us by?

Ever more poignant is the evening moment—*evening*, when light and darkness are *even*, and neither power can claim dominion—in front of the rather grand little toll-house on the railroad tracks by the river: two *gendarmes* are taking the air, and behind them the concierge's daughter is skipping rope on the cobblestones. The periwinkle blue of her dress is the only note of color, for the river is ashen now, and the sunset is quickly losing its chromatic identity—it merely *glows*. Oh yes, the red of the Tricolor is still luminous over the door, and upstairs the child's mother has lit one lamp. For the rest, the city might as well be uninhabited for all we can see or hear—across the river the smoke rises from some huge stack, and six windows are reflected in what appears more and more likely to be the Styx rather than the lifeless Seine. Even as the two officers—and now that we regard them closely, the red stripes down the sides of their trousers begin to glow as well, it is clear they belong to the flag over the door—hold their tongues (what is there to say? the skipping child is a symbol of whatever it might be) and wait for the first express to stop here on its way to Lyon, the street lamp comes on, and the magical moment of suspense is over. Night has begun.

Such paintings are often called *poetic*, by which I suppose we mean that every part of them seems to reveal a single harmonic statement: at three in the afternoon, a red two-wheeled cart in front of the church at the corner, the white horse, the white dog, the man in black who turns to see what the woman on the other side of the street is calling him for, the lilac sky, the lavender cobbles by which all that passes are measured . . . Wonderful that in French the image which halts everything for the lens is called a *cliché*.

PARKS AND ENVIRONS

A park in Paris, or indeed in France, is always a reminiscence of what the French call *la vie de château*, an allusion to that governance of nature which is so powerful that it affords an illusion of freedom. The *planted forest*, the *artificial ruin* are indices of that specifically French desire to exercise the will yet grant it a credence of its liberty. The park is where we play, or release our moods, our nostalgias, even our delinquencies—but only because such exonerations are *allowed*. Even the smallest park is the city's permission to relinquish the city.

Of course M. Delacroix is eager to engage our *purposes* in such places; how vividly he strews the gray lake with skaters, all so intent on their seasonal prowess, their romance of movement (even frozen, water affords us a phantasmagoria of ease!); and how pertinently he revives the excitements of Longchamp and Auteuil, the Parisian racecourses that have already awakened the vivacities of Degas, of Lautrec, of Dufy . . . Yet these splendid outings, where we yield ourselves up to the greatest apertures the city affords in order to do something, or to watch something, are less *taking*, finally, than other acceptations of such places (though even here, M. Delacroix has us skating round a fantastic feathery island, topped by a tempietto and shaped—scaped—till it has become a foreign site, a folly). M. Delacroix's *real* parks are more likely to be the terrains where we can invent our solitude, evoke the past and from it beguile such memories as we require. More often than not, the specific reference will be to Versailles, with its great basins set to retain the opalescence of the evening just a little longer than is quite *natural*.

And whether or not it is the Parc de Versailles which is evoked, it is that palace and its environs which have served as the model for the disposition of our dreams, the almost transparent statues waving us onward, or away, into a policed solitude. And it is something very much like the Trianon that we marvel at across the patient water—the horses drink, the dog barks, the child wriggles free from the nurse's arms, and the great trees stand behind the phony farmhouses, each one a reassurance that such peace can be, however connived. The French have never been quite comfortable with the notion that nature can be trusted, and they call those places in their parks where the bushes and plants are left to themselves an *English garden*. The French garden is always formal, each bed sculptured against a background of gravel or lawn. How emblematic, then, of all his atmospherics, that the painter should show us the little boy and his governess (though that is a hat Maman would not despise—perhaps it *is* Maman in a rather governessy gray-and-white ensemble) venturing between the wild woods on the left, and the carefully *fleur-de-lys*'d parterre on the right, toward . . . toward the great oaks which alternate with the white women on their tall plinths, together an ideal of all quests, the immortal (or at least ever-young) trees and the mortuary statues, mossy symbols of the dying away they pretend to ignore. Best of all, in all these noble parks, is the aura of obscure possibility M. Delacroix always grants these views: the mist seems to be forming on every blade of grass, between every leaf and stem, and if you look over there, past the corner of ornamental water and the broken Niobe, you will see the shadows rising out of the earth as if that was what parks were for, the generation of specters; with Baudelaire the painter might be saying:

> I thank these somnolent seasons which I love
> For offering to both my heart and mind
> So vaporous a shroud, so vague a tomb.

OTHER PLACES

Put the point of your compass in the heart of Paris—in the Sainte-Chapelle, say, that monstrance whose sacred relic is light itself—and

draw a circle of some hundred kilometers; you have described what
the atlas calls the Ile-de-France, the central atoll in a country surging
round it like a sea of changes. Except for that other island of Mont
Saint-Michel, our painter has confined—has confided—himself to the
mild, melancholy, household scenery of the Island of France, a land-
locked Crusoe.

Among these extra-urban views—which include a splendid panorama of the Château de Chantilly seen across the great carp-pond, the
hunt cantering in the foreground waved on by one of those allegorical
statues which make every château park a sort of figurative *text*, like a
page from the Limbourg *Book of Hours* (which is kept in the château
library)—are five images of country works and days, a sort of Gallic
georgics which are a wonderful pendant to what M. Delacroix does
with his chiefly urban preoccupations. All afford a partial view, in the
middle distance, of an old house, never magnificent but never modest,
never ramshackle but never unseasoned, around which are disposed
and displayed the activities of the turning year: 1) a boat is strenuously
poled along the little stream that runs through the rear of the property, keeping close to the alders and cattails of the far bank, for that is
where the pike are biting this silver spring morning, and we shall have
a splendid luncheon of *quenelles de brochet*; 2) in the fruit garden, far
enough from the house so only its tile roof can be seen, and a patch of
wall which would have appealed to Cézanne, old Jean is tending es-
paliers, which are so heavily laden this year that extra props are needed
if the plum and apricot branches are not to break under their own
bounty, and perhaps, Jean is thinking, some sort of scarecrow had better be devised if the birds are not to get the best harvest; 3) setting off
from the front terrace, where his wife and child watch him depart, the
Captain and his two white hounds are leaving for an afternoon's
grouse hunting, penetrating a thicket Corot would not have dis-
owned, one so teeming with mysterious patches of green that birds
must be everywhere, as the vigilant dogs attest: 4) it is a spring
evening, and the wild strawberries are especially fine this year, for it
has been a dry May, and while someone is tending a bonfire of last
year's vine-poles near the potting-shed, the ladies of the house are
berrying in the lower meadow, all but little Lucille, who is so busy
gathering daisies and cornflowers that she is no help at all; 5) there has

been an extremely rare March blizzard, and the woods are brilliant, as well as black, and it is easy to find the logs for the six fireplaces of the fine slate house behind the horse-and-cart, for the snow is not deep enough to cover them, merely to underline every likely trunk, stump, and branch that should be hauled home, while Neige, our black poodle, gallops through *his element*! These visions remind us of the remarkable uses to which nature is put in the French dispensation—not a twig from which you can fail to make an infusion, not a leaf which hasn't its place in the salad—everything has a purpose, everything *serves*, but only because it has been known to do so for so long and because no one has forgotten the lore transmitted for a thousand years. Even the Gothic ruin has its homesteading purpose, for we always pasture the horses there—somehow the grass is always richer, sweeter in the vicinity of those aspiring columns and stubborn vaults. It is a countryside where nothing is lacking, nothing is wasted—the middle of France, the *juste milieu*.

On Michael Lekakis

[1975]

This sculptor—who works in wood, or out of it; let me say that such works become, *through* the carved wood,* his pieces, for he cannot afford casting and he is averse, for reasons I shall consider, to welding—was born in 1907, in New York City.

Looking at him, listening (Lekakis can be voluble, he has "subjects"), you would not assume either biographical datum: facts are what require no meaning; where we are born, and when, are facts that defeat assumption. Perhaps it is characteristic of Greek men to age so little or so late (though it is a characteristic which may be disputed when the disputant evokes those stark peasants, gnarled as vine-stocks and still *young men*, to be met with on any path just outside Athens), but I surmise it is more an individual than a generic trait rehearsed here, a personal rather than a regional talent to submit to time and therefore triumph over it, without the marks and signs of a struggle. At sixty-seven, Lekakis is a stocky man with olive skin, very gentle eyes, and a galvanic spring in his still-black hair. He shakes hands with the same overwhelming courtesy that "disarms" his speech—the voice is low, rustling, reticent but not tentative, occasionally (when you appeal to his sense of the silly, of the impossible) exploding into a loud

---

*At the outset, it is well to remember that the "root" sense of *carve* grows out of the Greek verb *graphein*, to scratch, draw, write; and that a "carving" is, etymologically, a *grammar* of form, a *graph* of becoming.

giggle, even a delighted guffaw if you have appealed enough. There is, in his diction, the flexibility of the other language, the Greek he has always used in the intimate circumstances of life, the ordinary ones. Not that his English is accented, it is *insinuated* by an ulterior process—an English cited in adversity, as it were. The resonance of his speech, the reserve of his gestures, his capacity for stillness and for eloquence, make Lekakis an original without his being in the least an eccentric.

He has spent—or economized, in the Greek sense: he has ordered—all his life in New York's close-knit Greek community; he has traveled in Greece, but his habitat is not a place—it is people, people who talk Greek. His mother, with whom he lived till her death two years ago, never spoke English, nor did she know in any language (though we deduced a reckoning of about ninety) how old she was: it was of course the way she had of not being old at all, merely of aging, from within. Like Lekakis's own youthfulness, his mother's rejection of "counting time" is not an item extraneous to artistic biography, but has something, something indicative to do with the sculpture, and still more with the medium it takes shape, as we say, within—a medium being defined as a substance through which a force acts and an effect is produced. Neither age nor youth matters much in Lekakis's medium; it is process, the ecstatic realization of an identity given by growing, which is, literally, material. Wood, alone, of the sculptor's usual toys and toils can register the intimate action of gain and loss, that current which is lost, indeed, upon stone or clay or wax or metal, substances whose rhythm exceeds or stints human remarks. The branch, the root, the trunk through which such a force passes, and passing leaves a form (and forms a leaf), have their separate life in common, they share a singular passion. So that the various Greek names Lekakis gives to his pieces do not count for much, either, beyond the audible fact that they are Greek, one determination allied to so many others by which the sculptor—for all his New York promptitudes, his service in the American army (where he devised camouflage!), and his affection for the trees of eastern Long Island—regards himself, in temperament and philosophy and achievement, as distinctively Hellenic. The pieces, the sculptures might as well have all the one name which is *physis* or nature. All the works are strenuous recognitions of that energy which brings forth, which causes growth, which gets from here to there. Some of course are no more than nodes, knots, surds, and centers of such energy, brewing and brooding over the imminent act; but most—and the most ambitious, the most *realized*—of Lekakis's works are risks, reachings, exchanges, and efforts to transfer the force from one place to another, and thence back again; they are speculations, plunges as we say.

Risks indeed. Lekakis has never taught "art" within an institutional context, has never married, and his transactions with the market and museum establishments here—despite a first one-man show in 1941 and subsequent exhibitions of note—have been limited and "unproductive." He does not, being an original, pass himself on; does not pass himself off: there is nothing to show but the work. Problems arise in part because the work itself is not "reproductive"—because it is a confrontation, each time, with each piece of wood, here and now, as the shaping hand understands it in its past, in its becoming, past and becoming registered by the present grain, the gestures of protest and assent the organism affords. Lekakis is not easy about the few bronze casts he has been able (or enabled) to afford himself, and so the pieces—unlike those of all the other great sculptors of his period—stand unreproduced, one by one, unique in the splendor of their lonely joy, marked and signed by no more—and by no less—than the contours of the one immanence. Welding would be worse, worse than casting, I mean—it would be a violation of that gradual furnace which is the world, an over-acceleration of form-giving death to serve nothing but the will. Lekakis, though he works for years on any one piece, labors to escape the will rather than to impose it. That is what I had in mind when I said that Lekakis submits to time and thereby triumphs over it; his effort (and the paradox, surely, is that there must be an effort in order to relinquish the source of effort) is so to identify his imagination of form with his understanding of form that there will be nothing left over, nothing imposed. "The only problem," Lekakis says, "is to sustain my neutrality."

The climax of his work, if so much constant energy exerted upon so many occasions can be marked off in anything so separable as a climax, even illustratively, is to my sense the recently completed monumental piece* *Apotheosis*. It is carved from the trunks of three trees and their united root system; the group has been inverted—that is, has been placed to remind us of that other grove, that other sacred wood underground which is as ambitious in its reach downward as the branches and twigs and foliage stirring overhead. "Inverted" is an anthropomorphic impudence: in the maker's eye there is no up or down, certainly no right side up, there is but the realization of intricate energies, enabled . . . The three forms, the pulsating slender trunks and the more urgently excited linkings above them, have been set on a kind of table, surely it is an altar, and this upon one of Lekakis's characteristic bases or stems, itself gravely echoing the tetrahedral movement which suffuses, which links the entire group. Offered up on this pedestal, this dancing ground, we recognize in the three forms the most classic of all figural myths, the bodies we have learned to call the Graces bestowing, receiving, and returning—and what is it they bestow, receive, and return but the world itself, the energy which enables them to stand there, bearing down, bearing up? "There they were, still braiding together," says an eloquent contemporary poet of such a vision,

> Surfaces gently amove, one to another spilled:
> One giving, one accepting, one returning that flow,
> The benefits of the surface, light and awareness thrown
> Off them, through the eye, to the overseeing mind—
> And all this happening with barely a trace of motion,
> As if the three must be forever almost still,
> Fixed like an image so well known that memory
> Need never reanimate it even for an instant,
> There they were, unchanged, confirmed in their present selves,
> And all was silence, save the roaring of the world
> In its turning . . .

---

* "Each of these pieces," according to the Whitney Museum catalogue which illustrates *Apotheosis*, "has a history of work over a period of years. Some have been exhibited and reworked; exact dating is difficult." Like Bonnard, Lekakis is reluctant to let his art out of his hands, and always eager to get it back; there is always, he feels, more to be done, more life to be imparted, more rhythm to be discerned, attested to, asserted. No sculpture by Lekakis, then, is ever, by his own witness, completed: only abandoned. The sculptor lives among the sculptures, and they take their life, continuously, from him.

It is no accident that John Hollander is talking here not about Leka-kis's sculpture nor about some famous rendering of the Three Graces, but about a *natural phenomenon*, about three pools in Central Park. The apostrophe fits because it is to phenomenal nature that Lekakis seeks to return us in the most immediately sacramental of all his stat-ues, though whatever is rhythmic is religious (as any temple prostitute knew). It is to the linked images and figures, the joined emblems at the source of our understanding of what we later identify as bodies, objects, things, and persons, that Lekakis beguiles us; and so insistent is the dialectic between the measured and the found, the repeated and the spontaneous, the released and the constrained, that we cannot, at such a pass, call it abstract. Lekakis cannot, *for the life of him*, make an abstract thing, though he can make—it is the breath of life, precisely, it is the recuperative *breathing*—a ritual object, a figure which initiates even as it undergoes convention. As we say of verse, there is in Leka-kis's carved forms—tetrahedral, bulbous—the energy of repetition, of recovery, the rhythms of recognizance. In the wood—the logs, the trunks, the roots and branches as he finds them, searches them out— there is to start with only accident, only statement, only prose. Then they become, by that laborious prosody of his which has so much to do with time, with taking time—they become verse, capable of turn-ing back, of bestowing, receiving, and returning.

What singles out the works of Michael Lekakis from the sculpture of his age is, more significantly than their idiomorphic solitude, their at-titude toward the negative. By the negative I do not mean space, or the obverse of the full: I mean the impulses of destruction and erasure, of self-opposition (ranging from parody to suicide) which are the stock-in-trade of modernist art, and to a considerable degree the traded stock of our museums and galleries today. I believe it was Rodin who first exhibited (to a scorning audience) the evident *fragments* of the human body as finished *works*, as collaborations with catastrophe. The history of modernism is the history of that collaboration, usually in the form of an aporia—"I am writing this poem because I cannot write the poem I would write." All our modern art is an aporia, a confession of failure, though its successes, of course, are gigantic and gorgeous;

the point is not that they are successes, but that they operate within the decorum of failure. And since Rodin no sculptor, not even Henry Moore, has made works which do not acknowledge the very force which opposes their being. Indeed it is our modern piety to value the artist—consider the canonization we have accorded Giacometti, since World War II (and of course the Holocaust has a good deal to do with our accreditation)!—precisely in proportion to the amount of negativity (of destruction, of self-hatred, of unhappiness) he incarnates in his work. And if the negativity prevails, if the erasure triumphs then we make the artist himself (as we have done since Rimbaud) the succedaneum of the absent work. Our artistic pantheon abounds in such exemplary failures, and we keep their shrines well tended. Almost alone, then, among our makers of sculpture I single out Lekakis, whose sculptures have nothing to do, even, with those processes which—burning, melting, erasing, nailing—force upon matter its own despair, the recognition of its undoing. When Lekakis cuts into the wood, his action embodies a certain natural piety which seeks to observe (in both senses) the forces which produce the distinction, as Joseph Margolis calls it in his Whitney Museum catalogue, of every living thing. Lekakis carves to render the energies more explicit, less obstructed. But he never breaks apart, he never forces, he never, merely, fits. This is either the last sculpture of the pre-Socratic school, or the first of that post-modernism which, for once, agrees with Aristotle when he says that Plato, in the *Timaeus*, had proved that the good man was the happy man. Again, though, as in the matter of youth and age, I don't think *first* and *last* things are material to Lekakis: it is how you get from first to last which is his entire study, the substance of his revelation. The sculptures are distinct in their range: the warm worked waxed wood never opposes itself, never breaks off. As Nietzsche said of joy, it has the ring's will in it, and it is not by igneous but by ligneous conductors that the ring is closed: these are the statues of felicity. Theirs is a distinct morality, for by them we discover that happiness is not stagnant, never a still point. It is all in the reaching, the returning, the generosity or articulation that the bliss consists, the rhythm which proceeds from labor to work, from work to action. It is well to notice that in these days of privation, when so much is taken away, we can be—or we have been—given an art which is the antithesis of an art of suffering. Lekakis has made the works that Valéry's columns celebrate when they sing:

>Nous marchons dans le temps
>Et nos corps éclatants
>Ont des pas ineffables
>Qui marquent dans les fables . . .

We walk in time and our brilliant bodies have ineffable steps which leave their mark in fable.

Lee Listening

[1984]

Like *The New York Times* in its obituary, the rabbi in his eulogy emphasized the degree to which Lee Krasner Pollock was her own woman, promptly autonomous, prickly. And there is no doubt that the art world—ever since her husband's death (and probably before it, but I speak of her during the years I knew her: since 1956)—often rustled or rang with shock and vexation because of her clamorous insistence on what she felt, on *what she knew*, to be the truth. More than anyone I've ever met, Lee Krasner Pollock—who died this June, in New York, at age seventy-five—had a memory undistorted by apparent needs to inflect occurrence to her own advantage—or to anyone else's. Truth had its claims, and she served them; she observed them. It made her intractable, and to many people she became an obstinate, even an obstacular presence. Her independence was fervent and in the later years, more often than not, ferocious. Agreed. But there were other strands in the web, and because I prize them particularly—with the service at Springs cemetery still in my ears, as it were—I should like to invoke three moments of Lee's temperament that would otherwise not so readily be traced. We honor the dead we have loved by summoning them up immoderately, impatiently, as they lived.

It is May 1961. Work from Lee's own collection of Pollocks is to be shown in London the following month, and she is to go to England for the first time—indeed it will be the first time she has left the States since her return from southern France to Springs, New York, after Pollock's death. She is fifty-three and the idiosyncrasies of her figure loom (surely the right word) problematically for any dressmaker . . . What will she wear? Advised by her friend Alfonso Ossorio, she turns to Charles James, a grand old *couturier* neglected for a decade, once famous for his romantic, "architectural" clothes (created, as far as I knew, for society beauties who could "keep their figures," a retention out of Lee's reach). She commissions Mr. James to make her three "outfits" (I remember a stiff white-silk evening gown, a green woolen suit, a brocade cocktail dress—surely the whole wardrobe still exists somewhere). In those years Sanford Friedman and I were living on the place in Springs, and I recall the occasion: Charles James had asked Lee how she wanted to confront the English art world—"Do you expect to charm them? To astonish them? Do you want to take the room? I can make you look any way you want."

"I want to look invisible."

"That, Mrs. Pollock, is one thing I cannot do for you."

What he did do was indeed a surprise. The clothes emphasized all the apparent defects of Lee's body rather than attempting to conceal or compensate for them. I still see the sort of peplum tail that celebrated her can and the bunched up, almost medieval wadding over her belly—that Arnolfini suit. And lo! by some structural law unknown to "Mode," these clothes were a marvel: they made Lee look not invisible but invulnerable, not at all in fashion but beyond, entirely attractive and secure; and like no one else. But the woes of facture! There must have been a dozen fittings, buckram to silk, endless trips to the city for sessions, or rather standings—I think even on the way to the airport Mrs. Pollock was still being sewn into her traveling suit. But to our astonishment, Lee betrayed none of her now-celebrated impatience over all this process of dressing up. She was pleased, of course, to realize she would look her best—Kenneth Clark and "Sir Rothenstein," (as she called him) evidently made much of her company—but the point of my evocation is that she yielded entirely to the designer's vision, that she was willing to put up with any amount of aggravation in the service of an acknowledged art, her own or another's.

In that house on Fireplace Road, after Pollock's death, she could not stay by herself—she could not abide. If there was no house guest, if Sanford or I were unavailable, then a neighbor's daughter, a child! would do, but there had to be someone there. And if she could not sleep, even less could she concentrate on a book. What she loved, it turned out, was to be read to, and her appetite for reading matter, those summer nights, made the phrase more than a figure of speech: an almost material lack was being supplied, page after page. In any ordinary sense Lee was uneducated, but there are no ordinary senses for a mind as alert and inquiring as hers. She was obsessed, I think it is no exaggeration to say, by the romance of religion. Especially any religion other than the one in which she had been so severely reared—Lee was a good Jewess but a bad Jew, if you know what I mean. And after we had read many other books that were in the house, the one she wanted to hear (someone had given it to her, perhaps John Graham had left it on Jackson's shelf, I cannot imagine *how* we got to such a thing) was Cardinal Newman's *Apologia Pro Vita Sua*. We didn't get through it all, of course, but I remember Lee's absorption, her perfect attention, that power she had of fixing her mind without a moment's wavering upon Newman's vision, upon the argument that "the human race is implicated in some terrible aboriginal calamity, it is out of joint with the purposes of its Creator; this is a fact, a fact as true as the fact of its existence. . . . " And in the twenty-five years since those nights of reading aloud, I remember still how Lee stopped me with an almost whispered amazement when we came to Newman's departure from Oxford:

> . . . I called on Dr. Ogle, my private Tutor when I was an undergraduate. In him I took leave of my first college, Trinity, which was so dear to me, both when I was a boy and all through my Oxford life. There used to be so much snapdragon growing on the walls opposite my freshman's rooms there, and I had for years taken it as the emblem of my own perpetual residence even unto death in my University. On the morning of the 23rd, I left the Observatory. I have never seen Oxford since, excepting its spires, as they are seen from the railway.

Newman's *Apologia* had been written a hundred years before I was reading it aloud to her, and the doctrines it had been written to defend or dispute were essentially antipathetic to her spirit. But Newman's passion and his sensibility—she made me stop and read again about the snap-dragon, and she knew, she always knew, that what she was hearing could make her *see*. I think she mistrusted words—The Word—but if she did, it was because she knew the consequences of surrendering to their power.

In 1963, the Circle in the Square Theatre produced *The Trojan Women*, and Sanford and I took Lee, one bitter January afternoon, to see Irene Papas and Mildred Dunnock and the others in this play which Lee had never read—indeed she had never read, never seen a Greek play. I think she was ready to. Lee Krasner was the ideal audience for any articulated work of art, she was all there for it, utterly pliant to the demands of vision. Her attention to the Matter of Troy, to what Walt Whitman had called those vastly overpaid accounts, was a case of explicit rapture, and though I think the astonishment of Euripides' feminism, if we can call it that, made a part of Lee's delight, it would be simplifying to claim it was that only: the Greek image of our fate was what she answered with fascination, with fixity—the image of our fate to be met with just that plangent stoicism of Euripides. Sanford says Lee would have attended *Oedipus* or *The Bacchae* with the same utter conviction, the same enthrallment.

It is these moments of what I am calling submission, when perhaps all I mean is investment, that I hold dear. I want to celebrate Lee's talent for attention, for being present to any created vision. It is a talent I feel is concomitant with her talent for (merely) painting, and the memory of it is one that weaves another strand, I hope, in the received reticulation of all, besides her art, that remains of her among us.

Bald Heads

[1985]

Nearly two hundred headshots of entirely bald subjects, almost all of them men, posed full face, head on, close up, in the manner of police line-ups, without stipulation as to expression or emotion (no one has said Cheese), the absolute condition of flesh against a featureless outer darkness: the series of photographs Alex Kayser has taken is a meditation upon the responsibility of forms.* The form in question here, or rather the form responding, is that impulse of human identity we call the face, the visage, the countenance. In their etymologies, all three words suggest what the photographer's undertaking is to reveal, the made, the seen, the contained. Like so much else about ourselves—like our language, our food, our games—what we had thought was our nature is here revealed to be culture. Here the revelation is principally the effect of series art, which persuades us that each item in a set cannot admit the finality of any one member of that set. It is an art of erasure, in which each object or undertaking is superseded by a different version of itself. It has not arrived at or even acknowledged terminality. And because, by its inconclusive entertainment of the possible, this series of faces refuses narrative (or rather narrativity), because Kayser's photographs are inenarrable, they insist that our transaction with them is not "natural." It has none of the consecrated notions of beginning,

* *Heads*, by Alex Kayser, 1985.

middle, and end that are perceived to be the effects of biological life, as of stories. It is not nature here but choice, the assumptions and projections of culture, that produce their effect upon us. These faces are accountable for the way they look, for what they have in them. The beauty of these visages is a devised thing, not merely found but chosen, not merely chosen but invented, like—etymologically again—a poem, a fiction: something made.

But I speak too soon of the effect (the Beautiful) of these hypnotic images. In their formal insistence as Kayser has disposed them, none taking precedence over or leading up to the next (the sequence, although bound in a book, subject to your own progress or regress, shuffle and deal), they seduce us to generalization, they offer anthological proof. In the most abstract sense they *convince*. Indeed the French call the identifying photographs of criminals produced in evidence or exhibited along with the murder weapon *"pièces à conviction."* Just so. But let me loiter a little by noticing first of all what it is that the invariable absence of hair—these individuals are not so much bald as they are hair-free—constrains us to remark. In English, of course, we have no separate word for hair of the head, no current word, although we have the poetical and archaic *tress*. We have no word that, like *cheveux*, suggests discrimination from body hair and, by its very reluctance to form the singular, proposes something of hair's generic nature. This is a pity, for hair is our physiological myth of gender, of sexuality, of ecstatic growth. The grim assurance that our hair *keeps growing* on our dead skulls betrays something of its separate, elemental, mineral quality (like our nails, our teeth, our bones). Our hair relates us, and not only by analogy, to the movement of water, of fire, of foliage, and of wind—pulsing, undulating processes. Take away our hair and we are only human, mortal.

That is what these countenances present: the subtraction of hair, which in Western societies has been the readiest indicator of gender and in the governance of its wearing a clue to social docility or defiance. Without hair to tell us, we do not know much about the class of these persons Kayser has photographed. We cannot follow them into what used to be called their "walks of life." And upon continuous inspection, this inveterate feature—this having-no-hair—is perceived not

as a lack but as means and likelihood of recognition. The perfect geometry of the cranial arch over the faces (of every age, of every race) paradoxically releases the countenance from its ordinary obeisances to fashion,
to period, and brings us by the strange intensity of series art to a confrontation that must lead us to redefine what it is we mean by beauty.

Consider, as Paul Valéry used to say about a conch, a pebble, a
wave-whitened bone, whether, in their absence, it would be possible
to image forth—to invent—such faces, particularly in their juxtaposition, their endless *combinatoire*. Speaking as a creator, an artist, a sculptor, say, we might ask: Who could bring forth such things? And yet,
speaking as a consumer, say a lover: Who could imagine them as other
than they are? Is this not the spectacular beauty to which we are
brought down or raised up? Unable to conceive of such things, we yet
find them—once regarded—as inconceivable otherwise. It is, I think,
the absolute presence of the photographed flesh and its pointed symmetry that accomplishes this for us, and the polarities of black and
white camera work. In color, the incidentals would take over; the accidental nature of nature, so to speak, would prevail. But with only the
symbolic oppositions of dark and light to work with, the promptings
of shadow and the radiance of substance itself, we are lured to acknowledge much more readily the mathematical spell—if not of absolute black and absolute white, then of contrast between pale and
dark, between bright and dim—that Renaissance artists and alchemists
were always seeking to penetrate. We are lured to acknowledge the arith-
metic of interval, the geometry of transition, the algebra of expressive
analogy. The wars between singularity and parallelism are fought out
on these fields, and the kind of abstraction that Kayser has invoked,
has inveigled into his images by refusing to let his subjects *express
themselves*, convinces me for the first time that the fascinating analogies of the visage with the genitals that Freud so outrageously proposed are here evident in their simplicity, without distortion, without
the willful tugging of a Magritte or a Belmer. A centered singleness, a
framing doubleness (regardless of gender) seems to be the bilateral
essence of the face and of the reproductive body, the sexual self.

Further, the fact that all these faces are at first glance male (All? Are
there not some deceptions, some refusals of our easy contraries? Are

there not some women among these men?), male, yet without the signals of masculinity as a class society decrees them—faces without fashion beyond their own devising, jewelry and "facial hair" often of the most excruciating separateness—induces a further rumination on what the laws and license of pure gender might be. Notions of passivity and brutality, images of hardness and softness, of recession and advance are here reversed, flouted, and strangely erased. Surface and symbol exchange their customary positions, and the riddles of sexuality are proposed, proffered in a new way merely because of a simple radical alteration in the way we look at ourselves, time after time, head after head.

Certain correspondences of the exposed cranial arch with the chin, and the varying intervals of the zygomorphic frame around the mouth remind us here of what some news photographs of concentration camps and of shaved-headed collaborationists had hinted: that women look more like men than we had realized and that men look more like women. Or is it that in this artifice of abstraction both sexes approach a new framing of sexuality in which we shall have to reconceive what it is we want from the *other*? Do we want ourselves? Or perhaps the child, the *puer magicus* of the esoteric sciences? And are we ultimately appalled and repelled by precisely the beauty we cite in the transcendence of the accidental? That is, does our desire hang about the corners and crevices of perfection, unable to enter and act where it is displayed so elegantly, so ideally, so accurately? I am not teasingly withholding my solution, for I have none. I am merely prompted to these wonderments by the extraordinary *concordia discors* of all these pure masks, these pale apparitions on a nightmare ground.

And the final question to which Alex Kayser's series of photographs reduces or enlarges us is the matter of identity. (Is it a matter? Is it not, rather, the intersection, the collision, the subsidence of matters?) What is it that lets us, that makes us know a face? What can it be in the human countenance that enables the recognition of one out of a crowd of strangers? There are one or two celebrated visages among those in this book, and like as they are to the rest, we call out their names when we turn to their pages, as on the stairs of an opera house in some foreign city we call out the name when we recognize, among so many likenesses, one that is *unlike*, that is separate, singular—owned. But among these photographs, curiously enough, are so many samenesses, such congruence of form, that we finally wonder, as if by effect of the endless superimposition of transparencies, if the individuality of selfhood is not the greatest myth of all. Kayser's wonderful photographs make us wonder what we know about our looks and our looking. Are we known to each other (are we human) because we approach and fall away from the Beautiful? Are we beautiful because we are human? Or insofar as we are not? Surely the temptation of the total mask has not so much to do with secrecy (What is more accessible than even the most delicate of these lineaments?) as with an archetype of total sexuality, that magical image of the human enclosing and incarnating a self-nourishing desire. Not merely ourselves all over again and not merely the other, but perhaps what Frost meant when he said that what life wants

> Is not its own love back in copy speech
> But counter-love, original response.

Original response! The oxymoron thus reveals what the "facial mask," the face as fetish object, withholds and bestows by "giving itself away" in every sense. Only the camera, as I have suggested, can tell us such things; not our eyes, not the reality of the police line-up, the brothel selection. Consider the very word that governs these images, the word *bald*. When we refer to our National Bird, the bald eagle, we summon up that original sense of brightness, of shining, of "having a white head" that is also at the source of the word *black*. They both proceed from the Indo-European root *bhel*, what is burnt, bleak, and blinds us. That black and the bald, the white and the charred both have their roots in fire, the beginning of all things, as Heraclitus says. No accident then that we must develop a negative in order to have an image, that the blindness and the blaze, the blemish and the blank, all are reworkings of the one primal sound and scene, a blinding flash, a visionary impulse of delight.

The Nude

[1987]

In recent decades I have noticed that people attend "legitimate" theaters in order to see other people naked, not in order to see— as formerly in Batista's naughty Havana, 150 miles from home— Sensational Sex Acts. Of course the nakedness of pornography, on stage and page, maintains its old stand; although more accessible than ever, it is scarcely more inviting, scarcely more enviable—only less scarce. But it is not the transactions of an erotic agon that audiences flock to see. Not entirely. Nor is the naked body sought for contemplation as a respectable diversion on the pretext that it offers some sort of rhythmic kinesis or athletic prowess. Not entirely. Nor are the people who pay to see other people naked—or rather, nude—forgetting that they too have bodies much like those they pay to see: it is not a matter of overlooking the universal datum that all of us have a pair of these, or that none of us is born without one of those. Not entirely. There is, I believe, another factor involved in our patronage of these entertainments and of the publications, of every class and circumstance, of photographs of the unclad body. It is not entirely for vicarious sexual gratification that men and women alike seek out the show of nudity today as never before. What we seek is the *form* of the body, not its *accident* in the Thomist sense. I believe that nowadays we pay to see the entire flesh of both sexes disrobed, disclosed, displayed because we no longer possess an imaginative visualization of the human body long vouchsafed us by art. We no longer have a revealed image of the whole person that can sustain and satisfy our yearning for these most elementary notions of order and design within ourselves. Photography may be the only art (and only a pre-modernist aspect of photography at that, an ecstatic, lyric aspect committed to unity of being) that can still resolve our need, can answer our question: what does it mean to be—to look—human?

For five hundred years this need has been fulfilled by representations of the general body in art. As the art critic and psychoanalyst Adrian Stokes has observed in *Reflections on the Nude*, we cannot discover the nude entirely in our own bodies; narcissistic sensitivity obscures contemplation. Rather we must discover such integrity by a massive projection of ourselves, of *an image of ourselves*, onto the external that we then reabsorb. Therefore the conception of the undivided nude that is not ourselves is a singular and significant attainment, probably first achieved by Greek art and the Greek Olympians. For in a sense, without such a notion, such an image, such consciousness, we cannot be at home in a shared adult world. It is, as Stokes concludes, a premise of sanity that we are thus afforded, for this primary, impersonal love of ours for the whole figure is at the root of all human respect. Without what is so resonantly known as the state of nature, no State—or at least no citizens.

Yet despite our perennial cultural needs and political compromises, it is evident that the nude in art has altered its nature and even its aspect, as that art itself has altered. The change is a pervasive one, and it is generally expressed—or specifically identified—by the much-vexed word "modernism." Whatever modernism's manifestations in culture, we may remark this much about it: its modes and mechanisms are those of fragmentation, dissociation, erasure, and opposition. A work of literature, of music, of plastic art or architecture need merely exhibit these divisive, agonistic characteristics and energies with a certain insolence and determination (the names Picasso, Joyce, Pound, Stravinsky, Le Corbusier, Eliot, Webern will serve as a sort of shorthand here), for us to label them, with a certain resignation, a certain setting of the teeth "modernist." For modernism is habitually the arena of enormous repudiations, erasures, cancellations—in short, of negations. And it is evident that in all the arts, indeed in all the workings of culture, we have shifted from a poetics of *modulation*, whereby continuity is perceived to be the evidence of creative power, to a poetics of *collage*, an abrupt collocation or mosaic of shifting foci and citations functioning not by transformation but by transgression. I have always been struck by the coincidence of this development, actually of this explosion, with the advent of photography in our societies (photography both as a general practice readily available to any enthusiast, and as a singular art created by trained professionals). And I propose the phrase "the photographic moment" for that period (shall we say 1880? perhaps as early as 1870? the likelihood must in any case occur long before the century's turn) when the great upheavals of modernism took place in our visual culture, irreversible and inseparable from the technology—chiefly the internal-combustion engine and the film-loading camera—that circulated them to the ends of the earth and to the center of our psyches. As a poet I have been immensely taken with the notion that in order to produce most photographic images there must initially be *a negative*. This platitude of photographic technology has become part of the language itself, and most appropriately so.

For modernism is most appropriately taken as an inclusively negative concept, I think, one regarded as a field of conflicting energies, of sudden juxtapositions rather than of continuous modulation. Parody and critique, erasure and collage, are the characteristic dynamics of modernism, and they preside over, if they do not bring about, the disappearance of the old order, the structures and hierarchies of Western culture. Photography has of course been pursued and practiced as an art since its inception, and naturally its history contains instances and achievements that, although occurring within the chronological bounds of modernism, transcend negation. "The photographic moment" knows contradictions; the nudes of Weston and of Stieglitz are glorious examples of a virtually classical apprehension of wholeness, an almost Hellenic attainment of the whole nude. Yet I suggest that photography-as-technology made possible a sweeping, indeed a seismic, alteration in consciousness—or rather, it made possible a seismic alteration in the *manifestation* of consciousness in our societies. The destruction of the nude as a harmonious balance of forces is a representative process of modernism in *all* the showings of our visual culture; and such a carnage was most likely empowered by the (often horrified, certainly alarmed) recognition that for the first time in many centuries the nude body was not inevitably an entity in which to take pride.

The better to comprehend what has happened to ourselves (for there is an interrelation between our conception of the nude and our assessment of ourselves), I suggest that three significant new dimensions have appeared in our recognition of art that have immitigably converted what we understand, specifically, by the nude in art. This assertion concerns *all* the arts, those of time as well as of space, poetry, and music quite as much as those of imagery, plastic representation, and design.

Contemporary with and related to the assimilation of photography as a universal practice, we have assimilated three transmutations in our notion of what art might, indeed must, be. These three new organizations, or dimensions, oppose all that our forefathers held dear by way of critical determinations in high culture. They have implications so extreme they cannot yet be labeled with any neatness of phraseology, for they have not receded into the comfort of historical periods. If obliged to offer an identification, I should suggest "unconscious art." (Is the photograph not the supreme manifestation, as Roland Barthes has suggested in his essay *Camera Lucida*, of an art capable of emblematizing, of *embodying*, the unconscious?) Dissatisfied with labels, let me put it crudely in terms of our representations of the nude: for the first time in historical memory, we acknowledge in self-representation the Art of the Primitive (or the archaic, the tribal, the aboriginal—what cultural chauvinism calls "the savage"); the Art of Unreason (or of irrationality, madness, the absurd); and the Art of the Child (or of the infantile, the untaught, what Sir Herbert Read calls the innocent eye). It is easy to remark, in the very proliferation and slipperiness of this vocabulary, a considerable tendency to overlap. Frequently we are reluctant to distinguish between or among the art of the mad, the art of the tribe, and the art of the child—for are they not all crystallizations or floodings of what the poet Wallace Stevens identified as *a tidal undulation underneath*, an eruption of forces no longer ordered by those amassed and cumulative disciplines that were in place until "the photographic moment"?

Yet the remarkable thing is that we are nowadays quite convinced by our museum curators, our art schools, our aesthetic philosophers that all three dimensions are intrinsic to art. We are prepared to forswear all the salon pieties and to acknowledge that the Sepik mask, the schizophrenic's drawing, and the six-year-old's clay bogeyman (wherein the doll and the idol are indissociable) function as authentic avatars of art, an art that once dared not speak its name but that now fulfills its unspeakable purposes of terror, ecstasy, and apotropaism.

And it is through the lens of this triple transformation that we must perceive the image of the modern nude. First of all, though, we have discovered that the naked body can be parcelled out, can be fragmented, the more readily to be fetishized. It is here, I think, that photography assumes its greatest responsibility. I believe Rodin was the first artist to exhibit (not produce) as a complete work a fragment of the body, creating an erotic fixation upon a separate limb. And Rodin (along with Degas) is probably the first sculptor to make use of photography in the creation of his works.

From the fixated, fetishized, fragmented nude it was but a step to that impersonal cutting up of collage, which became the most distinctive invention of modern art. Where once—say from Phidias to Canova—we were obliged to conceive the nude body as a complex of thrusts and tensions whose reconciliation symbolized the principle of all the "figure arts," we now know that the naked body can be a "heap of broken images," of barely salvaged pieces, even a staccato dissolution whereby for the first time perhaps since Rodin's *Adam* (which in Hebrew means "red clay") man is unmade in his own image. If photography has identified itself with the glorious totalizing emblems of the past, it has as often dramatized the possibilities of the fragment and the fetish, thereby constituting much of the evidence of our knowledge.

The great witness to this transformation from the whole to the fragment-as-symbol-of-the-whole is of course the poet Rilke, whose account of the headless torso of an archaic Apollo ("archaic" is another of those ambiguous words we use when we are uncertain about the historical status of the "primitive," the "tribal") is the first great modern nude in poetry (the latest is surely Irving Feldman's ecphrasis of George Segal's white plaster bodies in "All of Us Here"). Without a head, Apollo's body looks at Rilke, and at us, from all its remaining flesh ("his gaze, only turned down, lingers and gleams"). There is no place in this flesh, Rilke says, that does not *see us*. Here the reversal of categories is ocular—the observer is being observed, in turn, by the fragmentary statue that has been transformed into a single though total eye. The reversal is possible precisely because the sculpture is broken, fragmentary. If the nude had actually incorporated Apollo's head, Apollo's eyes, the reversal could not occur. The absent eyes allow for an imaginary vision to come into being, making the eyeless sculpture into an Argus-eye capable of engendering by itself all the dimensions of space. It is absence that creates the space necessary for the reversal; it is fragmentation that finally leads to a totalization it seemed, at first, to make impossible.

The art of the child, the vision of the innocent eye, has had particular consequences for the envisioned nude. Think of the work of Paul Klee, of Joan Miró, of Jean Dubuffet, of Paula Modersohn-Becker, in easel painting alone, and it is apparent that the child's apprehension of function has triumphed over the post-Renaissance artist's comprehension of structure: in the art of the child, as it has been assimilated by the nude in modern art, there is no attempt whatever to separate the person from that person's body: every virtue resides in or is symbolized by the flesh, together with all humiliation, threat, and squalor. This indissociability is what modern nudity has learned from the art of infantilism. Indeed we note that children, perhaps because they are the portion of humanity most unceremoniously habituated to nakedness, do not make a point of representing the human figure as specifically unclothed. Of course there is nakedness in children's art, but there is no nudity, that idealized construct. For the child, nakedness is neither a customary nor an assumed condition; it is a functional dimension, and can quite readily be perceived *through clothes*, which become transparent indicators of status or category, but never hamper the perception of an infantile fantasy that has, so to speak, corporeal intent. But if the nude as an idealized whole is not a distinctive category for the child, the fragmented, partial body is very much one, and as such has entered into the canons of modernism. The "distorted" perspectives of the child create a strange proximity of certain organs, the impinging might of certain members, producing not so much a represented body in the child's artwork but a graphism of forces, a redistribution of powers that surrealist photography, for instance, has been quick to acknowledge. If nakedness exists at all in the child's art, it is as a version of need; and the grotesquerie of human need has assumed a certain grandeur in modern art.

This is one dramatic and vigorous transformation of the nude, and perhaps one of the most evident: what was once conceived of as an enduring figuration, a temple of the integrated adult psyche, is in modernism materialized—and often *broken down*—as a diagram of momentary interferences, sometimes with the character of an oppressive weight or listlessness left by the child's terrors and thefts, as well as by infantile delights and satisfactions. The celebrated commonplace once uttered so dismissively in galleries before a canvas by Jackson Pollock or Cy Twombly: "My five-year-old could do that!" has become a sort of accolade, the recognition of a truth of vision over and above any mere transmutation of matter into ideal form, of which the nude for centuries had remained the most complete example.

In the art that our Western societies have persistently called primitive, barbarian, archaic, there is also no such thing as the nude, nor even—as in children's art—the naked. There is the body, variously decorated and embellished, scarred and marked with ritual significances, but no state of "undress." The costume of the unclothed, when intended to be looked at, is subject to its own standards of what we call fashion, but it does not acknowledge the body in itself as in any way irregular or arresting. To some degree, this sense of the body's propriety—"a woman is always clothed in the dignity of her own nakedness," as our models are sometimes told—has pertained to the nude in Western art as well, but with an ever-fading sense of the sacramental, or the transgressive, and a constant trivialization of beholding that in modernism has been revitalized, even revolutionized, by a mimicry of tribal practices, as we could observe at the 1984 exhibition "Primitivism in Twentieth Century Art" at the Museum of Modern Art in New York. Although objects of African and Oceanic provenance, cult, and ceremony had been in some sense "available" in Europe since the 1880s—what I am calling "the photographic moment"—it was only in the first years of the twentieth century that they all at once became a numinous presence for modern artists in their representation of the nude: for Picasso, for Giacometti, for Modigliani, for Man Ray. These artists, and many others around them and following them, retained the notion of the nude, certainly as the consequence of a love of rational proportion. Yet the pattern of perfection that since the Renaissance has gradually become blurred, blunted, and bleached out required this unexpected and often frightening union of sex and geometry that was observably sacred, observably part of a spiritual function not to be evaded by even the handsomest obeisances to studio convention (Matisse) or to the integrity of materials (Brancusi). The idea of offering the naked body for its own sake as a serious object of contemplation nowadays erects a certain barrier of misunderstanding that I believe only our response to the primitive can overcome. It is a sad paradox that even as we have erased the reality of tribal cultures from our world, we have conceded the force, even the necessity, of their human representations among us. Malraux and Robert Goldwater pointed out in the 1930s that there is no modernity without primitivism—art's images of the body must reject the salon or not exist. Much of the work of Lucas Samaras and Robert Mapplethorpe, for example, is evidence of this, although "our" salon has managed to transform its thresholds in order to capitalize on their achievements. As André Breton once proclaimed, "Beauty must be convulsive or not be at all." The insertion of the primitive, the intercession of the tribal in our arts, has been so pervasive and so inveterate that we are in danger of forgetting—as when we look at Man Ray's famous photograph of the-nude-as-minotaur—that there was once a working method among Western arts that "proved" by representations of the human form that the gods were like men and could be praised for their life-giving beauty rather than for their death-dealing powers.

Most recent, I believe, of the three transmutations that have so profoundly altered our vision of the nude is the onset and acknowledgment of the art of the mad. The insistences of Surrealism—that first

constituted cultural movement whose artistic expression always included photography as a major resource—celebrate the unconscious
as a version of what is commonly called madness, the irrational (pop-
ularly, the "wacky"), unreason; not so much the nonhuman as the
nonhumanistic in culture. Yet Surrealism and psychoanalysis are but
two frequently interwoven currents of a stream that has many other
tributaries. Cruelty, brutality, and affectlessness are perceived to have
their part in the story. The great body of works—objects of the most
diverse provenance, often made by children and by "savages," of
course—that constitute Jean Dubuffet's *Musée de l'Art Brut* (and how
are we to translate *brut* save as: unmediated by consciousness and by
culture—primitive, infantile, and crazy?) entirely reorganizes our received and traditional notions of what a created work, *a work of art*,
might be. And particularly with regard to representations of the human body, the irrational, the unreasonable, even the irresponsible,
have their metamorphic contribution to make to our modernity. The
celebrated photographs of funhouse-like distortions of the nude by
André Kertész remind us, by their seeming reference to absurdity and
nonsense, how much we have recuperated since Nietzsche, van Gogh,
and Artaud from what was once dismissed as raving chaos. Henceforth, it is impossible for representations of stabilizing myths and beliefs to appear to encompass our actuality adequately. Among those
myths and beliefs is the confidence that the displayed naked human
body is something in which to take pride as a source of meaning and
delight. No longer a reconciliation and a harmony, the nude is often
represented in our art as an interrogation of existence, as problematic
of pleasure, and as a reliable cancellation of identity: so many corollar-
ies of the art of the mad.

If we are to recover our respect for the general body, which is the seal
upon our respect for other human beings as such, we must regain the
vision of the nude in art that these momentous transformations of the
infantile, the barbaric, and the irrational have so often alienated us
from (though it is to be seen, and celebrated, that photography has often been one means of a recuperation of the classic ideals and idealiza-

tions, the source of a recovery often despaired of in the other figure arts). I do not mean, of course, that we can squeeze the child, the primitive, and the madman out of our consciousness, as Chekhov said it was our human task to squeeze the slave out of ourselves. We know they are there, are part of being human, and in some sense the nude must henceforth be the container for the sum of their meanings, while it is also from a concatenation of their meanings that the nude, *the form of the body*, is constructed. Our innocence is irrecoverable, and therefore the reappearance of the nude as a whole and harmonious creation—what might be meant by the old phrase *the body politic*—will necessarily be a new invention, a new discovery.

Is it not possible that the audience for photographic versions of the nude are the catechumens of an elementary art, a new culture (of the nude) that might again afford us what we pursue so hungrily, so desperately: the rudiments of a civil art?

The Mapplethorpe Effect

[1988]

In a late poem, Jorge Luis Borges thanks the gathering darkness of amaurosis for rescuing him from the *prolixity of the real*: what is poetically singular is to be discerned by its disengagement from the world's plurals, necessarily prosaic. In any consideration of an artist's work, something of these constraints, these sunderings, must be invoked, even when it is the *prolixity of the unreal* which throngs the photographer's images, a congestion of fantasy and obsession. For in even the most schematic and fixated achievement, more meets the eye and the lens than the mind can discriminate. In Robert Mapplethorpe's work—granted, in his early work—there are a number of unexpected images, for example, of the sea, the one subject which cannot be made to pose; and in some of his latest work, anomalously in color, there are images of growing plants and of animals in the wild—granted, only an alligator's snout, but could even Mapplethorpe pose an alligator? As in the work of any venturesome artist, there are examples here which would appear to betray the strictness which the thematizing (and sense-making) onlooker must approve. It makes any effort of appreciation more arduous, having to register exceptions to what we were convinced—and happy with the conviction—was a kind of monomania. That Mapplethorpe is a gifted photographer of children, for example, or that he can allow the merest *furniture* to clog the attention so overwhelmingly bestowed upon *Brian Ridley and Lyle Heeter*, 1979, is an obstacle to our perception of him as a specific kind of artist—narrow, ensorcelled, not to be distracted.

No feature of a body of work, then, can be so important as it seems in our discussion of it—there will be, in Mapplethorpe's copious oeuvre, almost invariably a contradiction to the perceived drift, or even to the tyrannous current; he is venturesome enough, as I say, to inspect the nostalgias of the life we all live, of the sights we all see, as well as his own visions and vilifications. Yet for the rapt artist, the life we all live is not enough of a subject—and for the photographer, not enough of an object. It must be life with an inclination, a leaning, *a certain slant of light*, a tendency to shape itself only in certain forms, to afford its most valued and valuable revelations only in certain . . . darknesses.

And so it is with a crowding awareness of other pictures, a consciousness of their extension beyond my focus, that I shall discuss only some works, by no means a majority of the images Mapplethorpe has made, though I think they will be the ones he has made his own. I think, too, that in the general discussion of photography, the camera's powers are too generally received to permit their being looked at, effectively looked into and accounted for, unless they be isolated, epitomized—like something in an anthology of provisional faiths. Of course there are, in Mapplethorpe as in other photographers we call fetishistic or fanatical, experiences beyond such sudden identification; indeed the camera by the nature of its processes invites a diversity of experiences—for like every art, photography has its "interferences," its obstacles to singular realization, and an artist is never more than partly himself—"a Mapplethorpe," say, or "a Borges," at any one time. There is besides a kind of outward impulse which keeps our recognition of his specialty muffled quite as much as there is an inward motive which keeps his specialty going in the first (and last) place. My desire to constitute or at least to estimate an imaginative unity in Mapplethorpe's photographs will violate their loyal dispersion in experience. His is an extreme case, perhaps, but is it not always worth making the case, whenever we claim to identify what an artist is doing? Further constructions can be put upon these things, other things can be seen in them beyond or within what has been seen. Here, then, an essay in emphasis, for as Borges himself would surely have acknowledged, even the poems of darkness must be read in the light.

Mapplethorpe differs perhaps from other artists in photography by this insistence upon the darkness: if other photographers are artists precisely insofar as they *see the light* and register its capacity to seize and transform our response to the world, Mapplethorpe would be the photographer who sees the darkness. As he said in 1986, with suggestive grammatical disregard: "my work is about seeing—seeing things like they haven't been seen before."

I have presumed to say that he sees a particular darkness through three subjects: through flowers, through faces, through figures, discarding the prolixity, then, of the real and discarding the prolixity of the unreal. When we are not prolix (which means when we are not liquid), then we are concise (which means we are crystalline), and this indeed is Mapplethorpe's quality and his goal: to restore potency to flowers, to restore aesthetic dignity to the genitals, and to restore form to identity—and in so doing to set his images before us in such a way that we realize that what might never have been seen at all can never be seen as anything but what it appears. Which is, as Paul Valéry used to say, the realization of the beautiful.

FLOWERS

Flowers are the sexual organs of plants. In all Mapplethorpe's photographs of flowers I have seen, they are no longer a growing member of plants, but dissevered from them, their provisional status emphasized, their duration *on sufferance*, in bowls, vases—one exception: *Tulips*, 1983, still growing from bulbs but not in earth, not destined for any completion of their cycle, but clumped together in a wooden flat, a suffocating contiguity of bloom, as *contra naturam* as any of the arresting orchids and lilies thrust into a thimbleful of water or simply cropped, like *Easter Lilies*, 1979, which admit of no attachment to anything beneath a stem. Yet if Mapplethorpe's flowers are never shown in any kind of fertile continuity, neither are they seen to have any traffic with mortality—no fallen petals, no withered or faded parts. Whatever their complexity of structure and fragility of substance, the flowers are shown—sometimes leaning into the shot from the side, with no basis in fact—*to perfection*, in their heightened, erectile state, engorged with the liquids which make them such solids, driven through the green fuse by that force which, Dylan Thomas wrote, drives our human age as well. In these images, which are never afforded a landscape or even a setting where the condition of being indoors might be implied by the absence of weather or world, withholding any object that might serve as a reference of scale, the flowers are indeed fetishized so that we must perceive them not only as the sexual organs they are, but as analogies to our own. In his 1985 collection *Black Flowers*, Mapplethorpe plays this game of equivalents in quite explicit terms, setting the flower studies opposite his highly genitalized male nudes which counter a millennial convention of pelvic disregard or concealment—he insists that we confront what Yeats once called "the mystery which touches the genitals, a blurred touch through a curtain." But Mapplethorpe would focus that blurred touch, would compel us to see with the same focusing wonder the "expression" of the uncircumcised glans and the "assertion" of the cut flower. The penis, in all the images by Mapplethorpe I have seen, is never shown erect, the flower always so, its erethism undeterred "by any natural thing." (Yeats again: Mapplethorpe has certainly sailed to Byzantium, no country for old men indeed; unlike Rodin, his greatest rival in the adoration of "bodily shape," Mapplethorpe "sees" only the fulfilled, perfected physique as his subject, his satisfaction.) And even when the images of flowers and of the male genitals are not conflated, there are still extraordinary coherences: the photograph of *Michael*, 1983, in white tights which against a black wall make the genital contour more than explicit—which make it a decorative arabesque his stare defies us to disregard—leads us to the 1982 orchid in its prim white vase against a gaining outer darkness, with but the one iris leaf-spear to hold its analogously genital outline against our mind (even the verbal pun is presented: orchis-testicle). More surprisingly still, the 1976 photograph of *Mark Stevens*, in which the nude model arches over a stone altar so that his genitals are laid on the surface like some sacrificial first-fruits, annexes the 1985 *Eggplant*, in which the arcuate vegetable precisely echoes, in its identically shadowed realm, the phallic oblation. In all of Mapplethorpe's flower pictures, with their spe-

cific equivalents in his images of human sexual organs, we are granted
what one of his Italian critics has called, after Nietzsche, the retroac-
tion of form upon force. In these genital studies, human and botani-
cal, something very intricate, very particular, and yet very generic is—
I believe for the first time as a deliberate artistic manifestation—
articulated, studied, with curious consequences for our conventions
and decorums with regard to gender. Flowers—just think of Emily
Dickinson, of Georgia O'Keeffe, with their patient explorations of
bloom!—which have so traditionally been associated with female art
and female organs, are here, in their engorged, erectile, anti-chthonic
forms, identified with that "male" principle we so clumsily (and often
so reductively) decry as "phallic"—in the brutal sense that the word is
made to share with our related English word "bull." Indeed, much of
Mapplethorpe's enterprise, in the flower photographs made to
"match" photographs of male genitals, as well as in such images as the
one of *Ken Moody*, 1984, where the oneiric figure (eyes closed) holds,
on the rim of a bright circle, a fully open tiger lily: evident analogy
of the sexual organs here not revealed—much of Mapplethorpe's
enterprise urges us to see the male genitals as *potential forms* of great
delicacy and poise, paired with the thrusting, assertive, conventionally
female figurations of flowers. What is spoken, Heidegger says, is
never—and in no language—what is said. I might add: not even in the
language of flowers.

There is a further point to be made, or a perception (the word is a
translation of "aesthetics") to be reached with regard to these fiercely
present flowers—one that is suggested by Susan Sontag in her 1985 essay on the photographer: Mapplethorpe, she observes, could never
become a photographer of accidents. He wants to photograph whatever can be made to pose. "What he looks for, which could be called
Form, is the quiddity . . . of something. Not the truth about something, but the strongest version of it." An extremity of strength: that is
why these flowers are always, for all their artifice and their assertion,
perfect specimens, luminously disposed—as in *Orchid with Palmetto
Leaf*, 1982—to reveal the pinnacle, the crisis of *la condition botanique*,
of that kingdom where only a master of shadows can reveal to us,
without color, without odor, that all is yet Erotic Form.

And that is why the male genitals are often presented—as in the two notorious images of 1982, the *Untitled* naked man with the Klan-like pillowcase over his head and *Man in Polyester Suit*, 1980—as surrogates for the face, forming with the carefully included hands a new and quite recognizable expressive entity, though one for which our culture has no accommodation. It is without incident or anecdote that these flowers, like these unaroused genitals, are presented: not as dramatic power by as lyric potentiality—as what Valéry, speaking of the effect of light upon the sea, calls "a mass of calm and visible reserve."

Our received sense of "flower" as "epitome" is invoked by these images: to flower is to come to a point of physical perfection which has something of the *sacred* about it—the fine flower of manhood, not a frivolous word in the context, though by Mapplethorpe's evident parodies of Muscleman poses and *House Beautiful* arrangements, it is a word manqué even more than a word mocking; it is a sacred traduced by commonplace associations, and Mapplethorpe's task is to restore the gravity which has leaked out of what is unspeakable.

FACES

Mapplethorpe has made a great many portraits—recently even a commercial book of *50 New York Artists* (1986), with very little variation in the images, either head-on or profile shots, all but ten against a blank ground; and all his exhibitions and other publications have contained many portraits. Inveterately, he supplies the names of his nude models as if these works too were portraits, and of course he has made a number of self-portraits, including the sensational pair on the front and back cover of *Certain People* (1985), presenting himself as parodically male and as appealingly androgynous. (The appeal, of course, is to our sense of participation: nothing of Diane Arbus's fascinated repulsion in Mapplethorpe's exploration of drastic erotic identities; unlike most photographers, he is willing, even eager, to expose his own narcissistic fantasies, nor is there that sense of "dressing up"—or down—which makes Leonor Fini's self-portraits as the heroine of *Histoire d'O* so trivial a masquerade.) Mapplethorpe's portraits, as he said when Sontag asked what he does with himself when he poses, try to find that part of the subject which is self-confident. This is by no means a part of which the subject is readily conscious. We may identify Mapplethorpe's people if we are cognizant of certain social and artistic circles, otherwise we merely learn to know them as they appear. As early as 1971, he made the astonishing confession—or was it a challenge, even a defiance?—about his work as a portrait-maker: "I often don't know who these people are. It's not that important to me. I never had heroes."

If he never had them, he makes heroes now: the carefully arranged, cropped, lighted, or rather shadowed countenances assert just that degree of victoriously fulfilled flesh which—without envy or *schadenfreude*—exemplifies a heroic mode of being there. The great majority of these faces are of beautiful people, particularly of black men perceived as physiognomies so symmetrical as not to admit those "accidentals" which for most of us constitute the recognizable self (*Ken Moody*, 1983); and almost no one smiling. A remarkable exception to this general solemnity of regard is the portrait of Louise Bourgeois (one of three superb effigies of old-women artists in *Certain People*, the others, Alice Neel and Lee Krasner, revealed as flaunting the damages of a lifetime like a shield before them, stoically endured). Sometimes exhibited or reproduced in a cropped version, the Louise Bourgeois portrait then seems no more than a rictus of mysterious complicity. Seen in the version Mapplethorpe prints in the book, the complicity is accounted for: under her arm (and she is wearing a shaggy—monkey-fur?—jacket which accentuates the spooky side of things), she carries like a sidearm her own sculpture of a two-foot phallus-and-testicles, lighted and held in such a way as to form the base of a sinister—castrational?—pyramid. The livid light on Louise Bourgeois's face, explicitly tracing the seamed and wrinkled flesh, pronounces sentence on the entire composition: like some sibyl out of Petronius, the sculptor is on her way to a ceremony of puzzling erotic nature; she knows what she is about to do, as the shocking hand makes explicit: fingers can be taught, but that thumb was born knowing.

Within these faces, then, is a potential identity, not of necessity the celebrated or notorious ones associated with the name attached to the face (an exception: the portrait of the late Roy Cohn, made in 1981, is precisely the portrait of everything that name has come to signify, and the portrait is not so much a proleptic death mask as a Veronica's Veil of ill-omen, floating in a black void, bodiless and therefore soulless). A Mapplethorpe portrait *represents* a power of the flesh as a Mapplethorpe flower constitutes an effigy of sacred assertion: it figures Being taken—posed, beguiled, inveigled by all the sortileges of darkness—to the very limits of itself, all that flesh is heir to without the connivance of circumstance. I approach this instance of the sacred gingerly, as does Mapplethorpe himself: implicit in each of these faces, famous or obscure, desirable or desolate, is that pulsion of energy, a velleity within the flesh, *against* the flesh often enough, which seeks to transcend the given, which counters the pervasively downward pull, the gravity of substance. Sometimes this power, or this potentiality, flickers very near the point of extinction, as in the portrait of *Alice Neel*, 1985, where only the open mouth—open on the same blackness as that which surrounds the disarranged hair—signifies an effort to resist subsidence. But often the symmetrical delight of certain faces is so instinct with just the counterpoise of potency, as in the portrait of *Ken Moody*, 1983, that there is no need for the eyes to be open, no need for the features to *register*. What we call the *facial mask* has momentarily triumphed over individuality, over the personal, the human, and all that the merely human hides. Indeed, in the face of such an image I no longer know why we must praise an artist, a photographer, for being "human," when as Mapplethorpe shows us, all that fulfills and completes humanity is inhuman, is superhuman . . . is divine?

FIGURES

In Mapplethorpe's photographs, the world of inorganic form is absent save as it is defined by the organic. What we think of as Leonardo's circle, and Leonardo's square inscribed within it, are evoked by many of the astonishing bodies, astonishingly posed in *Black Book* (1986), and indeed the geometry of these cherished figures is insistently caressed by deliberate and theatrical lighting, by occasional props of flowers—

the sheaf of six calla lilies held by *Dennis Speight*, 1983, alludes to a potential orgasmic flowering, a sort of seminal bouquet—and by the
photographer's repeated assertion that it is the bodies of black men
which will take the light, and the darkness, with the most resolute formal determination. In most instances, Mapplethorpe's images of the
nude male are isolated, solitary. Exceptionally the drama is offered as
dialogue (an embrace, an agon between parallel black and white forms);
characteristically, the "subject" is a lyric efflorescence within the intervals and analogies of a single body. Moreover this single body itself
will not be taken whole but cropped (literally, anatomized) so as to
declare its symmetrical relations intramurally, as it were, without reference to classical canons of wholeness, of completed form—rather,
with regard to new proportions, new affinities, among them figures
which include the genitals in unabashed exploration of what has always been treated as the body's disgraced member.

In his studies of the bodybuilder Lisa Lyon, it is of course a reversal of stereotypes which Mapplethorpe effects. Precisely the kind of
lyric stasis so lovingly studied in male bodies traditionally granted
movement and power (in other words, a paradoxical anti-phallicism,
if we take our lead from the culture's interpretation of the phallic as
dominance, as inflexibility, as denial of the other's response) is withheld in the *Lisa Lyon* series: Lyon repeatedly subverts, in images of
sleek force and definition, the conventions of female iconography she
is made to criticize, to parody, to transform. "Seeing things like they
haven't been seen before"—Mapplethorpe's words hover over all his
nude figures, though I am convinced that the major revelation of
these studies, the burden of their enormous effort—in which the camera is compelled to acknowledge desire with an avidity not just optic
but haptic—is that of the body's implicit *energeia* to rise, to mount,
to erect itself into an insurgent principle.

Against what? What is the antagonist of these forms so suavely figured, so cunningly sectioned to reveal new anatomies, inadmissible
analogies, what Macbeth calls *understood relations* which bring forth
the secret'st man of blood? Perhaps the answer is given most diagrammatically in the photograph *Thomas*, 1986; in darkness, tangent to a
great white arc on the right, the frontal nude—garishly lighted so that

it has lost its bronze patina so prized by Mapplethorpe—yearns upward, strives, grasps (though the hands are cropped) for ascension
while the body *depends*, the very organ of erection limp, the double so-
cle of the thighs ponderous in their (also cropped) downward thrust.
In all Mapplethorpe's figures, though, each separate body is its own
repertoire of ascensional pulsions, reservoirs of potential elevation
against the gravity of its own structure, a headlong architecture of an-
titheticals.

The unified if never uniform impulse I would discern in Mapplethorpe's flowers, Mapplethorpe's faces, Mapplethorpe's figures is a
continuous struggle, the contestation of heft. Solemnity of effigy is
the consequence, I suppose, of a certain undecided outcome: flowers
spring up against their own weight; engorged with juice, they are
never shown attached to the cycle which would make their momentary victory more than just that. Faces are transpicuous with energy,
with appetite, yet there is always the gravity of the features, of the flesh
which pulls, which *ponderates*, in the sense of bearing down what aspires to rise, to mount to expression, to identity. And figures glow
with the potency of their rhythms, their newly revealed analogies of
form—yet even as these arresting pelvic landscapes can rise and indeed
reach beyond themselves, they are shown always in their dense and
onerous potentiality only, the long muscles and the delicate veins finally burdensome, unredeemed—impugning all we used to mean by
"phallic." If I reach for such terms as transcendence, redemption, the
apparatus of the sacred, it is because I used to think Mapplethorpe's
photography was grim with the restrictive occasions of obsession and
fetishism; but after a certain meditation, pondering their reasons and
their realizations, I discern these pictures—a good share of them—to
be emblems of contested mortality, grave with the contradictions of
organic life in their aspiration to ecstasy, as crystalline in terms of their
own art as the sonatas of Scarlatti or the last paintings of Mondrian,
but as problematic, as imprecatory as any representation of the body
I know, fond enemy and ally.

The Menil Collection

[1990]

They were palaces we wandered through, or were marched through in giggling squads—palaces and mausoleums, and we hushed our voices as they echoed across the vast interlocking halls, without accommodation for the likes of us. Such was the "museum experience" most Americans of my generation have had— may have still, in the provincial European cities, even in the capitals: the Louvre, the Hermitage, the Capodimonte, upon such models were constructed the antres dim of the National Gallery, the Metropolitan Museum, the Palace of the Legion of Honor (just so). Ungiving and apart, the world of art remained an alien dimension, gorgeously disposed and even when classically displayed, clearly *someone else's belongings*, defended against us by cords, placards, and plastic shields. There was no place to sit down; chairs were thrones, consular or papal, beds were the oddly tiny reminder of Other Lives, proprietary presences, and floors were marble paths between the cases, corridors to get us out of there as magisterially as we had been taken in. A museum was a place to look—respectfully—at other people's possessions, mostly dead people's, and since they were owned by others, their arrangement was properly other too. The formality of old-style museums was not altogether foreign to us, but it represented control; its guidance was that of authority even more than of enlightenment, certainly than of initiation into mysteries we left entirely behind us as we ran down the releasing stairs, free at last, once again.

There has been a remarkable transformation of such institutions within my lifetime, and even the New Wings of venerable galleries reflect something of what I suppose is a more democratic accommodation. For now it is the museums themselves which are *owners*; we feel that what we are being shown is not alienated property but what appears by rights in these spaces, on these beguiling walls. And the arrangement of space is no longer the orderly progression of corridor, staircase, gallery, vestibule, and exit, perceived as an invariable series, inhospitable but comprehensible, grim but to be grasped as we were lectured on our way . . . our way out. They have changed all that. In the chambers of the East Wing in Washington, in Dallas, in Berkeley, in Los Angeles—at the Beaubourg, the museum is no longer an aloof formality to be passed through rather wistfully, humbly aspiring; indeed, the difference begins with the fact that "chambers" have been eliminated. We are no longer to realize, to recognize where we are: seduced, beguiled, bewildered even, by a chaos of inviting areas, none of which evidently leads to or from any other; everything flows, everything runs, everything celebrates the delight of *being here*, a confusion of realms felt to be, at last, what art requires—a welter.

Stripped of its hierarchical status, art is shown to the public—*its* public?—in a cantilevered commotion of choices. The new museum is a much more intimate affair, but it is an intimacy of incomprehension, mostly: in the wonderland of popular access, we do not know where to turn, nor need we, so long as we keep turning somewhere. Around the next corner will be another . . . diversion; a new entertainment lurks or looms wherever we look, up and down and over there. If we are guided (manipulated) at all, it will be by subtler means than architecture: a color-coordination, a system of banners, Muzak perhaps. The one great exception to this notion of the museum-as-ferment, of the adorable Pandemonium of it all, was Wright's Guggenheim Museum on upper Fifth Avenue, the celebrated snailshell that instantly revealed its workings to the entering visitor. You took the protractor-shaped elevator to the top and tottered down the coils, art passing before you in a shallow spiral (you could see what was coming next, or what you had just seen already, across the well, distance lending enchantment to the view). It was not a shrine for possessions nor a free-for-all: it was a sort of machine for *having seen art*, and like the scroll or the tape, it was difficult to enter anywhere except at the beginning or the end, the top or the bottom. The Guggenheim is felt by artists to be the triumph of architecture over art, though not any more triumphant, I would suggest, than those notable buildings in Washington, Los Angeles, and Berlin which send you this message loud and chaotic: art is a world of wonderful impossibilities of choice with no way out or even in—there is only a labyrinth where anything goes, so long as it goes on. And now even the Guggenheim has mitigated the purity of its procedure, its time-machine status, by adding restaurant, bookstore, and (the endemic disease of the institution) BOUTIQUE. Still it is—or has been—the one contemporary contribution to the housing and display of art for the public which is governed by a comprehensible concept, a figuration of space so specific and so transpicuous that there is no moment when the visitor can fail to realize where he is, where he might be. All other new museums have fallen (and I speak deliberately) for the notion of art as continuous and unavoidable solicitation: you need never know where you are once you are in its toils, because art is that marvelous world which has nothing to do with the one you just came in out of, the world where confusion can be resolved and order rehearsed by means of comprehensible space.

What went up, to an overweening height of erection—towers by Philip Johnson, Pelli, Pei, embellished at their bases with statues by Dubuffet, Nevelson, Miró—has come down; excavation for a subsequent spire by Jahn has been filled in, black-topped, a provisional parking lot. Much of Houston today presents this stick-of-the-rocket effect: skyscrapers half-dead at the top, stores for lease, projects forsaken. Yet what has been "receded" from is not the only prosperity in view, and an odor of decay not the only effluvium. A sort of emblematic circumstance may be registered in the apparition—surely the right word—of two remarkable institutions and the structures which house them: the Wortham Performance Center (a two-theater opera house in downtown Oz) and, in the culturally permissive Montrose district, the Menil Collection, a museum which is the latest part of a complex of cultural functions generated here since the forties by Dominque and Jean de Menil (and the Schlumberger oil interests).

Hitherto, the Houston Opera Company performed in Jones Hall, where the Houston Symphony Orchestra also plays, but there were conflicts, obstacles to ambition (the Houston Ballet has also moved to Wortham) now assumed to be unconstrained, and what seems to be a vast tan railway depot will probably be seen and used by more Houstonians than the other structure, the one I want to linger in, simply because *performance* means audience—and art, for all the hype we bestow upon it, does not. Yet even the Wortham Center makes a gesture (a grotesque, perhaps obscene one) toward art. The lobby you enter requires that you mount a long, slow escalator through a cavernous interval before you can reach the auditoriums; this ascent is flanked—is hedged, is menaced!—by a double rank of metal sculptures (made by the same Rochester artisan who created all the hardware in the place, the doorknobs, the sconces, the EXIT-signs) spray-painted in all the colors of apocalypse and reaching for you as you glide past with the fearsome gestures of Conan the Barbarian, frozen in tormented steel, cast in effrontery. And already I have met Texans who claim they love this sub-Disney stuff—they love it because it is theirs, because no one else has anything like it, and it is part of the Houston repertoire of urban astonishments. The carnival—however diminished—continues.

The Menil Collection (notice the scrupulous elision of the particle here—contrasted, for example, with its insistence in the D'Orsay Museum in Paris) is the only structure besides the Guggenheim in which the exhibition of art is a matter of making clear to the visitor from the initial moment of encounter (not even entrance but encounter) where he stands and what the French call *le sens de la marche* (the way to go). One finds the collection on what seems the village green, surrounded by any number of gray houses with black awnings (all owned by Mrs. de Menil and rented out to artists; one is used as a bookstore—the moneylenders have been turned out of the temple). It looks rather like a huge country club golf-shop, for the exterior consists of gray clapboard—cypress; apparently a whole forest was *used up* to produce enough board feet without knots—with white trim and black canvas awnings, requested by the client. The client's charge to her architect (Renzo Piano, who had worked for Louis Kahn, and on the Beaubourg) was that the building be big inside, small outside. The building is 402 feet by 142 feet, maximum height 45 feet: for all its design modesty, it cannot be mistaken for a golf-shop. I am trying to suggest that the structure has maintained a certain distance from "architecture," especially in its elitist ranges. Mrs. de Menil wanted the institution to be not only a teaching collection but a place of work, "a little bit like a shop, or light industry," as Walter Hopps, the director, suggests. Piano's interest in an esthetic of minimalism runs counter to prevalent surface-ornamented and figurative compositions (think of Michael Graves and the new Whitney!); he has come up (or down) with what the magazine *Progressive Architecture* calls "a clean-industry aesthetic." The structure looks conventional in contrast to other Piano projects, and indeed the architect believes that the conventionality has an ideological basis. In an era of cultural mystification, art could be seen as inaccessible, and the purpose of this design was to break down such barriers. (The Collection is open until seven o'clock in the evening, and admission is free.) Certainly no carnival is going on here: an ascetic image is intended to enlighten the visitor as to the true meaning of the art it is designed to house. Piano, whose design contains no hint of function (historical or memorial function), meets our wonder with an interesting assertion: "historical memory of the past in America is not necessarily related to place." (So much for the Alamo.) In a region of tyrannical sunlight, the platform roof—the one dominant visual element which makes the collection appear more than just a responsive box—consists of ferrocement "leaves" suspended on ductile iron trusses, all cast with contours and textures to yield diffuse, shadow-free light. The galleries are also lit with windows, for Mrs. de Menil insisted on the need of the contemplating visitor to reconnoitre with what had been left outside, if not behind.

The platform roof overhangs the structure all around, providing a sort of veranda-effect. The entrance is in the center of the long sides, and runs through the building's utility core. Down the long interior runs a single hall from end to end, off which the galleries branch.

From the instant you enter, you can orient yourself in relation to this principal hall, and though there are secrets—one temporary exhibition gallery tends to disappear if you are not careful—even in the course of a first visit you will feel enlightened as to where you may go next and to where you have just been. The concept is one of "directed discovery," and it is neither tyrannical nor insouciant.

Basic to the construction is the sense of the active, even metamorphic nature of the collection. Its size (over 10,000 objects) means that exhibition spaces will continually change and that only a small percentage of objects will be on display. The reserve collection is in a raised penthouse (not a cellar: Houston is subject to extremes of street flooding), and storage is conceived as another issue of accessibility: Mrs. de Menil wants pieces available to ready viewing, to bringing out for the direct experience of scholars of classes.

The collection (and already the catalogue of the first selection, "from the paleolithic to the modern era," constitutes a prominent item on the Harry N. Abrams list) comprises four primary areas: antiquities, tribal arts, "modern" (school of Paris, surrealism), and American contemporary. Nothing is to be included beyond Jean de Menil's lifetime (1904–1973) or, as Director Hopps puts it, his regard. So carefully winnowed is this first showing that the effect is indeed as overpowering as I am sure it was intended to be: the Magrittes, the Cornells, the temporary exhibition of Chamberlain's crushed automobiles, the Cycladic and Alaskan pieces, the astounding Mali group— these are works which any Michelin would award three stars—*vaut le voyage*. What matters to me, beyond the matters of the collection itself, is the quite exceptional feeling that one is not to be *done with* the visit, that one is not to be *shown out* after the showing. The effort is all in the contemplation, with precisely the religious overtones which that word once had. The choice of the objects, the way they are placed in relation to each other, and the way they are embraced by the building in which they have come to rest, afford an experience unique in my museum experience. Not even Wright found so adequate a figuration for art (though his accommodation of the art-visitor is matchless). My visits to the Menil Collection have been punctuated, moreover, by comfortable sessions, or sittings, on the many chairs and banquettes provided for just that purpose. Austere, yes, but an auster-ity made manifest for the sake of a jubilation elsewhere, a hypertrophy of regard upon *works*, undistracted by the usual claims of commerce, sociability, or just heterogeneous *dreck* (the new MoMA).

It is an odd triumph in a city said to be in the grip of economic ter-ror. The convention center that has just opened, the opera house that is in full swing, are perhaps the more characteristic Texan rejoinders to the charge of decadence so often made these days in Houston. But I would instance the Menil Collection as the most serene building since the Taj Mahal and the most efficient since the Parthenon, for the au-thentic sign that there is life in Texas. Life and consciousness too, and perhaps most of all, life and consciousness and conscience. What an eightieth birthday Dominique de Menil has bestowed upon us all!

Brassaï the Writer

[1999]

Allof us dream, and in contemporary Western cultures, all of us write. Our dreams are our art, and our letters—the one mode of writing universally practiced, though hardly perfected— are our literature. Like our dreams our letters are that expressive form which, once completed—i.e., posted—cannot be revised: they are the products of culture we are most likely to regard as "natural"—not to be corrected, retouched, changed, as we like to say that nature, espe- cially "human nature," does not change. Yet when we read a man's col- lected letters—even, as in this case, the letters of a very young man—they seem, already, the evidence of culture, something more— or less—than nature. They seem, already, to present the portrait of a member (and perhaps of a victim, too) of a certain culture, but partic- ularly the indication of what spirit (enthusiasm, inertia, aspiration, dismay) possesses the letter-writer, affording the conviction so analo- gous to Freud's famous dictum about anatomy, that culture is fate.

The father of this particular young man—who is all of twenty-one when he reassures his parents in 1920, upon arriving in Germany from Hungary: "My first impressions are most favorable, and I do not re- gret for a second that I came here. I guess within a couple of days I will be totally acquainted with Berlin life and can start regular work"— is a teacher of literature, a writer, and the family milieu has prepared young Gyula from the age of five, when he was taken to Paris on a year's villeggiatura, for a life not only sweetened but indeed structured by culture. How pleasant it is to observe that this father is a constant "moral and financial support," as remarked in 1978, ten years after Professor Halász's death (at the age of ninety-seven!); that he actually encouraged his eldest son in his artistic ambitions from the first. The *Letters to My Parents*, which we may now regard as Brassaï's first book, are therefore charged with a sense of a justifying cultural mission. They are the record of the soul's (and the body's) laboratory.

The only odd—though understandable—thing about them is that the young artist is more likely to mention his relationships with fellow expatriate Hungarians—Sandor (aka Alexander) Korda, for example—rather than with such apparently marginal types as Pierre Reverdy and Henri Michaux, of whom his parents would not have heard. He does not want to scare them off, but here we may note for ourselves the immediate magnetism which draws this as-yet ill-defined intellectual youth to a certain kind of accomplishment in the arts. For Reverdy was perhaps the purest lyrical voice in that astonishing group of poets (Éluard, Aragon, Desnos, Breton himself) who eventually found it expedient to accept the leadership of André Breton in the literary and artistic movement known as Surrealism; and Michaux, though never a popular figure, was both a writer and a graphic artist of evident genius, certainly the greatest Belgian poet since Maeterlinck and one of the most remarkable image-makers of modernity. Friendship with such men—and such friendship was a characteristic of Brassaï's all his life, not just in the enthusiasm of youthful discovery and alliance—has a great deal to do with the photographer's subsequent literary achievement, though such "contacts" are unremarked in his correspondence with his parents, not a matter—yet—for family inspection.

After two preliminary years in Berlin, where he graduated from the Charlottenburg Academy of Fine Art, met Kokoschka, Kandinsky, Moholy-Nagy, and, most important, discovered Goethe (not the Goethe of *Werther*, but the later, naturalist, world-ordering sage), our hero, for that is how he is conceived by his addresses and by himself, moves on to Paris—it is 1924!—never to return to his hometown of Brassov in Transylvania, though in 1932 he adopts its name and modifies it for his own. Henceforth he will be the Representative.

Exploring Paris and eking out the life of a journalist (in two languages—Hungarian for the articles he sends to Hungarian papers and magazines in Transylvania, German for those regularly published by newspapers in Munich, Essen, and Cologne, and for caricatures sold to a Berlin paper) by taking on whatever employments fortune proposes (for instance, tracking down old photographs and postcards for collectors) in the fashion of Rastignac and Stephen Dedalus, the young outsider is determined to master the French language; according to the French wife he marries twenty-four years later, he studies French grammar and linguistics for the rest of his life; he lives to the age of eighty-five, and for him art is second nature throughout the decades.

(One might point out the analogy to the late Rumanian writer E. M. Cioran, Brassaï's contemporary, who indeed made himself a master of this same third language and became by constant study, as he avows, a great modern French rhetorician; Brassaï, I am certain, would have no such claim made for his writings, though it is my conviction that at least three of his many books are of permanent value as writing, and they are written in French.)

The letters home are good-humored, vivid, *lucid*, and constitute a sort of diagram of how a Young Man from the Provinces determines to conquer the Metropolis. He is wonderfully abetted by his evident capacity for making friends with remarkable people, and in the course of his Parisian discoveries (of which the sustaining ones, I suspect, are in books; Brassaï is a grand reader, marvelously responsive all his life to apparently all of literature in all its forms!) he decides, by 1929, to buy a camera and isolate, from the prolixity of the real, that vision of life which reveals itself to him in the labyrinth of Paris.

It is in these years that the artist Brassaï is formed. Often accompanied on his Baudelairean, even Dickensian prowls through nighttime Paris by Léon-Paul Fargue, already the insomniac poet and urban memorialist, the "ambulator of Paris" who had been a student in Mallarmé's English class and nonetheless, or perhaps for that very reason, remained the most intensely French of modernist poets; and by Raymond Queneau, the novelist and versifier and critic who was to remain a kind of clandestine eminence of French literature until late in life he conquered a flabbergasted public with *Zazie in the Métro*, that insolent romance whose demotic heroine is a sort of French Lolita;

and soon by another expatriate and another urban memorialist, though one with the perspective of Brooklyn instead of the Batignolles, Henry Miller, Brassaï creates his first images of what Baudelaire so canonically defined as the *fourmillante cité, cité pleine de rêves*; he sets up a darkroom in his Fourteenth-Arondissement hotel where—henceforth invariably—he does his own developing and printing, and becomes what Miller would call "the eye of Paris," though he cannot take more than twenty-four pictures a night because the photographic plates he uses are so bulky.

Until 1930, the young man had rather condescended to photography—if he was to be any kind of artist, it would most likely be a painter, a sculptor perhaps, or even a writer (and indeed Brassaï would succeed in becoming all of these). Photography—though by this time he had met Atget and had accompanied Kertész, a fellow Hungarian, on assignments—was not, to his mind (as it had not been to Baudelaire's, even in the intimacy of Nadar), an art, though it is important to note that Brassaï already shared Goethe's conviction that an artist might, indeed *must*, be "gradually elevated to the height of objects."

There is a mystery here, one which even these candid, often euphoric letters cannot quite penetrate, as to how Gyula Halász becomes Brassaï, just as there will be mystery, one which even the masterful visionary of Baudelairean Paris cannot quite penetrate, as to how Brassaï, "the eye of Paris," becomes the author of *Paroles en l'air*, *Les Artistes de ma vie*, and *Marcel Proust sous l'emprise de la photographie*. The two books on Miller and the *Conversations avec Picasso*, splendid portraits as they are, are not likely to constitute Brassaï as the significant author he will become by writing, in his later years, those ulterior three works. But the importance of mysteries is that they be accepted as mysteries, not degraded to the level of problems or even solutions. I shall assume that my reader knows the quality and value of Brassaï's images (and of his wonderful film *Tant qu'il y aura des bêtes*), and that it is not my task to account for the appearance, starting with *Paris de nuit* in 1932, of the continuously produced great photographic work. Since I am going to discuss further the work of the writer, it is perhaps apposite merely to observe how from the start Brassaï's photographic images were cheerfully accompanied by essays from the pens of such contemporary French masters as the polymath novelist, poet, and travel-writer Paul Morand; the poet, novelist, and playwright Henri de Montherlant; and the film-scenarist and poet Jacques Prévert (only the last, demotic lyricist of the Parisian petite-bourgeoisie, was Brassaï's friend who shared his sanguine vision of the lower depths). Contemporary French literature seized upon the new Parisian photographer as one of its own; indeed, the relation of Brassaï to the Surrealist poets, preeminently poets of the postindustrial city, is so complex that it has not yet been argued to a standstill (rather, only set in motion by Rosalind Krauss, whose exhibition of Surrealist photographs at the Renwick Gallery in Washington, D.C., was a revelation of the dimensions photography was to assume in the claims, assumptions, and methods of contemporary thought). Enough to say that long before he had reached the Middle of the Journey, Brassaï was acknowledged by the world of letters as by the world of art as a master, and that he had made magisterial accommodations to the world of commerce, arrangements which would assure him, through his transactions with Vollard, with Skira, as with the editors of *Verve* and of *Harper's Bazaar*, as with so many others subsequently, an entirely fruitful and prosperous creative life, one of the most attractive our century has to show. Like Balanchine in New York, Brassaï in Paris became one of the *marking* artists of his age, the two expatriates readily claimed and acclaimed by the world as reliably supreme artificers.

Though I am eager to accord Brassaï's brilliant and copious portraits of Picasso and Miller (those other expatriates, outsiders forever to be associated with the Paris to which they headed with all the force of bullets from Barcelona, from Brooklyn) whatever praise inheres, these days, to such *overheard revelations*, these volumes are not the literary achievements I want to salute in Brassaï's production. Let me observe merely—merely!—that they are, in the canon of classical journalism, the finest reportorial portrayals since Victor Hugo's *Choses vues*. Indeed, they are quite comparable, if we read Brassaï's account of his prowls with Miller among the Parisian brothels and then turn to Hugo's account of a midnight visit to Balzac's house to view the novelist's sudden corpse and perhaps even superior, when we proceed to the more succinct success of *Les Artistes de ma vie*, a very late work

(1982) consisting of the photographs taken, mostly for *Harper's Bazaar*, of nineteen painters and sculptors in their studios, usually in the process of making art and apparently undisturbed by the photographer's presence and processes (actually there are twenty studies, for Brassaï has included beautiful portraits of Kahnweiler and of Vollard), accompanied by as many essays which make the book something more than another volume of Brassaï photographs. If I were to name a single work of discursive prose identifying the qualities and character of the School of Paris between the wars, it is this book of Brassaï's, with its informal but grave designations, some of considerable length, others brief but always charged with observation, with what Macbeth calls "understood relations," that I would not only choose but assign to students already so remote from the makings of that great period. As Ann Wilkes Tucker has remarked, "Brassaï (a serious reader of history and philosophy as well as of literature) could just as easily have written *The Writers of My Life* and accompanied such a volume with equally marvelous photographs. Pity he didn't!" Perhaps in my eagerness to draw attention to the inclusive achievement of *Les Artistes de ma vie*, I have been less than fair to Brassaï's *Conversations avec Picasso*; here, it is Brassaï's own skill at becoming part of the furniture, the ambiance of the genius he is "conversant with," which may have dimmed his authentic gifts as a life-limner. Certainly we feel that no other contemporary can make Picasso heard not from a pedestal, not from the bedside, but uniquely from the easel, the workbench, the potter's wheel. But the very exposures in which Picasso has so vigorously cooperated make Brassaï's version of him less spectacular, necessarily, than the kinds of revelation he more trenchantly provides in the cases, or the constructions, of the artists of his life.

Sometimes, as with the texts on Maillol and Matisse, Brassaï is concerned to correct—properly to focus, one might say—the image of the maker; sometimes he is eager to disinter a buried friend, as in the case of the 1930s portraits-and-text of the forgotten painter Hans Reichel, a companion of Brassaï's earliest time in Paris. Indeed, the intimacy and insight of all the essays is what makes them so much more than reportage, so much more than what we tend to require of journalism: as Brassaï would later remark, it was not a matter of portraying images, but of presenting people *in their own light*: without any explanation, any psychological analysis, with no stage directions, as it were. This master of lighting is, in his literature, remarkably untheatrical: he is, rather, *photographic in spirit*, as he puts it in the essay introducing his finest literary texts, *Paroles en l'air* (1977):

> This "spirit" is not the exclusive property of photography. It existed earlier in the form of the artist's humble attitude toward the world, which was considered greater than his genius. When Goethe, having overcome his youthful romanticism, observed: "I have gradually been elevated to the height of objects," he was no doubt referring to the spirit of photography.

No doubt. And consequently in *Paroles en l'air*, that extraordinary work of humility, self-effacement, abnegation even, Brassaï offers a handful of recitatives—dramatic monologues, transcriptions of the spoken into the written, literary ventriloquisms—which belong with certain achievements in demotic French culture by Céline, by the contemporary experimental novelist Pierre Guyotat, by Proust himself, of whom more in a moment. These pieces—two uttered *en bistrot*, the first by a sort of group-consciousness under the Occupation, the second by a drunken clochard at closing-time; one in a taxi by a man demonically possessed by words; and the major piece, "Histoire de Marie" (first published separately with an introduction by Henry Miller), a series of distilled self-revelations by a *femme de ménage* as harsh, as ignorant, and as eloquent as the Françoise of Proust's *A la recherche du temps perdu*, and even more at grips with the household bonds of life as they are presented under the Occupation—constitute in their close tracing of voice a special peninsula in the geography of modern French writing. Their accuracy as "character studies," all of which are worthy of the author of "My Last Duchess" and "The Bishop Orders His Tomb" on the one hand (the hand of Demos), and of the author of *Claudine* and *Chéri* on the other (the hand of Melpomene)—that accuracy which in its excruciation becomes beauty, is achieved by a focusing of language, a condensation, or as Brassaï puts it, "not a strict copy of reality, but a *translation*"; Brassaï likes to quote Chekhov as an expression of the spirit of these texts of his, that strangely humble artist who had the greatest pride in a talent that could be conjugated with respect for "the object itself":

"The artist should not judge his characters or what they say, but be only an *impartial witness.* My role is only to have talent, in other words to know how to distinguish between what is important and what is not, to know how to illuminate my characters and make them speak." These lines by Chekhov express the *spirit of photography* and express it so well that I would gladly sign my name to them as my own *articles of faith.* The spirit of photography did not have to wait for Niépce before it could be revealed, but only the invention of photography, its processes, and the photographer's rapport with reality, was able to make *visible* and *intelligible.*

It is a splendid article of faith, one that enables us to see why, if not how, Brassaï made himself into the writer he is. But in store for us, in the very last years of the photographer's life, was one further surprise, one ultimate piece of literature, also a consequence of the photographer's dream, which crowns the great edifice of this man's multiple and complex creative energies.

Posthumously published, *Marcel Proust sous l'emprise de la photographie* (*Proust in the Power of Photography*) is a lucid analysis of the role of the camera in *A la recherche du temps perdu*; as Brassaï loses no time in pointing out, Proust's novel is the first great work of literature in which photography and the photograph play a major role, both as a *figurant* in the text, and as an *operator* of the text. Notions of cutting, framing, angle, and perspective, and especially the notion of involuntary memory (Proust's Muse) as the *latent image* to be developed in one's inner darkroom, are here explored with the most diligent concern for the integrity of the narrative itself. As I remarked earlier, Brassaï is a supremely gifted reader, always responsive to text-as-texture, as medium, yet ever alert to the grander consequences of the desire to halt the moment, fixing it forever in that sort of eternity to which

Proust found the photograph to be his best guide. In a characteristic
gesture of humility and eloquence, Brassaï has produced an invaluable
study of Proust and Photography, one which must henceforth be read
as closely as those we have so long consulted on Proust and Music,
Proust and Philosophy . . . Perhaps the humility is tempered by a certain pride as well, when we observe—as in this closing citation—how
readily Brassaï identifies the author of *A la recherche* with the maker
of photographic images:

> Just as the photographer, laden with images he has managed to
> capture from the visible world, withdraws into the shadows in
> order to bring them to light, so Proust has elaborated his clois-
> tered work in what he frequently called "my darkroom" . . .
> Like Plato's cave, the darkroom of the author of the *Search* only
> rarely granted him a direct vision of the world, but thanks to his
> remarkable visual memory, he could see it all the better, having
> stored up over the years everything of interest that the world
> offered to his eyes: flowers, women, girls, boys, steeples,
> churches, gestures, gazes . . .

A mind as concentrated and loyal as Brassaï's has readily identified
what Proust could rescue from distraction, could reprieve only by
finding certain repetitions or rhymes in experience. Indeed, Brassaï
has discerned in all his works, images, and texts, the scale of values
imposed on things by human nature, carried toward some by an innate love and away from others by a quick repulsion. As Santayana put
it in 1929, in an early essay on Proust almost as searching as Brassaï's
late one, and suggestive of the very qualities we shall find in the literature of this great image-maker, "we could not have asked for a more
competent or a more unexpected witness to the fact that life as it flows
is so much time wasted, and that nothing can ever be recovered or
truly possessed save under the form of eternity which is also, as he
reveals to us, the form of art."

On *Lepanto*: An Appreciation of Cy Twombly

[2001]

The triumphs and even the tyrannies of history endure for only a moment; it is their ruins which are eternal. It is tempting to say that in the battle of Lepanto, where Cervantes lost an eye, Twombly recovered a vision. Such paradoxes reveal the justice of art. To children, to foreigners (and in history we are all foreigners), such words as *Guernica* or *Anghiara* are alien indeed, yet they come to us demanding a posture of intimacy, of understanding, embodying, as they do, an artist's response to the wreckage they signify. Was it not Picasso who once called a painting the sum of its destructions?

For Twombly, Mediterranean *pathos* has always been an invoked phenomenon. Somewhere on his giant canvases, among glowing or effaced marks and signs, the glorious names are scrawled like so much scornful graffiti: Apollo, Virgil, Troy . . . When I had occasion to put together a program of poems alluded to in Twombly's work, it resulted in a veritable anthology of the classical world, from Homer to Cavafy. His response to the classical world which American genius has characteristically found unvisitable (is not Whitman more characteristic of that genius than Eliot, Melville than Pound?) is passionately singular, though it is scarcely as ordered as Pound and Eliot sought to be. Twombly's variations on the classical world, the classical past, are like jazz compositions—loose structures which go on their nerve, their necessary discoveries of a man's desire which lead to what he learns, by inspired guesses, of the weather of history, the climate of time.

There were, of course, particular manifestations along the way. For decades this artist—especially in his sculpture—has been concerned with the making of boats, recognizable solar barques of the kind ancient Egyptians buried in their tombs; vessels intended to conduct the soul to a transcendent condition. There has always been a kind of archaic splendor—both primitive and delicate—surrounding these little ships of Twombly's; they have reminded me many times of those late obsessive sequences of poems by D. H. Lawerence, "The Ship of Death," in which the self is abjured to prepare in a traditional yet home-made style the vessels that would carry across, would go over; would depart . . . In *Lepanto*, a work of twelve canvases offering a heroic series of variations on a Mediterranean theme of triumph and death, the boats are burned, thus signifying the destruction of the Turkish fleet by combined European forces under Venetian leadership. Yet there remains a mystery to what I am calling the splendor and the triumph, for they are often reduced (if that can be the word to use in such transactions, such events) to skeletal remains, to the elemental rudiments of what has been a terrible destruction. It is as if, for Twombly, the dozen panels of the tremendous sea-battle, which represented the rescue of Europe from Ottoman invasion in the sixteenth century, were a meditation on the destiny of the soul in terms of that vulnerable and fragile barque Twombly has so obsessively produced.

In the maritime museum of Barcelona, the star exhibition is the preserved galley of Don John of Austria, from which the victory of Lepanto was commanded. The vessel is astonishingly decked out with teak carvings and what Shakespeare called gold adornings, yet for all its embellishments it is one of the ships which, in decorative tapestries and frescos commemorating naval victories in all the palaces of Europe, represented the astonishment of Lepanto. There is no question, as we look at Don John's flagship, of the risk of the enterprise, of the value to the West of victory and the disgrace to the Ottomans of defeat. Twombly's canvases are concerned with precisely these issues— the showy glory of the ships on fire is what represents that victory, and the unscathed crudity of the linear (stick-figure!) European ships indicate the elusive triumph of the aggressor. Twombly has arranged his dozen panels to begin and end with the conflagration, which appears in scarlet and gold on every fourth panel, a sort of overall splendor, which signifies defeat. The second, fifth, and ninth panels describe the actual battle — the last in which hand-to-hand or ship-to-ship fighting occurred: from now on battles at sea would be won or lost by artillery and sail. A certain human prowess and brutality is registered here (though no human form is shown), amid the paradoxically opposed elements of fire and water, just as the desert sand swallows the solar barques in pyramid interments.

It is always dangerous for a maker to employ in a single project the entire range of his art — his whole armory, one might say. There is a kind of tombstone effect in the affair, as one feels about the elegiac mastery of Monet's water-lily panels at the Orangerie, where the whole project of the splendors and miseries of brushed vision is conducted to its conclusion. What if the artist — as in Monet's case — has something more to devise, some further invention? As we move along the swarming gamut of Twombly's sea-battle, there is a sense that we have encountered an anthology of creative invention — the vivid compression of painterly possibility, all-out and all-over. Yet the sheer exuberance of the twelve panels, and the decisive rhythm which this registration of the ambivalence of victory and defeat establishes, makes this work a much less totalizing enterprise than the anticipated spectacle of The Old Man's toys. As grim and sometimes uproarious as the panels are, their cumulative effect, as we move among them, or step back to take in the whole sequence as a single image, is one of luminous intensity. We witness historical evidence through a personal meditation on tragedy. Certainly *Lepanto* is an accounting, but not a final summing up. We are still, with Twombly, in 2001, in the thick of the fight.

Our art, certainly in the West, has inveterately seized upon the idea of Battle — having so often been obliged to commemorate, to justify the vexed occasion — as the likeliest, the most intrinsic condition of human life. From red-figure Attic vases to the calligraphic killing-fields of Henri Michaux, we readily accept the arena of fighting as high art's most evident and its most *eventual* categorization of experience. Twombly's version, his reading of our mortal lot, is sufficiently concerned to acknowledge the tradition — beginning with his very choice of Lepanto as a subject; after all, no admiral of the Venetian fleet or commander of the Turkish forces compelled him to exonerate or mourn the sixteenth-century carnage off the east coast of Greece. Twombly's version is also sufficiently discreet—distinguished by his refusal or inability to single out the winning side; or to celebrate those who sounded what poetry, with suitable ambiguity, has called "the wailing trumps of victory." The image of the "battle" has persisted ever since Atldorfer. I use the quotation marks by design, for as early as Rubens's *Feast of Love*, barely a hundred years after Lepanto, artists seem to have paired the portrayal of aggression on the most heroic scale, in mythological as well as historical terms, with the recuperation of an erotic totalization. Beginning with Rubens, polymorphic perversity is denoted by a stream of naked flesh, entirely embodied and eagerly active, in the significantly infantilized form of thousands of rosy *putti* gamboling around the beneficent figure of Aphrodite. By 1800 William Blake had envisioned the torrent of mortal lovers (illustrating the third canto of Dante's *Inferno*) looping in a sort of serpentine tide, easily pairing this image with that of War in Heaven after Milton ("I shall not cease from mortal fight"); and in another century, after Delacroix and his dutiful panoramas of the Napoleonic wars (of which I believe only two survive in all their circumferencing exactitudes of strategic futility), Ensor's satirical design of 1891, *The Battle of the Golden Spurs* (pencil, conte crayon, India ink, and gold paint), is exactly contemporaneous with Baron Frederic's *The Stream*, that deluge of fully sexed though perhaps unborn baby boys and girls charging together, indeed hurling each other, in countless thousands, into the pinkening struggle for existence. No wonder Freud found it imperative to report that in the imagination of children (so often put to bed in their parents' room), there was great difficulty in separating the perception of the act of love from that of the act of violence: "I thought Mommy and Daddy were fighting, but you say they were only fucking."

This great double-barreled proposition, as William James called it, in which two assertions can not be equated with each other but can not, by the same token, be separated from each other, is what Twombly has inherited. His twelve panels, which so elegiacally report the elimination, the *cancelling out*, of a fleet of ships that burned upon the water till they fell to so much charcoal, as lovingly assert a kind of *agape* at the very heart of chaos and night (to borrow a term from Montherlant, another writer of the double necessity of love-making and strife). Witness the thrilling conflagration of every fourth panel, on fire with passionate bursts of red and gold (burning ships or sexual discharges, now I ask you . . .).

I mentioned just now the *panoramic impulse* so frequently evoked in representations of the military imperative and of the erotic encounter as it is rendered in its most heroic terms. The American conscience at this present historical moment has a new, *ulterior* instance of this impulse: Hollywood in the film *Pearl Harbor* has just discovered that it can create a perfect verisimilitude of battle by digital special effects, computer-generated and all-encompassing to a degree never before possible. Something of this cinematic and technological triumph has already surfaced in Twombly's twelve panels as they surround us in their scrupulously ordered intervals, nicely accounted for by the historical succession of words we have used to describe the sexual climax: the Elizabethans called it *dying*, the Victorians said it was *spending*, we moderns have known it for a century as *coming*, but for Twombly the identity or at least the coincidence of love and war is simply (simply!), *being*.

Being is being moved, and notions of change, of difference and of loss, are registered in remarkable ways in Twombly's sequence. (The word "being" itself, as an account of what is *happening* in the Battle of Lepanto, is as suggestive as Chesterton's entire poem of that name, that Catholic hymn to the naval tactics of Shifting, a narrative of the deceptions necessary to produce victory at sea.) With a little patience, the lineaments of the story can be traced in Twombly's canvases, reading the twelve panels from left to right as he has desired. Having absorbed the story, however uneasily or traumatically, we can stand at the center of the series, letting it work its will upon us. These images have the power to communicate *in any order*. Yet, there is a narrative to be limned nonetheless. In the first movement of four panels, we witness the occasional hits and just as occasional misses of cannonfire. There is no indication here that any ships have escaped destruction by maneuvering. Ships are scattered on the sea, cannons manage to set many on fire. An incendiary pattern is produced at both ends of this first section with what I read to be a certain naivety, a certain detachment, as if the prospect of a devastating fire and an ultimate doom remained remote. The imagery of these first two panels after the initial salvo of fire is rather jaunty, considering the terrible conflagration on either side; the scribbled sense of oared galleys (quite similar to Twombly's previous experiments with the imagery of sacred vessels) has a measure of "childishness" (there, the naughty word is out—to be returned to shortly). Particularly haunting in that only a minority of the boat-figures has thus far escaped being hit and, at least in part, set afire. The insouciance of the blue surface, so halcyon in its color, is especially noticeable for being contained *between* the panels of total warfare, every clot and blob ablaze, whether it represents a flaming ship or merely a cannonball fired into the sea.

The second movement, the central one, of three ship-panels, appears before the intervention of another panel depicting fire-balls (these fire-ball panels occur at intervals rather like the horror-fanfares in Beethoven's ninth symphony). The second movement is the most "moving" in any sense: it shows the clearest progression of galleys, outlined with some suggestion of sails as well as oars against a less halcyon sea, grayed now but not showing any trauma, any touch of that terrible red and gold. If you took this one panel out of the sequence and proposed it as Twombly's representation of, say, a British fleet leaving port, no one could gainsay your impression from the mere evidence offered here, unless . . . unless the evidence of the next panel, in which there are several unmistakable raging fires, the desolation of all maritime adventure, were to revise your interpretation of the preceding panel: perhaps this is merely the charred skeleton of a fleet, the floating debris of the previous conflagration administered so thoroughly as to be without a spark of resistance? But no, there is, in this one blue and black-inscribed panel which is without flame, a certain vitality, a certain nonchalance, even, that carries us all the more tragically to the next two masterful images of destruction. On one panel, several ships on the right-hand side are shown badly leading an intense blood into a pale sea on which several vessels, shadowy and minor indeed, are clearly untouched by the horror happening and to come. In the third panel of this second movement, all the ships, which are at all visible, are hit and flaming, some reflecting upward their cadmium or sulfurous fate, most of them dragging straight down those awful strands of purple with their vermilion edges. This panel, and the firestorm which follows it, closing the second movement, are the most intimate expression of *the battle lost*, the fleet—any fleet—destroyed by enemy cannon.

The third movement is breathless in its immediacy and its suggestion, in at least the first of the three panels, of an attempted escape—the figuration of oars desperately stroking away, though the very vessels are clearly on fire or about to go up in flames. And the last two parts of this movement are quite like each other, as if to say all devastation is one: the innocent blue sea scarcely registering a total and terrible blotting out of what was once a fleet. Here there is no figuration of ships at all, merely versions of crimson, of madder, of scarlet, and the terrible gold edges to the flames. All is moving, but all is shapeless—so many smears and blobs with perhaps the faintest outline of what might have been a boat, but who knows? And the series is closed off by the last fire-storm, nothing but the painter's shorthand for deperition and despair; the red and gold clots without drawing, without any identifying marks of origin or destination, the blue surround grayed by the smoke of a hundred burnt . . . somethings, no longer separate items in a disaster but emblematic of the sheer condition of defeat, a canvas full of downward drowning fires.

Such is the narrative of Twombly's *Lepanto* as the painting's twelve panels tell it, though, as I have suggested, once the viewer has the successive experience of the work, he stands *in medias res*, no longer capable of determining that this occurred, then this, and because of that, this too. Now it is all the one disaster, a single anthem, as Chesterton would have it, to the war god; and if for Twombly the boats are an emblem of some spiritual passage, it is one of such consuming fire that no record of transcendence is possible; there can be only faith in things not seen, or despair without release or relief (certainly my own reading of the agonic scene; the sequence of destruction).

Some decades back, my friend Roland Barthes, whom I had served as a translator through ten of his works, told me that he planned to write . . . a novel. What kept him from doing so at the time was a confession of inadequacy as enigmatic as it was peremptory: "I don't know what to name my characters." As we know, Roland had no chance to think up names like Lepanto or Pearl Harbor, say, because a laundry truck jumped the curb and ran him down. But in his last years, for lack of a fiction, Barthes had been making paintings. He never called them that; the closest he came to identifying them, to giving them a name, was in the language of two essays he wrote about the paintings and drawings of Cy Twombly, essays which I translated into English in a book called *The Responsibility of Forms*. In these essays, Barthes remarked on the problem raised for any artist who attempted to replicate Twombly's way of working: "Try to do Twombly, you will find that you cannot; the clots and smears that seem so accessible to the performer, even the beginner, regularly elicit the famous phrase: 'Why, if that's art, any child could make art!'" Barthes had occasion to explain how he had learned from Twombly not to imitate the American artist's gestures, but to make gestures that were his own. Today there is a whole book, published by an Italian house, of Roland's drawings and paintings (as I must call them). As he noted in his two essays on Twombly, Barthes found the way to his own art-making through an acceptance of—indeed in the reliance upon—the "infantile" gestures, untethered by any allegiance to gender or to erotic choice, unencumbered by any historical or mythological identification.

Twombly's works of the last twenty years are probably the most intimate and the least personal art of our moment. So much of the familiar denotative world has been taken away. His works move upon the canon, as upon the paper, the wood, the twine, the painted metal that they come up with, as if their creator had become a child again, though no child's innocence could look as innocent as all this. Twombly's figuration, which has enabled him to accede to one of the great classical themes of Western art from within an anthology of transit, is so simple, so childish indeed that many have been baffled by its rhetoric. His creation of *The Battle of Lepanto*, recapitulating as it does an entire career, was a perilous undertaking, since it could have marked the tombstone stage of his making, a terminus indeed. But the terms in which this work is cast, its *rhetoric*, enable the artist to slip out from under the net of identifications which culture itself imposes upon the inveterate maker. His sequence, therefore, does not have the air of The Old Man's Toys, that dread notion by which we may defer or defuse our engagement with an artist's late works. If anything, the twelve panels connote "the child's weapons," the means by which an innocent eye confronts battle, whereof both the losing and the winning convey the doom of human experience. Twombly's work cannot be accounted for within a rhetoric of "old mastery," but only through an encounter with those marks and signs, the smears and squiggles, which he alone knows how to make. With them, Twombly has created a Lepanto we have all won and lost, the battle of making art.

ON PROSE

What Is a Neo-classic?

[1965]

How the heart sinks—where else, as she would say, might it go?—at the thought of reading Ivy Compton-Burnett's eighteenth novel, *A God and His Gifts* (her nineteenth, if you count *Dolores*, an unobtainable and uncharacteristically titled work, published ten years before the Blisters and Blasters series that began in the 1920s).

For the uninitiated reader—and who else is to be trusted in such matters?—the tidy rhyming uniformity of all these double titles, the "special taste" one is supposed to cultivate for this author's "difficulty," like Greek olives or marzipan, and the inescapable comparison to Jane Austen ("I do not think myself that my books have any real likeness to hers. I think that there is possibly some likeness between our minds.")— all point to the dreary Womrath's conclusion that Miss Compton-Burnett is but a fiercer, tighter avatar of the tireless Angela Thirkell, turning out a fake Trollope with real toads in it every other year. . . . Though she has taken a degree in classics—which I find no excuse for all those liaisons with Greek tragedy that have been attributed to her like *la* Lupescu's affairs with exotic royalty—and though she claims she is "interested in all kinds of literature"—which does not keep her from making another claim: "I cannot tell why I write as I do, as I do not know. I have even tried not to do it, but find myself falling back into my own way"—and even though she is the wittiest writer in English since Congreve and the meanest since Hobbes, there is no basis for regarding Miss Compton-Burnett's works as an exploration of the world, or as the creation of one. They are only—only!—a judgment, a regression, and thereby a reiterated self-indulgence, which of course is what they are for the reader as well. As she has it, "doing things in your own way is not really doing them."

I have been self-indulgent indeed, for I have read all eighteen of these indistinguishable novels—or at least I know I have read fourteen, the other four might be any one of them that I have read twice by mistake—and it is with mixed feelings (the mixture as before) that I acknowledge *A God and His Gifts* to be every bit as brilliant, and every bit as tiresome, as all the rest.* It has the by now familiar features: a family in a great but decaying house, tyrannized by a larger-than-life villain who is brought down so terribly that his defeat becomes a source of appeal; the overheard presence of many generations, split-level hangers-on from anterior marriages, harmless but straight-talking senescents, hydra-like children ("'A child is a strange thing,' said Cassius, as they were left alone. 'It is a natural thing,' said his wife, 'that is why it strikes a civilized person as strange.'"), a chorus of domestics who mirror the gentry's pecking order *en jaune*, the personnel of the Other Household, a counter-family of just one generation—a menage consisting of a queer brother and sister, for example—who are confessedly unimportant (though the modesty of such people is rather like that of Paul Valéry telling Einstein he had only the most rudimentary notion of the tensor calculus).

This dramatis persona talks, my God how they all talk, and what keeps them at it is the Terrible Event, usually involving incest, bigamy, and adultery (Miss C.-B. prefers all three to be committed at one fell swoop, so to speak, as here by a father and his daughter-in-law who is probably his daughter by a previous liaison with his wife's sister). The Event, and the plot which resolves it, is carried forward by the devices of melodrama: the wrong dose of lethal medicine, the concealed will

*It betrays, actually, a larger sense of exposure to the World Outside than the author has ever permitted before. Her talent has been in her exploitation of "two inches of ivory," but in this latest book, which has a sort of Hall Caine for its eponymous "hero," she runs the risk of letting fresh air leak into her vacuum. It is a risk easily absorbed.

that turns out to be forged, the disaster at sea, the purloined letter, the overheard secret, the sliding panel, the marked deck, the false bottom . . . Yet the author's peculiar genius is most flagrant at precisely this point: she manages to convey her preposterous tale *even while* and *because* her puppets are chewing at their lines, a preposterous scenery of the soul. Miss Compton-Burnett manages, in other words, her transitions, the refinements of modulation, the inflections in which she envelops her changes of pace and direction, with astonishing accuracy and effect. It is not true that these highly fenestrated novels, as Leslie Fiedler once called them in the only good nosology I've seen of Ivy Compton-Burnett's tragedies of manners, eschew description and narration in favor of repartee. In an early book like *Brothers and Sisters*, for example, there is quite as much of the one as of the other, and it is only in the latest books like *A God and His Gifts* that the talk goes on without narrative guidance—the difference is simply there, so that there is no need to make it, beyond saying that a character's eyes are "of the color that is called grey because it is no other." (There is always a lot of tautology-as-wit in these books; characters are forever saying "Well, it is what it is," or "My dear Megan, you are what you are," and smacking their lips over the jest.)

Though the expert, or the addict, may discern, as I say, such signs of "growth" or let us call it mastery at least, in the warp of Ivy Compton-Burnett's novels, it is certainly true to say that there has been no development of the woof, the mind that regards itself as resembling that of Jane Austen "possibly." And that, for the new reader, is where the real trouble lies. Our emblem of literature, of authorship at its most valuable, is the career of Shakespeare—the long curve of convention, experiment, and repossession of means—and, in a modern instance, of Yeats. Or even of Jane Austen herself, all of whose works represent an exploration, a venture into the possibilities of unexposed technique, a development of feeling beyond the resources of mere judgment. We tend to discredit the—call it neo-classical—notion of an artist producing no more than what he has set out to make, progressing from the arbitrary toward a previously defined necessity, from a certain disorder toward a certain order. Even from painters and composers, after the career of a Picasso or a Stravinsky, we expect "transformation," though here we are still often content with the anthological satisfactions of having "a" Poussin on the wall, "a" Scarlatti sonata on the phonograph. Surely this prejudice of ours thrusts against a sympathy for the perfected art of Miss Compton-Burnett. Further, and deeper, we have learned to distrust a presentment of order and necessity which does not seem to have to struggle against a constant sense of arbitrariness and disorder resisting the thing that is coming into being. It is the sense of such a conflict that I miss in Ivy Compton-Burnett's work, and its absence keeps me from suggesting that *A God and His Gifts* crowns the long career of this magnificent artificer, for such careers, by their nature, cannot be crowned, but only further bejeweled.

Jane Austen: Poetry and Anti-Poetry

[1986]

Writing almost fifty years ago, the poet W. H. Auden, beginning what was to become his famous "Letter to Lord Byron" from Iceland, of all places, acknowledged a momentary doubt as to the propriety of his choice of correspondent; perhaps he should address his epistolary lines,

—looking round for something light and easy—

not to the wild-hearted poetical nobleman, the exile, the spoiler, the rake, but to the plausibly less formidable and altogether more domestic author of *Sense and Sensibility*, that wise ironist whose first and basic understanding is that Spirit—what we sometimes call "life" or "affirmation"—is not free, that it is conditioned, that it is limited by circumstance, that the expansive virtues have a consented-to cost at which they are to be gained and exercised. So Auden wavered, initially, as he cast about for a sponsoring genius, between the rebellious aristocratic poet and the more tractable bourgeois novelist:

There is one other author in my pack:
   For some time I debated which to write to.
Which would least likely send my letter back?
   But I decided that I'd give a fright to
   Jane Austen if I wrote when I'd no right to,

And share in her contempt the dreadful fates
Of Crawford, Musgrove, and of Mr. Yates.

Then she's a novelist. I don't know whether
   You will agree, but novel writing is
A higher art than poetry altogether
   In my opinion, and success implies
   Both finer character and faculties.
Perhaps that's why real novels are as rare
As winter thunder or a polar bear.

The average poet by comparison
   Is unobservant, immature, and lazy.
You must admit, when all is said and done,
   His sense of Other People's very hazy,
   His moral judgements are too often crazy,
A slick and easy generalization
Appeals too well to his imagination.

It's true, of course, m'Lord, that you were dead
   Before the four great Russians lived, who brought
The art of novel writing to a head;
   The help of Lending Libraries not sought.
   But now the art for which Jane Austen fought,
Under the right persuasion, bravely warms
And is the most prodigious of the forms.

She was not an unshockable blue-stocking;
   If shades remain the characters they were,
No doubt she still considers you as shocking.
   But tell Jane Austen—that is, if you dare—
   How much her novels are beloved down here.
She wrote them for posterity, she said;
'Twas rash, but by posterity she's read.

You could not shock her more than she shocks me;
   Beside her, Joyce seems innocent as grass.

It makes me most uncomfortable to see
   An English spinster of the middle-class
   Describe the amorous effects of "brass,"
Reveal so frankly and with such sobriety
The economic basis of society.

Auden's ulterior choice of Lord Byron, then, rather than of Jane
Austen as the recipient of his contemporary report on The Way We
Live Now (the way we lived in 1938), is the other face of his alarm (expressed in a very '30s phrase which identifies Miss Austen as a sort of
Marxist *avant la lettre* and which a similarly period label would file under Castration Anxiety); his reluctance to direct his letter from Iceland
to this novelist who on the face of it might seem a lot more comfy, as
he would say, than the gimpy nobleman who once observed that a
lady should never be seen eating anything but lobster salad and champagne, is pretty much of a piece with most of the (male) defenses
against Jane Austen's authentic authority; ever since her books
appeared—anonymously, of course—she has been presented, praised,
and pilloried as a cameoist oblivious to her times or a stern propagan-
dist on behalf of a beleaguered ruling class; as a good, self-effacing
maiden aunt or a nasty, mean-spirited old maid; as a subtly discriminating prose stylist or a homely songbird unconscious of her art. This
last version comes, alas, from Henry James, whose condescension to
this author may puzzle us until we recognize that it was his surest
method of releasing himself from her mastery; always reticent and at
times even misleading on the subject of the real formative influences
upon his own art, James's loftily disparaging comments on Austen
need not extend our outrage beyond mere mention of their inadequacy here. What for my purposes we need to note is that when
Henry James observes that Miss Austen leaves us "hardly more curious of her process, or of the experience in her that fed it, than the
brown thrush who tells his [*sic*] story from the garden bough," he is
quite as determined as the twentieth-century poet who became an
American citizen in one World War, just as James became a British citizen in another, to characterize (and to undervalue) Austen as a *novelist*, no other kind of writer, certainly not a poet, songbird though she
may be . . .

Of course it is Jane Austen herself who has been chiefly responsible for this hedge against poetry which bristles so around all her enterprise. Today, women novelists of some wit and concision who concern themselves with those aspects of genteel life which can be viewed from the coffee-table and the desk-top computer are almost invariably compared by reviewers to Jane Austen. From Ivy Compton-Burnett to Fay Weldon and Anita Brookner, the imputation is invariably made, probably as exasperating to the modern makers as to their great predecessor. If they share one impulse—Mrs. Croft's untroubled insistence in *Persuasion* that women are "rational creatures" who can and indeed who must seize the reins lest the carriage overturn—yet it is very rare indeed that they have much in common with Austen's tough eighteenth-century mind, her severity of values, her inveterate sense of form. But it is interesting that a new woman poet of analogous lustres and apparent limitations—that Elizabeth Bishop, say, or May Swenson—is never compared to Miss Austen, nor Miss Austen to a poet, ever since Ruben Brower called her "Pope without couplets."

How different is this from major English novelists (except Trollope) since her time. Think of the Brontës and of George Eliot, of George Meredith, of Hardy and of Stevenson, even of Thackeray and Kipling—eager poets and assiduous verse-writers all; why even Dickens and Conrad are frequently characterized as prose-poets, and the enormous metaphorical flights of Henry James himself are seen by many critics of his last phase as a sort of excruciated poetry.

Whether or not Jane Austen was a conscious practitioner of the novel as an acknowledged literary form (and only Virginia Woolf among her first century of critics seems to have insisted that she was from the very start a committed artist), she never *regarded herself* as in any way allied with *the poets*. Nothing amused her more than to throw cold water on the enthusiasm (absurd condition!) they were able, if not likely, to inspire. Even in her last completed novel, so often felt to be composed with a sort of autumnal *obbligato*, the heroine chastises Mr. Benwick by "venturing to recommend a larger allowance of prose in his daily study." And I don't think Jane Austen was even *amusing* herself, I think she was speaking from her carefully guarded heart when, in the same book, she (indirectly but so powerfully) observes:

It was the misfortune of poetry to be seldom safely enjoyed by those who enjoyed it completely; the strong feelings which alone could estimate it truly were the very feelings which ought to taste it but sparingly.

Consider with me, for a moment, what she actually is saying: the very concept of "safe enjoyment" is asserted to be irreconcilable with "complete enjoyment" (as if the ordinary reader of poetry ought to practice a sort of *coitus interruptus* or safe sex, and leave the unprotected experience to those poor adepts—doomed to the "misfortune of poetry," she calls it!—who are willing to lose their legacy if not their lives in an unprotected exposure); the strong feelings which are the only proper qualification for judging this awful art are to be invoked (in order to taste this dangerous fruit) with the most fastidious caution.

In practice, right to the end, this response is quite consistent. Here, quite conclusively in her unfinished last novel of 1817, known as *Sanditon* though that is not a name she gave it, is the sensible heroine's response to the inflamed enthusiasm of her would-be seducer Sir Edgar:

He began to stagger her by the number of his Quotations and the bewilderment of some of his sentences. "Do you remember," said he, "Scott's beautiful Lines on the Sea? Oh what a description they convey! They are never out of my Thoughts when I walk here. That Man who can read them unmoved must have the nerves of an Assassin! Heaven defend me from meeting such a Man unarmed . . . But while we are on the subject of Poetry, what think you of Burns's lines to his Mary? If ever there was a man who *felt* it was Burns. Montgomery has all the Fire of Poetry, Wordsworth has the true soul of it—Campbell has touched the extreme of our Sensations—'Like Angel's visits, few & far between,' can you conceive anything more subduing, more melting, more fraught with the deep Sublime than that Line? But Burns—I confess my sense of his Pre-eminence. If Scott *has* a fault, it is the want of Passion. Tender, Elegant, Descriptive, but *Tame* . . . Burns now is always on fire. His Soul was the Altar in which lovely Woman sat enshrined, His Spirit truly breathed the immortal Incense which is her Due—"

"I have read several of Burns's poems with delight," said Charlotte as soon as she had time to speak, "but I am not poetic enough to separate a Man's Poetry entirely from his Character; and poor Burns's known Irregularities greatly interrupt my enjoyment of his Lines. I have difficulty in depending on the *Truth* of his Feelings as a Lover. I have not faith in the *sincerity* of the affections of a Man of his Description: he felt and he wrote and he forgot."

"Oh no, no!" exclaimed Sir Edward in an ecstasy, "He was all ardor and truth. It were Pseudo-philosophy to expect from the soul of high-toned Genius, the grovellings of a common mind. The coruscations of Talent, elicited by impassioned feeling in the breast of Man are perhaps incompatible with some of the prosaic decencies of Life—nor can you, loveliest Miss Heywood, nor can any Woman be a fair judge of what a man may be propelled to say, write, or do, by the sovereign impulses of illimitable Ardour."

This was very fine; but if Charlotte understood it at all, not very moral. She gravely answered, "I really know nothing of the matter. This is a charming day, the Wind, I fancy, must be Southerly." She began to think him downright silly. Why he should talk so much Nonsense, unless he could do no better, was unintelligible. He seemed very sentimental, and very much addicted to all the newest-fashioned hard words—had not a very clear Brain, she presumed, and talked a good deal by rote.

Now I am not so besotted a reader that I take Sir Edgar for Austen's exclusive representative of poetry and poetry-readers, nor do I account her heroine merely a mouthpiece for herself. Nevertheless, if we are to understand these lines at all, we are obliged to recognize that though she was a close contemporary of the first generation of great romantic poets—Wordsworth was five years, Coleridge three years older than she—Miss Austen was untouched by the romantic movement. Or rather, good Augustan daughter of Samuel Johnson as she

was, she refused to be so touched: she would have regarded such pal-
pation as an unwarranted and an unwanted intimacy. Since she died at
the age of forty-two in the year before *Endymion* was published, we
can only wonder what would she have made of Keats (though I believe I can hear quite distinctly her witty repudiation of the famous
Ode's famous assertion that "heard melodies are sweet, those unheard
are sweeter" as, simply, "unsound"), and what *could* she have made of
Shelley, whose behavior was ever so much more extreme than that of
poor Burns, and who in so many words observed that "in the infancy
of society every author is necessarily a poet." After all, Miss Austen did
not regard herself as living in the infancy, or even in the adolescence of
society—she was a grown-up among grown-ups, and if ripeness was
not quite all (as the poet had claimed), it was, as dear Dr. Johnson had
said, highly desirable: Sunday *should* be different from another day,
he remarked. People may walk, but not throw stones at birds.

It was in Jane Austen's defense that G. H. Lewes, one of her first
impassioned critics, wrote to Charlotte Brontë "Miss Austen is not a
poetess" (this assertion offered without our advantage of reading
Austen's own observation, which I have already cited, that *she was not
poetic enough to separate a man's character from his poetry*); and it was in
opposition to this claim that the author of *Jane Eyre* wrote back "Can
there be a great artist without poetry?"

Probably not; but as long as a man's poetry is identified with a man's
character, and a woman's poetry with what is felt to be her lack of character, and as long as being *poetic* is regarded as coincident with a certain
carelessness, it will be necessary for this unmarried, middle-class, scrib-
bling woman, publishing her work without her name attached to it and
arguably a kind of exile in her own country, launching a tactful challenge to the gender injustices of both those militant institutions marriage and private property, and secretly committed to uncovering, with
great delicacy but still uncovering, the ideological underpinnings of
many cultural myths, to separate herself from poetry and all its works.

Well, not from quite all. If she was Pope without couplets she
wasn't much of Pope—indeed she speaks approvingly of a gentleman
in *Sense and Sensibility* who *admires Pope no more than is proper*. The
poet she admired quite properly is Cowper, whom Fanny Price actu-

ally quotes in *Mansfield Park*, and whose long poem *The Task* of 1785 endeared its author to Jane Austen, perhaps precisely for its subjugation of the natural to the human, as in these lines from Book III:

> Strength may wield the pond'rous spade
> May turn the clod, and wheel the compost home;
> But elegance, chief grace the garden shows
> And most attractive, is the fair result
> Of thought, the creature of a polish'd mind.

Thirteen years later, Wordsworth was to recommend, in *Lines Composed a Few Miles Above Tintern Abbey*:

> . . . those steep and lofty cliffs
> That on a wild secluded scene impress
> Thoughts of a more deep seclusion; and connect
> The landscape with the quiet of the sky.

This sort of thing would never do. Mr. Knightly's dislike of picnics in *Emma* is characteristic of Jane Austen's entire approved personnel; *his* idea of the simple and natural, it will be recalled, was "to have the table spread in the dining-room. The nature and the simplicity of gentlemen and ladies, with their servants and furniture . . . is best observed by meals within doors." (This is probably the place to report that if Austen showed no fondness for Wordsworth, the great Lake Poet had not much for her; he admitted that her novels were an "admirable copy of life, but he could not be interested in productions of that kind; unless the truth of nature were presented to him clarified, as it were, by the pervading light of imagination, it had scarce any attractions in his eyes.")

Cowper, therefore, is Jane Austen's man, with his entirely anti-Wordsworthian, and certainly anti-romantic notion of what is to be done with the out-of-doors:

> Who loves a garden, loves a green-house too.
> Unconscious of a less propitious clime
> There blooms exotic beauty, warm and snug,
> While the winds whistle and snows descend . . .

As for the other Austen-sanctioned poet, George Crabbe—whom most of us know as the source, in his poem *The Borough*, of Benjamin Britten's *Peter Grimes*—I cannot believe Jane Austen, despite her registered approval in a letter to her sister Cassandra, really cared so much for Crabbe as for Cowper; nonetheless, if he no longer paid his principal attentions, not to speak of devotions, to a domesticated nature but rather to the misery and distress of the improvident poor, at least he entertained, in sturdy couplets, the fate of *other people* a good deal closer to Miss Austen's chosen milieux, in tales like "The Frank Courtship" and "The Lover's Journey" with their scenes of village middle-class wooing and romantic deceptions coolly unmasked. At least he did not, like Lord Byron (and like all other poets, according to Auden), deal only with himself, and (as in Byron's case) with an errant, wanton, peccant self at that!

But Jane Austen's languid esteem for a couple of minor Augustans is no argument for any authentic and active interest she might take in poetry. I think we must look deeper into her commitment, from her first satirical efforts, to the art she had seized upon—her consecration, actually, to novel-writing and to prose. There was no place for poetry in the world of a committed novelist, for poetry, ultimately, is utterance which is valued for itself, not for what it connects or leads too. Poetry was not only of no help in her chosen profession, it was a distinct hindrance—for poetry was that pause, that silence, that cessation effected in the conversation, and in the career, the romance, the *life!* when no relations could be understood, no judgments applied, no sense made. Jane Austen the novelist was not interested in silences; unheard melodies were quite sour to her—she had her story to tell, her conversation to extend, her career, her romance, her life to lead, and if poetry could decorate the progress, well enough; but since, for the most part, it could do no such thing, away with it! For poetry was precisely a part of life dissociated from the conduct and character of human beings as they were to be observed by this sharp-eyed outsider who centered her novels in the consciousness of unempowered characters—that is, of women.

"Seldom, very seldom," she wrote in *Emma*, "does complete truth belong to any human disclosure, seldom can it happen that something is not a little disguised, or a little mistaken." It was Jane Austen's genius to disclose more while disguising less, and she accomplished this by rejecting altogether that one human enterprise which, from the earliest organization of all our societies, has meant that language was to operate for itself, without immediate social consequences.

If she was to rewrite the lexicon of conservative discourse, she would have to eschew that one art which depended on the constituted language which functioned only, as she so wittily observed, for its own sake. Will it seem paradoxical if I conclude my report as to Miss Austen's antipoetical stance with a poem about Jane Austen? It seems to me the only revenge a poet might take, and I shall take it now, in closing, with a poem of my own.

Awareness of Austen *as an author* was extraordinarily limited in her lifetime; as late as 1803 her nosy cousin Egerton Brydges did not know that she was "addicted to literary composition," as he put it, and the memoir of the novelist by her nephew tells us that "few of her readers knew even her name and none knew more than her name; it is not possible to mention any other author of note whose personal obscurity was so complete." This snobbish family chronicle did not appear until 1870, then stimulating a mild rediscovery; perspective was, so to speak, far to seek, especially since there was still such a fierce debate among critics and famous authors, who numbered among themselves certain genuine Austen haters, like Mark Twain who in describing a ship's library in 1897 exulted that "Jane Austen's books are absent. Just that one omission alone would make a fairly good library out of a library that hadn't a book in it." Informed scholarship and even judicious criticism, in such an atmosphere, are unlikely (recall that Carlyle called her novels "dish-washings" and that Jane Carlyle said they were "too washy, water-gruel for mind and body"); praise was not much likelier, making this author into the sort of angelic icon which recent centuries most distrust—for example, the official (family) biographer asserts, having prodigiously destroyed all Jane Austen's private papers, that she "never felt any attachment which affected her happiness"; the picture we have inherited of this author leaves us uncertain whether to put it over the fireplace or into it. Scholarship, as I say, is likely to be belated in such a case, and it is not until the 1920s that R. W. Chapman, who among many other editorial and critical tasks, such as providing editions of the novels which have now satisfied more than two generations of critics, compiled a famous *Jane Austen Bibliography*. It is a clubman's volume, omitting essays open, as he says, to the familiar objection that their subject would not have understood them. As Chapman writes, Austen would turn over in her grave if she heard scholars describe her novels in terms alien to her apprehension, the apparatus of literary history and textual scholarship, to say nothing of post-structural interpretation, being regarded as likely to misrepresent her enterprise. To Chapman, Jane Austen is in the canon not because of her social vision or her artistry, but because she had the good fortune to be able and the good taste to be willing to record the elegant manners of her time. Hence with an inexorable circularity, Chapman's edition of Austen creates the author it presumes, and the history it desires, a graceful monument to country life in Regency England, inveterately given to graciousness and tranquillity. Such is not the writer we read at the century's end, though I bet she has such readers still. There is a small library of feminist, Marxist, Lacanian, and deconstructive criticism now, and its excesses are indeed a corrective to what happens when, as my poem has it, we lately look into this Chapman's Jane Austen, even as the Keats unknown to her first looked into Chapman's Homer. I leave you, then, with this poem in the matter of Jane Austen, a novelist with whom poetry has, apparently, so little to do.

ON LATELY LOOKING INTO CHAPMAN'S *JANE AUSTEN: A CRITICAL BIBLIOGRAPHY*

"The passions," Charlotte Brontë was at pains
to notify her correspondent (male),
"are perfectly unknown to her. Of course
a lady! all you like—I see you do—

but as a woman, incomplete." "She is
unpleasant—English in the snobbish sense:
a mean old maid," wrote Lady Chatterley's
creator, and the list goes on from there.

Can we forgive her? Even Henry James
was likely to be snappish on the score
of "our dear, their dear, everybody's dear
Aunt Jane . . ." who had never trifled with Keats

and travelled not at all in "realms of gold"
or any other glamour, if we trust
her answer (after *Emma*!) to the Prince,
that she confined herself to "pictures of

domestic life in country villages,
and could no more engage to write Romance
than Epic Poems!" Keats, who could, affords
a clue. Consult *our* Chapman (anything

but "loud and bold"—amazingly discreet),
and feel instead "like a watcher of the . . . *depths*
when a new *species* swims into his ken":
for her—for the species Austen—love, like death,

is the great leveller, but not because
everyone loves (or dies), but just because
no one—not even Lawrence—understands
what love (or death) can mean. And we are left,

eagle-eyed or even a little dim,
to ogle each other "with a wild surmise,
silent on a pique" (ah, Charlotte!), still
commanded to acknowledge what *she* knows:

that Wisdom's secret is detachment, not
withdrawal. And that nobody is damned
except by his own deliberate act. Or hers . . .
Perfectly unknown? "If we have not lived

within a family, we cannot well say
what any of its members' griefs may be";
holding her method by that end, she pulled,
and as she pulled, it came. Homeric Jane.

Apart: Hearing Secret Harmonies
in Esther

[1987]

These stories were told us—very young children, disaffected Jews in a Midwestern suburb—before we read them, before we could read at all. At first they were told as *Bible Stories for the Young*, but very soon they were read to us from the Authorized Version. Greek myths and Shakespeare could be diluted almost indefinitely, but the Old Testament—like the tales of Andersen and the Grimm brothers—soon came to us in what passed for original strength. It never occurred to us that such things were translations.

And out of the stories, as they were told, as they were heard, loomed a sort of wandering wonder we associated with any telling—it could be Alice, it could be Artemis—a cloud of conjecture inseparable from its source in "ancestral voices prophesying. . . ." There was always the implication, of course, that eventually we would be reading—for ourselves, as it were—that we would bestow upon all such received matter the resolved and rectified attention which *reading* inveterately signified. I think we understood, even in our passive condition, even in our delight, that a time would come when we would be reading *on our own*, that we might at that time *correct* the promiscuous and irresponsible suppositions of hearing by a more severe indoctrination. We would leave off the appropriate response to telling, which was speculation, and take up the appropriate response to reading, which was acquiescence. No wonder, then, that we were encouraged to learn how to read for ourselves, which meant for others, whereas when we listened to others telling, we heard—and hypothecated—for ourselves.

Indeed, in the ensuing years I was informed and sometimes admonished that my own excessive bookishness was evidence of my Jewishness. I was one more bespectacled child who had learned to read "too soon"; my literacy was a symptom of my lineage. Were we not—as ignorant of Islam as we were knowing about the *Arabian Nights*—the people of the Book? But as I loiter more inquisitorially over my early experience with these stories, with the histories and apocrypha of the Bible as I heard them, I must acknowledge that we were the people, initially, of the Tale. Telling, and hearing, came first, and the process was marvelous, metamorphic, meant. We were beguiled by, and brought together upon, narratives which in their recounting allowed for—indeed which compelled—all kinds of speculation as to their outcome and as to their ongoing likelihood. The Scroll of Esther was merely a characteristic wonder as it unwound in the telling. Perhaps because of the doubleness of its method it was more resonant than the others, more resplendent, and could lead more easily, by the very contrast of the eponymous half of its substance with the rest of its matter, into the auguries of imagined life.

In the largest, cloudiest apprehension, I knew that Esther was about my mother, and that Mordecai was about the world—about my stepfathers and the struggle for survival. Esther was magic, Mordecai was management. Exactly apprehended, the process was accounted for by Michelet, though neither a Jew nor a child, in *The Bible of Humanity* (1864):

> The history of the Jews, at whatever level of seriousness, transpired against a fictive background—the arbitrary miracle, in which it pleased God to choose among the lowest, indeed among the unworthiest, a liberator, a savior, an avenger of His people. In the Captivity or in Court intrigues, sudden fortunes cast imaginations on the path of the unexpected. The splendid historical novels of Joseph, Ruth, Tobit, Esther, Daniel and many more appeared. Always based on two figments: *the good exile* who, by the interpretation of dreams and financial astuteness, becomes minister or favorite; and *the woman beloved of God*

who makes a great marriage, attains to glory, seduces the enemy and (astonishingly enough, in contrast with Mosaic notions) becomes a deliverer of her people. But it is precisely the unexpected choice which fiction seizes upon: God makes the woman a snare, utilizes her seductiveness, and through her brings about the downfall of a man he has doomed. There is the essence of the novel: it is the contrary of history, not only because it subordinates great collective interests to an individual destiny, but because it does not favor the ways of that difficult preparation which in history produces events. The novel prefers to show us the lucky throws of the dice which chance occasionally produces, to flatter us with the notion that the impossible frequently becomes possible. By this hope, this interest, this pleasure, fiction wins its reader, spoiled from the start, who will pursue it avidly—to the point where he foregoes talent, even skill. The chimerical mind is interested in the story, in the *affair*, wants it *to turn out well.*

Esther (and, scarcely to a lesser degree, Susannah and Judith) was the heroine in whom, as soon as I had heard her story, I invested *that hope, that interest, that pleasure,* for she was less arbitrary than Alice (after all, from my perspective she was a grown-up) and less absolute than Artemis (after all, she was a mortal). And if, as Michelet so uncannily perceived, I was spoiled from the start, it was not just because I wanted the story to turn out well (though I did, I did—I lingered over every seductive detail likely to establish Esther's invincible appeal; or, rather, I did not linger, I ran ahead, I devised every possible allurement out of whatever lay around the house, out of anything I deemed likely to move the Ahasuerus of South Park Boulevard, my imminent stepfather), but also because I entertained [*sic*] so many fears of its turning out otherwise, because there was so wide a margin for error. Only the story of Scheherazade—not the stories she told, but *her* story, her situation, her discovery that silence was death and *telling* was life—could rival the enchantment of "Bible stories," and indeed the reason for that rivalry, for that equivalence, would become apparent to me as I marveled over Esther.

My amazements here began at the beginning, began with what

narratologists would call the prologue: the repudiation of Vashti. For, in order to produce Esther, in order to bring on the heroine, if there was to be a heroine at all, place must be made for her. And was there a hero? Why was Mordecai given such minor billing? His was a position comparable to Joseph's—obviously Joseph's story had exerted a strong influence on the writer of Esther—and indeed in the *Book of the Chronicles of the Kings of Media and Persia* referred to at the end of Esther it is "the greatness of Mordecai" that is proclaimed, not the greatness of Esther. Emphasis in the early sources on Mordecai rather than on Esther suggests that there were indeed two stories, two *affairs*: the *history* of Mordecai, engaged in court intrigue, jealousy, and persecution of the Jews in Susa, and the *story* of Esther, who won her king's favor and prevented the persecution of her people: *i.e.*, the *tale* of Esther, the *book* of Mordecai. The heroine must replace the old queen. Who was no such thing, this offstage Vashti: she was young and lovely—so lovely that her extravagant and impulsive lord commands her to exhibit her beauty to the people and princes at a feast, wearing the royal turban or *Megilla*. (*Megilla*, in our house, was not known to be the Hebrew word for "scroll"; it was the word assigned to anything complicated or intricate.) Here was a story, or at least a circumstance, which I could commit to speculation, for I knew it already; I had heard it already, as I had heard of Artemis and Alice. I had been told a Greek story of King Candaules, who was so proud of his queen's loveliness that he contrived to have his servant see her naked. . . . I knew how that story ended, if it was allowed to end. But in the story of Ahasuerus (which scholars in Göttingen as recently as 1958 related to the story in Herodotus through an original Persian New Year festival), the ending was altered. The story changed. For the lovely queen, whether or not she must appear naked at the feast (some rabbis actually suggest that Vashti was commanded to attend the feast clad in the *Megilla* and in nothing else), was but demonstrating decorum in refusing to appear before a crowd of drunken men. Indeed, was she not asserting her royal prerogative? For when the drinking began at a feast, that would be the signal for concubines and courtesans to join in. If Vashti appeared at the feast then, she would no longer be queen, but would by her mere presence be degraded to the status of a concubine. And were there not some commentators—they were Christians, but even so—who recognized in such reluctance a propriety so pervasive that they declared Vashti to be the only admirable person in the entire tale, precisely by virtue of her refusal to accede to her giddy husband's perverse and perilous command? ("I am so hostile to Esther," Luther remarked in his *Table Talk*, "that I could wish she did not exist at all; for Esther and Maccabees judaize too greatly and contain much pagan impropriety.") Thus Vashti became, to my obstinate hypotheses, one of those haunting, secret figures in literature, like Lot's wife, who make one decisive negative gesture, who violate a commandment and then vanish forever, leaving only a symbolic transgression for memorial.

Here the story diverged from the Candaules theme and braided itself into another, one equally familiar to the ears of childhood: the story of Scheherazade. If we were to have Esther, Vashti *had* to be deposed. And the king, after half a year of feasting in his winter capital (which the Greek geographer Strabo declared to be so hot that snakes and lizards trying to crawl across the roads at noon were burned to death), his anger having subsided and his appetite revived, upon sober reflection *had* to be supplied with a new queen, "better than Vashti," to be chosen not just out of the harem of existing wives, concubines, consorts, and courtesans, but out of all the virgins of the realm. Certainly Memucan's suggestion of a nationwide search presented a much more exciting prospect to the king than the quotidian selection. It was easy to understand that the splendid postal system of the Persian empire ("nor snow nor sleet can stay these messengers from the swift completion of their appointed rounds": Herodotus's words were on the post-office cornice), later invoked to such purpose in this very story, would be employed in making sure that the *irrevocable decree* against Vashti was publicized. Those advisers would hardly want to confront the displeasure of a reinstated queen! But disobedience for disobedience—a subject of consuming interest to myself and my coevals in those days, when we were also told stories about the insubordinations of Brunnhilde and the last Mrs. Bluebeard—it seemed to me that Vashti, in refusing to appear, was no more refractory than Esther would later prove in refusing to stay away. But perhaps I had already learned, with regard to kings and fathers and husbands, that there were *degrees* of transgression, and that one violation of the rules provokes anger, and another may elicit, just as readily, mercy. . . .

Now, what happened, I wondered, to this wife who had been put away? Where had she gone? Deposed . . . Repudiated . . . Was it like "divorced," as I identified such abjurations in my own family, in Cleveland? My mother had already been divorced—twice. And I knew her to be a vivid figure, still, in the world of those discarded—and discarding?—figures. Was Vashti still accommodated somewhere in the palace, despised perhaps but not altogether disposed of? I knew of households, no grander than our own, in which some awkward aunt, some senile grandmother, had separate quarters at the top of the house, visitable but not receivable. After all, the virgins whom Ahasuerus condescended to inspect (I could imagine that the king's servants were eager to smooth away his discontent), and to whom he eventually preferred Esther, were not eliminated in the manner of Scheherazade's predecessors. Following a night with the king, apparently an unsatisfactory one, such women were not beheaded but merely relegated to a "second" harem, where they would wait—apparently the rest of their lives—for the king to summon them, to call them by name. Of course, I had some clues as to why Esther had been preferred to these women, and what mistakes the others had made—beyond sexual incompetence, which I failed to take into account, though I was fascinated by the notion of a year's preparation to please the king: six months of massage with oil of myrrh and six months with balsam and other unspecified cosmetics. Each virgin, the story went, on her way to the king was permitted to take with her anything she desired. Esther alone, it would seem, required nothing, and obtained favor by requiring nothing. Evidently the compunctions of Cinderella were in force here, and I recognized the merits of modesty and an unassuming demeanor, even one that had been massaged and perfumed for twelve months.

Esther herself was only called "queen," of course. She did not rule, once the king set the *Megilla* upon her head and threw her a party ("even Esther's feast"). And later, though she had been acknowledged queen for five years, she occupied a precarious position still, at least in her own mind. She did not put herself forward in any way, therefore, and made no claim upon her lord, but remained all that time in the harem, waiting. And if all the concubines and even the wives who did not find favor in the king's eyes were confined along with the approved "queen" to that world of women which the word "harem" signified to me (and where, after all, "to die" might have meant nothing graver than not to be alive in the king's imagination, not to be present in his thoughts), did Esther and Vashti never meet there? What might such an encounter be like—the confrontation at the well, or in the baths (I had seen reproductions of Ingres's uterine fantasy of the women's baths as well as Gérôme's)—between the new queen, still unfamiliar with Ahasuerus, and the once-favored queen, who had been so arbitrarily thrust aside? As yet Esther had not "showed her kindred nor her people." Universally popular in the harem and elsewhere, Esther must have eaten, dressed (and undressed), and behaved like a Persian harem-girl, rather than like an observant Jewess. What, then, would she and Vashti say to each other? What precepts might be passed on, what experience shared? This was not a situation Scheherazade was ever obliged to contend with—rather, it was one that could crop up only in a thoroughly modern harem. I pondered the relationships—marital, divorced, adulterous, matronly, and virginal—which I could identify in the society around me (Cleveland 1936, say, as opposed to Susa 500 B.C.E.), and I marveled at Esther's *astuce* in beguiling the king's impulses rather than expressing her own, in showing the docility and submissiveness so notably lacking in her predecessor. Though perhaps—and here I began my own embroidery, my own affabulation—with the wisdom of hindsight, it was Vashti who had advocated such attitudes in her successor. I could imagine the scene all the more readily for having witnessed analogous encounters between present wife and "ex," between *maitresse en titre* and old flame: deprecating or implacable, as the case might be. The story of Esther, as I mused upon it, was one that transpired in an astonishingly alien world of sultans and viziers, as in the *Arabian Nights*, and yet in a world of reassuring familiarity, as in Hollywood movies and at our own dinner table. The Oriental despot who would hand over an entire people to his cruel vizier without even inquiring as to that people's name was the same tyrant who had just repudiated his wife on a whim and who would shortly execute his vizier on a new wife's word. As one ancient Jewish commentator put it, Ahasuerus sacrifices his wife to his friend and later sacrifices his friend to his wife. Even the names of the (ultimately Jewish) hero and heroine were instructive as to this doubleness, this ambiguity: Esther and Mordecai bear not only non-Hebraic but even idolatrous names (so that Esther, a Daniel in reverse, must be given a second name, the Hebrew name Hadassah, which is interpreted to mean "myrtle—for as the myrtle spreads fragrance in the world, so did she spread good works"). Ishtar and Marduk are pertinently proposed as the Babylonian gods whose ritual became a historicized Jewish myth, "a Jewish adaptation of a popular Persian novella."

Certainly, with the introduction of the second story, the story of Mordecai, a history of manipulation and intrigue, it was clear to me that Hadassah was the heroine's appropriate name when she figured in the Mordecai tradition, and Esther was her appropriate name when she belonged to the magical tradition. Once Vashti had been spirited away (as in so many apocryphal harem tales), there was every indication that the Scroll of Esther was no more (no less?) than a conflation of two texts. Indeed, one French scholar, Henri Cazelles, found evidence for this duplicity in the pervasive "twoness" of episodes and situations in the tale: two banquets; two lists of seven names, one the reverse order of the other; the second house of the women; the second contingent of candidates for the king's favor; Esther's two dinners; Haman's two discussions with his wife, Zaresh, and his friends; Esther's twice risking her life by appearing before the king. One text, Cazelles asserts, was "liturgical" and concerns Esther/Ishtar, the provinces of the empire, and non-Jews at the time of the Persian New Year (so that Purim is to be identified with a bacchanalian Persian festival—this, of course, is also Frazer's reading of the story); and the other text is "historical" and concerns Mordecai the Jew, the persecution of Jews in Susa, and the working out of Court intrigues.

Even on an early hearing—before *reading* taught me to conflate, to correct, and to revise rather than to remember, before I learned even to glimpse what Professor Cazelles and his like might be suggesting

by the operations of higher criticism—I knew that there was a difference in the kind of interest I might invest in the Esther who exposed
herself for her (as yet unacknowledged) people, and the interest I was
expected to take in Esther/Hadassah, Mordecai's "daughter," the instrument of political manipulation. I know now what the difference
was, for I have learned that in all cultures what is known as Wisdom
literature is another thing altogether from law and history and prophecy. Wisdom literature is not Jewish, of course—it bubbles up out
of Egyptian and Mesopotamian sources—and it is primarily concerned with happiness and success in this world. As Dr. Moore tells us
in The Anchor Bible (Esther, volume 7B, where I have found so much
grist that I can barely persuade my mill to grind), it is noncultic and
detached in spirit, "prudential and pragmatic." It is what stories depend on. The story of Esther—the Esther we are asked to regard as a
heroine, the Esther for whom the scroll is named, though it is Mordecai who outstrips her in all the earliest sources—is a Wisdom narrative,
the kind I must also have recognized in the attitudes and even in the
costumes of those other women, the conspicuously attired or abluted
Susannah, Jael, Judith, all the way to Salome, perverse echo of these
heroic ladies. In the Cleveland Museum of Art, and in books of art reproductions, I had pored over the magic effects of their appearance:
Susannah observed in her bath by the elders, Judith adorning herself
to beguile Holofernes. And I had watched my mother getting ready
for those evenings with those men, one of whom would become, I
knew, another of my stepfathers. I also knew (I *learned*) what significance might be attributed to the proper placing of a jewel, the right
choice of a perfume: secrets of the harem! In them was to be discerned,
to be discovered, why it was that Esther was a heroine, why she was so
brave and so brilliant. *The toilette of Esther* was a subject for mannerists
and the Baroque masters, for Tintoretto and Veronese, Rubens,
Poussin, and Claude Lorrain. It was what appeared to be her particular heroism: preparing herself to appear, unasked, before the king.

There was a detail here that always held me fast in the hearing, a
ritual detail which I felt I understood in a secret way. Until this moment I have never sought to confirm my understanding, but was not
Esther's decision to broach the king's presence unasked (an apparition

which jeopardized her life) a form of sexual violation, a reversal of male and female roles which would dangerously suggest autonomy in a woman and submissiveness in a man, at odds with the orthodox view? Was this not the sense of the scene's climax? "When the king saw Esther the queen standing in the court, she obtained favor in his sight, and the king held out to Esther the golden sceptre that was in his hand. So Esther drew near and touched the top of the sceptre." Is this not an expression of a certain sexual understanding between suppliant and sovereign? The condign phallic recognition which is granted to the "inadmissible" woman, and which is responded to by her dumb show as well: the king extends the golden scepter (it is licit that she rouse his desire) and the queen touches its top (she acknowledges phallocracy). Then they can talk. Then she can ask a favor, can ask anything, even unto half the kingdom. This, I remembered, was what Herod offers Salome to forestall her demand for the head of John the Baptist. But no one ever wants half the kingdom. Esther, in fact, wants the whole kingdom for her people, to whom she then and there reveals herself as belonging.

Though I had realized, as the Mordecai themes of the story were brought closer home by the developments of world politics, that it was cunning of the author to have managed to braid the two narratives together, there were still discrepancies. Why had Esther not heard about the edict which Haman had persuaded Ahasuerus to let him issue against the (unnamed) Jews? Had Mordecai taken up his lamentations in the king's gate so quickly that word had not yet reached the harem? Was Esther so isolated there that she had heard nothing? Or was she so indifferent to the problems of the outside world and of her people that she did not care? No, I think I understood even then that Esther simply had no part in *that story*, that Haman does not even mobilize royal forces against the Jews—he marks them as outlaws. The king's protection is withdrawn from them: they may be killed and plundered by anyone with impunity. Whereas Mordecai's edict grants the right of self-defense to the outlawed Jews, who may "stand for their life" and with impunity kill those who would kill and plunder them. In other words, in the Mordecai story, parity is established between the Jews and their enemies. These enemies are never named, we do not know who they are, and Haman is isolated so that his decree against the Jews is really a decree against Mordecai, an act of personal vengeance. As far as Jews in general go, the city of Susa is said to be *perplexed* (grieved) when Haman's edict is published, and the same city rejoices in Mordecai's appointment as vizier in Haman's place. And Esther only returns to the story here, having passed up two splendid opportunities to intercede for her people, the king in each instance having committed himself to granting her even half the kingdom.

Esther's return to the story is part of her fascination—her fascination with regard to that preliterate audience of which I was such an impassioned member. For her "action" is a passion, indeed a passivity. "Had we been sold for bondmen and bondwomen, I had held my tongue," Esther says, "but we are sold to be destroyed, to be slain, and to perish." Whereupon, once she has named Haman, Esther's part in the story is eliminated, or, rather, is emphasized: she lies upon her couch, unmoving, as Haman falls upon it ("upon the bed whereon Esther was"), permitting the king to reach the most damaging interpretation possible. As with Vashti, it is essential that Ahasuerus be removed from the room. Commentators have offered a long list of explanations for the king's tempestuous withdrawal and return ("the king arising from the banquet of wine in his wrath went into the palace garden . . . then the king returned out of the palace garden into the place of the banquet of wine"). The story comes to its magical (as opposed to managerial) conclusion with a tableau of retributive justice: Haman—who should have sought mercy from the king, not from his revealed racial enemy—at Esther's feet, was actually *lying on her bed*, and either seizing her feet or kissing them. And Esther simply allowed her position (in every sense of the word) to do the rest. For, according to harem regulations, even if Haman had prostrated himself a foot away from the queen's couch, the king's reaction could still have been justified—though many scholars have characterized that reaction as excessive, unreasonable, or just plain drunk. Esther's *petition* is no such thing, of course—it is an admission. She has not so much unmasked the villain as she has unmasked herself. Esther's heroism is self-revelation—the rest is politics. *Tout commence en mystique*, Péguy says, *et finit en politique*. Certainly that is the arrangement arrived at in the Scroll of Esther.

Furthermore, the response of world literature to this theme has been similarly doubled, similarly divided. The tale became a preferred subject of miracle plays of the religious theater, from Spain to Moscow. *La Hermosa Ester* is Lope de Vega's version, and the first play in Russian, produced in 1672, is based on the same tale. Racine's version complicated the magic, for the court of Louis XIV recognized Vashti as Madame de Montespan, the Hebrews as Huguenots or Jansenists, and of course Esther as Madame de Maintenon! Handel's oratorio— whose words were long thought to have been written by Pope and Dr. Arbuthnot—restores the tale to a less clearly keyed articulation, and thereby both Voltaire and Tom Paine found Esther "execrably cruel" and the book "fabulous." How appropriate that Jefferson, our most inexorably political Father, should advise reading such books "as you would read Livy or Tacitus," historians—not as you would read Ovid or Virgil.

Just as I knew that human beings, not Jehovah, delivered the Jews, so my delight in the Scroll of Esther, by the time I could read, was a delight that there was a power disparate from that of politics, a power that inheres in Wisdom literature, though that literature might well be called the literature of folly. For that power is merely and magically that of showing forth, apparition, epiphany of the person, of the poor, defenseless, and, as I could determine now, invincible human body. Mordecai and his machinations enabled the Jews to escape Haman and to meet his wicked enmity with a countervailing force. They had nothing to do with the story of Esther as I had *heard* it, as I immediately and inwardly understood it, the story of the revealed mystery of presence. That story was a much cruder, much earlier, much more primal one. It was no longer the master of the deliverance of the Jewish people through a brave woman. It was a reminder, urged as by a tidal undulation from an unacknowledged depth, of the body's power, beyond argument, beyond art, to beguile. Michelet was right about the kind of attention, of allegiance the story required: only it was not the "chimerical mind" which was at stake, for that mind was the reader's; it was the substantial body, and that body was the listener's.

A Description of Susan Sontag's "Description (of a Description)"

[1988]

B y this text and even by its title (and by ours, if we would acknowledge what hers intends), we are faced with a process Sontag has invoked before, particularly in her fictions (novels, tales, fables, allegories, emblems, screenplays) but not only there, for her essays and meditations frequently engage with it, almost as a method, particularly when the argument profits, as she conducts it, from being not ongoing but circular; it is a process so frequent—if not popular—in modernity that we are prepared to find it wherever there might loom or lurk a resistance to narrative thrust, to linear time, to a merely mimetic scription.

This process has no name in English critical discourse, though its most celebrated instance occurs in our most celebrated drama, and though we recognize its existence throughout our literature—indeed we recognize its existence as an essential device of representation, and perhaps of culture itself. The French (whose name for it we must borrow, as we have borrowed *novel* or *nocturne*, *enjambement* or *paysage moralisé*) call it "putting (*x*) *en abyme*," an old expression from heraldry, whereby in the center of the shield is set another tiny shield, its replica in every respect, except for its diminution. We recognize it as the Quaker Oats effect, of course, or to catch up my reference to *Hamlet*, as the play within a play, the story inlaid within the story and, being thus compressed, adjuvant to the nature of the environing enterprise. But useful as such a figure may be (we recall how eagerly

Gide would hail the device in his notes for *The Counterfeiters*), it be-
wilders as well, perhaps as much as it enlightens, by its suggestion of
infinite regress. The word comes from the Greek *abyssos*, "bottomless."
Bewilderments already abound: we commit a contradiction in terms
when we speak of *the bottom of the abyss*, and a pleonasm when we
speak of a *bottomless* one. Perhaps that is why Sontag, in a text of
only four pages, finds it so prone to her purposes, among which—
inveterately—is the mirroring of writing by itself, so that her title
invokes the geometrical sense: the tracing or traversing of a course, as
the *description* of an arc or a circle; and of course the ingenious parallel
to *deconstruction*—the de-scription of a description, the conversion
of (any possible) function to WRITING.

Look first at her prose, as it takes the page. Many short paragraphs,
the longest ten lines, each appended (what we may call an *adscript*) to
a fragment given in italics. We recall examples of this not from fiction,
of course, but from the literature of exegesis, most recently in Barthes's
S/Z. It has been apparent to several writers of Sontag's generation—to
Barthelme, to Gass, to Davenport—that there were figurations and
contraptions which a new, or a renewed, fiction would find generative
in Barthes's criticism, for just as the genre of such works as *Camera
Lucida* or *A Lover's Discourse* is uncertain, so the fictions that have
found a resource there make less of a claim to be fiction in the "story"
sense, and more of one in the "poetic" sense, which is to say, a *made
thing*, for in that sense a fiction and a poem are one.

There is no identification of the italicized text, much fenestrated so
that each of its fragments—what Barthes would call a *lexeme*—is given
the proprietary and instigating status of a *scriptural* utterance. Indeed,
there is no identification of a great deal in the piece. We do not know
even the sex of the speaker(s), and we are warned early on that the
more elided, the more *comes back*. And many things are elided—it is almost as if Sontag had determined that she could set our narrative
processes working without the usual bait, without the determinations
which so much of modern fiction has appeared distressed by: where?
who? when? But to keep to my observation, initially, of the way the
piece *looks*, we notice that there is no paragraph *without* an italic *in-
scription*; apparently there must be something to get the commentary

going in each case; the commentary or *midrash* cannot break away
from its incitement, though it can argue with it, question its authority, wonder about its rightness. There has been something that has
come first, that goes before, and Sontag's text manages to dramatize
this response to predecession by the italic/roman script alternation,
though neither the instigating text (the *prescription*?) nor what will become the extraordinarily personal gloss (the *subscription*?) is accounted
for, is *ascribed* to a particular speaker. Let us search for some clues. No,
clues are what we have—let us consider them.

The initial italic phrase offers us a triple temporal shoehorn, and
though for all its detail we still have no certainty what year, what season, what century is intended, we recognize in the formality and the
elaboration of the three elements that the italic phrase may be earlier
in time than the comment, has perhaps an *old-time* flavor—with which
the commentary immediately takes issue. If the person writing the
commentary is to be perceived as the same person who *has written* the
italic phrase (does this not appear to be the case? Certainly a kind of
responsibility is being taken: "I give the time but not the village"),
then a certain self-criticism is being made. Here we are on familiar
grounds in Sontag's fiction, all of whose protagonists are—as this one,
too, will be—self-doubters to the point of pain and debilitation. Yet
the final italic phrase (skipping four pages ahead), disturbingly gno-
mic, sounds like something we remember, something we recognize:
that notion of experience as invention, of truth as acknowledged lie—
where have we heard that before? Where *will* we have heard that before, as it turns out? Certainly the commentary, here at the last, enters
in the most forceful manner possible. We are given an identification,
we are given a literary allusion, and we are given a powerful sign-off,
a devastating coda that sends us circling helplessly into the abyss of exegesis and narrativity alike, compelled like the Ancient Mariner to repeat a "story," obsessively to suffer a fate, endlessly inscribed, even
within *someone else's* expression. If the "I" of the commentary wishes to
be known, to make himself/herself known, he/she latches onto the
grand if familiar myth of Crusoe, invoking another set of recessions
(Defoe over Selkirk, the novel over autobiography, revision over
scripture—"an *urban* Robinson Crusoe"—a further impetus into the

past) in order to do so. Only in the last phrases do the italic phraseology and the roman commentary overlap, indeed coincide. Between the testy beginning—are we in the nineteenth century? is it a New England village? is it Switzerland? Can there be thatched huts and a film preview in the same world of discourse?—and this mini-maelstrom of an ending, there are extraordinary divergences to be reconciled or at least acknowledged, room must be allowed for discrepancies of the most wildly confessional order, and a sense rehearsed that *any* experience—evidence, happening, continuum—will permit, if not compel, the author of the commentary to question once again his/her failures, obsessions, a dolorous stoicism.

The division in experience suffered by the author of the commentary takes on a decisive tinge not accommodated by the italic text, though the "I" there proposes the dilemma too: would the subject have done this rather commonplace humane thing, have responded to another's distress, had it been foretold? Can we rely upon ourselves, beyond the spontaneous (and irresponsible) fact, to project an hypothesis of selfhood that will account for and anticipate how we may (must) react to any and every occasion? It is one of Sontag's constant preoccupations, this location and vocation of the self. And I find it capital that the expansive speaker here, the author of the commentary (if that is what it is), chooses precisely this moment of uncertainty and hysterical supposition—if forewarned, would that speaker not have done just what the "victim" has done: fall down and become another prone, felled, resourceless being?—chooses, indeed, precisely this moment of indetermination to dilate upon that other world of experience not even hinted at by the italic text. The world of "you."

It is just the knowledge or the foreknowledge of response—the conviction that, under a given circumstance, this is what the self would do—which brings to the surface of the discourse what separates the experience of the italic text from the experience of the commentator. And suddenly there is a kind of solution of continuity, there ceases to be the rather snappish, resentful querying of the italic text, as if the commentator had been reading a translation not entirely trustworthy ("*For in the meantime . . . all possible drives would have had time to imagine. . . .*" "Drives? Forewarned, I could have. . . . But why should I?"). And instead, the commentary ventures at last on its own submersion in the destructive element. Precisely the recognition that one fallibility makes us all free, or at least fallible, releases the commentator to that *self*-recognition which is decisive: "I discover who I have become," *i.e.*, I suffer, therefore I am.

Between that inception which appears so querulous in its dealings with detail, so quizzical about the premonitions of a pathos to come ("mailed you so many abject letters"), and that decisive close which commits the speaker to a fetishized anamnesis, the glorification of what is sometimes called repetition-compulsion, Sontag's text proceeds by a device, or is it a division? which has become, over the years, her way of walking, her *enjambement*, precisely. If her structural metaphor is the figure *en abyme*, the principle of infinite regress, her metaphor of surface is the aphorism: a wisdom broken, a suspension between poetry which is always recurrence and prose which is always singularity. It will not surprise us that some of her most celebrated essays have been undertaken in this guise, or wise: fragmentation as voracity, break and enter, divide and conquer. And ever since *The Benefactor*, even her means of fictive characterization has been *this* means, epigram or aphorism; concision is her antidote to what Hegel calls *the prose of the world*, her saving grace in a medium that is damned for its mendacity. Barthes and Canetti are latter-day masters of the elliptical and the oblique, the aphoristic consciousness, and it is they, of course, whom Sontag eagerly salutes, along with Cioran and Pavese; not to mention, in its wilder ranges, Cage and Artaud. . . . The very international savor of these contemporary virtuosi of broken wisdom is one of Sontag's strongholds. Of all American writers of her generation, she is readiest to hurry after strange gods, aware that they may very well be the ones to shore up the holiness that has so continuously leaked out of the home-ground divinities (Emerson, so astutely hailed by Nietzsche, says little to her, or is not honored for saying it). As for the apothegmatic penchant, take "my love for you my idyllic self"—this is concision indeed, the reduction to seven words of an entire theory of ethical consciousness. What good is a theory, Sontag might say, that cannot be thus reduced? The awareness of being wounded, of flagrant pain ("to snatch composure from my insignificant terrors"), enables her stoicism, her widened awareness, what she calls, at the very end, "my watchful solitariness."

Momentarily it has seemed that I fail to separate Sontag from her speaker, her characterized commentator on that italic meditation which leaves us with the query *"To experience is to invent?"* I think my lapses into such an identification (who can doubt that it is Sontag who turns on herself and asks "is it true that we were happy once?") are warranted by the nature of the enterprise itself. Any text by Sontag, discursive or fictive, mistrusts a high mimetic surface, and she will go to strange lengths to puncture our ease in the narrative carapace, our security. The strangest length, as I have been surmising, is the explosion of narrative altogether (*Death Kit*, with its Dantesque allusions, is the largest instance), the recognition that in any story, any incident, any acknowledged *event* ("that which befalls us, that for which we are not prepared") is the likelihood and even the necessity for self-discovery, for self-recognition.

I think, our clues thus brooded upon, our devices grilled, we can now revert to the grander sort of identification: The description that Sontag has de-scribed, has pursued into its interstices, where she can lodge her own remarkable evidence of a wisdom shattered and thereby glinting, is a text by Friedrich Nietzsche, the merest anecdote from *Daybreak* (1881). I suggested, all unfairly by my reference to an untrustworthy translation, that of course we might recognize the tonality of "Must we go so far as to say that / in themselves / [our experiences] *contain nothing? / To experience is to invent?"* It is the tonality—questioning, subversive, liberating—of the early Nietzsche, before even *Zarathustra*, before *The Genealogy of Morals*, and Sontag has found within it—dividing it up into the lexemes that will enfranchise her own lacerations, her own liberations—the detonating mechanism, the trigger, the release that the modern writer readily finds in the work of the predecessor, the forebear, recalling that to find, *invenire*, is to come upon, is to invent.

A constant application to Nietzsche has been Sontag's resource from the beginning. I recall, some twenty years back, getting a glimpse of her notes for a series of lectures "Beyond Personality," and on one three-by-five card being startled to see the scrawl: *"NIETZ-*

SCHE—my hero!" It has been ever thus. And so this text becomes, beyond its sorties into storyland and confession country, a prepossessing *homage* to the enabling genius of the place. It is a kind of tribute by *collage*, a discovery of what there is to say, of what has to be said, by the force of juxtaposition, broken sentence against broken *sagesse*, past *versus* present, and otherness exacerbated into selfhood. I suggested, starting out, that Sontag may enjoy compelling us to respond to her plot without the usual linear inducements. For them she has substituted other temptations, other powers, and it is precisely the reversals and paradoxes of the Nietzschean resonance (*"What then are our experiences? / Much more / that which we put into them than / that which we already contain"*) that let her get in her own licks, that allow her to discover or invent her *native strain*, in any sense that phrase will bear. Promptest exponent of the "modern" resonance, Sontag has always scrutinized the masters for what would make them "her" masters. She is the most generous of our critics because she has discovered that the excellence and the ingenuity of art is precisely what will empower her to an autonomous rage of actions. Admiration is her analytic device, Penelope's web which she will pluck apart by night (in the darkness of critical texts) so that she may weave it again by day (in the dazzle of fictions and fables like *Description [of a Description]*). I daresay there is no more poignant self-explorer ("I am always starting up, straining to hear a change in the sound") among her contemporaries than this resolutely errant venturer into the acknowledged mysteries of mastery.

What is remembered and what is forgotten are—Sontag is here to remind us—one and the same. It is the faith of our modernity: we remember what we wish to remember, what we regard as important (Freud); and yet we truly remember only what we did not know we remembered, what our senses bring back to us involuntarily from the abyss of the past by a kind of art, a reconstruction of that lost paradise that is the only paradise we do know (Proust). This is Sontag's pursuit, what I call her errantry. In the present text she proceeds by the *use* of memory (citation, much fragmented, of an unobtrusive Nietzsche text) to the use *by* memory or deeper incitations, what Wallace Stevens calls "ghostlier demarcations," a willingness to submit or surrender mere conscious process which engages the reality of what I call *scrip-*

tion, that writing without purposive prefix which is the secret of our texts, our fabrications ("one can forget everything and then it all comes back"). How prescient she is when she (necessarily) concludes: "I have told this story many times—it is the "one story only" that all her fictions and all her discursive forays tell, and will continue to tell, not always so diagrammatically as here through the battle of the Nietzschean web, but always with the same passionate capacity for recognition, for admiration—for wonder and awe.

An International Episode:
Henry James and George Sand

[1989]

By the time of his death in 1926, my grandfather Isaac had accumulated—by catalogue purchase through "specialist" booksellers who also sold him, as I was to discover, manuscripts (Whitman, Eugene Field), autographs (Presidents of the United States), and rather gentlemanly erotica, usually labeled "curious," all of these suitably encased in buckram envelopes—a library of impressive proportions, a library which to my child's eyes, even a decade after his decease, was remarkable for its glistening, apparently unscathed *sets*, as I eventually learned to call the collected and uniform editions—sets usually of dead authors (for how inconvenient it would have been to match the bindings had a living writer continued to produce works beyond the specified series). I was born three years after my grandfather joined the authors of his sets, and I grew up in a house in Cleveland which contained—in a big room called The Library, with a coffered ceiling and a fireplace large enough to roast the ox whose hide had been used to bind a set of Goethe or Voltaire—that library which I inherited almost half a century later.

To this day I possess a number of those handsome *sets*, chiefly of the English-language writers, for the collected editions of translated authors* were all—can there have been an exception, even the Verne

---

*Balzac in red Morocco, fifty volumes, with alternating fleurs-de-lys and swastikas on the spines—a confusion to me in the 1930s, though doubtless to the binder a harmless Hindu embellishment; and Gautier, and Hugo, and fortunately, for those same years of confusion, Jules Verne, ten olive-green crushed-leather quartos which I devoured over and over.

with its *atmospheres of pressure* and *leagues* under the sea—there were
only twenty, not twenty *thousand*! in the original—and its mysterious
and never-explained *versts* in *Michael Strogoff*?—were alas, *all* abom-
inably translated, verse, prose, and dramas.*

I have sold most of it: the autographs of the Presidents to the Taft
family, ever aspiring; the Whitman manuscript (smudgy pencil notes
for a lecture on Tennyson) snapped up by the Library of Congress; the
curiosa (was I wrong?), and almost all the *sets* of foreign authors, of
Maupassant, of Daudet, and of a farraginous series (though identically bound in crisp ultramarine linen) gilt-stamped *Roman Contemporain*: another confusion to my pre-Francophone youth, for what, I
wondered, *was* a contemporain, and how did a Roman version differ
from other kinds? Why were there so many Roman contemporains
and not any Venetian or Neapolitan ones? And right next to this mysterious array (it was in English, of course, despite the eventually deci-
phered legend on the spines, and it boasted works by such luminaries
as Erckmann-Chatrain, and the Goncourts, and Charles-Paul de Kock)
was what glistened and glowed as the finest *set* in the room: at least
four feet (or perhaps a *verst*) of turquoise shagreen volumes, consecu-
tively numbered like all the other sets but, unlike them, identically labeled, all twenty-five volumes: MASTERPIECES OF GEORGE
SAND. How many years I was to marvel at the genius—and the
industry—of Mr. Sand, of whom these turquoise productions were
but the *masterpieces*! Who knew—certainly not my grandfather—how
many botched works, how many more merely competent compositions this copious Sand fellow had created, and discarded, in order to
bequeath to the binder's sumptuous art so many Masterpieces. You
understand, I was never allowed so much as to touch these books, to
break the set, as it were: not that these specimens of literature were denied to an inquisitive child for internal reasons, *for curious reasons*, as it
were, but in order to safeguard the merest and clearest and dearest external proprieties. Or properties—for that is what it came down to, or

---

*Which I believed to be neither prose nor verse, but some other kind of thing: *perverse*, perhaps; but given, or taking, the translated dramas of Victor Hugo—where Hernani shrieks:
[No, I shall not depart, I shall *disappear*!—]was I so wrong?

owned up to. And of all the *things owned* in that big room, none loomed larger or bulked more illustriously to my unspecifying appreciation than the masterpieces of George Sand.

I sold them too, of course, forty-five years later, with all the rest—even the Jules Verne. Sand in English was just like sand in lettuce, a bother. I did not sell the Dickens or the George Eliot or the Thackeray or even the Poe (whose prose was certainly no better than translated Sand, though what Frenchman would ever believe that?); and it is of a certain significance to note, before I leave the much-curtailed library, what contemporary novels, what *Roman contemporain* in his own language my grandfather had considered worthy to share the shelves with the masterpieces of the mistress of Nohant. There was—I have it still—the Sundial Edition of the works of Joseph Conrad, Volume 1 signed by the author; there were two dozen volumes of Kipling (with more swastikas on the spines!) and George Meredith even, and Arthur Machen, but among my grandfather's contemporaries, no representation whatever of Henry James. Certainly nothing like the monumental New York Edition (which Edith Wharton had persuaded and *paid* Scribner's to publish), nor even a miscellaneous assortment of tales, travels, essays. In the library of an upper-middle-class literary and leather-fetishizing Jewish family man, the message was clear enough to a grandson willing and even eager to sell his patrimony for a pot of message: "masterpieces of George Sand," whose very profuse and persistent enterprise made against any such thing, and not one work by Henry James, whose every other novel from *The Portrait of a Lady* (1880) to *The Golden Bowl* (1904), easily bears the magisterial imputation. So much for the received taste and discernment of ancestors—so much for the Situation of 1926, let us say, which has been so curiously reversed by Literary History in half a century: "All my books," James once remarked, "will one day kick off their tombstones," and indeed here in my university's library (and still in print, even now) is the *second* New York Edition of the *Novels and Tales of Henry James*, with additional volumes, a *set* indeed, whereas neither in translation nor in her own tongue can we obtain, currently, the *oeuvres complètes* of Aurore

Dupin Dudevant, who unflaggingly produced George Sand's novels
and tales. Her *oeuvres autobiographiques* we can obtain, in the Pléiade
edition which runs or seeps to some two thousand pages; and we can
obtain (if we are very rich and very robust) her complete correspondence in twenty volumes, at about a thousand pages per volume—I
have seen such a thing in the university library, though hardly dared
heft it—but even in France there is no standard edition of the *works*
(novels and tales) of George Sand today, and certainly no such thing
as an agreed-upon *set*: it appears that the masterpiece of George Sand
is only herself, not her literature. And oddly enough, or perhaps it is
not odd, only curious, the reasons for this highly symbolical reversal
in literary standing, in literary access, are best to be sought in the account of the lady provided by the gentleman in the case—in the essays
of Henry James, which so obsessively engage the life and work of
George Sand.

Eight times he wrote about her *in extenso*, from the age of twenty-five
in the *Nation*, when Sand was still very much alive, still very much
writing, or writing very much, to the age of seventy-one in the *Quar-
terly Review*, when Sand had "passed away as a 'creator,' suggesting the
immense waste involved in the general ferment of an age, and how
much genius and beauty, let alone the baser parts of the mixture, it
takes to produce a moderate quantity of literature." Except for Balzac,
no European writer provoked Henry James to comparable lengths
(and *provoked*, I think, is the right verb, though *seduced*, even *usurped*,
come to mind), and none provoked him over such a spread of time:
fifty years, and he could not put her down (in any sense of the phrase),
though sorely *tempted* to consign her to the realm of creative chaos:

> The mind producing this narrative, gushing along copious and
> translucent as a deep and crystalline stream, rolling pebbles and
> boulders and reflecting all the complex vault of nature, seems
> not to have isolated and contracted itself in the regions of per-
> ception, but to expand with longing and desire.

Yet even before I take up James's formal transactions with Sand, which
like all his essays, now gathered in the splendid pair of 1500-page volumes of the American Library, and his reviews and his merest notations, stand for consistent sophistication of surface and conviction of
depth, as something of a lion in the path of any interpretive effort—
before I track James tracking Sand, I must—for a compositional purpose which will eventually be apparent and even inevitable—record
James's frequently reverted-to youthful relation to *his author*; at the
very age when I was still marveling over the handsome but unhandled
volumes of her *oeuvre*, Henry James was reading her through, was being, as we say in such connections, *imprinted*, for indeed she—the ir-
repressible George, as James's brother called her in a letter—seems to
have constituted something of a family figure, though in the light (or
lueur) of Henry James, Sr.'s, response, a disputed one. There had been
a time, the imprinted son tells us in his first review, "when Mme
Sand's novels were translated as fast as they appeared, and circulated
half surreptitiously, as works delightful and intoxicating, but scandalous, dangerous and seditious," and perhaps this accounts somewhat for the outraged father's disapprobation:

> I try vainly to read George Sand's *Francia*. I have come across
> nothing of that lady's that reflects a baser light on her personal
> history. What must a woman have been through to want to
> grovel at this time of day in such uncleanness? Don't buy it—I
> wish I hadn't.

But Henry, Jr., did buy it, as he had bought all of Sand's writings, and
accounts at some length, in his late *Notes of a Son and Brother*, for the
effect:

> I happen to remember perfectly the appearance of the novel of
> Mme Sand's that my father so invidiously alludes to. I hadn't
> gone to the length of my father [says this Oedipal champion],
> who must have taken up the tale in its republished form, a so
> slim salmon-coloured volume: oh the repeated arrival, during
> those years, of the salmon-coloured volumes in their habit as

they lived, a habit reserved, to my extreme appreciation, for this particular series, and that, enclosing the extraordinarily fresh fruit of their author's benign maturity, left Tamaris and Valvèdre and Mlle La Quintinie in no degree ever "discounted" for us, as devotees of the Revue des Deux Mondes, I make out, by their being but renewals of acquaintance. The sense of the salmon-coloured, distinctive of Mme Sand, was even to come back to me long years after, on my hearing Edmond de Goncourt speak reminiscentially and, I permit myself to note, not at all reverently, of the robe de satin *fleur-de-pêcher* that the illustrious and infatuated lady, whose more peculiar or native tint didn't contribute to a harmony, *s'était fait faire* in order to fix as much as possible the attention of Gustave Flaubert at the Diner Magny; of Gustave Flaubert who, according to this most invidious of reporters, disembroiled with too scant ease his tangle of possible incurred ridicule from the declared sentiment of so old a woman, even in a peach-blossom dress, and the glory reflected on him by his admirer's immense distinction. Which vision of a complicated past doesn't at all blur its also coming back to me that I was to have found my parent "hard on" poor Francia. I see that general period as quite flushed and toned by the salmon-coloured covers; so that a kind of domestic loyalty would ever operate, as we must have all felt, to make us take the thick with the thin. . . . When I say all, indeed, I doubtless have in mind especially my parents and myself, with my sister and our admirable aunt thrown in—to the extent of our subjection to the charm of such matters in particular as *La Famille de Germandre*, *La Ville Noire, Nanon* and *L'Homme de Neige*, round which last above all we sat ranged in united ecstasy; so that I was to wonder through the after years, and I think perhaps to this day, how it could come that a case of the "story"-strain at its finest and purest, a gush of imaginative force so free and yet so artfully directed, shouldn't have somehow "stood out" more in literary history. . . . I hover for instance about the closet of *L'Homme de Neige*, I stand outside a moment as if listening for a breath from within; but I don't open the door, you see—which must mean, in all probability, that I wouldn't for the world inconsiderately finger again one of the three volumes. . . . Isn't it relevant to my listening for the breath of life unquenched that our dear mother was at the time reading "over" *La Famille de Germandre*, which confirmed her in the sense that there was no one like this author for a "love-story"?—a conviction, however, that when made articulate exposed her to the imputation of a larger tolerance than she doubtless intended to project; till the matter was cleared up by our generally embracing her for so sweetly not knowing about *Valentine* and *Jacques* and suchlike, and having only begun a *La Mare au Diable*, and even thereafter been occasionally obliged to skip.

I quote at such length not only because it is difficult to extricate oneself from this python's adorable coils, but also because, as always when an author tells us more about the circumstances which color his reading than about that reading itself, we are being made party to a sort of Primal Scene—to what in the case of the elder Jameses we might call a Swedenborgian Primal Scene. Does it not strike you, in all this breathing about the bush, that George Sand represents for young Henry James a figure of the Beloved Mother, a sort of extended and developed mother, beyond the actual maternal timidities and naïveties, who can be sequestered from the Forbidding Father, who can be relished and reveled in and even run off with, a figuration of bliss—that "gush of imaginative force so free and yet so artfully directed"—which was to stand, long past the Family Romance, yet through it as well, for everything desired yet dreaded, everything required for a life of plastic conceptions yet reproved and even, in the long shadows of paternal power, repudiated? Let me leave the suggestion, at least, in your minds as we consider no longer the memories so artfully tinted and touched up, but the essays and reviews themselves, coming back, at the end, if you are still with me, to one further intimate—excruciated—resonance, in a letter of 1912 to Edith Wharton.

It is as if Henry James had just got up from that family argument under the library lamp to do his first piece on Sand, which we must remember—for all its high-handed locutions—was written before he had published any volume of fiction, before he had indeed laid any kind of claim to a fictional region of his own. He is thus impressed by Sand's profusion—of talent as well as of tales:

> Since 1845, the author has produced a vast number of romances, and exhibited a greater fecundity, we think, considering the quality of her work, than any writer of our day. With all her precipitation, not one of her tales (we believe we have read them all) can be said to have forfeited the claim to literary excellence. . . . She handles men and women, the rich and the poor, the peasant and the noble, the passionate and the joyous, with equal sympathy and power.

And of course by her *désinvolture*, her *sprezzatura*—here, evidently, we need some foreign word to express just the quality that comes so reluctantly to the Anglo-American novelist—think of George Eliot, of James himself: "it appears to be flung upon the paper absolutely without effort and without the consciousness of doing a fine thing."

The claim to have read all of Sand's work, and to have found that work all so unconsciously plastic, so "free, comprehensive and sincere," is James's first identification of Sand with those qualities of fertility and figural energy which he was to cherish all his own long career as a writer. And his career as a writer was to become his only career, an acute and widely diffused emotional demand for a new mode of self-validation. Sand is initially prized as the *exemplum* of a world in which experience is shaped by mouths in speech, a world in which James functions even more superlatively than Sand herself, I suppose, though she is perceived as setting the tone, as giving the high sign: when Henry James met an acquaintance in the street, or wrote a letter to his brother, or a note to himself, or a book, he was there in it entirely, there as the maker. Who else was there to be? For him, verbal artifact was all. And in this first account, there is almost none of the moralizing fuss, a sort of conventional regression for James, which I shall discuss in its place, when we first hear the sound of harpies' wings over the Sand banquet. Here, the praise is almost unbroken, so that the fracture itself must be specially attended to:

Mme Sand's literary career has been, as the reader knows, a very long and eventful one. It is marked by a vast number of moral and intellectual stages or stations, and now, towards its close, it assumes a form in which the sagacity and serenity of age are very finely blended with the freshness and lightness of an immortal imagination. The tale bears the stamp of an intellect weary of the contemplation of disorder, and of an inventive faculty for which, not to move and act—not to frolic through space like another Ariel—is simply to die. Herein resides both the strength and the weakness of Mme Sand's imagination. It is indefatigable, inexhaustible, but it is restless, nervous, and capricious; it is, in short, the imagination of a woman.

In its failure or refusal to judge—just like Henry James's mother—the temperament which characterizes Sand's choices (all artistic as these are, never dismissive, never restrictive) is, James says, "almost too limpid, too fluent, too liquid. The creative spirit is well-nigh too impersonal, too impartial, too ethereal." And of course when you are given over to the rule, or the anarchy, of such a creative spirit, you have no control over the ultimate excellence or inadequacy of what you write. How quickly my grandfather's bookbinder would have smiled at James's summing up, which so warranted his own golden identification: "Madame Sand's masterpieces are scattered throughout her career, and in many cases stand cheek to cheek with some of her most trivial works. . . . But taking it as a whole, and judging it in a liberal fashion, what a splendid array does this career exhibit! From our own point of view there has been none in modern years to compare with it, and to find a greater magician we must turn to the few supreme names in literature."

Only eight years later, in an obituary note to the *New York Tribune*, part of his fortnightly "Letter from Paris," James renders a qualified justice to the late author ("I confess I do not find her earlier novels as easy reading as I once did"), yet relishes still her "extraordinary art of narration. This was Mme Sand's great art. The recital moves along with an evenness, a lucidity, a tone of seeing, feeling, knowing everything, a reference to universal things, a sentimental authority, which makes the reader care for the characters in spite of his incredulity and feel anxious about the story in spite of his impatience. . . ." But something has entered the picture, or the tone of voice, which I suppose we must connect with that reductive identification of "the imagination of a woman" as "restless, nervous, capricious." It is as if James no longer trusts the qualities, the virtues he acknowledges to be Sand's and in some ulterior sense his mother's as well, and in the struggle for a position in a world of men, of fathers, feels obliged to impose certain judgments, to invoke certain (highly conventional) repudiations:

> She was essentially a scribbler; she wrote unceasingly from the publication of her first novel to the day of her death, and she had always been fond of a quiet life, even during that portion of her career in which our Anglo-Saxon notions of "quietness" are supposed to have been most effectively violated. . . . She was an *improvisatrice*, raised to a very high power; she told stories as a nightingale sings. No novelist answers so well to the childish formula of "making up as you go along." Other novels seem meditated, pondered, calculated, thought out and elaborated with a certain amount of trouble, but the narrative with Mme Sand always appears to be an invention of the moment, flowing from a mind which a constant process of quiet contemplation, absorption and reverie keeps abundantly supplied with material. It is a sort of general emanation, an intellectual evaporation . . .

You will notice that Sand's characteristic excellence, throughout, is always associated with the liquid element—gushing, flowing, even evaporating. In the kinetics of consciousness, I suppose there is no more immediate analogy to be made than that of fertility and profusion with the movements and materializations of water. To its powers James now opposes what will become something of a fetish, even a perversion in his later novel-theory; meditation, calculation, and elaboration. By 1876, then, James is in the grip of what we have learned to call ambivalence about Sand—a grip that will tighten to a pathological degree in later essays: on the one hand, he will maintain that she had a natural gift of style which is certainly one of the most remarkable of our day; her diction from the first was ripe and flexible, and seemed to have nothing to learn from practice. The literary form of her writing has always been exquisite.

Yet he cannot quite endure to let this appreciation stand; the very achievements of the woman whom Nietzsche called *la vache à littérature* seemed to necessitate a gainsaying:

> Some of her novels are very inferior to others; some of them show traces of weariness, of wandering attention, of a careless choice of subject . . . In her bright voluminous envelopes, it must be confessed that Mme Sand has sometimes wrapped up a rather flimsy kernel; some of her stories will not bear much thinking over. . . . Her novels have a great many faults; they lack three or four qualities which the realistic novel of the last 30 or 40 years, with its great successes, has taught us to consider indispensable. They are not exact or probable; they contain few living figures; they produce a limited amount of illusion; her people are usually only very picturesque, very voluble, and very "high-toned" shadows.

Surely James knew that some writers concentrate and construct their experience into words, as he was to do for another forty years. Others, he must have realized, expand and extend and exhaust their experience, like George Sand; their unity is in all their work, not in single efforts, where the unity may indeed evaporate. Where there is no generalizing power, all the novels together may make a generalization. Perhaps we cannot say what that generalization is, however intensely we feel it. Who can say what the sphinx generalizes—and it was George Sand who liked to call herself a *sphinx bon enfant*, a good-natured sphinx, an appellation James was quick to cite, for was he not heroically to answer certain questions this monster was to put to him, to answer them and in a sense thereby to defeat her powers—the powers of darkness, antinomian powers which must include the dangerous realm of sexual autonomy, sexual freedom?

Condemnation, in these two necrologies for the *Tribune*, is not yet
so baffling, or rather, is still baffled, in this response:

> As she advanced in life, she wrote her stories more and more for
> the story's sake, and attempted to prove nothing more alarming
> than that human nature is on the whole tolerably noble and
> generous. After this pattern she produced a long list of master-
> pieces [that word again!]. Her imagination seemed gifted with
> perpetual youth: the freshness of her invention was marvellous.

And later in this one, where the bitchy resonance begins to emerge,
even to protrude:

> It has been said wittily, in reference to Buffon's well-known ax-
> iom that "the style is the man", that of no one was this dictum
> ever so true as of Mme Sand; but I incline to believe that at bot-
> tom the man was always Mme Sand herself. . . . It is a misfor-
> tune that she pretended to moralize to the extent that she did,
> for about moral matters her head was not at all clear. . . . Her
> didacticism has always seemed to me what an architectural
> drawing would be, executed by a person who should turn up
> his nose at geometry.

I have invoked, in connection with this ambivalence of response,
Freud's concept—here quite transformed into a Swedenborgian
variant—of the Primal Scene, fantasies of which may leave the child
unable to envision or endure any kind of active sexual response in later
life. James's mother and father, whose disputes over Sand I have
pushed into the sexual arena, seem to have produced something of
this effect in their observed, and imagined, representations of freedom
and order, for as James continued, with a certain fanaticism, to attend
to Sand's career—even more than to her work—in ulterior essays, he
seemed increasingly to be troubled, even pained by the evidences of a
certain acknowledged and enjoyed sexuality in her relations, in *all* her
relations. The very language in which he obsessively repeats the
episodes of Sand's sensational erotic career—especially the story of her

journey to Venice with Alfred de Musset, of Musset's illness there and return to Paris, shortly followed by Sand and Musset's doctor, who had become her lover over the poet's sickbed and now constituted, as James puts it on one occasion, no inconsiderable part of her luggage. What bothers James most, in the frequent recensions of this incident, is that Sand and Musset for a while actually resumed their intimacy after the physician's provisional . . . ministrations. In James's first full-dress study of Sand of the following year, we are made aware from the start of the romancer's erotomania, which is given a certain hereditary taint:

> If it is a fair description of Mme Sand to say that she was, during that portion of her career which established her reputation, an apostle of the rights of love *quand même*, a glance at her pedigree shows that this was a logical disposition. She was herself more sensibly the result of a series of love-affairs than most of us. In each of these cases the woman had been loved with a force that asserted itself in contradiction to propriety or to usage.

And of course, as we have had intimations already, the ultimate responsibility for Sand's unacceptable preoccupation with sex—in a word, her sexuality—is attributed to her being a woman in the first, or the last, place.

> What we have called briefly and crudely Sand's want of veracity requires some explanation. It is doubtless a condition of her serene volubility; but if this latter is a great literary gift, its value is impaired by our sense that it rests to a certain extent upon a weakness. There is something very liberal and universal in George Sand's genius, as well as very masculine; but our final impression of her always is that she is a woman and a Frenchwoman. Women, we are told, do not value the truth for its own sake, but only for some use they make of it. My present criticism involves an assent to this somewhat cynical dogma. Add to this that woman, if she happens to be French, has an ex-

traordinary taste for investing objects with a graceful drapery of her own contrivance, and it will be found that George Sand's cast of mind includes both the generic and the specific idiosyncrasy. . . . In spite of her plausibility, the author of *Consuelo* always appears to be telling a fairy-tale. We say in spite, but we might rather say that her excessive plausibility is the reason of our want of faith. The narrative is too smooth, too fluent. . . . The effect it produces is that of a witness who is eager to tell more than is asked, the worth of whose testimony is impaired by its importunity. . . . But if other things come and go with George Sand, amatory disquisition is always there. There is to our taste a great deal too much of it; the total effect is displeasing. The author illuminates and glorifies the divine passion, but she does something which may be best expressed by saying that she cheapens it. She handles it too much; she lets it too little alone. Above all she is too positive, too explicit, too businesslike; she takes too technical a view of it. Its various signs and tokens and stages, its ineffable mysteries, are all catalogued and tabulated in her mind, and she whisks out her references with the nimbleness with which the doorkeeper at an exhibition hands you back your umbrella in return for a check.

In the course of this very long essay, which James himself reprinted in his *French Poets and Novelists* of 1878, the rejection of romance, of "the author's romances" is conducted to the brink of rejection of the author: "We have lately been trying to read the author's romances over, and we frankly confess we have found it impossible. It has been said that what makes a book a classic is its style. We should modify this and instead of style say *form*. Mme Sand's novels have plenty of style, but they have no form. . . . Is this because after all she was a woman, and the laxity of the feminine intellect could not fail to claim its part in her?"

One can scarcely believe what one is reading. Is this Henry James, the admirer of Jane Austen, the staunch advocate of George Eliot, the author of the only gallery of adequate and intelligent women in all of American literature? What can account for such preposterous reversals, regressions, indeed repudiations in the creator of Isabel Archer and the critic who claimed to "know and never cease to know by George Eliot's name a great treasure of beauty and humanity, of applied and achieved art"? I think we have already seen what it was that James, in the acquisitive phase of his vocation, had gained from George Sand—we have seen, I mean, that vocation confirmed in its feeling that *expressive form is being*. And literature the sum of being. For James, human action simply—simply!—consisted in the recorded play of consciousness and referred to nothing independent of the fabric of the work itself. It is why his characters must all sound more or less like the master, just as Sand's figures must all exhibit that peculiar power of self-defense, that constant need to justify, to glorify, to place in a becoming light those errors and weaknesses in which her own personal credit may be at stake. But once James was sure in his lesson, once he was fairly launched (it is in this year that he writes *his* first masterpiece, *The Portrait of a Lady*), a certain revisionism sets in—indeed, from now on becomes, I should say, a disease, a pathology of disapproval and dismay. The essay from which I have been quoting is the last one to register, in the very turn and tendency of its prose, as normal, as nominally sane, in the entire series of essays on Sand; hence it is fair, it is even cheering, to pluck from it a final citation, one still within the rim of a just discrimination:

> When the world is given over to a "realism" that we have not as yet begun faintly to foreshadow, George Sand's novels will have, for the children of the twenty-first century, something of the same charm which Spenser's *Faerie Queen* has for those of the nineteenth. For a critic of today to pick and choose among them seems almost pedantic; they all belong to the same intellectual family. They are the easy writing which makes hard reading.

Twenty years later, Henry James is found to be not only in the thick, or at the height, of a triumphant literary career, but in possession—alarmed possession, Leon Edel tells us—of secrets of his own. The terrors of *biography* were upon him when, as he says, "the cunning of the inquirer, envenomed with resistance, exceeds in ferocity and subtlety anything we have known till now, and the pale victim, with every track covered, every paper burnt and every letter unanswered, can then, and then only, stand in the tower of art, the invulnerable granite, can withstand the siege of all the years." It was events like the publication of some fifty pages of new documents, letters from George Sand to Alfred de Musset "in the course of a famous friendship," which provoked James to his own conflagration of forty years of private papers in his back yard (for how else keep them private, unless they were reduced to ash?), and to a very long essay in *The Yellow Book*. "If you sacrifice all delicacy," he upbraids his now long-dead author, "show at least that you were right by giving us a masterpiece"—and of course the novel (on which these letters are the diacritical marks, so to speak) is no more a masterpiece than any other of what James now calls "the loose lucid liquid works of its author." Here again the interesting words occur under James's pen—the word *masterpiece* and the word *liquid*, the one denied because of the other's presence, we might say. The entire story of Sand's affair with Musset is rehearsed yet again, and James seems to take shelter, for his present disapproval of the sexually explicit and loquacious Sand, in the most invulnerable postures of respectability:

> The lovers are naked in the market-place and perform for the benefit of society. The matter with them, to the perception of the stupefied spectator, is that they entertained for each other every feeling in life but the feeling of respect. What the absence of that article may do for the passion of hate is apparently nothing to what it may do for the passion of love. Of course there had been floods of tenderness, floods of forgiveness, but for Mme Sand in her so much longer life, there was no hush, no letting alone; though it would be difficult indeed to exaggerate the depth of relative indifference from which, a few years after Musset's death, such a production as *Elle et Lui* could spring.

The phenomenological note which James always strikes in association with Sand—"floods of tenderness, floods of tears"—is here invoked again; it is indeed the sign of an immitigable anxiety, a doubt, to put it quite directly, as to what in the case is mother's milk and what seminal fluid:

Her immense plausibility was almost the only sign of her sex.
She needed always to prove that she had been in the right. . . .
It is not too much to say of her gift of expression that from beginning to end it floated her over the real as a high tide floats a
ship over the bar. She was never left awkwardly straddling on
the sandbank of fact.

This is the one case I know, in the immense career and construction of
James's critical enterprise, where his discernment fails him. Not that
he is mistaken about the writer he cites as so often being called *la mère
Sand*; he is not mistaken, he is just not writing literary criticism any
more, he is arguing himself out of a certain engagement, out of that
mode of incorporation which was to be his own salvation and which
therefore had to be snatched from her grasp: Henry James is pro-
nouncing an exorcism.

In 1899 the first two books of a vast three-volume biography of George
Sand—a sort of life-and-letters raised to the highest inclusive power—
by a Russian woman writing under the striking pseudonym Wladimir
Karenin was published in Paris. Hearing the challenge yet again, James
returned to the charge, and in 1902 published a very long essay which,
twelve years later, he "completed" at the age of seventy-one, when
Mme Karenin at last published her third volume starring, one may say,
Chopin, just as volume two had starred Musset. Though James appears
to have admired Chopin's character more than Musset's, he acknowledges that Chopin's relation to George Sand was very much of the
same type, appealing both to the motherly and to the decidedly male
aspects of Sand's nature. Of course, in the Musset instance, Sand's own
children had been offstage while the lovers were in Venice, while
Chopin was actually siding with the abominable Solange, Sand's disagreeable daughter, during the dramatic days at Nohant, after Majorca.
I don't mean to suggest that James has for a moment overlooked the
various intervening lovers, celebrated and obscure:

Her relations with men closely resembled those relations with
women that have been complacently commemorated as stages

in the unfolding of the great statesman and the great poet. It is very much the same large list, the same story of free appropriation and consumption; and if millions of women, of course, of every condition, have had more lovers, it was probable that no woman independently occupied and so diligent has had more unions. She strikes us as in the benignity of such an intercourse even more than maternal: not so much the mere fond mother as the supersensuous grandmother of the wonderful affair.

In these final, very obscurely written but evidently ironic and "distancing" or, as Nietzsche would say, "perspectivizing," essays of James's penultimate year, he can no longer treat Sand as a writer at all, merely as a phenomenon of virtually transsexual vitality. He can defuse his anxiety, then, by no longer dealing with her as a woman—though he still invokes the liquid metaphors to suggest the perils of female authorship, as in these two instances:

> It is hard to say of George Sand's productions, I think, that they show closeness anywhere; the sense of that fluidity which is more than fluency is what, in speaking of them, constantly comes back to us, and the sense of fluidity is fundamentally fatal to the sense of particular truth. The thing presented by intention is never the stream of the artist's inspiration; it is the deposit of the stream. . . .

And again, pages later, reinvoking a figure invented years before:

> She had, in spite of herself, an imagination almost of the first order, which overflowed and irrigated, turning by its mere swift current, without effort, almost without direction, every mill it encountered, and launching as it went alike the lightest skiff and the stateliest ship.

But the terrors of liquidity need not loom so devastatingly if Sand is no longer perceived as an initiatrix, as a woman in possession of just that expressive secret which would allow her—and indeed allow

James in her wake—to possess a lifetime of promiscuous writerly energy, in which assumptions about the world, horizontal relations, count not as limiting data but only as material for the self, writing its survival onward.

> The scene quite changes [James writes] when we cease to expect these graces. As a man, Mme Sand was admirable—especially as a man of the dressing-gown and slippers order, easy of approach and of *tutoiement*, rubbing shoulders with queer company and not superstitiously haunted by the conception of the gentleman. . . . She keeps here and there a feminine streak—has at moments an excess of volubility and too great an insistence on having been in the right; but for the rest, the character, confronted with the position, is an explanation.

By the time he is seventy-one, then, by the time he has completed his tremendous trajectory through the world of letters, James has managed to reverse the terms—has taken from George Sand those elements of an undivided consciousness which Freud called polymorphous perversity, and has transformed his great inductress and adversary into a mere male: what we in fact most recognize, James says, "is not the extension she gives to the feminine nature, but the richness she adds to the masculine." In other words, Henry James has resolved his Oedipus complex.

My pursuit of James through his formal Sandist exercises and functions would be complete—though there is always more to say about James's odd lapses from his customary feminist identifications, about his exacerbated references, in these Sandy wastes, to "liberations of the subordinate sex," luxations which occur only in treating the matter of what we might call the Sand-woman. But there is a final utterance, an intimate one symmetrically framing James's concern with this astounding woman, symmetrical, that is, to James's intimate glimpse in *Notes of a Son and Brother* with which I began. In 1912, having "read over" Volume 3 of Mme Karenin's biography, James writes to Edith

Wharton what he calls "the last word about dear old George"; in this letter he is commenting on Mme Sand's ability to "post" a friend as to "all her *amours*." It is the final incident in this international episode—the one that erases Sand entirely from the scene, leaving nothing but language, finally—as we hear:

> To have such a flow of remark on that subject, and everything connected with it, at her command helps somehow to make one feel that Providence laid up for the French such a store of remark, in advance and, as it were, should the worst befall, that their conduct and *moeurs*, coming *after*, had positively to justify and do honor to the whole collection of formulae, phrases and, as I say, glibnesses—so that as there were at any rate such things there for them to inevitably *say*, why not simply *do* all the things that would give them a *rapport* and a sense? The things *we*, poor disinherited race, do, we have to do so dimly and sceptically, without the sense of any such beautiful *cadres* awaiting us—and therefore poorly and going but half—or a tenth—of the way. It makes a difference when you have to invent your suggestions and glosses after the fact: you do it so miserably compared with Providence—especially Providence aided by the French language: which by the way convinces me that Providence thinks and *really* expresses itself only in French.

You will have noted that in this communication from Henry James to Edith Wharton, any reference to George Sand herself as a writer, as the writer who provokes or inspires such reflections on language taken to such an expressive extreme, has been altogether elided.

It is, ominously enough, a final solution. One symbolized by the fact that until I wrote this paper, I did not possess, in the current version of that library of my grandfather's, now mine, a single work of George Sand, though I own, indeed, all the Henry James available in print—which is to say, all of Henry James.

INTRODUCING
NEW POETS

Eleanor Ross Taylor, *Welcome Eumenides*

[1972]

"After you I go, my life! Was it chase or flight?"

I n Castalia, not far from where I was raised in northeast Ohio,
there is a place called The Blue Hole, which I used to be taken to
see as a child: it is a small pond, apparently without source or
outlet, blue indeed and said to be bottomless—there is the inevitable
story of the team of horses accidentally driven into it one winter night
a century ago and never found, though grappled for at unimaginable
depths. The Blue Hole is a mysterious site, nor can its mystery be vul-
garized, even in northeast Ohio where windshield souvenirs attest
your visitation, for there is a silence about this body of water (the expression seems only justice, for once), an unexpected presence from
below that keeps the gum-wrappers from polluting such fountains
with which poetry has always been associated, as the name Castalia itself reminds us. Of course The Blue Hole is not really bottomless,
merely the sudden surfacing, among trivial mediations, of an underground river which then vanishes once more; the team of horses cannot be dragged to the surface because it has been carried away, perhaps
the skeletons, or, who knows—say the water is a marinade and the
team entire, rolling eyes, streaming manes and tails—will reappear the
next time this subterranean source remounts, abstergent, unplumbed,
clear, giving back whatever it took into itself.

This natural miracle is before us—it has occurred in the work of
Eleanor Ross Taylor. A dozen years ago her first book of poems,
Wilderness of Ladies, was published with a brilliant introduction by

Randall Jarrell "to make it easier for the readers to consider the possibility of the poems' being what they are"; what they are, as our great poet-critic exulted, is a world, like Hardy's or Janacek's, "the water / meeting me around the curve . . . the waiting womb! the waiting tomb—the empty antique sitting room!"—precisely, birth, life, and the process that divides and unites them. Now, after long silence, we are given that speech again, "etched with inheritance and fate," eager yet reticent, reckless and still patient, solicitous, attentive, nursing (it is capital that one of the major pieces here is a dramatic reverie uttered by Florence Nightingale, a poem which gives the book its startling title).

I think Jarrell's prose did make it easier for readers, but perhaps it became harder for the poet, after such praise, such precision ("the world is a cage for a woman, and inside it the woman is her own cage . . . life is a state of siege, a war to the last woman"), to surface again, to welcome the Eumenides which are, we must remember, not the Erinyes, the Furies, but the Kindly Ones, mediators of ritual, functionaries of acceptance.

This new book of Mrs. Taylor's is our fortunate particular and proof that what had seemed a singular welling-up, an exceptional outpouring, is more for being carried on, for returning to observable earth, not just The Blue Hole but a longer look at what Matthew Arnold calls "the unregarded river of our life." We have watched, or at least we have waited, for that American talent which would seal the pact between Emily Dickinson and Walt Whitman, between that private extremity which is a crying need and that public extremity which is an inward wound. And here, with this second collection which includes "A Few Days in the South," the best poem since Whitman about the War Between the States, here is that talent, that reconciliation ("fever, flesh, ash into ashes burn") which is of course a new aggression, a new demand. It is a demand upon the poet herself, an insistence that she come to terms with her resources, with her impoverishment, and it reminds us that Eleanor Ross Taylor is the wife of Peter Taylor, one of our finest narrative writers to concern himself with the voice of a region, the vision of a class, the vaunt of a generation. It is a great thing for a poet to be married to a great prose writer, for his achievement shows her what she must keep overcoming in order to become what she is: a diction out of the shadows which does not erase itself as it is raised. Whereas the prose voice rubs itself out as it goes along, *her* voice must be somehow suspended, held up on its rhythms, its intervals, its silences, until no message is left but a resonance, no communication but an echo: persistent, yielding, heard.

Lest I, too, seem to outspeak Mrs. Taylor who is quite likely to sink back into her garden ("earth to earth, inside you yet / in the garden to come"), the buried stream proceeding to its next unpolicied embodiment, I would not claim for her more than her own purpose, so aptly asserted by her title. *Welcome Eumenides* (the diary notation of Florence Nightingale) is a rehearsal of what Jane Harrison means, in her famous chapter of the *Prolegomena*, "The Making of a Goddess," when she describes the growth of a function from imprecation and warding-off to acceptance and nourishment (nursing!) to welcoming and prayer. That is why the word *attendance* holds both the word for shelter and the word for tension within its etymon, and why, magnificently, Eleanor Ross Taylor will say—it is the way to read her, to let her reveal herself—

> Our language exists but in silence,
> Our mortality in immortality.

Cynthia Macdonald, *Amputations*

[1972]

. . . Years in which to become detached.

S he had, like the rest of us, to start somewhere, and luckily for her poetry, Mrs. Macdonald started late. Of course there is no such thing as a late start or an early one in poetry, that is no more than a critical convenience, no less than a critical fiction, for there is no starting, there is only coming out, coming up, *reaching the surface* from somewhere which is not the surface—subcutaneous, ventral, deep; nor is there an end, poems are not finished but excused, and what matters is the terms between starting and finishing, or between the excursion and the excuse, the armistice between torment and terminal which is acceptable to both sides. So what I mean by a late start in Cynthia Macdonald's case is that she started *as* Mrs. Macdonald, as a mother twice over, as a woman who has been around, specifically, the world; and I mean that she got a *head* start, as well as a diaphragmal one, by becoming a musician, a singer, a professional performer. She learned, that is, the shape of a made thing not of her own making, yet which had to be produced or made over by her as if it *were* her own. She learned cunning, therefore, and she learned compliance— invaluable resources for a poet—and she learned, as it has turned out, how the appearance of the random must somewhere join the reality of contrivance. Then she started writing her poetry.

Of course it is musical, but in the formal sense in which poetry can be musical, not in the accidental and careless way in which we say that poetry is musical because it labors the sounds of vowels and by imposing a grid or pattern upon them keeps us from advancing *through* them. The poetry of *Amputations* is musical in the strict sense: it resolves a series or sequence of discords, it accounts for and enables movement, it moves onward, and its diction, as Northrop Frye says of all truly musical diction, is better fitted for the grotesque and horrible, or for invective and abuse. It is irregular in meter, leans heavily on enjambment, and employs a long cumulative rhythm sweeping the lines up into larger rhythmical units such as the paragraph. It is poetry of a particular kind, then, and all of one kind—not uniform but unified, collected from experience which has sunk in. Or else it has originated wherever *in* may be. What is significant about this poetry is that it has moved from its origin or source (being, then, no longer merely original but resourceful), has reached what I have called the surface— nothing less than the eye, the ear, *other people*—and in performing this trajectory, it has had every occasion to discover its own nature, to *reveal itself.* What had been held down is now held up to utterance, the voice raised, brought from the unsounded center to the circumference of expression, that part of our lives where things *take shape.*

Hence the ideogrammic or iconographic aspect of most of her poems, their design on the page being a design upon us: the page is the arena, the circus, the stage. The work of Cynthia Macdonald figures itself out, there, as the barker's pitch, leaves from the sibyl's cookbook, the diva's farewell—undertaken by necessity, overtaken by prowess— the vaudeville turn, earthworks, the *lazzo* of Commedia dell' Arte, and—I hope I have got the right sow by the ear—the commentary for a suburban chatauqua travelogue (splendors of Iowa); out of these unlikely *numbers*, which is after all the old name for poetry, she has made up her *sum*, which is after all the old name for a result reached by coming out on top, at the *summit* (the Romans counted upward), as well as a Latin word meaning what all poetry means: *I am.* The arithmetical processes employed here are the ones the Walrus used in the School of Fishes: *ambition, distraction, uglification,* and *derision*— with some other additions to the curriculum in the form of *mystery, ancient and modern, drawling, stretching, and fainting in coils,* and of course the classical subjects *laughing* and *grief.* It amounts to saying that Cynthia Macdonald is a poet of the grotesque.

It is the wrong preposition. What I mean is that she is a poet *from* the grotesque. For by the grotesque we mean—the *language* means—something to do with the grotto, the originating cavern (womb, skull, lung) where it all starts. We call it the unconscious, that place where Lord knows what could be daubed on the walls of *living rock*, and where the goings-on, by smoky torchlight, were anything but edifying. The point is to get *out* of the grotto with that dark or dubious knowledge intact, to examine by some other illumination what could not be dealt with by the light of day. The unconscious is exciting, as we know from our dreams, but not interesting, as we know from other people's dreams. The conscious is interesting, as we know from other people's words, but it is not exciting, as we know from our own. What is both interesting and exciting is the passage from dreams to words, from the unconscious to the conscious. A poetry *of* the grotesque would be worthless, for we could not tell what we had; a poetry *from* the grotesque is what we have here, a cast of experience seized as it proceeds from the cave, out into sunlight.

Mrs. Macdonald's stratagem is generally to suppose that the worst has happened, to divine the consequences, as if the worst were not what does happen:

Today I rejoice: I even treat myself kindly
Because I have uncovered a crucial self-secret:
The reason for my defective memory, the why of my forgetting . . .

And then she proceeds, she gets on with it as if the worst were not to be shut back in the grotto, as it is by most of us, but were to be lived with, on and on, an ordinary evening in Purgatory. As she says, in another (awful) context, but with immense bearing on her poetry:

I have more subjects than I can handle,
But only volunteers. It is an art like hypnosis
Which cannot be imposed on the unwilling victim.

She constitutes herself the willing victim, and her poems are reports—spiels, arias, inventories, laments, dirges, even eulogies—of the handling. There is an immense trajectory evident in her wit, in the delicacy of her phrasing, in the distinction of her ironies, in the sharpness of her ear for caste and class, for circumstantial "placing"—a vast parabola between what lies or lurks behind her and what she has made it into up front. By hilarious management, or one might say by a cool hand, she has taken the *terribilità* of her experience and made it, merely, operatic—which is to say that she has *worked* on it enough to make it ours, which is again to say that she has made it unmistakably, recognizably hers.

One word more. She has made it, also, prototypically American. There is nothing in her poetry which participates in the "international school"—half great plains, half grubby Paris—of easy surrealism being trumpeted (or kazooed) in some quarters. Mrs. Macdonald engages the capitalist realism of our culture from within, and her achievement can best be summarized or at least suggested by Hermann Broch's beautiful aphorism: "We are a *we*, not because we hold communion, but because our contours overlap."

Frank Bidart, *Golden State*

[1973]

"Hell came when I saw MYSELF . . . "

Not familiarity but recognition is the craving here, a thirst not for knowledge but acknowledgment, not likeness but identity. And it must be put this way—in the way of choices entertained and rejected, hesitations, bewilderments, refusals. It would be out of the question to speak (as we are so fond of speaking) of "unerring aims," of "sure instincts," when their object is precisely errant, indeterminate: when the target is the realization of life itself, and the errors the very means whereby any aim—focus, concentration, scope—may be achieved.

A young man, a young poet, cannot discover the true goals of his endeavor without discarding the false ones. The wrong turns, the missing links and mistaken signals are no more than evidence of what may be right, given, understood. Over this book is suspended, like a ceiling of swords, the threat and indeed the doom of the negative. In his prosody, as in his convulsive pursuit of a voice which will, accountably, speak in the first person singular—and of course the achieved value here is that the prosody is not apart from but is a part of the pursuit, it *is* the pursuit at its incandescent brimstone pitch—Frank Bidart is as evasive as he is venturesome. "Don't turn into the lies / of mere, neat poetry . . ." he implores his father *in his own poetry*, and he will be at pains to keep the utterance from being *mere*, from becoming neat. Everywhere is the effort to vary the cadence, to elude that kind of recuperation of energy, that avowal of a constant in verbal behavior which (precisely because it can be repeated, violated, returned to) we call *verse*. This is a poetry which is, as Heidegger calls it in his 1950 essay "Language," *purely spoken*; its roots are not in assent, which is silent, but in declaration, in contestation, which is the lesson of all speech. "The opposite of what is purely spoken, the opposite of the poem," Heidegger says, "is not prose. Pure prose is never 'prosaic.' It is as poetic and hence as rare as poetry." Prose, then, is the basis of Frank Bidart's prosody, his organization of language to suit and serve his need, which is his quest: a poetry in search of itself. Such a petition will necessarily invoke a warp of the formal enterprises—the novel and the play, ever since Proust and Pirandello made *The Search* explicit thematically, which is to say formally, afford the clue here, the way into the labyrinth. The way out, however, is one that Bidart has had to find by himself: if poetry is prose, then the poem must have that form of its own which is *not* a novel, *not* a play. And he has found that form (cunningly enjambed, weighted with the varying shifts of the raised voice, the wounded utterance) in the *terrain vague* between the dream and the letter, the only two forms of human expression which are not subject to revision, but merely to creation. Bidart's *dream letters*, then, are that form, as astounding in their mythologizing remove as in their intimacy, their avowals.

Undressing, Oscar Wilde once told someone, is romance, dressing philanthropy; and the poet who is neither romantic nor philanthropic, merely questing his own creation as a poet, is indeed endangered, likely to be severed from himself by the one sword or the other. It is interesting to see how Bidart avoids the cutting edges: he begins and ends his book with "other lives," mirror-images of what, in his center section, he explores indeed as the *given*. Shocking as "Herbert White" is intended to be—and shocking it is—there is every reason for it to precede the rest, for this poem's real horror is its parallel with the discovery made in the closing poem "Another Life," the *identical* discovery that the self must become one with its unacknowledged obsession, that there is only the one life, not other lives. Dressing, then, is how the book begins, for it is Bidart's tactical decision to open with an "autobiographical" narrative which is not his own, thereby preparing us to accept his ulterior revelations, his undressing as fictions, as mythologized identities, not confessions:

> . . . The way to approach freedom
> was to acknowledge necessity:—
> I sensed I had to become not merely
> a speaker, the "eye," but a character . . .

The ambitions of a self which can engorge Catullus and Aeneas—versions of the poet and the hero which would seem, everywhere else in this troubling, attractive book, to be cut off from expressive means: what a thing it is to have an education!—are immense indeed, and they are ransomed (if ambitions can be ransomed, rather than merely reduced or rewarded) by the earnings of *presence*, which we sometimes call wit:

> . . . leave me *alone*!
>
> He smirked, and said
> I was never alone.
>
> I told him to go to hell.
>
> He said that this was hell.

Which way I fly is hell, myself am hell is the ultimate Satanic assertion, and one which Bidart has made, wittily and sometimes with a wonderful lyric warp to his prose ("I turned, and turned, but now all that was left / was an enormous / fresco;—on each side, the unreadable / fresco of my life . . . "), into a thesaurus of detestations, heresies, the scandal—for poetry—of the negative. A clear case, then, or a clarified one, of diabolic possession; the recording angel of Bidart's world is a fallen one: himself. "What *reaches* him," he asks in the poem "Self-Portrait," "except disaster?" By the end of the book we know—it is no longer what reaches him but what *he* can reach, the colonization of inferno. And hell lay all before him, where to choose. . . .

Kenneth Rosen, *Whole Horse*

[1973]

"I rise and enter the hardware and the light"

S electing his psychopomp with the acuity which characterizes an entire cavalry of work written before and since *Whole Horse*, Kenneth Rosen (a teacher of literature, a runner of roads; reader by profession even as he is writer by preference, by self-preservation) puts his book, with its epigraph from the love-deluded Antony, under the sign of dissolution. That water which is indistinct in water is of course—out of its course, *discoursed*—the Tiber, which melts into the Nile as Antony capitulates to the Egyptian queen: with an energy for-ever about to be extinguished, muddy, ultimately fertilizing. The gift here is all in the submission to the dissolving element, the gift is in the giving way: Antony as Adonis, Rosen as the risen god:

> O women, death, you are the everyness
> of countryside and time. I bleed
> upon your wood, my body
> gives the leaves their lime . . .

The poet's overwhelming identity is just that—to be overwhelmed, to let his imagination sway him from the vertical and sweep him (protesting: "Is this art? I asked myself. Have I gone insane?") on and out, unchecked by those mere proprieties of time and place, what used to be called the unities, which mark our waking lives. In our dreams, nothing holds its shape, nothing is reformed—there are too many

meanings within the images of our dreams for them to remain one
thing or another: they are anything, or nothing, but they are not determined. They are over-determined, and what meanings we assign
them, if they are to be significant, must proceed from several parts of
our lives at once, of our bodies as well:

> We remain until something breaks
> and we are diffused, fluttering
> our foolish ions, our limited valences . . .

That will be one aspect of the strangeness of these poems, then (for
they are strange, they are estranged from *rendering*; instead they
embrace) — and their predictable indeterminacy, their disjunct consis-
tency of metamorphosis. Another salience in the oddity of it all is
Rosen's delight in precisely that American wonderland one might assume to be inimical to poetry, or to poets: the plastic suburbia, the
campus wasteland, the quonset pastorale:

> Excelsior, I murmured where none
> could hear. Let your lakes become sewers
> and your sewers overflow, rats sleep and nest
> beneath the beds on every floor, or lava come
> and petrify all before any can scrawl
> Gomorrah on any standing wall.

Just when our country is most jeopardized, most exposed ("All is
twisted, All is withheld."), this goofy eloquence comes to redeem it, to
take those journeys by automobile and canoe, to cover the ground in
those pilgrimages which in our dreams are always our life itself, in the
initiation to vulnerability which when we wake is survival:

> I stayed in the car and waited
> for ordinary passage, my salvation.

My temptation is to correct Kenneth Rosen, to smooth out his
pop corrugations, to make him accountable to the culture — the high
culture — when it is just such bookkeeping he evades: "I decided I

could write poems like a man hangs wallpaper," he writes, "lay the first line and unroll the poem. It became a more complicated ethics of courage and being—if the chief way for one to *be* is in the poems one casts—but at first and for a while, it was just, as it were, WHOLE HORSE. . . . " It is a temptation I need not resist now, *after* reading the poems; for instance, I might assert the contrary—I might insist that when a man has made his imagination coincide with his experience as Rosen has, there is no "just," no justice. If the line-breaks seem indeterminate, it is because there are no breaks at all in Rosen's poetry, there are only consistencies: colloidal, viscous, warm. But I would not rub the strangeness off these oneiric eclogues too rapidly: their diction is as deliberately peculiar as that of Auden's first little book, though it is Mick Jagger rather than Thomas Hardy who looms behind them, the confiscating figure, an anxiety. Rosen's poems, as I began by saying, are not much concerned with proprieties of time and place—with ownership, with decorum, though he is hysterically responsive to decor:

> my sick clams
> and lost ejaculations, O ocean, city, sky,
> my heaven effort!

—they are concerned with giving in, giving way, giving out, giving up, the enterprises of surrender we associate with Tammuz, Osiris, the torn god who is always the male avatar of sexual infantilism. "Managing myself with weakness, yearning," he boasts, and falls once more upon his amazing phrases, "a crisis of wild embroidering" but also a crazy illumination of the possibilities. Nothing is to be corrected here, for if we tamper with the evidence we shall perhaps hamper the prolegomenon to any future resurrection—which is what Rosen's poetry, here and now, amounts to. He must not "denature" the given world by too much fingering, or he will miss that restoration to which he aspires, of which he is assured by precisely the depth of his here-and-now abasement:

> There is an anguish our planes and burnishes
> are unable to shed, a desolate landscape,
> a finger of wrath, rancor for wealth, an
> aesthetic of painted glass, love's mystery.

So that the poems take the page with a certain insouciance, not jaunty but not jointed, either—without those evidences of artisanship I have always thought were requisite to convince me of an authentic arrival, a new mastery. In Rosen's work I find a different thing, an alien force which I am at some loss to characterize, though perhaps because loss is where Rosen is at, and easy there. Without the usual marks and signs, then, I find myself compelled by these twenty-nine spiels— games indeed, and sweet airs: the music Antony heard when the gods abandoned him, music from undersea:

> I heard a guitar and singing, "O to live on Sugar Mountain," with more words, more beauty than I knew I knew, and there I saw my mother, holding a guitar, smiling, ready to join the song, and your mother, and you, the most beautiful person, were there, light in darkness, not even knowing, and I was happy, and I was saved. Saved! Not wasted, saved.

Kenneth Rosen will write much more poetry—he has already written it. But he will never touch the language with the strangeness of this spell again, he will never come this unpropped to his diction, this naked to the intervals of his energy. The poetry of WHOLE HORSE is "cast" indeed, as Mr. Rosen says—cast off, cast away, the vestments of a given life. A life given.

ishment. For she is supremely aware of the metamorphoses—even in the cemetery, even in the nursery, in the nursery most of all. Death is not something that comes from outside and takes life away; death in her poems is there, a presence within, which affords life its careful meaning, its meaningful care. And the poem will be accountable to these immense perceptions

> by the glass, wherein all images are clear
> by the needle, that pricks and lets no one rest
> by fire, that burns and is not consumed
> by song
> by praise
> by silence

A lot of winnowing, a lot of paring, a lot of *undoing* has gone into these charms and hexes. Their patience is exemplary, for it has accommodated the eager hopes of what will not be stilled, as well as the pressure of what will be only still. They do not make grand gestures, though they have the presence of a certain grandeur in them: the grandeur to hold still and watch, to sit by the fire and wait. Laboring, waiting, noticing—these are the actions which afford, sometimes, a cosmic insight, as in the poem "Nightfall," and sometimes a comic one (though the joke is always on her, on the properly named Constance), as in "MidAmerica." They are poems of wisdom which has shucked off knowledge, which has shucked off information—there will not be many facts here, and there will not be many fables. There will be the sediment, the precipitate, the residue of facts and fables, and we call it wisdom, a word whose root has something to do with our word *guide* and with that word for appearances *guise* or *wise*, as when we say a thing is done in a certain wise. Hence the cool *sagesse* of a poem like "The Fruit," which appears to come out of the ritual practice of proscribed lineages, but which is no more (no more!) than the long, loving look at the guise of things, and the guidance such a look yields up. It is the look I have seen on the Etruscan funerary figures, and the likeness, too, of this poem, which will do—if the reader goes no further than this note—as a liminary specimen of this remarkable artist, this wise woman who, like a man, is never disgusted:

Those who have not yet been abandoned
know about abandonment

Those who have not yet been afraid
know about fear

Those who have not yet been betrayed
know about betrayal

So that the surrender is unconditional
so that they go down not into the comforting darkness
but in the full glare of artificial illumination

In the anteroom of the narrow house they wait
while doctors haggle over fees and ethics
while scientists peer for angels through microscopes

They know they have not always been patient
or suffered in silence, or been kind to children

Once, some were loved, whose rags of flesh
under moon-colored hair, are still visited by a smile

Those who have been spared
know that none will be spared

The authority of that poem speaks for itself—indeed that is for whom it must speak. The beauty and the justice of it is that there is a "whom," that there is a person *paying*, as the French say, for the wisdom achieved, won from nothing less than the whole range of the life lived, the suffering known, the joy divined.

Turner Cassity, *Yellow for Peril,*
Black for Beautiful

[1975]

"The music that has made them real will let them see."

When James Merrill refers, characteristically and character-
izingly, to the structure of this peregrine poetry as "an
opera house in the jungle," we must not—in our imme-
diate rush of assent to the *rightness* of the edifice and its environing
wilds so identified—we must not mistake the whereabouts of that
barrens, the location of exoticism: the jungle is ourselves, the way we
live now; and the freakishness, the spectral singularity of Cassity's
open-all-night casino, is that it should stand, towering under us, looming downward in all its derisive shapeliness, amid our noisy parking
lots and plastic trees which encroach, as jungles do, upon the civil
space of speech. Architecture, as Walt Whitman once observed, is
what you do to a building when you look at it, and our transactions
with this poet's oeuvre suggest that we turn a building into a "folly"
when we don't look at it enough. It is our neglect which is playing the
fool here, not Cassity's capacity, not Cassity's veracity, not Cassity's
sagacity.

Crisp from his encounters with the Yvor Winters memorial frigi-
darium, this poet sets a mark, a stamp, a *frappe* upon utterance which,
from the first, has been unmistakable—"these outlines have an anthem," he says somewhere, and of course these anthems have an outline, a temperate *moulage* which is the consequence of their trust in
that old ceremonial of keeping, of returns and recuperations which we
call verse, meaning thereby something that keeps turning:

> They hold no promise. Forward or reverse
> Impels them only to where what occurs
> Occurs. Such is, at least, the chance of being terse
> And is their grace . . .

Though he is describing the ferries at Sydney, surely Turner Cassity is here constructing the entire justice of his prosody, and the esthetics of its justification. Unmistakable from the first, then, because unmistaken: "the first" goes back some little ways—to *Watchboy, What of the Night*, a book of lyric epigrams published in 1966, verses so terse one might expect to find them incised on any stele under the name EUROPA, transliterating the grave of colonialist schemes in the backlands, the outlands, the hinterlands whose earlier laureates, subsiding with imperialism's swell, have been Kipling, Conrad, Dinesen. Then in 1970 came "The Airship Boys in Africa," occupying an entire number of *Poetry* (whose founder, back in 1912, called her periodical, remember? "A Magazine of Verse"), and preoccupied to the point of perversity with a tale, the story and personnel of a German junket in Africa (1917), observed not only from the hawk-eye view of history, but from a Zeppelin view of process, metonymic, inflammatory, more humane than the marmoreal, dismissive lyrics could afford to be. "Divinity embarrasses," Cassity remarks in another connection, "and who were gods / In retrospect seem their machine." The astonishing identity of the dirigible with its crew and their mutual disaster suggest a persistent thematics of downfall in this poet: "we are each defeated by the actual," is one of his ways of putting it—whereupon we welcome such defeats, joyful martyrs to what is real, for of course it is imagined reality that is, more than anything else, actual. The narrative conventions, the working-up of connective tissue into a cantatalike flourish of retrievals, continues the following year in "The Return of Ming the Merciless," a fifteen-page epyllion, quite simply—simply! with such decors: "their columns are of jasper and their orders chrome"—the best Hollywood poem ever written, a kind of Fu Manchu *festspiel* as it must have been scribbled by the gnomes of Parnassus on a forced diet of Saturday-afternoon serials washed down with lots of spiked Kool-aid. In 1973 Cassity published an even more masterly volume of lyrics,

Steeplejacks in Babel, and when he refers to them as "pages from the last Big Little Book" he is casting no aspersions on the high seriousness of his endeavor, he is not even type-casting himself as Don Winslow about to ask Madame LaMort for another hesitation waltz, he is merely informing us as to the provenance of his passions, the origin of his actions. As the titles of his first works suggest, we are here in the mythological world of American adolescence, "the crescent margin that is life" ever and again trodden out by monstrous emblems, figures from a disreputable *collective conscious*: the heroics of boyhood lore. The same year appeared another masterpiece, *Silver Out of Shanghai*, a feature-length scenario for Von Sternberg starring wicked nobles, depraved nuns, Imperial Marines, person in blue, and of course Resurrection Lily:

> On her face the twin deep shadows fall
> As they would fall upon a skeleton . . .
> The husky voice, whose perfect consonants,
> Ever so slightly, rattle, forms in German,
> Then in English: "Red Sails in the sunset,
> Way out on the sea. . . . "

That is Dietrich as Gioconda, colder than the rock candy and popcorn among which she lounges, and a characteristic snippet of the luminous fabric Cassity has woven out of Movieland cobwebs. It is a reclaiming, a civilizing process, this career of Cassity's as I trace it, in which "anecdote falls heir to all," and "style gives back a time but takes its terrors." *Where id was, there shall ego be* is the swamp-draining motto of our modern Faust, which Cassity recasts: where *kitsch* was, there shall culture feed. The energies of a bitter wit, a *turner*, indeed, of the most intricate contours upon the lathe of prosody, are bent or at least curved to transform what had been merely waste—public consumption, rated G—into particular delights, the significance speech has when it is no longer public but personal, obsessively individual, idiopathic, its own man: rated X.

The new book by Cassity toward which I am loitering here is exceptional in this already exceptional configuration, as I have tried to make it out, because it combines, it conjugates the impulse to tell with the impulse to toll, the narrative with the knell, the epic with the elegy. Here are twenty new instances of Cassity's ziggurat wit, preposterous True Comics, like the resurrection of Ibsen to do a script for High M.G.M. (though what could ever be "like" this?):

> . . . Presentations in brief; the lights in Klieg.
> "Herb Stothart. What we have instead of Grieg."

> Blue eyes behind the granny glasses smolder.
> "And this is?"
>   "Adrian."
>   "Your button-Moulder?"

> "Rich, is it true," inquires Louella Parsons,
> "Your plays all deal with syphilis and arsons?"

> "What about Sonja Henie," breaks in Hedda.
> "Will you date her?" Silence. Enter Greta.

> "We should like to be alone," says Ibsen.
> "Send us Aquavit."
>   "I vant a Gibson."

> Age and youth, Norway and Sweden, arm
> In arm they leave forever the broken charm,

> The circle—jungle—of her beauty sleep.
> The Kliegs go out; the other light will keep. . .

And as even this savage cartoon suggests, here is a verse play (in hexameters, some in Afrikaans) on or around—capering wildly around—the death of Cecil Rhodes, biggest daddy of them all, a Lament for the Dead Hero which is this poet's own snarling version of the collapse of the Knights of the Grail—a kind of *Boys Own Parsifal*, wherein the Fellowship dissolves into . . . Rhodes scholarships! and the Men of the Great Man secede to their private purgatories, out of the shared contours of Empire's splendid inferno.

The lyric epigram, the dramatic narrative: one watches these two impulses of Cassity's come together, coalesce from opposite ends of the book, with a sentiment that is something like terror. For they are opposing tendencies, the energy of metonymy, narration, prose, and the energy of metaphor, ecstasy, verse. To have them even in the same book gives off a certain pre-explosive glow, satanic and suburban both (Kierkegaard said you could not, if you found him, tell the Knight of Faith from the law-abiding citizen); now black, now yellow, the light is anything but light-hearted, however giddy. It is to me apparent that we are in for a cataclysm—hysterical tears in the Children's Section— for Cassity's gifts, his talent to amuse and his genius for being amused, are about to coincide. This little book serves notice to a largely negligent world that the human artificer has assumed Klingsor's powers, or Alberich's; we remember that for such wizardry, the renunciation of love was a condition. But what if you are not only obsessed by what you renounce, but pursued by it? The answer is here, imminent and audible, the physis of a giant art, a little Big Book of Revelations, news from a defunct oracle, Intimations of Immortality from Recollections of Early Childhood. . . .

Norman Dubie, *The Illustrations*

[1977]

"Some inevitable sadness that will visit each of us"

What are they illustrations *of*, these irregular, even rugged but ever rutilant poems in Norman Dubie's third book? The word itself will tell us, for we regard being, even our own being, as *illustrious* when it is purified and illuminated by light—when it is lustrated. But is it our being which is in question, and in answer, here? Look down the table of contents: from Lascaux to D. H. Lawrence, from a painting by Van de Velde to a novel by Gide, these poems of Dubie's are "brief lives" of other people, hell itself (as Hegel said), invited into the poet's own speech, invented by the poet's own words in one of the great Flirtation Routines of our moment. Or is it always the poet's life, as the insistent dedications to family and friends suggest . . . a world of derived identities?

If I ask so many questions, it is because so many answers are afforded by the poems, because so much light is cast, is shed by the poems themselves that we are choked, blinded: we know too much. For example, we know what it is like to be Horace on the Sabine farm ("the Goths have been defeated, and Maecenas was his friend"):

> Here in the hills
> Caesar is a spectacle of dead trout
> Washed with smashed mint and lemons.
> What have I kept back?
> Only this: there is no way to leave him.

And we know what it is like to be Aleksandr Blok ("at night St. Petersburg is empty"):

> Once when you were very young you watched peasants
> Shoot a horse in a pasture: it fell over
> Like a table. And what I've kept from you, Aleksandr,
> Is that you were cruel and handsome!

In such knowledge, as the two citations show, the poet keeps something, which he then bestows in the poem—indeed, it is the poem which becomes the bestowal, the relinquishment of some final totality otherwise merely lost or evaded in the *private life*. We cease to be dazzled, endangered by so much experience, if we respond to the one thing the poems ask of us; for they ask of us the one thing that art must ask, not all the other things which it may: they ask of us submission. Submission to one life, then to another, picked up and put down (revealed, redeemed perhaps, in the moment's audacity of attention):

> My father?
> One stormy night in 1927 he rode a train in New England
> While trying to memorize a poem by a Frenchman:
> It said something about a mirror rising from
> The sea. You know: *un miroir de la mer* . . .
> Some men postpone orgasm by reciting poetry,

taken here, and then there, the perpetual *next*, at crucial ventures within the biography, at critical instances: we are always, with Dubie, upon the verge of extinction or of ecstatic renunciation, some grand romantic fantasia upon broken themes of dispossession and metamorphosis. Proust and Ovid, silver-age Russians (Blok, Babel, Mandelstam), Klee and Breughel, the deposed Czar ("I teach the children about decreasing fractions," he writes from his captivity in the Ekaterinburg barn, "that is a lesson best taught by the father"): it is always the experience which has the root of *peril* in it, the ripple of danger which enlivens the seemingly lovely surfaces, the "ordinary" existence. And as I say, Dubie identifies that experience, by reciting it, with his own life to a hallucinatory degree: we are not to know what is given and what is taken, what is "real" and what "made up." What we know is that three things can be said about all of us—that we were, that we are, and that we will not be. We listen then (no clue who is speaking) to a recital of experience with no hint of recurrence, no hope of repetition, yet not in prose even so, for there is Dubie's rage for unity from the start and throughout, making even the most intricate and weird of his notations (mostly declarative utterance: "the bald heads of two priests can be seen / like the white buttocks of the lovers fleeing into the trees," or more tenderly:

> The water is green. The two boats out at a distance
> Are silver, and the two gulls coming in
> Off the water are, also, silver . . .)

round on themselves and form a whole, even if it is a whole enigma, a whole labyrinth, a mystery entire. We listen, then, in what I recommend as a posture of submission. Best to let the poet tell, in that shocking way of his, what you can see or hear by his lights, what morning looks like on the curtains, and what century it is. He is, as they say, a natural (they mean: we do not yet understand such art), and he will often be able to compel a recognition-scene from just the moments most alien to your experience: it is because he has *created* your experience in the poem, has preempted you as he has assimilated Boehme and Mme. Blavatsky, and there is no pulling apart the intestinal warp now, no mine and thine about the texture, as in this aperçu from "The Boy Breughel":

> Ice in the river begins to move,
> And a boy in a red shirt who woke
> A moment ago
> Watches from his window
> The street where an ox
> Who's broken out of his hut
> Stands in the fresh snow
> Staring cross-eyed at the boy
> Who smiles and looks out

> Across the roof to the hill;
> And the sun is reaching down
> Into the woods
> Where the smoky red fox still
> Eats his kill. Two colors.
> Just two colors!
> A sunrise. The snow.

It is because Dubie has created *your* experience by the words in his poem (his? who is "he"? Breughel? The reader? The painting?) that he obtains the submission he requires (Dubie is very chary about revealing his *other* means of obtaining it, hides his rhymes and rhythmic insistences within a hugely idiosyncratic method of enjambments, "the regalia inside"). We yield to these poems because they value our confusions, our shames.

Indeed so intimate is his scrutiny of the nostalgias, as Wallace Stevens would say, that Dubie appears unable to forget—to subordinate any experience to some other; thereby he occludes what we have agreed to call meaning (to mean is to see resemblances, repetitions), but he enlarges what we have agreed to call value (to value is to see differences, singularities). As the poet says:

> And my mother pale with her red hair rests,
> At midnight, looking out the kitchen window where
> All summer the fat moths were knocking their
> Brains out against the lamp in the henhouse,
>
> But now the moths are replaced with large
> Flakes of snow, and there's no difference, moths
> Or snow, for their lives are so short
> That while they live they are already historical. . . .

That you may grant this assertion—that the poem can create your experience of the world rather than that your experience must create the poem—is the risk Dubie takes, his cherished peril. He has put *himself* as medium in the service of an art which, of us, asks that submission merely. Of him it asks everything else.

Madeline DeFrees, *When Sky Lets Go*

[1978]

"Day Rolls Over Me And Still It Wears Somebody Else's Sign"

In one of her letters, Louise Bogan speaks of the poetry of Sister Mary Gilbert, published in 1964: "She sees things rather panoramically, and is not at all pietistic—hardly any Jesus and NO Holy Mother. Unusual." It is one more reason to wish that Louise Bogan were alive still, this new book of poems by the woman who was once, in religion, Sister Mary Gilbert but who writes now from, and into, another life. How much *more* unusual than the diligently administered, serviceable poems of *From the Darkroom* are the extreme and charged ones of Madeline DeFrees—and how I should like to know what Bogan would have made of them, and of the fact that the same woman made them, as I say, for and from another life. What I make of them is mainly a wonderment, marveling as I do at the authority and, still, the solicitude: the authority which comes from the solicitude of their making, and the violence which works out of them, from the center to the surface, discharged there in the only enduring function, the only *effectiveness* violence can have, accommodated by art.

Not that Madeline DeFrees is immensely or immediately concerned to show us her art—but she has enough of it, she has sufficient *style*, we may call it, to control the human violence of the talent, to turn it to account. I think that in her other life, what she has, and what she does, would be called prayer, though in the life exhibited, in the life exposed here, one is not so easy about the precision of the paranoia ("One star is out to get me" . . . "Nothing here / the wind can use against me") as to be able so to call it. Until we remember Blake's beautiful definition, and we are a little easier about the metamorphosis of this poetry into prayer—unmixed attention, Blake says, is prayer.

These are poems of terrible weather, chronic vicissitudes of climate and season which will not permit us to rest in them, nor the poet to repose until she has wrestled with them and rid herself of them:

> Sisters,
> The Blue Nun has eloped with one
> of the Christian Brothers. They are living
> in a B&B Motel just out of
> Sacramento . . .
> > ("With a Bottle of Blue Nun to All My Friends")

The "other people" in the poems seem maddened, driven beside themselves by some awful contention of the landscape and the lost or lawless meteorology (what Newman, if I may have my little joke with this poet of an abjured theology, called some dark aboriginal catastrophe); yet all the others—the "irremovable pastor 20 years too late," the widow Damascus, that other widow whose parrot calls her Mama, the residents from the State school for the handicapped, the rest: for there is a gathering personnel in these poems, and if they are paranoid, it is a paranoia of work done with others, pleasures shared and mourned with others, the paranoia we call, in our saner moments, life itself—are versions, try-outs, experimental takes of Madeline DeFrees, whose rages always turn upon, or against, herself and whose verses always enjamb to reveal something unexpected:

> . . . The old and strange collect around me,
> names I refuse pitched at my head
> like haloes. This one is a dead ringer.
> It rings dead. I pat the head of the beagle
> nosing in my crotch and try to appear
> grateful. A witch
> would mount the nearest broom
> and leave by the chimney. At ten I plot

    my exit: gradual shift to the left,
    a lunge toward the bourbon . . .
                                        ("The Odd Woman")

a turn indeed. When we say our experience has given us a turn, we are speaking, or might be, of such an art as that of this deciduous woman, casting off the very selves—

    . . . Weeks trickled off. Rouge drained
    from wimpled cheeks. Warm air came back. It caught
    us on the swollen porch, limp coifs
    and windy veils, throwing out the garbage.
                            ("Reply to an Irremovable Pastor")

—which once had chastened her into habitual service: casting off the habit. It is difficult not to speak personally in this matter, in this spirit; what after all can be less exceptionable than to speak personally when you are speaking about a *persona*? about a woman who has made herself intimate with us without making herself less private, public without making herself known? It is difficult not to acknowledge and even affirm that here is the poetry—a cause for wonder—of a woman who has spent and gained enough of her life and her death in the one acceptation, so much that now that she has altered the acceptation, transformed the provenance, her earlier giving and taking cannot be regarded as a parenthesis.

    Better, then, to take this poetry as all the one thing, sutures and splints for the one life growing together. It is not easy, as I have suggested, but it is literally wonderful. Best to take it as the snorkel diver learns to take the sea; the mask fits close, the breathing must be through a tube clenched tight between the teeth, and the movement afforded by the flippers is abrupt and unaccustomed—we move and breathe and have our being in an alien element, and these tools, the means of locomotion, are merely there to keep us going. In the destructive element, Conrad said, immerse—let *us* say, revisional, in the alien element submit, and you shall see wonders, taken for signs:

> . . . I drive ahead
> Towards a dead end, a new freeway. Which?
> The labels don't match. Signs double back
> between the eyes. On two-lane roads
> I list toward open sea and salt, kill
> my plants at home with small attentions.
> Nobody's fault. Wreckage the stars relate
> in drifting light ought to form a scene.
> Even on Mars there is water. What
> does it all mean, this neighborliness of disaster?
> Barnacles stud the necklace of my bones.

It all means a sea-change into something rich and strange. It is how
Miranda, middle-aged, renders the real.

J. D. McClatchy, *Scenes from Another Life*

[1981]

"the power to answer outcry with insight"

While we are living it, we cannot conceive of "our" life as given over to *scenes*, discrete, dramatic fragments with a glinting finitude of recognition to them, scenes we recognize only in our own past—the intolerable gift—and in the parade of others' lives from the window of our own, the voyeur's balcony. If there is "another" life for us and scenes from it to be considered, enjoyed, deplored—as this new poet suggests—it will be precisely because this is not the life we have, the life we live. There will be a certain alienation, a necessary distancing before the poems come. Yet that is how this other life is generated, looming up out of the losses and sorrows of the life we do live:

> . . . expanses once you
> Held in thrall are deserted now by all
> But broken views of their domain . . .

And in American poetry of the last quarter-century, the emphasis has been on the abiding possession rather than on the alienated scene; our poems are difficult to see apart from ourselves, to hear at any distance from the instances of utterance. And what a fruitful selfishness it has been, this hugging of the reft ego, close enough so that its accents are never divided, nor divisive, from such eloquence as we recognize to be incontrovertibly our own. To acknowledge an alien eloquence is indeed to be cut off (or relieved?) from the messy me, and for these remembered decades, the power of our verse has been there, in the argument with holdings close to home. The strength, the enlivening and peculiar interest of McClatchy's poems, I find, is their capacity, their energy for attending to *both*: to the realities of the merely lived life, experience, which means death, and, on the other side, to the splendors of the life imagined, vision, which means—for him, at least—love. He is a poet who has recognized the significance of otherness if there is to be a sameness, the dialectic of self and surroundings that we minimize by calling it worldliness.

It is a theater of confirmation, McClatchy's poetry, and as he says, "there is poise in this regret." There is more: his balancing act ("inlaid flux and pendent atmosphere together") sounds a new note in American poetry or, at least, a tonality rarely sounded these days, as I suggest. It is a language reaching past the immediate murmured solicitude for the very widest range of effects, light to darkness, gaiety to pain; for McClatchy, it is the rhetoric that *enables* the world out there, exploring it to present a possibility of the world in here: "to house what gods may yet arrive."

One figure seems inveterate and is worth seizing upon as a handle to so much that goes up in smoke, "the least particular now hovering, now / settling in the globe I carried home." Just so, if a globe is carried home, one needs all the help one can get in holding onto it, and help is at hand: in consummation. In burning. In release from mere possession: "rising from fire to ash to the very air / of an indrawn breath." And again: "shadow / risen from the ashes of another nightmare." The sense is that we shall be nothing nor have what is worth having, something new, until we have incinerated all we had. No increment without incremation. Or as the poet has it, "morning, when it comes, will burn off his dreams." It is a very old notion, original in the true sense, this submission to loss and destruction so that all may come round and begin again. Perhaps it is why we call a marriage a consummation. The poet plays, if such ardent manipulations can be called playing (they can, they must!) for

> still higher
> Stakes, that all will be undone, restored
> To something like itself.

The poetry is not to initiate himself; it is the consequence of that initiation, but it is to enable us "to learn this tomb / has always been a gate"; how consistent McClatchy's imagination is, how congruent his practice with his perception! *Another Life* is not, in these poems of wryest wit and yet most gullible exultation, merely the past ("overdrawn drafts of forms") but the future as well, the enormous possibility that comes to us only when we have consumed—consummated—our losses: a phoenix.

The profit of loss, then: "such advantage as this pain affords." The poems come out of some such transaction with what is not the comfortable and comforting ego. The maker

>   . . . sees all this and so creates
> Pretended ruins of a city he does not know
> Once was his. He may as well be lounging
> In a stuffy museum room, benched
> Before overdrawn drafts of forms that call
> To mind "the past," another of our handles
> On what contains us. It takes time to tell
> How much is owed to private slants of vision.

Time, and a mind as active as phosphorous: McClatchy has put these things together, willing to let the poems work their way out from the center until they have left him altogether, scenes from another life indeed. If this is a consummation, as I see it to be, it is that marriage which is the perpetual struggle of energy with fear, and that incineration which leaves the place bare for the next egg to hatch, and the next singular bird to appear, "restored to something like itself," yes, but different from itself as well—different and disconcerting. As the poet says:

> One loses all but confidence in its redundant
> Uplifting illustration, just the right
> Effect of mind over the matter at hand.

Rika Lesser, *Etruscan Things*

[1983]

We touch, we hold, we keep / one another free

I t is the imperative, as well as the privilege, of all such through-composed works as *Etruscan Things*—of all those covens and clutches of poems confederated to arrive at a structure, a meaning from contiguity, contrast, and recurrence, rather than disposed to afford the pleasures of merely circulating among separate feats, discretions—that we *have read* the entire production before we linger over, before we pluck out any one member of the concatenation, any particular limb of the body. We date our modernity, almost, from such affairs as *Leaves of Grass*, as *Fleurs du Mal*, whose "secret architecture," as Baudelaire called it, articulates a vision beyond the anthologist's dream. Rika Lesser has learned, translating Rilke, translating Ekelöf, the likelihood such structures have of resisting not only the intelligence but oblivion as well, of sticking to the mind because they make a shape in the memory. She has gone to some trouble to devise a scheme of this kind, a map of earthly ruins which corresponds, it would seem, to that map of the skies by which a repressed culture once secured its wisdom and its joy. Nothing appears less *actual*, of course, than the question of the Etruscans (who were to the Romans what the Jews were to the Germans, and to the Romans as well, according to Tacitus) and their sky maps, their divination from the courses of lightning through the starry sky, until we realize that we bear, still, within our language, vestiges of this practice. Each time we *consider*, each time we *contemplate*, we make a sidereal temple of the stars, setting them in significant order, a constellation. So I would suggest that the first way of dealing with this new guide to the ruins is to read it through, notes and all, without stopping over bright particular beauties, though there are plenty of them, and even without trying to "figure out" what the "intellectual" intentions of left and right, near and far, intimate and hostile, might be. It is my experience with these poems that their tephromancy—their divination by ashes—can be trusted, and that by the time you come round to the celebrated couple in the twenty-fourth poem, the *sposi*:

> Sharing the single bed, how close
> we lie; fingers curved over palms
> whose fable reads: *conjugal bliss*
> *is possible*.

—you will feel that you have experienced—suffered, recovered, enjoyed—a version of vision which, perhaps for being so fragmentary, so supputative, is the more *telling*, the more striking for being stricken.

Cunning and compassionate, resourceful and responsive Rika Lesser has been (perhaps they are the same thing—not a thing at all but a mode of *taking in*, whereby the poet is made merely a vessel, a means of rendering justice to the visible world which, thus pronounced, replies in *sentences*: " . . . transformed the words. They entered my flesh, / became whole inside me. Black ink on / white cloth: opaque remains. The meanings / lie in the lacunae")—so submissive to the evidence that I am at a loss, and happy to be there, whether what I am calling the presented vision of a whole culture, a society, a way of being human, proceeds more vividly from her recuperation of the Etruscan things themselves, or from their wreck: is it the story of loss and ruin which tells us more, the evidence of destruction, than any restored emblem ("reconstructed from about 400 fragments") might dissert?

In either case, or in the accumulated pressure of both at once, the Etruscan *gestus* and the text of fragmentation, these poems contest the primacy placed by most of us, most of the time, on a life defined by reason, utility, and discursive order. Here the attention is bestowed upon those practices and attitudes which acknowledge death as a force of life rather than its tragic demise. Solitude, isolation, and despair are—however momentarily—overcome within ecstatic instants, apprehensions of continuity labeled sacred in "archaic" cultures. These are poems which rehearse the affirmative willingness to lose things, meanings, and even the self (the self most of all, for if the self is the God in everyone, it cannot be fully entered into). Rika Lesser has determined upon the intuition of ruins secretly awaited, where the sustained value is intensity, a concentration of energy antithetical to the husbanding of scarce resources, disdainful of immediate ends, resolved upon the transgressive violence of sacrifice, a rite where paradoxically the moment of eroticism transcends sexuality (eroticism being to sexuality as the nondiscursive is to language). As we see in the final poem, to look at a person laughing—it is the subversive insight of Georges Bataille which I borrow here—can be a form of erotic encounter.

These conclusions or reductions cannot, evidently, be warranted by any one poem, or even by the eminently quotable and cunningly enjambed movements within any one poem, though I find these lines irresistible as a liminary invitation (and admonition):

> Nothing our own hands fashion
> endures intact. Weather will
> have its way, eating into
> these faces, making queer shapes
> of our work. And some future
> race will worry these contours,
> forcing open its false doors.
> None but the Hand of Sky—palm
> blazoned with thunderbolts, streaked
> with burning stars—on the day
> it clasps the Hand of Earth
> (crushing our bones to powder)
> can bring the temple down.

One is obliged to read *Etruscan Things* in the way Eliot suggested we read *Anabasis*—by yielding to its serial pressure, letting the stubborn center be scattered where the poet, in her will-to-vanishings, intends her artifice to be undone. Then we discover the dire, fastidious significance of Rika Lesser's poems, which are of course a meditation on what happens to the open secret of her life, what becomes of *now*; we discover, in so many Etruscan things taken out of their Etruscan places, that the past pollutes AND saves.

Paul Kane, *The Farther Shore*

[1989]

. . . little boulevards
of phrases become the avenues of approach

When a new poet beguiles us so readily, *without apparent effort*, by the charm of his diction, by the aspiring rise and the dying fall, by what Hopkins would call the *carol* of his voice moving back and forth between gentle margins, we suspect— as I began to suspect when I noticed Mr. Kane's poems some years ago, in the easy evanescence of a university milieu, then of magazine verse—that we are being deceived, toyed with, charmed in the sinister sense of the operation, as a bird is charmed by a serpent. Nothing this deliberately amiable can be so amiable as all that: such seductions must be paid for, accredited by what this poet cunningly identifies as "significant pain."

It would seem at first that we are being invited to enjoy "a season of no regret, an / afternoon beyond compulsion." So formidable are the accomplishments of this latest student of all the nostalgias that for once we appear to be in the presence—and ever so happy to be there, revelling even, if that is not too vehement a word for our satisfactions— of an art without the usual exactions, without that clutch upon our efforts of attention which is the regnant character of *the modern* in its dread avatar among us. As if the poet were merely casting into the cool inscriptions which are his gift and his gaud (his *guile*, I have called it) our intransitive contemplation, producing from a collection of accidents, cryptically presented, a design of reverential rhetoric which but stands, stock still, a monument. But once we have read through his collection, his series, his *structure*, we learn more, we think better of ourselves for discerning that these poems of "older travels, other travails," of "a pastoral world [that] is forever past," are not mere blandishments, adorable winding sheets around our reassurance. Rather, it seems to me, they are, ultimately, quite insistent presentments of that mortal energy of alternation which for Paul Kane constitutes what it is to be "human: the flood / and withdrawal of the tide." Repeatedly the figure occurs:

> And no misgivings could mar this moment—
>   the very waves, beating the shore, withdraw
> in foaming undertow and carry with the tide:
>   exhausted, redeemed; exhausted, redeemed.
> It is the fever of our lives that we
>   compel the sudden changes and all the while
> ache with an alien solitude, knowing what
>   changes us flows from a sea beyond change.

And again, in the title poem where Kane declares we have not fallen, we are falling still, sliding down the waves forever, he offers that program of systole and diastole which is our anatomy, our fate:

> The far shore cries out with the voices of leaves
> whirled in the wind: "farther, farther," the sound
> in the rustle lifts, dies down and lifts again.

We are taken back to Shakespeare's *ebb'd man*, and to the sense that the self is never immune to a sort of vegetable repetition-compulsion,

> this common body,
> like to a vagabond flag upon the stream,
> goes to and back, lackeying the varying tide
> to rot itself with motion.

But attend how lovingly this anything-but-innocent voyager offers us the booty of his helplessness ("The Whores of Algeciras," "Canada," even his pretended, his projected, his *dramatized* helplessness in "Mr. Emerson Assisted on His Walk"); not that he is a Tiresias-figure—far from it! He has not yet eroded his illusions, his sexuality (are they the same?), but he has premonitions, he has doubts: "the past has yet to happen—these are figments of presence."

And if it seems to me that on one occasion certainly Kane goes past premonitions into the region of prophecy (in the alarming poem "Stellar Junk," where he declares in a panic beyond the personal "We hope it will end there. We are looking / forward to uncreation, to beyond our own time"), the point to loiter upon, as if it were no more than a palm extended, is the vivid ease of these semblances: "we live in the mirror world of our waking, the crystal / refractions, the prison of our prism." This poetry makes itself "easy" on us so that we will the more efficiently understand what is arduous, what is intolerable; so that we will turn the poet's own words back upon him, declaring:

> We search the sound of what you say,
> We wish to come close to what you see . . .

S. X. Rosenstock, *United Artists*

[1996]

To *make free with culture* is perhaps the last action of Eros to be exploited by a member of our society—certainly the last behavior to be looked for from a poet. (Our escutcheoned poets, nowadays, are culture-*bound*, and it is that bondage, that mansuetude, which secures, even when it scares, their poetry at all.) Yet such *making free* is just the conduct of Ms. Rosenstock, a new and startling poet not so much in our midst as on our margins, our outskirts, as it were, to be noted, to be identified, and to be saluted with a certain hilarity. She is at liberty—she *takes* the liberty—to move among the monuments, and among the ruins, with a strange (to my ears) insouciance (she is not insolent about the masters, except perhaps in the case of "acceptable feminine behavior"), and the consequence of her movements, these poems, are surely the most affectionately aimed spitballs ever lobbed into the courts of High Culture.

Her specific pleasure, even more than her stories, her *imaginary lives*, surely, is the business of syntax, overheard sentences braided over and under the grammatical hurdles like a sort of technicolor wickerwork, though it is just these jumps over the barricades that she takes so handsomely, so gleefully. Her delight in the preposterous, the unavailing, the not-to-be-cloned is apparent from the inside out; her diction, her tropes, her allusions all tend to carve up the funeral baked meats (Coole Park) into designer hors d'oeuvres (Coole Jerk)! Wharton and Plath, like Mme Bovary's daughter and Pauline de Rothschild's decorator, are prodded into patterns wickedly subservient to Rosenstock's will. Hers is a will to challenge (more than to change), and what it challenges are certain patriarchal codes revealed by her experience to be . . . uncertain. Pleasure does not always mean pleasing men.

These are evidently poems written to beguile Rosenstock's ear *first*, before canonical considerations flatten out the silly or sorry sublimities into sensible ones. Like Florine Stettheimer (whom she resembles in her palette and her impasto), this poet is unconcerned to *mind*, as Nurse used to say. She wants, in her eager, trusting way, to *matter*, and caresses the gorgeous syllables, the odd words, the amazing references, the forced temperatures, until she does. On the way, she wants you to have a good time, even a redeemed one, but if not, not. That one doesn't do it? Try this. As Nurse would say: Did you ever?

If there is any Advice to the Reader which might be offered on the threshold of this glistening echo-chamber of imaginative utterances, it is to abandon all anxiety of allusion-catching here. It will be even more fun if you can guess who Marcel might be, if you will bother to look up the Marschallin or (Lord help us!) Ray Bradbury. But not before you let the poems work their cooing, buzzing, garrulous way into your innocent ears.

The Thesaurus of Pleasure welcomes a new work within its narrow purlieus: to Ms. Rosenstock arms are extended from such *doyens* as Valery Larbaud, Daisy Ashford, Raoul Dufy, and, breathless with adoration, Richard Howard.

Sarah Getty, *The Land of Milk and Honey*

[1996]

Ｎone of the obstacles, the problems, the bafflements which poetry presents, these days, to the Common Reader (who of course may not, these days, exist at all—and to the Uncommon Reader poetry presents no more than a request for attention, a claim on the time otherwise allotted to science, or to history, or even to the domestic economy) is to be found in this collection with which Sarah Getty begins her life as a poet.

Neither the disjunctive shades of Jorie Graham nor the daunting intimacies of Sharon Olds (to stay with the women, merely) are operative here, to any degree. If there is a mentorial figure behind the ease and entertainment which these well-made, worked-out poems afford, it is not so likely to be a poet at all (though Mona Van Duyn does float to the surface of association) but rather a chef or a shrink such as Julia Child or Anna Freud (to stay with the women, merely).

Getty makes no trouble: she wants us to get into her poems, to get through them, and to get out of them with a minimum of fuss; her emblem of duration might well be the effective recipe, the revelatory psychoanalytic session. Just look at her poems on the page—carefully counted out, the stanzas leaving plenty of room to breathe, the long lines promising that all will be confided, in due time. Just listen to her sensible music:

> . . . The Only Child leans back
> into my arms and I lean

> back into my mother's, home again. Rocking
> we watch the west for omens unfolding in the gold.

The varied enjambment of *back* and the long O's of *Only* and *home* and *omen* sealed with the rhyming of O's of *unfolding* and *gold* are sufficient to inscribe the lines in the aural memory, to finish, as Julia Child would say, with a demiglaze. Sarah Getty doesn't go in for more spectacular effects, she wants neither to intimidate nor to dazzle, but her poems always function at a level just above the tension of the lyre, as Wallace Stevens called it, where the language has its way with us, even while we are having ours with it. Such is the plain style, its eminent dignity and its secret design.

Of course some notice might be taken—this is where Anna Freud comes in, I guess—of the interesting commitment this poet has made to the gynaeceum; her poems are all "about" that wonderful concatenation of experience which moves from mother down to maiden, from maiden back up to mother, by way of the married daughter—Getty is good at all the parts, she does the female in different voices—without much attention given, or even loaned, to the father, the husband, the son. If love is blind, marriage restores its sight with remarkable acuteness in these poems, and I believe we are in the presence of a new, a post-feminism here, an attitude which is neither militant nor resentful, but remarkably exploratory and resilient. As Ivy Compton-Burnett reminds us, and Sarah Getty exemplifies, there is more difference within the sexes than between them.

But if she is personal (always a good idea when you are talking about a person), this poet is never private; and if she is heterogeneous (always a good idea when you are talking about a gender), this poet is never public: she is identical, and her poems are the elated statements of that self which delights to be conscious of its duties. A poet is someone who has invented a poet; I am happy to welcome Sarah Getty's invention, her identity on the pages of our attention. Chesterton said it was unwise in the poet to goad the sleeping lion of laughter. On the contrary, it seems to me, in Getty's poems, that the highest wisdom, and the truest value, is to be found in the presence of her waking lion on almost every page—or is it lioness?

Robert Hahn, *All Clear*

[1996]

A nything but a raw recruit to his art, indeed more likely to strike the reader as a practiced, though hardly hardened, veteran (his adept and much-exercised voice has not been heard, been *scored*, for some while: almost a decade since the last chapbook), Robert Hahn is a poet of what Emerson calls "beyonding"—it is necessary for him to ground his perceptions, his discoveries in a specific circumstance, to write around the occasion, *to circumscribe* in order to ascend. As he says so powerfully in "False Dawn":

> . . . How one loves the impassioned drudgery
> of names, decoding a bunker, a mosque enjambed
> with Venetian stone, the world demystified.

(As for veteran expertise, I rest my case with the axiological force of *enjambed* here, a truly beguiled usage.)

Throughout Hahn's knowledgeable book such "impassioned drudgery" will be strenuously indulged (though for us, of course, it is no such thing: naming is glamour, glossy as well as glossary, on the receiving end) in order to reach the risen condition, the *state beyond* which is the purpose of all his poems. I cite the poet once again in order to assert the Understood Relation (which will bring forth the secretest man of blood, as Macbeth calls it):

Simple men, we like to assume,
Obedient to the blunt instructions of [our] master: be
composed. Tell the truth.

As often as not, such orders come from the painters and novelists,
who are faithfully studied here as docents of levitation. How studious,
indeed how worldly Robert Hahn appears in his inspection of the
nostalgias, the makings, the shrines. Not much escapes the punctual
cunning of his notation as he observes what Wordsworth called "fallings
from us, vanishings." . . . The acknowledgment of imperfections, of
veritable collapse, the abasement of culture seems to be necessary, or
at least concomitant, if we are to soar to any height; it is a measure of
Hahn's passionate elevation in almost every one of his grand poems
that the scrubbed missions, the underminings, the duds, are so inveterately accounted for, ruefully, gingerly, but with all the sharpness of
some other ripened spice, a secret ingredient.

It is a great privilege to partisan the poetry of a master—but I want
to clarify the kind of mastery involved here (and *involved* is surely the
right word, the sense expressed of being at the heart of the matter, in
deep): not so much the delighted control of the medium, the eager
display of the wonderful articulations, though these are the first matters to come to light, as the mastery of what we call "experience," the
mystery of a world revealed when the conditions for apprehension
are, yes indeed, *all clear.*

James Cummins, *Portrait in a Spoon*

[1997]

s a literary phenomenon, as a category of received poetical circumstance, the Second Book—particularly when a poet's First
has been notable and nonesuch—calls for special regard: poems here are likely to be found closer to the bone (what is criticism, after all, but in the wisdom of our etymology a cutting-at-the-joints?) than
those incipient performances wherein the flagrant distractions of merely
making inveterately loomed or lowered somewhat *apart*. It is these ensuing texts—anything but *secondary* except in the temporal dimension—
which tend to incarnate what the poet *can do* rather than what is but
obligatory, but needful to get poems written *in the first place*.

As first books come and go, James Cummins made something of a
sensation, a few years back, with *The Whole Truth*, which many readers gleefully characterize as "the Perry Mason sestinas"; a relentless,
sometimes goofy, and always graphic sequence wherein the dread con-
cepts of plot and character were goaded through the most unyielding
formal baffles that occidental poetry has yet devised. Virtuosity emerged,
even protruded, as the justification which modesty proposes in such
cases, an expedient of *desperate measures*.

In the present instance, an alleviated reader will find, still, a few inevitably expert sestinas, as well as poems ("Portals" is a good example)
that appear to be convalescing from sestination; but for the most part—
and for the best part, it seems to me—these subsequent Cummins poems require far less tending, many fewer props and struts in order to
articulate their identity, their essential pain (their essential pleasure: all

one, as the poet reminds us). It is, that identity, the matter and the (sometimes grand) manner of a relished solitude, for all the jokes at the expense of Rival Poets, Star Athletes, and Family Counsellors, and for all the voiced (or under-voiced) claims that it is dark in here, and cold, and wet, and hard to breathe . . . *Sotto voce* stage directions from the heart, the lungs, and what used to be called the liver and lights.

Henry James remarked somewhere in *The American Scene* that New England villages afforded so little possibility of "conversation" that introspection had become a social resource; Cummins makes us realize that in southern Ohio, loneliness is a spectator sport, a recreation in which he may triumph over Rilke and Hemingway, Hamlet and Jackson Pollock, to name but the big-league contenders. Family and Profession are the easy losers here, and not even a new daughter can offer much in the way of competition:

> . . . you'll know what I know,
> the sadness of most things a little before
> their beauty.

Of course it is love, famous opponent of all our solitudes, that Cummins has *really* seen through, the inevitable result of such transparency being that no matter how many may give themselves to this lover, no matter how many he may take, there is always a third party to their intercourses—the third party is time, which makes cuckolds of them both:

> We sit in middle age, the snapped-
> off languages lying close,
> like toys we have succeeded
> in demolishing. Will touch
> proceed from this, or scorn—
>
> scorn of the human? And that's
> the story within the story:
> the scorn or love that once
> were different, yet now
> mean one and the same thing.

Cummins's odd and entirely appropriate title for his new book frames the enterprise between the inevitable solitary reflections; he begins with George Eliot's derision of "various small mirrors," extending to "Milton, looking for his portrait in a spoon," an inevitable source of grotesque likeness, and he ends with the classical adjuration to his book:

> Go, little mirror. You hold up to me
> only desire, not what I long to see.

Of course by laying (pressing?) so much weight on the heartbreak of the matter, I have badly neglected the hilarity; Cummins is a genuinely funny poet, though not a comical one—it always hurts when he laughs—it hurts *us*.

Sidney Wade, *Green*

[1998]

. . . wayward words that suffer
time, the dark romance of disappearing, all
flawed and hopeful, flushing with nobility

It was Hopkins, I recall, who waged a certain war on the kind of secondary poetry he called *Parnassian*; how eloquently he raged against its all too imitable eloquence, how cruel his animadversions upon those careful embellishments which were all too evidently *applied*, added to things—it was generally *things* that received the treatment—from outside, so many embellishments. I am not all that dead set against such beautifications myself (nor is the poet I wish to endorse, who can be as Parnassian as any Hérédia, when the Byzantine fit is upon her:

> Copper is shaped with rhythmic strikes
> in crabbed streets where in older days
>
> the golden insects of Apollonius
> sang like brazen parakeets . . .

Indeed some degree of such—after all, admirable—work is probably necessary if we are to tolerate a poetry spoken *above the level of the poet's mind* with any sense of invited pleasure, of recognizable ease. But it is because Sidney Wade's passionate discourse comes so pervasively *from within*, because her powers so inveterately seek their expression from the center, moving outward upon whatever occasion she is chosen by, that I would offer her new poems as a particular and splendid instance of what Hopkins meant by "poetry proper, the language of inspiration."

The way you can tell, Hopkins goes on to instruct his Oxford correspondent, that a poet has eschewed the Parnassian and all its works, is when, reading that poet, you cannot imagine yourself going on in that way—in that guise, as it were—whereas it is a mark of the Parnassian that you could conceive yourself writing it if you were that poet. This is where I could ring in Sidney Wade as a remarkably consistent *proper poet*, the poet of inspired language, unimaginable by us in her ecstatic apprehensions. Yet once *she* has imagined her poems, has written them down, they cannot be otherwise to us; they seem, merely, her poems. The beautiful, we are told, is what we cannot conceive of existing otherwise. This is the effect of Sidney Wade's poems as I read them, the quality of experience rhetorically seized and followed up the staircase of surprise (Emerson) to extreme elevation—in this instance, a library carrel suddenly illuminated by a shaft of sunlight:

> A pure pacific entertainment
> weighed into the scheme of things beneath
>
> the mansard roofs of higher education
> and I felt for a hefty and eternal minute
>
> like a strongman bearing up with splendid fortitude
> beneath the unbearable barbells of bliss.

The occasions which find her out are various, multiple in their fulfillment of the mythology of A Woman's Life—the record of the dying mother, of the daughter, of the daughter's father perhaps, of the lover, of other lovers—and in their exploration of the Scene of Enchantment, in this case Istanbul. Here is where *Green* is most astonishing, for it is in transactions with exotic or even with merely exalted locale that poetry succumbs most readily, most greedily indeed, to the Parnassian; her intensities of feeling and what I might call her chastity of perception preclude such capitulation, and Sidney Wade is never just the Pierre Loti of the enterprise. What she says of the "Turkish Bath" is indeed the truth of all of her poems of this place, to which she is as inwardly steadfast as Wordsworth ever to Rydal Mount:

> The chamber is cruciform, a circlet of columns
> supporting a breath-filled central dome
>
> where language moves, substantial and firm
> through the humid air of a woman's throat.

Indeed in all these poems, there is a loyalty to the Ego and its own, to revive a dangerous notion, which remains oblivious to solicitations of the exotic as of the "merely" personal. So that when Sidney Wade writes of a domestic incident—

> . . . seduced by the brilliant green lie of the duckweed,
> my two-year-old daughter steps off the low dock and onto the fabulous
> figment of landscape composed by a million small fraudulent islands—

she is as delicate ("unlike the unfortunate / Demeter") and as decisive ("the tug on her hair / that drew her up over the glistening fringe of the splintery dock") as when she celebrates the union of the Bosphorus with the Golden Horn, say. In old-fangled terms, Wade is a poet who has been found and possessed by her authentic daemon, creating memorable verbal objects of great freshness and power for which we may be, as Mr. Auden once said in another connection, honestly grateful.

Vickie Karp, *A Taxi to the Flame*

[1999]

There is a kind of thinking, or of knowing—of *cognizance*, to sweep the two together—which proceeds, when it comes to expressive endeavors, by the recognition of objects, by the discovery of circumstances, by the awareness of situations, in terms of their resemblances and analogies to *other* objects, circumstances, situations. Such cognizance we call metaphor or trope, and we correct it, when its excesses are beyond us, by the idiot rehearsals we call identity. For these are the only instruments we have, metaphor and identity, with which to account for how the world strikes us, and in the enterprise of poets there are varying degrees, diverse densities of the one or the other. Of course words themselves are metaphors in some stage of decrepitude, so that even the austerest poet of identity is discovered to be metaphorical *deep down*. Perhaps because we do not choose to read that far down, we tend to accuse the poets of identity of a certain poverty, a certain bleakness—what Yeats called (and acclaimed as) *the desolation of reality*. On the other hand, we tend to accuse the poets of metaphorical richness of a certain confusion, a certain derangement; Shakespeare is *hard to read* if we are not trained to metaphorical cognizance. Though I wonder how hard . . . When Antony complains about "the hearts that spanieled me at heels," it seems to afford the (presumably untrained) playgoer no trouble at all to understand the trope even as the syllables flicker past. I guess the trouble begins as the out-of-favor warrior continues his complaint:

. . . The hearts
That spanieled me at heels, to whom I gave
Their wishes, do discandy, melt their sweets
On blossoming Caesar; and this pine is barked,
That overtopped them all. Betrayed I am . . .

Thick and fast the metaphors arrive—the spanieling hearts turn into dissolving confections which then, disconcertingly, somehow offer their delights to a rival Caesar perceived to be in flower, which flourishing at once summons the contrasting figure of a stripped fir that once towered over "them" (no longer hearts but Romans). Incidentally, there is no record of either verb, *to spaniel* or *to discandy*, occurring anywhere in our language except on these sole occasions in Shakespeare, whose capacity to trope finds no obstacle in the *hapax legomenon*, a verbal form used but once.

Of course this is all very well for Shakespeare . . . (if it is). But when a contemporary poet invests in such creative behaviors, contemporary readers may repine, and that is where I should like to intercede in Vickie Karp's behalf. This poet thinks metaphorically, with a Shakespearean luxuriance, and may, as in "Getting Dressed in the Dark," disconcert:

. . . The body rises, shifting its inner tropic from swamp to tree,
Pats the floor for its shoes, places a thumb

On each side of a sock—the mugging grin of a boy
About to stick out his tongue—

And slowly, as if dipping a foot into cold water,
Rolls the puddle up over each ankle.

Such metaphorical cognizance is endemic in Vickie Karp, and as a post-Shakespearean reader I revel in it, though I concede that you may need to give some time and attention to the exactitude of this poet's expression before you join her on the other side of consciousness. Of course what makes her the distinguished writer she is, the poet of re-

sponsible delight, is her awareness of this rare plenitude; she has a remarkable capacity to switch into a diction of great plainness, a lingo of
what Shakespeare calls *the self-same*, which balances her poems wonderfully between the figural and the literal, between economy and ex-
travagance, as in "Endless Greetings," her apostrophe to Monet which
I believe to be her masterpiece, from which I cite the last six lines:

> Now a green smoke rises.
> An underwater bursts up and spreads its mackerel skin.
> The white rings of birch spin in solitude.
> The fragrance of the bank infuses the anticipation
> Of someone running towards you,
> The flash of her white dress.

Here the equilibrium between metaphor and identity is perfect, and
the poem, thereby, unforgettable. The process is perfectly accounted
for in another poem in Vickie Karp's remarkable book, an elegy in
which she commands (or implores) herself to

> Close my well-repaired eyes, open my unrepaired heart.

Such is the method of Orpheus.

Carl Buchanan, *Ripper!*

[1999]

A letter from the poet acknowledged, as long ago as 1994, "I began writing it fourteen years ago." His book is as intricately formed as that long gestation would suggest (compel), a series of structures within structures, like those Chinese boxes which sanction entrance—and egress—through an invisible sliding panel, itself to be discovered only by a process of trial and error (what a phrase for this subject!); and once inside the innermost (and empty!) chamber, nowhere to go but out again, the Gentle Reader's tormented spirit seeking release as it had first sought enthrallment.

This systole and diastole, a dialectic of confinement and compurgation that makes for the doubleness of all rhythm, is wonderfully observed in *Ripper!*, a text which for merely *narrative* purposes would otherwise confound the reader. I mean that given the nature of what is being returned to and issued from, any regular compositional procedures among those which we associate with verse, any ceremonial of recurrence, would afford us a kind of discouragement, a hypnosis of horror.

After all, the poet has chosen to assemble his great inquiry—what is the self? how is an individual to be identified, who am I?—around the most sensational (and unsolved) serial-murder case in modern history, and he has been unsparing in the freshness and frequency of the details. Only by ringing changes in his formal enterprise, by keeping the reader guessing (and hoping that the guesses are *wrong*), can Carl Buchanan be certain that we do not go the way of all crime buffs, all enthusiasts of detection who abandon their text once the solution is achieved, to the point of forgetting the phraseology itself. Here of course, as in all poetry, it is *the phraseology itself* which is at issue, and at closure, and Buchanan has ensured the avoidance of any monotony, any favor of forgetting, by an interlocking configuration of poems of the most iridescent variety; indeed *Ripper!* is actually what the classical rhetoricians call Menippean satire, wherein debate and disguise replace any (mere) linear occasion.

The *frisson* afforded by a celebrated (public) criminal instance has been of great appeal to writers in our developing media culture—from Dostoievsky down to Don DeLillo, and from Thom Gunn (songs for Jeffrey Dahmer, no less) back to Robert Browning, whose discovery of the "square old yellow book," a baroque Roman murder story, was to generate one of the two greatest nineteenth-century English epics of murder and adultery (the other is *The Idylls of the King*). Yet even so virtuosic a manipulator of blank verse as Browning collides with the problem of formal *longueurs*: why should every member of his (extremely varied) personnel employ the same prosodic structure? Here is where Carl Buchanan has discerned and seized a great advantage: conscious that today's readers are by no means so ready to invest in extended iambic-pentameter discourse as Browning's more acquiescent public (by the time he was writing *The Ring and The Book*, Browning actually had a public), Buchanan has sought, and with the permission of our incomparable modernity has found, the most sensitive variations within free-verse utterance, where finding must mean *invention*, that chief virtue of the grand poem, as is asserted, once again, by the classical rhetoricians.

Inevitable bewilderment is a part of this learned maker's stratagem—it is only when the whole poem has closed over us that we know where we are, and where we want to be: at the heart of the mystery disclosed *as mystery*, not dismissed as solution. We stick with the poem, or rather it sticks with us, because it is not resolved, not settled, not *known*. It is a difficult, very modern beauty which is the consequence of Carl Buchanan's architecture and interior design; *Ripper!* is like one of those disquieting new buildings—examples in Tokyo, in Bilbao, in Mexico City—in which and from which we may learn to renegotiate space, to reconceive desire, to redefine the self.

Stella Johnston, *Without a Witness*

[2000]

Now give me a drink of water. Here's
to all that's done but still unfinished.

Take my hand. The Gods can never die.

P oets seem to discover their own forms, their own formalities —
the kind that really help them say what they mean to say, rather
than the ones learned or loaned (these lapse), usually in the
course of a considerable initiation period, during which the trials and
tactics of the art may be apprehended or, more likely, be warded off. It
is extraordinary to me that Stella Johnston arrived at, actually *landed
on*, the necessary diction of her dramatic lyrics from the very start,
without the usual huffing and puffing that characterize the tyro in
matters of verse, that ceremony of returns. Her speech is, as I say, dramatic, which means it is also distilled. Take any handful of lines, such
as these from "Ball Lightning":

> There's someone standing in an open door.
> There's a sickly smell of sulfur
>
> and back in the kitchen, a kettle's
> boiling over on the stove.
>
> It's morning.
> When nothing else can happen, the rain begins.

And it appears, it *resonates*, that there is a certain density, even a *man-
teia* about the words and the way their edges meet. Her language, that
is to say, has passed through the stage of being rhetoric, and has come

out into the light and darkness of revelation, an unveiling indeed.
Only a couple of the poems are specifically about her own somatic
disasters, though more concern the sequels and backwashes of such
disorder:

> We are in a dark room together,
> myself and my breathing machine.
>
> I am lying on my back
> when the doctor's shape moves in.
>
> I press the usual questions.
> Today, in this room without a witness,
>
> he answers:
> "Your father's dead and you'll never walk again."

Even when she mythologizes her experience, as in "Andromeda" or
"Of Being Alive," what beguiles Johnston most is aftermath, consequence, actually *survival*.

The mysteries of how the new poet (and none I know of is so new
as Johnston, taking the brilliant air like a morpho butterfly just out of
its cocoon, wings still damp and not yet rid of their creases of constraint) compels her utterance leave me wondering on the threshold of
her poems, entering and leaving and quite happy to be there.

This is the authority, these are the accents of Marina, daughter of
Pericles rescued from shipwreck, "given by one that had some power."
Her poems begin often enough in Texas, but they end—rather they
do not end, but echo ever after—in the territory of *legend*, what must
be read, as *memoranda* must be remembered, as *delenda* must be
destroyed.

Bryan Dietrich, *Krypton Nights*

[2002]

For a poetry as convincing and accomplished as this, for a mythology as exhaustively researched, one looks for models, prototypes, antecedents, wondering where to plant the bars of the cage when the captive has been so cunning so long. The best I can come up with is Turner Cassity, our Klingsor of the Serials, who back in the eighties published a grim little jape on "The Southeastern Comic Book and Science Fiction Fair to be held in Atlanta," wherein the Enemy speaks thus to a deaf-mute in search of dog-eared Marvels:

> . . . If I promise, I your Tempter,

> All the world and tights that never crease,
> How will you answer, dumb, Get thee behind me.
> You will not? Well, if you need to ease
> Clay feet, I shoe them. You know where to find me.

But Cassity requires the pathos of History, and of her wayward daughter Class Consciousness, for his poetical heartbreaks, and sends only this minor grimace in the direction of Superman and Co., a popular religious fantasmagoria which Dietrich has mined so deeply that it is only his garrulous deftness which keeps him from being the exhaustive Aquinas of the affair.

No, there is no antecedent High Versification in our theology of

Comic Books, though we can immediately recognize the subject in its place and wonder why not? Perhaps because the stern stipulation for the Tinsel City of God is not only a proud and interplanetary imagination (Hollywood, Here We Come!) but a metaphysical sympathy I should expect to find only among the most loosely lapsed of Catholic readers—readers of *Superman Comics* as an epyllion to Dante's divine version.

When you're working with elements as "elementary" as the Lost Babe of Krypton, as crude, not to put too fine a point on it, as the Doomed Planet which has given its All, or its Best, to an analogously doomed Earth (do we not all feel?), it is Order that is the one thing needful, Device which must serve the turn, and Dietrich is of course wonderfully armed and outfitted with orders and devices of every kind, from Clark Kent's crown of seven sonnets climaxing in the inevitable Adam-to-Jesus muddle:

> . . . for Clark, Superman, me: Fruit, fig-leaf, fakery,
> Coming home to a hard day's Gethsemane.

to Lex Luthor's wicked complaint from the Arkham Asylum:

> Should I lift a leaf from Lovecraft, from Poe?
> Explain, oh-so-lucidly, just what sort
> of mad I'm not? Tell you all the gorgeous
> things I've done were done for my father's sake . . .

And wiliest of all, the poet of Krypton Nights has taken the omnipresent *dialogue* of comic strips (even comic *books* are all talk, nothing *behind*) and made it too, even it, into a structural order which is the prosodic justice of his entire art. As Henry James once remarked on the exceptional use of talk for architectural [poetic] purposes, "really constructive dialogue, dialogue organic and dramatic, speaking for itself, representing and embodying substance and form, is among us an uncanny thing . . ." For Dietrich the thing is indeed uncanny, but so inveterate as to be—for his readers—only natural, only nurturing, only necessary:

. . . This is what we are,
Not supermen, not perfection dressed
in our garish red, blue and yellow Sunday
best. We, the world we read, are Torah.
Superman, the constancy of his concupiscent star,
is less than this. A big red S. A text
we read too lightly.

The author of *Krypton Nights* has made a remarkable contribution to American literature: he has added another scarlet letter to our alphabet of heroic undergoing, and his "big red S" embellishes the breast of a fondly interpreted icon. Move over, Hester Prynne, make way for Superman!

AN EXCURSION
TO THE
EXTERIOR

Manila Clipper

[1987]

An American writer of stoical bent and belittling straightfor-
wardness had left Manila a few days before I arrived, and after his visit and his pronouncements, Philippine PEN—which
I was visiting on my way to the 1977 PEN Congress in Sydney—was
in a dither. The writer had declared that the members couldn't manage
English properly, not to say expressively, and they suspected he was
right (certainly they couldn't manage English the way he did). Still, in
a much-scattered country of many languages, English was the literary
language they used, the choice they had made, and it seemed hard—in
their avowed (and castigated) struggle against a despotic regime—to
acknowledge along with those political difficulties the more intimate
defections of which Mr. Gass had left them so bitterly conscious.
Though that regime was even then building some sort of culture palace,
the writers I listened to that first morning in Manila were skeptical
about ever seeing the inside of it—at least from the stage. Van Cliburn
would be welcome there, they said, but native literary types were perceived as far too dangerous for public consumption on a . . . public
scale. Why right now there were two Filipino writers—a theater director and a "prose-poet"—in jail, and in this instance such treatment
was entirely unwarranted: neither man was political in the least; indeed, the director was a "harmless faggot aesthete" and the prose-poet
had innocently run afoul of the censors but was not concerned with
"issues." (Here everyone giggled, and before you could say Pier-Paolo

Pasolini, the subject was dropped.) But might I, that evening, when I would be dining at Malacañang Palace—might I at least speak to their outward grievances? At dinner I would be meeting, they said, the regime's cultural counselor, a young man of attractive aspect and ambiguous affect with regard to writers ("like someone in Mrs. Mandelstam's books"), and through him I might reach the boss. In such matters, and on such occasions, the boss was Imelda Marcos.

I spent the rest of the day being shown around the capital by an elderly man who had operated the best bookstore in Manila (closed by the regime for its back-room sessions, deemed subversive; my host had plenty of time to do the honors). We visited the *beaux quartiers* where the American officers from Clark Air Base lived, and the friends of the regime as well; and we visited the *tondo*, a sort of vast floating slum which in mere extent surpassed anything I had ever seen in Istanbul or Barcelona, cities quite enterprising in shantytown life. I am no connoisseur of the *bidonville*, but even I recognized a superior specimen here. In her capacity as mayor of Manila, Mrs. Marcos had announced that the *tondo* was to be transformed (into what?) and that the regime would have no patience with inhabitants—however numerous—who might offer to defend their squalor. Reform was imminent, it was said: had not all pornographic materials been banned in bookstores and magazine racks throughout a city of many millions, only that month? (It was only halfhearted, that ban, as I discovered on the streets of Manila around the hotel, yet it gave evidence of the characteristic puritanism of the rulers, whose tastes in these matters were to be defined for me rather specifically.)

At six that evening, I was admitted to The Palace through the usual series of checkpoints (we have them in the White House) and waited in a variety of vestibules, the Aubussons thickening underfoot, while my invitation was checked and matched with my identity; in the last of these I was joined by the cultural counselor or whatever he was, who explained to me what a hard job it was mediating between Mrs. Marcos and the touchy writers—he was, however, doing his best. We passed through increasingly splendid Spanish decor (Malacañang is— except for ruined forts and a cathedral—the only vestige of Hispanic colonialism; Forbes Park is the evidence of ours, I suppose). The country had been under martial law six years already, and would be for another three. The assassination of Benigno Aquino would not occur for six years. So a series of routine examinations of my papers seemed hardly excessive, even in the company of this important, and evidently knowledgeable, functionary. We reached one of the main salons, I would guess, and there, in the center of a very large, dark room (only the ceilings, gilded in the Spanish manner, were distinct) loomed up four gilded bridge chairs, occupied—it turned out—by President and Imelda Marcos, and by the Swedish ambassador and his wife, watching the last reel of *Elvira Madigan*.

The president vanished as the lights came up, and I was presented—by her cultural adviser—to Mrs. Marcos. I recall my disappointment: so blurred and blunted a countenance, so coarsened and, yes, thickened a figure, when I had been led to expect—whatever it might be that former beauty queens become. The introductions continued, and Imelda Marcos announced that she had enjoyed the film—it was so refreshing to see a Swedish film which wasn't dir-ty. The Tagalog burr or drawl in her voice gave the last two syllables a particular savor; Georges Bataille would have appreciated the tone, the distinct lilt. . . . The Swedish ambassador blushed (as northern folk will do) and said nothing. We waited as other guests arrived: in particular for a friend of Mrs. Marcos, a columnist ("like Suzy—you know Suzy?") in one of the Marcos papers; she wrote, I was coached, a lively society piece every day, and was much appreciated for her insolence—no one knew how far she might go, even at The Palace. Apparently this guest managed to make her deadline, for she arrived straight from the paper, and we all went "in" to dinner: another vast salon, and a tremendous feast laid out—it was for the Swedes, of course—in the manner of a shipboard buffet. Lots of Filipino specialties elaborately distributed on green leaves. Marcos never reappeared. The columnist, vividly dressed and vivacious indeed, opened a conversation about censorship—after all, I had murmured that I was on my way to a world congress to discuss the writer's right to freedom of expression—by asking if I knew about the old pre–Hayes Office rules of self-censorship in Hollywood, whereby almost any transaction between couples could be shown on screen so long as both parties "had one foot on the floor."

No, I had never heard of such a thing, we marveled together, the table marveled with us, in the heart of porn-free Manila. And then Mrs. Marcos spoke. She had been staring into the distance, as though watching another movie, or Banquo, and she said, in a reverie that was quite consciously comical: "But suppose—suppose they were doing it on the floor?"

Except for Napoleon's saying that to be believed you must make truth unbelievable, I have never known dictators to make jokes—and good jokes! It took some time, I recall, for conversation to find its way back (back?) to my purpose, my mission. The columnist asked me—it might all have been worked out by the counselor and the columnist, they knew the ropes, and the strings, and were pulling them—asked me what I was doing in the Philippines. And that led to my account of the two unjustly jailed men, the writer and the director. Oh yes, the columnist knew of them, no, she knew *them*, of course, were they in prison? whatever for? they were indeed harmless. "Then let them out!" Imelda Marcos exclaimed, evidently eager to see justice done.

A telephone was brought to the table—I forgot to say we were eating on a gold service, my first experience of that kind; I have also forgotten what the phone was made of, but it appeared, Mrs. Marcos spoke into it rapidly, forcefully, and the instrument was removed. "You can tell your friends those fellows are free now," she smiled, and her graciousness was entirely convincing. It was evident she was readily satisfied by the assurances of the columnist, who appeared to abound in the sense of my PEN friends that morning. The counselor looked relieved that the sensitive matter had gone off so well. The evening ended early, and I remember nothing else about it but this: when we got up from table (everyone had addressed Mrs. Marcos as Ma'am throughout, even the columnist), I saw that we had all been sitting on tapestried straight-backed dining chairs, except for Ma'am, who stood up from a gilded armchair and led us to the next vast room.

It had been arranged that I would return to The Palace for one more meeting the following morning. There had been some allusion to meeting the president, but he did not appear. Mrs. Marcos, on this occasion in a very elaborate rainbow gown, took me into the corner of yet another salon, and we sat down a moment together. This was the

Heavy Lies the Head moment. From a large receptacle beside her she extracted two large, glossy, illustrated books. "These," she said, and she put on some gold harlequin glasses to say it, "are President Marcos's writings, they are studies of Philippine democracy, with outlines of his plans for our people's future. You know"—and here she looked at me sternly through the gold harlequins—"Marcos is a profound believer in democracy. And I am sure that as the president of American PEN you will be interested in what he has to say. It is not an easy task to protect democracy, and how hard we must work . . . "

Evidently this was my clue for dismissal, which I seized, though Mrs. Marcos urged me to stay on in the Philippines, to visit her in their country place on Mindanao. At present, I knew, that island was in the midst of the most vehement insurrections, and I could not believe such an offer was being extended seriously—it sounded like an offer of the last resort. But my hostess appeared entirely unconscious of any obstruction to a pleasant weekend. In any case, I was obliged to get on to Sydney and the debate in our congress over some amendments to the charter—concerning free speech, I believe.

So I left The Palace, and after being checked out in the opposite direction, was released to the purged streets of Manila and my long taxi ride to the airport. I turned over the bright pages of the books Mrs. Marcos had given me: the democratic vistas of Ferdinand Marcos. There she was, beside him, smiling up from my lap into the camera, much less coarse-looking now, much grander than the thickening matron who had so disapproved of Swedish porn. And I thought: Lord, if these people are ever deposed, they can claim to be *authors*, and PEN will have to defend them!

And I opened the taxi window and flung the ridiculous lying trash into the ditch, and left for Sydney on time. I still wonder if, once the plane was past Mindanao, those two men were clapped back in jail, or were they released for good? There has been no news from Philippine PEN since Mrs. Aquino's presidency.

Bibliographical Notes

ON POETRY

"A Consideration of the Writings of Emily Dickinson." *Prose*, 1973.
"To Be, While Still Becoming: A Note on the Lyric Verse of Mark Van Doren." Preface to *Good Morning: Last Poems*, New York: Hill and Wang, 1973.
"Dreadful Alternatives: A Note on Robert Penn Warren." *The Georgia Review*, Spring 1975.
"The Resonance of Henry James in American Poetry." Unpublished, 1988.
"Marianne Moore and the Monkey Business of Modernism." *Marianne Moore: The Art of a Modernist*, edited by Joseph Parisi, Ann Arbor: UMI Research Press, 1990.
"Sharing Secrets." Lecture, 1992.
"Things Forgot: The Education of a Poet." John R. Adams Lecture in Humanities, San Diego State University, 1996.

ON FRENCH LITERATURE

"Childhood Amnesia." *Yale French Studies*, No. 43, 1969.
"A Note on Barthes's *S/Z*." Preface, New York: Hill and Wang, 1974.
"A Note on Renaud Camus's *Tricks*." Translator's note, New York: St. Martin's Press, 1981.
"A Note on *Les Fleurs du Mal*." Foreword, Boston: D. R. Godine, 1982.
"A Note on *Past Tense: The Cocteau Diaries, Volume One*." Translator's note, San Diego: Harcourt Brace Jovanovich, 1987.
"A Note on Julien Gracq's *Balcony in the Forest*." Translator's foreword to the Morningside Edition, New York: Columbia University Press, 1987.
"From Exoticism to Homosexuality." *A New History of French Literature*, edited by Denis Hollier, Cambridge: Harvard University Press, 1989.
"Invitation to the Voyages of Xavier de Maistre." Introduction to *Voyage Around My Room: Selected Works of Xavier de Maistre*, New York: New Directions, 1994.
"Yourcenar Composed." *Salmagundi*, Summer 1994.

"Divination by Ashes: An Introduction to Claude Simon." *The Georgia Review*, Spring 1995.

"A Note on *The Charterhouse of Parma*." Afterword, New York: Modern Library, 1999.

"A Welcome Return: On Gide's *Journals*." Foreword, Urbana and Chicago: University of Illinois Press, 2000.

"The Cruel Guest: Alphonse Daudet's *In the Land of Pain*." Review, *The New Republic*, April 7, 2003.

"An Introduction to *In Search of Lost Time*." *In Search of Lost Time, Volume 1: Swann's Way*, New York: Modern Library, 2003.

ON THE VISUAL ARTS

"People Figures." *Craft Horizons*, January–February 1970.

"Fragments of a 'Rodin'." *Shenandoah*, June 1974.

"Eleven Caprices on the Work of Michel Delacroix." *Michel Delacroix's Paris*, New York: International Archive of Art, 1990.

"On Michael Lekakis." *Shenandoah*, June 1975.

"Lee Listening." *Grand Street*, Autumn 1984.

"Bald Heads." Afterword to Alex Kayser's *Heads*, New York: Abbeville Press, 1985.

"The Nude." *Legacy of Light*, edited by Constance Sullivan, New York: Alfred A. Knopf, 1987.

"The Mapplethorpe Effect." *Robert Mapplethorpe*, edited by Richard Marshall, New York: Whitney Museum of American Art in association with New York Graphic Society Books, 1988.

"The Menil Collection." *The Gettysburg Review*, Summer 1990.

"Brassaï the Writer." *Brassaï: The Eye of Paris*, Houston: Museum of Fine Arts, 1999.

"On *Lepanto*: An Appreciation of Cy Twombly." *Cy Twombly: Lepanto*, Gagosian Gallery, 2001.

ON PROSE

"What Is a Neo-classic?" *Partisan Review*, Winter 1965.

"Jane Austen: Poetry and Anti-Poetry." Lecture, 1986.

"Apart: Hearing Secret Harmonies in Esther." *Congregation: Contemporary Writers Read the Jewish Bible*. San Diego: Harcourt Brace Jovanovich, 1987.

"A Description of Susan Sontag's 'Description (of a Description)'." *Facing Texts: Encounters Between Contemporary Writers and Critics*. Durham: Duke University Press, 1988.

"An International Episode: Henry James and George Sand." *Grand Street*, Spring 1989.

INTRODUCING NEW POETS

"Eleanor Ross Taylor, *Welcome Eumenides*. New York: George Braziller, 1972.

"Cynthia Macdonald, *Amputations*." New York: George Braziller, 1972.

"Frank Bidart, *Golden State*." New York: George Braziller, 1973.

"Kenneth Rosen, *Whole Horse*." New York: George Braziller, 1973.

"Constance Urdang, *The Picnic in the Cemetery*." New York: George Braziller, 1975.

"Turner Cassity, *Yellow for Peril, Black for Beautiful*." New York: George Braziller, 1975.

"Norman Dubie, *The Illustrations*." New York: George Braziller, 1977.

"Madeline DeFrees, *When Sky Lets Go*." New York: George Braziller, 1978.

"J. D. McClatchy, *Scenes from Another Life*." New York: George Braziller, 1981.

"Rika Lesser, *Etruscan Things*." New York: George Braziller, 1983.

"Paul Kane, *The Farther Shore*." New York: George Braziller, 1989.

"S. X. Rosenstock, *United Artists*," Columbia: University of South Carolina Press, 1996.

"Sarah Getty, *The Land of Milk and Honey*." Columbia: University of South Carolina Press, 1996.

"Robert Hahn, *All Clear*." Columbia: University of South Carolina Press, 1996.

"James Cummins, *Portrait in a Spoon*." Columbia: University of South Carolina Press, 1997.

"Sidney Wade, *Green*." Columbia: University of South Carolina Press, 1998.

"Vickie Karp, *A Taxi to the Flame*." Columbia: University of South Carolina Press, 1999.

"Carl Buchanan, *Ripper!*" Columbia: University of South Carolina Press, 1999.

"Stella Johnston, *Without a Witness*." Columbia: University of South Carolina Press, 2000.

"Bryan Dietrich, *Krypton Nights*." Lincoln: Zoo Press, 2002.

AN EXCURSION TO THE EXTERIOR

Manila Clipper, *Yale Review*, 1987.

Index

Napoleonic wars, 272
narcissism, 162
Nation, 320
National Gallery (London), 194
National Gallery (Washington, D.C.),
    253; East Wing of, 254, 255
National Poetry Month, 92
Natural History (Urdang), 353
Neel, Alice, 249, 250
Nemerov, Howard, 69
Nevelson, Lois, 255
Newman, Cardinal John Henry,
    226–27, 367
Newton, Vernon, 16*n*
New York Times, 189, 224
New York Tribune, 325, 328
Nicholas II, Czar, 363
Nietzsche, Friedrich, 7, 116, 121, 157,
    161, 165, 241, 247, 313, 334; on Sand,
    327; on joy, 82, 222; Sontag on,
    314–16
"Nightfall" (Urdang), 355
Nightingale, Florence, 340, 341
Nijinsky, Vaclav, 123, 191
Noailles, Anna de, 133–36
Nobel Prize for Literature, 148,
    151
Noon Wine (Porter), 137
"No Swan So Fine" (Moore), 60
Notebooks of André Walter, The (Gide),
    120, 161, 162
Notebooks of Malte Laurids Brigge
    (Rilke), 120, 139
Notes of a Son and Brother (James),
    321–22, 335
Notes from Underground (Dostoievsky),
    129
Notre-Dame Cathedral (Paris), 208,
    210
Nourritures terretres, Les (Gide), 119,
    121–22, 125, 126
Nouvelle revue française, 163
Nouvelles Litteraires, Les, 143
Novelli, Pietro Antonio, 148

nude, the, 233–42
Numquid et tu...? (Gide), 162

O

Observations (Moore), 60, 66
Oceanic art, 239
"Octopus, An" (Moore), 60
Ode on the Morning of Christ's Nativity
    (Milton), 140
Ode to Saint Cecilia (Dryden),
    140
"Ode to the West Wind" (Shelley),
    59
Oedipus (Gide), 163
Oedipus complex, 335
Oedipus Rex (Sophocles), 227; opera-
    oratorio by Cocteau and Stravinsky
    of, 112–13
"Of Being Alive" (Johnson),
    398
O'Keeffe, Georgia, 18, 67, 247
Old Courtesan, The (Rodin), 191,
    198
Olds, Sharon, 382
Opéra-Comique (Paris), 205
Opoponax, L' (Wittig), 101, 166
Opposing Shore, The (Gracq), 115,
    117
Or Else (Warren), 40, 41
Orangerie (Paris), 271
Orchid with Palmetto Leaf
    (Mapplethorpe), 247
Oriental Tales (Yourcenar),
    147
Orion aveugle (Simon), 149
Orwell, George, 150
Ossian, 131
Ossorio, Alfonso, 225
Ottoman Empire, 270
*Ouevres complètes de Xavier de
    Maistre*, 128
Ouro Preto (Bishop), 48